REAL PROPERTY

A Study Team Report
to the Task Force
on Program Review
May 1985

Available in Canada through

Authorized Bookstore Agents
and other bookstores

or by mail from

Canadian Government Publishing Centre
Supply and Services Canada
Ottawa, Canada K1A 0S9

Catalogue No. CP 32-50/7-1985E
ISBN 0-660-11977-3

Canada: $32.50
Other Countries: $39.00

Price subject to change without notice

CONTENTS

FOREWORD

The Task Force on Program Review was created in September 1984 with two major objectives - better service to the public and improved management of government programs. Recognizing the desirability of involving the private sector in the work of program review, assistance from national labour, business and professional organizations was sought. The response was immediate and generous. Each of these national organizations selected one of their members to serve in an advisory capacity. These public spirited citizens served without remuneration. Thus was formed the Private Sector Advisory Committee which has been responsible for reviewing and examining all of the work of program review.

The specific program reviews have been carried out by mixed study teams composed of a balance of private sector and public sector specialists, including representatives from provincial and municipal governments. Each study team was responsible for the review of a "family" of programs and it is the reports of these study teams that are published in this series. These study team reports represent consensus, including that of the Private Sector Advisory Committee, but not necessarily unanimity among study team members, or members of the Private Sector Advisory Committee, in all respects.

The review is unique in Canadian history. Never before has there been such broad representation from outside government in such a wide-ranging examination of government programs. The release of the work of the mixed study teams is a public acknowledgement of their extraordinarily valuable contribution to this difficult task.

Study teams reviewed existing evaluations and other available analyses and consulted with many hundreds of people and organizations. The teams split into smaller groups and consulted with interested persons in the private sector. There were also discussions with program recipients, provincial and municipal governments at all levels, from officials to cabinet ministers. Twenty provincial officials including three deputy ministers were members of various study teams.

The observations and options presented in these reports were made by the study teams. Some are subjective. That was necessary and appropriate considering that the review phase of the process was designed to be completed in a little more than a year. Each study team was given three months to carry out its work and to report. The urgent need for better and more responsive government required a fresh analysis of broad scope within a reasonable time frame.

There were several distinct stages in the review process. Terms of reference were drawn up for each study team. Study team leaders and members were appointed with assistance from the Private Sector Advisory Committee and the two Task Force Advisors: Mr. Darcy McKeough and Dr. Peter Meyboom. Mr. McKeough, a business leader and former Ontario cabinet minister, provided private sector liaison while Dr. Meyboom, a senior Treasury Board official, was responsible for liaison with the public sector. The private sector members of the study teams served without remuneration save for a nominal per diem where labour representatives were involved.

After completing their work, the study teams discussed their reports with the Private Sector Advisory Committee. Subsequently, their findings were submitted to the Task Force led by the Deputy Prime Minister, the Honourable Erik Nielsen. The other members are the Honourable Michael Wilson, Minister of Finance, the Honourable John Crosbie, Minister of Justice, and the President of the Treasury Board, the Honourable Robert de Cotret.

The study team reports represent the first orderly step toward cabinet discussion. These reports outline options as seen by the respective study teams and present them in the form of recommendations to the Task Force for consideration. The reports of the study teams do not represent government policy nor are they decisions of the government. The reports provide the basis for discussion of the wide array of programs which exist throughout government. They provide government with a valuable tool in the decision-making process.

Taken together, these volumes illustrate the magnitude and character of the current array of government programs and present options either to change the nature of these programs or to improve their management. Some decisions were announced with the May budget speech, and some subsequently. As the Minister of Finance noted in the May budget speech, the time horizon for implementation of some measures is the end of the decade. Cabinet will judge the pace and extent of such change.

These study team reports are being released in the hope that they will help Canadians understand better the complexity of the issues involved and some of the optional solutions. They are also released with sincere acknowledgement to all of those who have given so generously of their time and talent to make this review possible.

TERMS OF REFERENCE

BACKGROUND

The federal government, on behalf of the Crown, is the largest real property manager in Canada. It is estimated that the value of real property holdings is between $40 and $60 billion, annual operating and capital expenditures are $2.0 billion and some 17,000 person-years are directly involved with property management functions. Annex A contains a list of 74 programs, within 18 different departments and agencies, which are directed in whole or in part to real property management.

Real property programs serve a variety of purposes and uses and are managed through several different forms of organization. Real property programs included within this review can be divided into three categories:

Common Service. This category includes programs whose primary purpose is to manage accommodation as an administrative support to other programs; examples include the accommodation programs of Public Works, External Affairs (overseas property), Correctional Service (penitentiaries) and National Defence (bases).

Direct Program Delivery. This category includes programs for which the management of real property is an integral part of the delivery of services to the public. Generally, these programs concern the economic infrastructure (airports and ports) or the social infrastructure (museums and parks, and property held in trust by the Crown for Indian Bands).

Property Development. This category includes programs whose primary purpose is the control or development of real property for broader socio-economic reasons; examples include the National Capital Commission and the Public Works Lands Company.

These terms of reference have been reviewed by the Deputy Ministers of Public Works, Transport, National Defence, Environment, and the Secretary of the Treasury Board.

PURPOSE

The Ministerial Task Force on Program Review seeks information and advice regarding improvements to the efficiency and effectiveness of real property management. The review will encompass all government organizations, with the exception of crown corporations which manage real property as part of their commercial operations. Included in this advice could be observations regarding:

Groups of property functions or programs which could be privatized, consolidated, reduced in scope or eliminated;

Changes in the organization of government for the management of real property;

Changes in real property management policies or practices;

Legislative actions that would be required to implement any changes;

As far as possible, the resource implications of any changes, including impacts upon costs and the number of staff.

As outputs of the review, the study team is asked to provide basic facts on the nature of real property activities of the federal government, to identify major issues and concerns related to real property and to outline observations and advice on these issues and concerns. In developing these outputs, the study team is asked to provide information regarding:

Delivery Structure

Principal organizations and programs responsible for real property management within the federal government;

Resources (capital, operational, human) expended by organization and by regional distribution;

Advantages and disadvantages of privatization or the use of crown corporations, and other special organizations to manage real property and carry out major construction programs;

Use of municipal-provincial-federal 'port authorities' to manage federal real property;

Use of revenue dependency concepts in real property management;

Overlaps between provincial and federal government real property management programs;

Approaches used by the private sector, provinces and other countries to deliver similar programs;

The legislative base and existing conflicting objectives and impediments for efficient and effective real property management.

Efficiency and Overlap

Lines of responsibility among government organizations including:

the responsibility between Public Works and other departments and agencies within the National Capital Region;

the relative responsibilities of Treasury Board, Public Works and other program organizations for real property management.

Multiplicity of design and construction responsibilities and organizations across several government organizations and the implications for accountability;

Duplication and overlap of property administration staff between tenants and Public Works;

Advantages and disadvantages of expanded use of contracting out to the private sector for property management services;

Complex processes which effect the planning, approval and execution of acquisition and construction programs;

Management of accommodation standards to ensure control of tenant demand and improved utilization of accommodation;

Relationship between investment decisions for renovation, replacement or acquisition and government accounting and resourcing practices;

Asset management: the scheduling by departments of surplus properties and their disposal by Public Works Canada.

Gaps and Omissions

Programs which should be taken into account in this review but are not in the list of programs in the Annex.

LINKAGES WITH OTHER PROGRAM REVIEWS

As a common service, real property management is an element of all government programs. Many of the programs are or will be subject to review by other study teams under the Ministerial Task Force. When a potential for overlap of study teams exists (for example, the review of the Small Craft Harbours program), the two teams will develop work programs to avoid duplication.

COMPOSITION OF STUDY TEAM

The study team will be led by a senior executive from the private sector. The Team Director will report to both the Public Sector Advisor and the Private Sector Liaison Advisor serving the Chairman of the Task Force. The Team Director will be supported by three government executives, a matching number of private sector representatives and other public sector officers seconded to provide research assistance to the team. The team, or its Director, shall meet with the Public Sector Advisor and Private Sector Liaison Advisor at their request.

WORK PROGRAM

To cover the many programs and organizations involved in property management, the study team will be divided into sub-teams responsible for specific programs and for specific cross-program functional topics. Early in the review, the study team will submit for consideration by the Ministerial Task Force a revised list of programs and a detailed

PWC	102	ACCOMMODATION - LEASED PROPERTIES
PWC	103	ACCOMMODATION - LEASE PURCHASE PROPERTIES
PWC	105	ACCOMMODATION - CROWN PROPERTIES
PWC	106	ACCOMMODATION - PROGRAM PLANNING AND CONTROL
PWC	107	REAL ESTATE SERVICES
PWC	110	SERVICES PROGRAM - DREDGING AND FLEET SERVICES
PWC	113	DESIGN CONSTRUCTION AND REALTY TECHNOLOGY
PWC	114	FIRE PROTECTION
PWC	115	EMERGENCY PREPAREDNESS
PWC	116	MUNICIPAL GRANTS
PWC	117	SPECIAL PROJECTS
PWC	119	MARINE TRANSPORTATION AND RELATED ENGINEERING WORK/DRY DOCKS
PWC	120	MARINE TRANSPORTATION AND RELATED ENGINEERING WORK/PLANNING AND CO.
PWC	121	LAND TRANSPORTATION PROGRAM - HIGHWAY SYSTEMS
PWC	122	LAND TRANSPORTATION PROGRAM/BRIDGES AND OTHER ENGINEERING WORKS
SLSA	6	THE JACQUES CARTIER AND CHAMPLAIN BRIDGES INCORPORATED
TC	35	AIRPORT MARKETING PROGRAMS
TC	37	AIRPORT SECURITY
TC	47	MARINE AIDS TO NAVIGATION
TC	69	PUBLIC PORT FACILITIES
TC	90	MOTOR VEHICLE TEST CENTRE, BLAINVILLE, QUEBEC
TC	91	URBAN TRANSPORTATION ASSISTANCE PROG (TERMINATED)
TC	98	COASTAL LABRADOR AIRSTRIP PROGRAM
TC	99	FINANCIAL ASSISTANCE TO CONSTRUCTION AND OPERATION/AIRPORTS
TC	100	CONSTRUCTION OF AIR TRANSPORTATION INFRASTRUCTURE/NORTHERN QUEBEC
TC	104	ATLANTIC PROVINCES PRIMARY HIGHWAY STRENGTHENING/IMPROVEMENT PROGRAM
TC	105	FEDERAL/PROVINCIAL HIGHWAY AGREEMENTS - SRCPP
TC	108	FINANCIAL ASSISTANCE FOR HARBOUR IMPROVEMENT
TC	260	VICTORIA JUBILEE BRIDGE
TC	300	WATERWAYS DEVELOPMENT
TC	410	AIRPORT FACILITIES AND AIRPORT SERVICES PROGRAMS
VAC	7	COMMONWEALTH WAR GRAVES COMMISSION
VAC	8	HOSPITAL TRANSFER PROGRAM
PWC	108	REALTY MANAGEMENT SERVICES
PWC	109	ARCHITECTURAL AND ENGINEERING SERVICES
PWC	111	CORPORATE AND ADMINISTRATIVE SERVICES
PWC	112	FEDERAL LAND MANAGEMENT

STUDY TEAM MEMBERS

Team Leader	Mr. Edward (Ted) Elford, C.A. Senior Vice-President (retired) Trizec Corporation Calgary
Deputy Team Leader	Mr. Al Clayton Director Bureau of Management Consulting Department of Supply and Services Ottawa
Private Sector Members	Mr. John Rand Vice-President Barnicke Real Estate Toronto
	Mr. Bill Niles Senior Financial Officer (retired) Canron Inc. Toronto
	Ms. Gloria Fougère Controller, Quebec Division Marathon Realty Co. Ltd. Montreal
Public Sector Members	Mr. Paul Migus Senior Advisor Program Branch Treasury Board Secretariat Ottawa
	Col. David Edgecombe Director Construction Engineering Requirements Department of National Defence Ottawa

Dr. Hari Johri
Director
Bureau of Management Consulting
Department of Supply and Services
Ottawa

Mr. David Carter
Director
Corporate Policy and Strategic Planning
Department of Public Works
Ottawa

Professional Support

Mr. Ted Tunis
Bureau of Management Consulting
Department of Supply and Services
Ottawa

Mr. Jean Petitclerc
Department of Labour
Ottawa

Dr. Tony Quon
Bureau of Management Consulting
Department of Supply and Services
Ottawa

Mr. William Lye
Bureau of Management Consulting
Department of Supply and Services
Ottawa

PREFACE

This report to the Ministerial Task Force has a slightly different format than reports prepared to date by other study teams. This structure was necessitated by the highly integrated, system-wide issues reviewed by the team.

The report is divided into four types of papers.

Overview. Section 1 contains an executive overview summarizing the themes and conclusions of the study team.

Functional Assessments. Functional assessment papers are grouped in Sections 2 and 3. An introduction appears at the front of each section. These papers contain observations and recommendations which cross individual program lines. The papers are divided into organization issues and policy and procedures issues.

Program Assessments. Sections 4 to 20 contain assessments of property programs and are grouped by organization. An introduction appears at the front of most sections. These assessments contain observations and advice which are specific to that program, as well as observations on system-wide issues covered by the functional assessments.

Information Summary. Section 21 contains papers, for information purposes, on real property responsibilities and expenditures, and a record of consultation.

SECTION 1 - OVERVIEW

There is a vast minefield floating just beneath the surface of a sea of federal real property. The minefield has resulted from generations of investment in new real property. Disarming the mines will be difficult and dangerous; but if not disarmed, they will explode. The explosion will be in the form of increasing demands for capital for regeneration of the property portfolio and enormous and ever increasing expenditures for its maintenance.

Real property has been one of the most highly politicized functions of government. In addition to providing support for the expanding set of government programs, real property has been used as a vehicle for furthering socio-economic objectives and distributing benefits across the country. It is no accident that the federal government's central inventory of real property holdings is organized and published by electoral riding.

The result is that unneeded properties have been retained and upgraded for purposes of local employment. New properties have been overbuilt in the name of federal presence. Properties which could be better managed at provincial and municipal levels or by the private sector have been acquired and developed by federal departments. New property has been used to meet operational needs without resort to less expensive and more imaginative program delivery techniques. Each of these investments may be laudable in itself, but the cumulative effect is a real property system which is bloated with inventory, undermanaged and overstaffed.

No one has his finger on the pulse of these property holdings. Government-wide data on costs and people for real property are not available. When this study team developed terms of reference in January, the best estimate was that 17,000 person years and $2.0 billion annual expenditures were consumed in property activities. In our March, 1985 interim report, we estimated 20,000 person years and $3.0 billion. In this final report, our tabulations of programs shows 35,000 person years, $6.0 billion in expenditures and $2.3 billion in revenues.

Our report contains 62 assessments of property programs, 11 assessments of common property issues and 13 overviews. However, our options flow from a handful of core proposals and two themes. These themes are:

- the need for a rigorous program of divestiture of federal property; and
- the need for changes in the organization of government for real property management.

Our divestiture proposals involve a fundamental shift in the approach to real property management. The government has too often owned, operated and funded properties in order to achieve program objectives. Consequently, the government has operational responsibility for properties which are best managed by the private sector or provincial and local jurisdictions. Once ownership is assumed, individual properties create their own political and bureaucratic constituencies and unneeded properties become difficult to abandon, sell, or transfer to other governments. Federal policy should depend more heavily upon joint participation or contributions and incentives without ownership and operational responsibilities.

A divestiture strategy for existing properties should be implemented immediately. Divestiture will not happen overnight; nonetheless, a clear direction is needed now. Within this direction, the study team recommends to the Task Force that the government consider:

- transferring the ownership and management of federal airports from Transport Canada to local authorities;
- selling surplus federal property through an active program of identification and disposal;
- transferring to local governments and/or selling federal urban development projects in Quebec City, Montreal and Toronto;
- reassessing the base and station infrastructure of the Department of National Defence;
- reassessing the land and property holdings of the NCC;
- transferring federal responsibility for canals, dams, bridges and highways to the appropriate level of government; and
- rationalizing Transport Canada's public ports and Fisheries and Oceans' small craft harbours by closure of inactive harbours, transfer to local authorities, sale to private interests and implementation of investment strategies based more clearly on economic considerations.

Our proposals for changes in government organization are designed to resolve three weaknesses of the present system:

- a void at the centre for real property management responsibility;
- the impossible combination of roles assigned to Public Works Canada (PWC); and
- the irrational fragmentation of real property responsibilities.

Our options are based upon the principles that the ownership (custody) function is best carried out by the occupant/user organization and that property services should be contracted out to the private sector, whenever economic, as a matter of public policy, with the remaining internal services being accounted for on a full cost basis. Given these principles, the study team recommends to the Task Force that the government consider:

- establishing a new Real Property Unit charged with central functions now carried out by the Treasury Board Secretariat (TBS) and Public Works Canada (PWC);
- outside the National Capital Region, maintaining the current custody responsibility as split between PWC and numerous program departments;
- within the National Capital Region, transferring custody responsibility (including capital budgets) from PWC to program departments for all special purpose buildings while transferring custody for designated properties of national interest (Parliament, official residences) from PWC to the National Capital Commission (NCC);
- establishing the PWC role as follows: the management of general purpose properties on behalf of tenants and, at the option of its clients, the provision of operations and maintenance, architectural, engineering, real estate and contracting services;
- transferring all architectural and engineering staff performing design functions and real property contracting staff to PWC, with these services being charged to clients on full cost-recovery basis;
- transferring NCC property operations and maintenance and architectural and engineering staff to PWC, with the NCC initially being required to purchase such services from PWC; and

- instituting a systematic program of increased contracting out of engineering, architectural and operations and maintenance services across all property programs.

The implementation of the divestiture and organizational changes will take two to four years to complete. Major labour-management negotiations and policies will be needed to implement the organization changes. Divestiture will be equally difficult. Provinces and municipalities may be reluctant to accept ownership or funding responsibility because of the long-term liabilities associated with some properties. The private sector may be equally dubious. To facilitate the process, we recommend to the Task Force that the government consider a strategy in which the federal government negotiates transfers within the context of a broader federal-provincial framework, 'abandons' a few selected facilities and transfers ownership under funding arrangements.

Following, we present a more detailed overview of our report. We start with general observations on real property, follow with options on organization and process issues, then outline options related to major property organizations and conclude with comments on implementation.

OBSERVATIONS ON THE STATE OF REAL PROPERTY MANAGEMENT

Any review carried out in a short time frame involving so many different organizations, with so many diverse activities, creates a tendency to identify individual weaknesses and generalize them across the whole system. We must emphasize that the property management programs of government generally fulfill the purpose for which they were intended. The runways at airports are cleared of snow and aircraft do land safely. Military bases meet military program requirements. National historic sites are popular tourist attractions which contribute to a sense of national identity. The performance of many individual property programs is acceptable. Yet, the overall system does not work and requires reform.

The management of real property has been studied to death - Royal Commissions (Glassco and Lambert), the Senate

Committee on National Finance, the Auditor General, the Public Accounts Committee and numerous internal government reviews have recommended reform. Several reforms have been completed or are underway. Yet, despite generally competent professionals and managers and effective performance by many individual property programs, the whole is somehow less than the sum of its parts. Following are some of the key characteristics of current real property operations which contribute to the problems of the system.

The conflict between efficient service delivery and broader social economic objectives is not well managed.

Treasury Board policy states that:

> "real property be managed economically and efficiently and that it be managed so as to combine the efficient provision of government services with the achievement of wider social, economic and environmental objectives".

Most government activities face such conflicting objectives. But in the case of real property, there is a lack of norms, policies and practices for adequately resolving such conflicts. The result is that almost any decision can be justified and accountability can be avoided in the name of 'political considerations'. In reaction, public servants at several organizational levels anticipate political decisions. Reform is needed so that property management objectives are understood primarily in the context of efficient provision of services and that decisions on broader objectives are funnelled to the appropriate political levels.

The system is fragmented. The Public Works Act assigns the custody of federal real property to the Minister of Public Works, unless another Minister is so designated by another Act of Parliament. This study team identified 46 different organizations - 18 departments and 28 corporations - with such separate authority. While decentralization of authority is not a weakness in a management system, in real property the decentralization has occurred piecemeal, without a rational framework.

There is a void at the centre. Property management has been viewed primarily as a line responsibility of program Ministers and their officials: and this principle should remain. However, central management is required for such functions as capital budget analysis, property acquisition, major changes in land use, property disposal and policy development and monitoring. Treasury Board and Public Works, which are assigned such functions, have been unsuccessful in carrying out this central role. Treasury Board has lacked the intention and the staff. PWC has lacked the authority, the leverage and the credibility. An essential step in improving the property management system is to fill this void.

PWC has been given a nearly impossible combination of roles and has serious management problems. PWC is asked to be both service-oriented to clients and to act as a central control agent. It is placed in the position of deciding the allocation of capital funds among competing program departments in the National Capital Region. It provides services to tenants under unclear policies and practices regarding tenants' rights. It is being held 'hostage' by its major client, Canada Post, which threatens to use its option to withdraw from PWC services to exact special concessions. PWC has an aging management cadre, is undergoing the revolution of converting to revenue dependency and has a low level of credibility with many clients and with central agencies. In fact, since January 1985, PWC has been under a great deal of scrutiny.

There is an obsession with PWC issues, and a corresponding neglect of other property programs. Property management as viewed by central agencies and the public has been centred on PWC and its problems. Because property is the PWC program and due to the visibility of its office towers, the spotlight on PWC is understandable. Meanwhile, the 73 per cent of federal real property managed by other authorities is given minimal attention or scrutiny from the centre.

The quality of real property management across government is inconsistent. Some large property holders such as National Defence, the RCMP and Parks Canada have well-established, professional property management organizations and practices. Other major holders such as Agriculture Canada and External Affairs undermanage their property. Some PWC tenants, such as Employment and Immigration, have established strong organizations to fulfill their property functions, but the property organizations of most PWC tenants are weak.

The 'regular' real property management system was frequently abandoned during the past decade. Crown corporations were set up to construct, develop and manage high profile projects. With the Special Recovery Capital Projects Program (SRCPP) of 1982, the government created a coordinating committee and office to cut through its own red tape. When capital budgeting practices became a barrier to effective property management, the government used lease-purchase arrangements. These deviations were not necessarily ineffective. Rather, they reflected a dissatisfaction with the regular system and the need for better delivery mechanisms.

The incentives in the system are against the highest and best use of property. Government users of property do not pay property taxes. Revenues from sales are not credited back to the seller and the cost of money and depreciation are not included in financial statements. Capital for the acquisition of new property is acquired within a competitive resource allocation process which encourages program managers to land-bank property against possible future needs and provides little incentive to dispose of surplus properties. Such bias is exagerated by a system in which it is easier to obtain maintenance funds for uneconomic property than to get the capital to sell, regenerate or replace properties.

The organization and process for design,construction and contracting are cumbersome. Many major property authorities have in-house architectural and engineering staff and contract out to the private sector a large portion of services. Other property authorities use PWC as their design and construction agents. There is excessive double-checking and supervision of private consultants by public sector professionals. This is caused by a lack of trust between PWC and its clients and, most particularly, between public sector architects and engineers and private sector consultants. At the core of this distrust is a contracting process which is slow and expensive for both the consultants and the government. This process has created barriers to further contracting out.

There are opportunities for increased cost recovery from users of federal property. Many property programs receive revenues from users ranging from token payments for national parks to 'full cost recovery' for major ports. As described in the paper on "Cost Recovery for Government Services", prepared by the Study Team on Services and Subsidies to Business, there are opportunities for greater cost recovery, possibly leading towards privatization.

However, cost recovery is retarded by the lack of a policy framework, by widely varying practices and by inadequate financial information on the real total cost of individual government property programs.

ORGANIZATION OF GOVERNMENT FOR REAL PROPERTY

Improved accountability and control are at the centre of the need for organization change for real property management. We found confusion in the system between the 'custody' role of planning, budgeting and control and the 'services' role of design, construction and maintenance of property. Government property organizations are often dominated by a technical orientation, at the expense of the custody role. The organizational options we recommend centre upon improving the custody function - in the vernacular of the times, make the managers manage!

To correct the current fragmentation of the system, the government could move in one of two directions: it could consolidate custody responsibility in one agency (PWC) thus turning all users into tenants; or, it could assign custody whenever possible at the user level. The British consolidate all custody, including Defence and Foreign Office properties, under one Property Services Agency. We found the model to be less appropriate for the Canadian federal government due to the volume, variety and geographic dispersion of government property. More significantly, the key issues facing real property organizations should be divestiture, contracting out and accountability. A massive move towards consolidation would create several years of organizational jockeying while avoiding the key issues. Such consolidation would even further confuse accountability.

Our organizational options are based upon placing the key management decisions at the right location and level. The resulting thrust is towards greater devolution in the system by clearly designating, whenever possible, the user organization in the custody role. This concept is based on the principle that accountability is strongest when financial planning and control decisions are integrated in the program organization that is ultimately responsible for the delivery of services. While implementation of this principle will have minor impacts outside the National Capital Region, in the Region it will require:

- transferring the custody function for special purpose properties from PWC to program departments; and
- transferring the custody function for designated properties of national interest (such as the Parliament buildings and official residences) from PWC to the National Capital Commission.

Devolution does not imply dilution of central control and authority. On the contrary, it requires strengthening the current structure. But central authority should not be confused with increased review and approval of transactions (contracts, leases, expenditures). Rather, central authority requires more informed and professional strategic analysis of long range capital plans; greater leadership in developing norms and standards for property management; and improved operation of such system-wide functions as acquisition and disposal of properties, property information and payments of grants in lieu of taxes. The current arrangement of shared Treasury Board Secretariat and PWC responsibilities has not worked; hence the study team recommends to the Task Force that the government consider creating a separate Real Property Unit to undertake this central role.

Custody does not require that each organization have its own staff to provide service functions. In the private sector, major developers contract out almost all of their design, construction and maintenance needs to other firms. This is done, in part, to achieve the economies of scale of specialized services, but also to focus attention on the key ownership (custody) role. The federal government operates many properties with functions and under circumstances quite different from private developers, but the private sector model is generally appropriate for the federal government.

The NCC, PWC, National Defence, External Affairs, Parks Canada, Transport Air and Indian Affairs and Northern Development all have significant internal organizations providing architectural, engineering, maintenance, contracting, and project management operations and services. (For other major custody organizations such as the RCMP and Correctional Service, PWC acts as the service agent.) The study team recommends to the Task Force that the government consider a partial consolidation of these services under PWC based upon the principles that:

- custody organizations retain the minimum necessary staff to fulfill their custody responsibilities as a knowledgeable client;
- subject to an A-base justification, custody organizations retain any required in-house staff for property maintenance; and
- architectural and engineering design and contracting responsibilities be consolidated under the Minister of Public Works.

CROWN CORPORATIONS FOR REAL PROPERTY

Several real property programs are currently delivered through Crown corporations. Major examples are the NCC, Defence Construction Canada (DCC), Canada Harbour Place Corporation, and Canada Lands Company Ltd. (and its subsidiaries). There have been proposals that PWC be converted to a Crown corporation similar to the British Columbia Building Corporation and La Société Immobilière du Québec.

Crown corporation structures for real property cannot be isolated from the broader context of the organization of government. Crown corporations (Schedules CI and CII of the Financial Administration Act) are intended for organizations which combine public policy and commercial purposes. The Crown corporations named above, as well as a PWC corporation, do not meet both these criteria. Their major rationale is the circumvention of the financial and personnel regulations of government. It is time to change the regulations, not to create more corporations.

Thus, the study team has recommended to the Task Force that the government consider folding existing corporations back into departmental status and establishing no new real property corporations. Organizations which require an arms-length relationship to government, such as the NCC, could be made into Schedule B departmental corporations. The remainder would become Schedule A departments and agencies.

FEDERAL ROLE IN URBAN DEVELOPMENT

Through its major land holdings in urban areas, the federal government has always had a role in the development of Canadian cities. Starting in the late 1960s, this responsibility increased through a proactive approach involving federal expropriation, acquisition and consolidation of existing lands, backed by major capital expenditures on redevelopment. The result of this initiative are several corporations (Vieux-Port de Québec, Vieux-Port de Montréal, Toronto Harbourfront) and funding arrangements under the PWC Federal Land Management program.

There are two issues related to the federal role: should the federal government be involved in such urban development plans and what form should this involvement take? The federal government as a major landowner must fulfill a responsibility of harmonizing its plans with those of local authorities. However, there is a policy vacuum as to whether the government should be proactive in such involvement. The issue requires more in-depth consideration than carried out by this study team.

Regardless of the conclusions of the review, the form of federal involvement should be changed. Once established, development organizations become difficult to terminate or adjust. The federal government becomes a permanent landlord in urban areas. Henceforth, such involvement should be limited to joint ventures, contributions or incentives, with private or provincial/municipal authorities responsible for ownership. In this light, the study team recommends to the Task Force that the federal government should take the necessary steps to divest itself of present urban development corporations.

The urban area where the federal government has the largest property holdings and impact is the National Capital Region. We support the concept of the NCC as the federal planner for the National Capital Region. We also support the need for the NCC to own sufficient strategic property to exercise leverage in planning the National Capital. However, we question the continued relevance of the extent and nature of NCC property holdings. The NCC objective does not require it to hold vast areas of rural properties for uncertain and undefined future needs. A review of NCC property holdings and policies is suggested.

REAL PROPERTY PROCESSES AND PRACTICES

> The 1983-84 report of the Auditor General stated: "Government policies on the management of real property by departments are generally adequate; however, there is frequent failure to comply with these policies."

While the study team is in general agreement, we believe the existing framework for property management, designed in the name of control, probity and prudence, has created unneeded barriers to economic management of real property. As noted earlier, the existing statement of the purpose of real property management has been interpreted with a bias towards social and economic objectives. While recognizing that these objectives exist, the policy statement should be re-worded to emphasize more strongly efficient delivery of government services.

The process for planning and approval of capital projects is lengthy and time consuming, requiring frequent decision and transaction review by Treasury Board following the Ministerial decision to proceed. The study team recommends to the Task Force that the government consider creating a simplified system based upon real property capital requirements being presented to Ministers as part of the operational planning decision process and with increased delegation to line Ministers to execute approved plans following funding approval.

Since the mid 1970s, the government has been pursuing a contracting out policy for services which can be more economically performed by the private sector. In real property, virtually 100 per cent of construction and approximately 70 per cent of design and 40 per cent of maintenance is now contracted out. The study team recommends to the Task Force that the government continue contracting out, while intensifying implementation. The policy should be changed so that in-house staff are retained only when it can be proven that private sector expertise is not available or that the in-house service can provide the services more economically. Government in-house services should be accounted for on a full cost basis. Furthermore, we suggest that specific plans be established for each department for the reduction of in-house services.

The current process for contracting for services needs simplification. If further contracting out is to be successful, the responsible Minister must be able to contract to qualified individuals and firms within a reasonable time frame. We recommend that the government consider consolidating the contract processing for real property under the Minister of Public Works, with line Ministers retaining final approval authority. To simplify the process, we suggest greater use of 'standing offer' contracts and prequalification lists for the selection of consultants for design and renovation work. For larger contracts, the current process should be continued. However, we recommend design/build and performance specification methods of design and construction become the preferred technique for major capital projects.

In the view of the study team, the policy and process for identification of surplus and underutilized property requires change. Under current policy, individual authorities are responsible for identifying such properties to PWC and there is no incentive nor central authority for encouraging such declarations. Accounting and budgeting systems are designed so that there is no formal cost to holding such properties. We recommend the government consider a new policy framework which increases incentives by charging grants in lieu of taxes to individual properties and which establishes the Real Property Unit in a challenge role over the use of individual properties.

Revenue dependency for the Accommodation Program and Services Program of PWC has been a topic of debate for many years. A 1980 Cabinet decision approved revenue dependency in principle, subject to future evaluation of PWC readiness. In 1983, PWC was deemed unable to meet its April 1, 1984 start date. Partial implementation is now proceeding without firm target dates. We recommend that the government consider re-stating its commitment to revenue dependency for PWC, without qualification, and establish April 1, 1987 as the new target date. Furthermore, the Real Property Unit and Office of the Comptroller General should review the information systems of other custody organizations to increase the quality and commonality of real property reporting.

PUBLIC WORKS CANADA

PWC has some 8,800 employees and in 1984-85 expended $1.238 billion, $232 million of capital funds and $1.006 billion of operational funds and grants. Our organization proposals define a limited but strong role for Public Works. There are two areas for PWC focus. The first is custody of general purpose office properties. The second is the provision of design, contracting and operation and maintenance services. Given this new role, the study team recommends to the Task Force that the government consider reorganizing PWC so as to clearly separate management accountability for carrying out its custody and service functions.

Our proposals suggest the transfer of PWC custody responsibility for designated properties to the NCC, custody for special purpose buildings in the National Capital Region to program departments and responsibility for central management functions to the new Real Property Unit. Our proposals also suggest the transfer of NCC operations and maintenance responsibility and all government design and contracting services to PWC. We also suggest that PWC custody responsibility for highways and marine properties be transferred to provinces or other federal program departments. We agree with the suggestions of the Study Team on Services and Subsidies to Businesses to divest PWC of dry docks and operate PWC dredging services on a contracted out full cost recovery basis.

In addition to these changes, we also suggest to the Task Force that the government consider the need for several management process reforms within the department. These are:

- priority conversion of the PWC Services Program to full cost recovery and establishment of the PWC Accommodation Program on a full revenue dependency basis; and
- establishment and implementation of a program to increase contracting out of operation and maintenance services.

MARINE TRANSPORT PROGRAMS

Marine programs of the federal government involve a massive investment in real property infrastructure. This investment comprises over 2,500 ports and harbours, the St. Lawrence Seaway, bridges, canals, and other diverse assets. Total annual expenditures of $540 million are reduced by $340 million of revenues leaving an annual cost to the government of $200 million. Approximately 3,500 person-years are employed in marine real property related activities.

The Minister of Transport is responsible for 15 ports administered by the Canada Ports Corporation (CPC), nine harbours in Ontario and British Columbia under autonomous Harbour Commissions (HC), 301 public harbours administered by Transport Canada (TC), Canadian Coast Guard bases and the St. Lawrence Seaway Authority. The Department of Fisheries and Oceans (DFO) administers 2,232 fishing and recreational harbours under the Small Craft Harbours program.

Marine properties constitute a ramshackle proliferation of infrastructure as the result of more than a century of incremental growth based largely on loosely defined notions of socio-economic benefits and a perceived imperative to disperse and perpetuate federal presence in the name of the 'national interest'. This infrastructure is largely inefficient, costly to administer, of arguable economic benefit, and politically difficult to dismantle.

This trend should be reversed through inventory rationalization based on: withdrawal from operations more properly handled by other levels of government; divestiture of assets to the private sector; and management of the remaining infrastructure based on maximum local autonomy, financial self-sufficiency and market driven levels of service. Specifically, the study team recommends to the Task Force that the government consider that:

- identifying and retaining Transport Canada and DFO harbours required to support isolated communities;
- selling remaining TC, CPC and HC ports and harbours for the best prices achievable;
- operating all ports and harbours which remain unsold on the basis of financial self-sufficiency;
- selling all recreational harbours as soon as possible;
- declaring as surplus unneeded fishing harbours and disposing of them; and
- operating remaining harbours, within the context of the overall rationalization of the fishing industry, on the basis of financial self-sufficiency.

AIR TRANSPORT PROGRAMS

Since the 1930s the federal government's role has been one of ever-increasing ownership, operation and subsidization of Canadian commercial airports. No other western national government is so heavily involved in airport operations. This intervention has resulted from the policy of successive governments - there is no legislative requirement that the federal government operate airports.

There are over 600 licensed airports in Canada: Transport Canada owns 154 and operates 103. The 154 airports account for over 90 per cent of Canada's total passenger traffic. For airport operations and air navigation services, operating expenses in 1984-85 were about $850 million against revenues of $650 million, leaving an operating deficit of $200 million. These programs involve 10,600 person years including 4,700 for airport operations and administration and 5,900 for air navigation.

For several years, TC operated the 23 major airports under a revolving fund, with losers and winners combining to create self-sufficiency. The remaining airports were funded through separate net appropriations. Last year, it was estimated that the 23 airports in the revolving fund would require in excess of $1.0 billion from the federal treasury over the next 10 years. The 'solution' was to decrease the revolving fund to only nine airports and transfer the others to regular appropriations.

Airports are capital intensive operations which must respond to market demand for facilities. Capital expenditures over the next three years for the airports will approach $700 million. Because airports compete with a wide variety of other programs for federal government capital appropriations, they face a high degree of uncertainty and delay in capital projects. Greater access to sources of capital (i.e. private markets) would provide airports with the flexibility they need to operate effectively.

Various reviews have shown that the costs of running the system are excessive. The existing management structure has three distinct levels of authority over federally operated airports. This creates work duplication and places excessive overhead on the airports. Moreover, airports are not able to maximize revenue opportunities. The financial performance is the result of the federal government taking upon itself the ownership and operation of what is essentially a commercial business under the structures and regulations which are not designed for such purposes.

Various reviews have stressed the need for greater local autonomy for Canadian airports. We support this direction. The study team recommends to the Task Force that the federal government consider retaining its role and financial responsibility for national and international air navigation, aviation safety and security; however, the government should also consider instituting a fundamental change in policy for airport operations from ownership and centralized public service operations to locally managed and owned airports.

Implementation of the change will require extensive involvement by every major interest group at each airport, e.g. all levels of government, airline industry, users and unions. The implementation may have to be done in stages and may take three to five years but care should be taken so that the objective of non-federal ownership and local operations is not altered as a result of transitional or intermediate steps. In the short term, to provide financial self sufficiency, the federal government should ensure through legislation a weighted allocation and payment to airports of the Air Transportation Ticket Tax. A large number of airports can be financially self-sufficient through restructuring of cost and increasing revenues. The costs of airports which cannot be expected to reach financial self-sufficiency within a reasonable time, but for which there are compelling reasons to continue operating, should be borne by the local or regional community or recognized as a social subsidy.

DEFENCE SERVICES PROGRAMS

The Department of National Defence (DND) is the custodian of the largest inventory in the government in terms of building area (space of almost 10.7 million square metres) and of the largest number of buildings (more than 36,000 of which more than 24,000 are married quarters). It is the third largest landholder in the government, with more than two million hectares. In 1984-85, DND spent $150 million in capital and $535 million in operational funds on property activities.

If military requirements were the only criterion, the study team is of the view that the number of bases in Canada could be reduced by a least seven, from the 33 which currently exist. The number of stations could also be reduced substantially. Such bases and stations have been retained for local employment reasons. Prolonging indefinitely the life of defence installations which have no essential military function is expensive to government, reduces military capability and is not the best way to encourage the social and economic evolution of host communities.

The study team recommends to the Task Force that DND plans include a systematic medium and long term infrastructure rationalization plan. The plan should include provision for cooperative planning with provinces and local communities for the socio-economic adjustments which would have to be made.

Recent audits and evaluations, most notably those of the 1982 Barton Report on Defence Procurement and the Auditor General in his 1983-84 report, have commented favourably on DND's real property acquisition and management generally.

One of the reasons DND receives such plaudits is its determination to "stay out of trouble politically". To do this DND has developed an elaborate fail-safe property management process, which is designed to ensure full compliance with administrative policy. The process is particularly heavy and lengthy at the front end (the construction project justification and development phases). In the view of the study team it could be simplified and shortened without serious risk, and with immediate benefits in terms of speedier project implementation, enhanced relationship with the private sector and reduced overhead.

DND employs civilians in a support role to military functions. Some 10,700 (or 28 per cent) of DND's 36,000 civilian employees work in real property functions chiefly under the supervision of military personnel in Operations/ Maintenance. The total number of military personnel involved in real property (construction engineering) activity is 2,280 or 2.7 per cent of the Forces. About 30 per cent of the design, 10 per cent of the construction and 70 per cent of the operation and maintenance work of DND is done in-house by these 12,350 military and civilian personnel.

Most of the 70 per cent of operation and maintenance work done in-house is simply routine maintenance, there is considerable scope for contracting out this work to the private sector. The study team recommends to the Task Force that the government consider directing DND to develop a program for the reduction of civilian employees in real property retaining only those required on isolated sites or justified for military operations. The reduction of civilian employees should be phased to take into account the high attrition rate for civilians expected over the next 5 years.

Similarly, in-house civilian architectural and engineering services could be contracted out to a greater extent since the majority of the in-house design work is for buildings that have no special military purpose, such as officers' quarters. In fact, design for such military specific properties as the ship repair unit in Base Halifax and the hangars for the F18 fighter have been sucessfully contracted out to the private sector. We suggest that the government consider transferring civilian design services staff to the PWC design organization. We further suggest that the government consider changing the DND contracting agency, Defence Construction Canada, from a Schedule CI to Schedule B organization and transferred to the Minister of Public Works.

PARKS CANADA

Parks Canada, which is part of the Department of the Environment, is the government's largest custodian of raw land - some 12.77 million hectares. Parks operates 31 national parks, 69 historic parks and sites and 9 historic canals. In addition, the National Battlefield Commission, a Schedule B departmental corporation, operates the Plains of Abraham park. In 1984-85 Parks Canada operating expenses were $56.4 million, revenues were $7.9 million and capital was $60.0 million. Parks Canada used 1,598 person-years in real property management.

Parks Canada has emphasized acquisition and development at the expense of the maintenance and recapitalization of existing assets. The recapitalization back-log is now estimated to be in the order of $320 million. The initial and long-term costs of some parks are excessive and could have been lower had the park agreement with the ceding province or territory not included such non-park items as highways, golf courses, gondolas, etc. In spite of these problems, once a park has been established, the formal development planning process used by Parks Canada appears to be most effective.

The Parks Canada philosophy should be supported that all park and park-related activities not central to the conservation/ preservation/display mandate should be privatized. Privatization of existing in-park services should be accelerated where possible and development of such services should be severely restricted in wilderness parks.

Parks Canada has responsibility for 2,500 kilometres of highways and roads, the majority of which pass through, and in some cases, between parks. This infrastructure consumes a disproportionate 48 per cent share of the capital budget. The canals, which were transferred to Parks from Transport Canada when they effectively ceased to be essential to trade, impose a similar distortion on the Parks budget. It is considered that both through-park highways and roads, and the canals should be transferred to provincial jurisdiction.

Leasehold properties in the National Parks, particularly in the Mountain Parks, have been a source of controversy for years. Rents on Banff and Jasper properties are to be adjusted again in 1990. The study team recommends to the Task Force that the government consider forming a review committee chaired by a private sector real estate expert with representation from Parks Canada, Treasury Board, Justice and the residents to recommend new rental rates. The establishment of rents should be based on sound business grounds.

Parks Canada is the townsite manager of Banff and Jasper. Residents receive municipal services that are heavily subsidized. In fact, in 1983-84 they paid only 21.1 per cent of the cost of providing those services compared to the Alberta formula where 46 per cent of the cost of municipal services is borne by the ratepayers. The study team recommends to the Task Force that Parks Canada's objective of moving to the full Alberta formula should be supported. Furthermore, negotiations should be started to transfer townsite management from Parks Canada to the Province of Alberta.

Although there may have been good cause for the establishment of the National Battlefields Commission in 1908 to acquire, restore and operate the historic battlefields at Québec City, there appears to be no good reason for its continuance. The use of 47 person-years to operate a relatively small park in the centre of an urban area is excessive. The government should consider transferring this function to Parks Canada and contracting out the majority of the operating and maintenance activities.

HOUSING FOR FEDERAL EMPLOYEES

There are many departments which provide housing for federal employees, the two largest being National Defence and External Affairs. Others include the Royal Canadian

Mounted Police, Transport, Environment, Indian Affairs and Northern Development, Health and Welfare, Fisheries and Oceans, Agriculture, Communications and Employment and Immigration. Employee housing policies are set by the Treasury Board and negotiated through the National Joint Council.

Public Works acts as a common service agent for some departments and provides 'pool housing' in designated northern areas for all departments. Many other departments have their own housing programs. Particularly in areas 'south of 60°', there appear to be better delivery options for government through the greater use of private accommodation, the privatization of housing management or the transfer to provincial and local housing authorities. This subject was beyond the scope of our investigation. We recommend that it be the subject of detailed review by the Study Team on Housing.

IMPLEMENTATION CONSIDERATIONS

There are several implementation questions to be resolved before the improvements and savings resulting from our options can be realized. Considering the various options will require participation of all departments and agencies and many Crown corporations. A central coordinating mechanism will be needed to lead the highly integrative nature of many of these options. The establishment of the new Real Property Unit to act as the implementor would appear to be the highest priority.

A second overriding consideration is the decisions regarding public service employment. In some cases, the available options involve considerable reduction in public service person-years through contracting out, divestiture and better organization design. In other cases, the options involve transferring positions from under the aegis of the Public Service Staff Relations Act to the Canada Labour Code. In many programs, particularly in National Defence and Public Works, the anticipated natural attrition rate is expected to be high over the next five years. But attrition will not be enough! Special reassignment programs as well as employment agreements with firms receiving contracted out work should be developed.

A third consideration is that the bulk of the financial improvements may be three or more years away. The benefits of organization change will take time to be realized. Policy and practice changes will impact on future actions involving expenditures several years in the future. The proposals to transfer federal property programs to other jurisdictions or to divest of programs will require hard bargaining and have far-from-certain final results.

But the process must start somewhere. Rare capital funds must be allocated strategically across a leaner portfolio of holdings with clearer accountability for decision and execution. The real property business of government has been for too long the subject of paralysis through analysis. It is time to enter the troubled waters.

SECTION 2 - ORGANIZATION OF GOVERNMENT FOR REAL PROPERTY MANAGEMENT

INTRODUCTION

The study team believes that the organization structure for real property management in government requires clarified and strengthened managerial accountability and control. The study team recommends that the government consider accomplishing this objective by:

- creating a strong, but limited, central authority through a Real Property Unit consolidating functions now carried out by Public Works and Treasury Board;
- placing the custody (ownership) accountability more clearly with the user/program departments; and
- establishing the Minister of Public Works as responsible for common Design and Contracting services for government real property.

The implementation of these principles will have major organizational and financial impact within the National Capital Region, the most significant being the transfer of the majority of staff of the National Capital Commission to Public Works Canada. A minor effect will be felt outside the region.

BACKGROUND

The Public Works Act gives custodianship to the Minister of Public Works for all properties except those which are assigned to other Ministers by other specific acts of Parliament. Such acts have given separate authorities to some 46 different departments, agencies and corporations of the federal government. Each of these organizations have internal staff responsible in varying degree for the planning, design, construction and administration of property. A further 90 organizations are exclusively tenants of Public Works Canada (PWC) and assume responsibility and employ staff for effective administration of their occupied space.

PWC has custody of 27 per cent of the building area and 22 per cent of the land area of the federal government. The major departments with separate authorities are National Defence (bases), Environment (parks), External Affairs (overseas properties), Transport (airports and harbours) and Indian and Northern Development (reserves).

Crown corporations with separate authority can be divided into two general categories: those with a prime objective of managing federal property, major examples being the Canada Lands Company Ltd. and the National Capital Commission (NCC); those established to meet other purposes but which are authorized to hold, operate and maintain property in support of their operations and/or as an asset base, major examples being Canadian National and Canada Post.

The allocation of responsibility is substantially different between the National Capital Region and other locations in Canada. In the National Capital Region, the NCC has control of land use and exterior design of all federal properties and custody of the majority of federal land area and buildings located thereon. PWC has the custody responsibility for all other buildings (and associated lands) except the airport, the military base and properties of Crown corporations. Across the rest of Canada, PWC responsibility is generally limited to office complexes while most other real property is in the custody and under the management of user organizations. Thus, although 25 per cent of public service employees are in the National Capital Region, the region contains almost 50 per cent of the PWC inventory of building space.

The responsibility for central coordination of real property management in government is divided between the Treasury Board and Public Works. Treasury Board reviews and approves capital and operational budgets for property, approves individual major capital projects, develops and distributes government-wide property policies and approves individual transactions (leases, contracts) above the signing authorities of individual Ministers. PWC advises Treasury Board in the development of policies and, on behalf of the government, maintains a central inventory record, pays grants in lieu of taxes, maintains and disposes of surplus lands, expropriates property and funds urban development projects.

PWC, NCC, National Defence, Indian Affairs and Northern Development, External Affairs, Environment Canada (Parks) and Transport Canada (Air) each have significant internal organizations providing architectural, engineering, operation and maintenance, contracting and project management services. On the other hand, major custody organizations such as the RCMP, Correctional Services, Agriculture and Health and Welfare purchase such services from PWC. Several reviews have been conducted in the past 20 years on the feasibility of consolidating some or all of these resources in PWC to reduce overlap and duplication and to better utilize rare professional resources. These reviews have generally favoured consolidation: no consolidation has taken place.

OBSERVATIONS

Improved accountability and control are at the centre of the need for a change in the organization for real property management. The study team found confusion in the system between the custody role of planning, budgeting and control of real property programs and the services role of design, construction and operation and maintenance of property. Government property organizations are often dominated by a technical orientation, with the effect that the custody role is neglected. The organizational options the study team has identified are centred upon improving the custody function - in the vernacular of the times, making the managers manage!

To improve the current fragmentation of the system, the government could move in one of two directions: either consolidate custody responsibility in one or two agencies, thus turning all users into tenants; or assign custody whenever possible at the user level. The British consolidate all property custody under one Property Services Agency, including Defence and Foreign Office properties. We found the model to be less appropriate for the Canadian federal government due to the volume, variety, and geographic dispersion of property. More significantly, the key issues facing real property organizations should be divestiture, contracting out and accountability. A massive move towards consolidation would create several years of organizational jockeying while avoiding the key issues. Such consolidation would further confuse accountability.

The thrust of our options is towards greater devolution in the system by clearly assigning accountability for the custody role to the user organization. Accountability for real property is strongest when financial planning and control decisions are integrated into the organization that is ultimately responsible for the delivery of the program. The implementation of this principle will have minor impacts outside the National Capital Region, but in the National Capital Region the study team suggests:

- transferring the custody function for special purpose properties from PWC to program departments; and
- transferring the custody function for designated properties of national interest such as the Parliament buildings and official residences from PWC to the National Capital Commission.

Devolution does not imply dilution of central control and authority; on the contrary, it requires strengthening the current structure. But central authority should not be confused with increased review and approval of transactions (contracts, leases, expenditures). Rather, central authority requires more informed and professional strategic analysis of long-range capital plans as part of the budgeting process; it requires leadership in developing norms and standards for property management; and it requires improved operation of such system-wide functions as acquisition and disposal of properties, property information systems and payments of grants in lieu of taxes.

It is the view of the study team that current arrangement of shared Treasury Board and Public Works central responsibilities has not worked. Treasury Board staff have lacked the critical mass to establish a centre of expertise in real property and have been developing policies in isolation of operational realities. PWC has lacked the leverage and credibility with the property community to carry out its central operational duties. The study team recommends to the Task Force that the government consider creating a separate Real Property Unit with responsibility for both central policy and central operations and that this unit contract with PWC to carry out its operational functions. The unit should be headed by a real property executive from outside the federal public service.

Custody of real property does not necessitate each organization having their own staff providing service functions. In the private sector, major owners contract out almost all of their design, construction and operation and maintenance needs. This is done partially to achieve the economies of scale of specialized services, but more importantly, to focus attention upon the key custody (ownership) role. Although the federal government does have some properties with truly unique operating characteristics, we consider the private sector model as generally appropriate for the federal government.

The services required by custody organizations should be available from two sources - the private sector or PWC as a common service agency to government. In this framework, the study team recommends to the Task Force that the government consider allocating architectural, engineering, operation and maintenance and contracting staff as follows:

- custody organizations should retain the minimum, necessary managerial and professional resources to fulfill their custody responsibilities;
- custody organizations should retain operations and maintenance staff but substantiate them from a zero-base;
- NCC design, contracting and operation and maintenance staff should be merged with PWC and contracted back to the NCC; and
- the Minister of Public Works should be assigned responsibility for providing common design, operation and maintenance and contracting services with respect to real property.

The cumulative effects of these changes would have a profound effect upon the Department of Public Works. Its responsibility for central management functions, for designated properties and for special purpose buildings in the National Capital Region would be transferred to other organizations. PWC would remain with two primary businesses: custody of general purpose buildings and an increased role in the provision of architectural, engineering, contracting and operation and maintenance services.

These options would also profoundly change the character of the NCC. The NCC would retain its present design and planning control responsibility and would retain and even increase its custody responsibility, but its services staff would be transferred to PWC. This would allow for better rationalization of services in the National Capital Region as well as for better focus by the NCC on its key roles.

These options envisage the transfer of an estimated total of 500 to 600 design and contracting staff from National Defence, Parks Canada and Indian Affairs and Northern Development to PWC. This includes the transfer of Defence Construction Canada from the authority of the Minister of National Defence to the Minister of Public Works.

The study team considered the feasibility of creating a Crown corporation to deliver real property functions in general, and PWC functions in particular, but rejected this approach. It would continue the practice of the last decade of avoiding the problems of real property by creating corporations to circumvent the system. Crown corporations should not be used for organizations whose sole purpose is to deliver real property services to government or to avoid the restrictions imposed by Parliamentary appropriations and by government rules and regulations. Emphasis should be placed on changing the rules and regulations.

Attached as Annex A is a list of major government organizations and their functions within the organization approach developed by the study team.

ANNEX A

ORGANIZATION STRUCTURE FOR REAL PROPERTY MANAGEMENT

CENTRAL MANAGEMENT

Real Property Unit - budget/capital analysis
- policy and monitoring
- central operations (contract with PWC)

CENTRAL SERVICES

Public Works Canada - operations and maintenance (optional)
- design (optional)
- contracting (mandatory)
- real estate (optional)
- central operations (mandatory)

Defence Construction Canada (under Minister of Public Works)
Department of Justice - legal services
Supply and Services - construction goods procurement

CUSTODY ORGANIZATIONS AND TYPES OF PROPERTIES

Agriculture - research labs and lands
Communications - research labs
Energy, Mines and Resources - research labs
Environment - parks, historic sites, canals, research labs, weather stations
External Affairs - overseas residences and chanceries
Fisheries and Oceans - fishing harbours, recreational harbours, research labs
Indian Affairs and Northern Development - reserves and northern properties
National Defence - militiary bases and stations
Health and Welfare - medical stations, research labs
National Revenue - customs ports
Public Works - general purpose office, common use properties
Transport - airports, harbours, ports
Veterans Affairs - hospital
Correctional Service - penitentiaries
Supply and Services - warehouses
RCMP - detachments, training facilities
National Museums - museums
National Research Council - research facilities
National Capital Commission - lands, national interest buildings

CENTRAL MANAGEMENT OF REAL PROPERTY

BACKGROUND

Central responsibility for real property management is diffused among several organizations within the federal government. Treasury Board under authority granted by Section 5 of the Financial Administration Act is given lead authority. Four of the five branches of the Treasury Board Secretariat have related responsibility.

- **Administrative Policy Branch** (APB) develops and distributes real property management policies including contract regulations and monitors and assesses submissions from departments against these policies; it dedicates eight person years to these functions;
- **Program Branch** (PB) reviews and assesses multi-year, annual and individual project requests for funds from departments; program officers are organized by department, thus real property projects and activities are reviewed as an element of each department, not as a consolidated set of expenditures;
- **Crown Corporations Directorate of Program Branch** (shared with Finance Canada) reviews and assesses annual expenditure plans and/or the capital plans of corporations; program officers are organized by corporation and review property as an element of each corporation;
- **Personnel Policy Branch,** among its functions, develops government policy in such areas as working conditions and health and safety; these areas can have direct impacts on future real property expenditures and programs; and
- **Staff Relations Branch** represents the government at the National Joint Council at which labour-management consultations take place on such non-compensation issues as working conditions, employee housing and health and safety.

The Treasury Board Advisory Committee on Federal Land Management (TBAC/FLM) is responsible for reviewing and advising Treasury Board concerning major land acquisitions, changes in land use and disposals. TBAC/FLM is chaired by a middle-level officer from APB/TBS and has permanent members representing PWC, Environment, Canada Mortgage and Housing and the NCC, in cases of National Capital Region properties. The TBAC/FLM commissions PWC to carry out land use studies, particularly Area Screening Studies of federal holdings in major urban areas.

Public Works central management responsibilities result from its designated common service role, from Cabinet directives and from its residual role under the Public Works Act. These central management functions have been grouped under the Government Realty Assets Support (GRAS) program. The activities under GRAS are:

a. **Federal Land Management** - management of surplus and designated properties, development of properties, federal land studies and maintenance of the Central Real Property Inventory (equivalent of 473 PY of which 300 are assigned to the Goose Bay base);
b. **Fire Prevention** - development of standards, inspection and education (63 PY);
c. **Emergency Preparedness** - planning national construction and federal emergency operation centres (20 PY);
d. **Design, Construction and Realty Technology** - conduct of research, development of standards and distribution of information on property technology (equivalent of 44 PY);
e. **Municipal Grants** - payment of grants in lieu of taxes (equivalent of 35 PY); and
f. **Special Projects** - currently federal identity, accessibility and asbestos contamination (equivalent of 11 PY).

This grouping of activities under one PWC program is an innovation starting in the 1985/86 fiscal year; thus, there is no operational experience. There is no corresponding PWC organization. These activities are delivered by many different organizations in PWC headquarters and by all regions.

A third agency with a central role in real property is the Department of Justice. Through its Legal Services offices, located within individual departments, it provides legal advice to each separate authority on such items as property contracting, leases and lettings. Justice headquarters has two sections specializing in real property (Quebec and Common Law) which provide general advice and have prime responsibility for property acquisitions and disposals.

Several other organizations, as part of their normal central responsibilities, also impact on property management. They include the Department of Finance (general resource levels), the Comptroller General (financial and management practices) and the Privy Council Office (cabinet secretariat roles).

OBSERVATIONS

The Interim Report of this study team noted that there was "a void at the centre" of real property management. Except for the full Cabinet, there is no central real property manager within the federal government. The Public Works Act, which dates back to Confederation, was intended to assign this role to the Minister and his department. Section 9 of the Act gives the Minister responsibility for all federal property; Section 10 gives Parliament the authority to assign control to other Ministers by specific Acts of Parliament. As government grew in complexity and size, individual departments and Crown corporations were given such separate authority reducing PWC to one of many program departments in managing and operating real property. (Currently, PWC manages only 27 per cent of federal building space and 22 per cent of federal lands.) The GRAS program elements of PWC are central management functions, but are more a potpourri of tasks than a coherent package of responsibilities.

The Treasury Board through its funding approval can exercise strong leverage on the real property management system. For example, in the last two years it has required all departments to develop and submit long-range capital plans. Due to the departmental focus of Program Branch (PB) and the Crown Corporations Directorate, this leverage has not been applied on a consistent basis across all programs. Thus, PB has not been reviewing capital funding for real property on a government-wide portfolio basis.

The Administrative Policy Branch (APB) issues policies but has limited compliance capability. It is the responsibility of deputy heads, through internal controls and audits, to ensure that policies are followed. The major APB compliance leverage is through its review and advice to Treasury Board on submissions from departments of contracts, leases and other required reports. Such submissions do not comprise a comprehensive set of property reports, rather, they involve individual transactions within larger programs.

The communications between PB and APB are often poor concerning an individual department or an individual transaction. Common information is often not shared. Moreover, the two branches often have different approaches and agendas related to property issues which leave departments in either a state of confusion or provide an opportunity to play the two branches against each other.

The Treasury Board Advisory Committee on Federal Land Management is a paper tiger. It collects extensive information but has had little authority to recommend change in property use and disposal. It primarily reacts to submissions concerning minor transactions from line departments as part of a routine approval procedure.

PWC has been unable to effectively carry out its central management responsibilities. The PWC management thrust for the last decade has been to increase its client focus, not to emphasize its control role. Under the Common Services policy, several central service organizations perform both service and control roles. In other cases this dual responsibility may work, but in the case of PWC there are two mitigating factors:

- The PWC organization is too weak. The dual role of service and control requires an organizational sophistication and credibility which PWC does not possess; and
- PWC lacks the leverage to carry out the role. It is not the dominant property manager of government; it is one of many.

Conceptually and practically the PWC/TBS relationship has been flawed. Treasury Board has in fact assumed the role of central manager of real property. It has issued policies which are difficult to administer and not assumed accountability for implementation. PWC has been placed in the position of administering policies related to other line departments without adequate leverage.

CENTRAL MANAGEMENT FUNCTIONS

The central authority issue must be viewed in the context of the recent history of government organization. The Treasury Board has not assumed the full role of the government's Board of Management; it has tended to restrict its role to the budgeting, policy development and transaction control functions. Furthermore, several horizontal coordinating agencies have been eliminated during the past few years to simplify accountability, to emphasize the responsibility of individual Ministers and their officials and to reduce overlap and duplication in the central decision-making structure.

The feasibility of central authority is also governed by the diverse nature of real property management in the federal government. Property programs are delivered by organizations with many different types of relationships, with operations scattered all over the world, in support of programs with very different purposes. Some organizations, such as National Defence, have sophisticated, well managed property programs; other organizations have major property holdings but lack the expertise to adequately manage these assets.

Finally, the nature of central authority must reflect a basic philosophy of the management process of government. Strong central authority is needed over a few critical elements of the real property management process, so that the execution of programs can remain within the program departments. The roles which should be carried out at the centre include both coordination and operations functions. The coordination functions are:

- review and analysis of capital plans on behalf of Treasury Board;
- identification of and recommendation on the approval of land acquisitions, changes in land use and disposal of unneeded properties;
- development and monitoring of government-wide real property policies;
- development of government-wide real property information and reporting systems;
- leadership in the real property community through development of common technical, personnel and management practices;
- negotiation with other Canadian governments on real property transactions; and
- conduct of special reviews and studies.

Central operational functions are:

- management and development of 'surplus' property;
- maintenance of central information systems;
- acquisition and disposal of property;

- fire prevention; and
- payment of municipal grants.

The most critical of the functions is the capital budgeting analysis. On the bases of the options developed by the study team, the central authority would ensure that proposals are assessed in the context of an overall real property strategy and that proposals clearly differentiate between real property needs and broader social and economic objectives. In fact, Treasury Board and Public Works are currently responsible for the budget analysis as well as all other functions except for the personnel, technical and management practices and participation in intergovernmental negotiations. The problem is how to better organize to carry out these roles.

One option is to create an independent Real Property Unit reporting to the Minister of Public Works. To be seen to be independent of PWC programs, this unit would be separate from the department. The unit would have both coordinating functions and selected direct operational responsibility. The unit would have about 30 staff with the remainder of services being 'bought' from PWC. For responsibilities formally assigned to the Treasury Board, the unit would serve as a staff group to the Board.

A second option is to locate the same unit under the Treasury Board. The operational functions would be carried out by PWC staff under 'contract' to the unit. This relationship would be similar to that between the Personnel Policy Branch of TBS and the Public Service Commission and Supply and Services. With this option, as well as with the first, the Real Property Unit would be headed initially by a real property executive from the private sector. This would provide internal neutrality and external credibility.

A third option is to create a Real Property Unit reporting to a new Committee of Ministers or to the Planning and Priorities Committee. In either case, the unit would retain its contracting relationship with PWC.

A fourth option is to maintain the present split between Treasury Board and Public Works but improve the coordination through the 'two window' approach. Within Treasury Board a single property management directorate could be established. Within Public Works, the GRAS program could be assigned its own accountable senior executive.

There are advantages and disadvantages to all four options. The first more clearly assigns responsibility for real property to the Minister of Public Works, but it organizationally separates the budget analysis function from the approval authority of the Treasury Board. This budget function is the key leverage which the central authority should have over the real property process.

The second option more clearly assigns responsibility to the Treasury Board, but the operational role of the unit would be inconsistent with the traditional role of Treasury Board. However, under this option the budget function is consolidated under the Board and operational activities are 'contracted', not delivered by the Board.

The third option would provide high visibility to the real property function in government. It would create interface difficulties with the Treasury Board on funding matters; however, it would give the unit the leverage required, particularly in the short run, to initiate action.

The fourth option is an improvement of the status quo. It would maintain the present confusion in accountability between the policy development role of Treasury Board and the central implementation role of PWC.

We do not recommend the fourth option. The real difference among the other options involves the role of Ministers within the Cabinet structure - a subject beyond the scope of our review. The first option would be a major departure from tradition by giving the Minister of Public Works authority to analyze and recommend to government on the property programs of all Ministers. The second option is more consistent with the recent tradition of the role of the Treasury Board. The third option would be the most radical departure from tradition.

OPTIONS

In view of its analysis, the study team recommends to the Task Force that the government consider:

- establishing a Real Property Unit to be responsible as the lead organization for real property management in government; and
- assigning the Real Property Unit the central coordination and advisory functions now carried out

by the Treasury Board Secretariat and the central operational functions now assigned to PWC and formally contract with PWC to carry out operational responsibilities.

The study team suggest that the unit be headed initially by an real property executive recruited from the private sector.

ORGANIZATION FOR REAL PROPERTY IN THE NATIONAL CAPITAL REGION

BACKGROUND

The responsibility for real property in the National Capital Region is different than in the rest of Canada. In other regions, PWC has custody of general purpose office buildings and some multi-user buildings (such as some post offices and customs ports) but program departments under their separate authorities have custody for special purpose buildings and associated lands. In the National Capital Region, PWC has custody of all general purpose office buildings and nearly all special purpose buildings such as the Parliament buildings, official residences, museums, court houses, research laboratories, and the experimental farm. Properties in the National Capital Region which are managed by users include the military base (DND), airport (MOT), communications research (DOC) and properties of the National Research Council and National Capital Commission. As a result of this split, PWC has about 50 per cent of its total inventory of 6,682 million square metres in the National Capital Region. In the remainder of Canada, PWC is the custodian of about 11 per cent of the space occupied by the federal government.

At one time, PWC did not have the overall custody responsibility in the National Capital Region, program departments had independent authority. The current system was instituted because there was no central coordinating mechanism for government real property and, in the National Capital Region in particular, this resulted in departments competing with each other for rental of space and for services from the private sector.

Budgeting in the National Capital Region has anomalies due to the custody role of PWC. Individual departments requiring capital funds for properties are expected to have their projects completed within PWC's capital budget. On rare occasions they receive separate Treasury Board approval through joint PWC/department submissions but custody and funding responsibility rests with PWC. As priorities change and new projects get approved, Treasury Board will often direct PWC to make adjustments to its planned programs, thus PWC is faced with being the arbitrater of competing interests among program departments. For all capital funding outside the National Capital Region, these same program departments deal exclusively with Treasury Board for funding approvals and have control over priority setting among their own regions.

Another major difference in the National Capital Region is the role of the National Capital Commission (NCC). The NCC is a Schedule CI corporation. It has custody of 48,200 hectares of lands, which is about 10 per cent of the land in the region. These lands include the Gatineau park, 'Greenbelt lands' around Ottawa, parkways and various buildings of architectural and historical significant. The NCC manages, designs and maintains properties on these lands. The NCC also has authority to expropriate property, pay grants in lieu of taxes and dispose of properties. The NCC also has overall planning and design control of federal lands and it negotiates with, and funds work projects for, the two regional governments and 27 municipalities in the National Capital Region.

This split responsibility between PWC and the NCC creates overlap and duplication, particularly in operations and maintenance. There are many cases where PWC maintains the interior of buildings and the NCC maintains the outside grounds. The NCC maintains its parkways and parks while regional municipalities maintain adjacent roads, streets and parks. The NCC practice is to provide such services with their own staff while PWC and muncipalities practice is to contract out such work.

OBSERVATIONS

Due to the heavy concentration of government properties in the National Capital Region, there is a need for central coordination. The NCC through its design and planning control, the Treasury Board in its funding role, and the new Real Property Unit suggested by this study team, could fulfill these functions. It is the study team's view that there is no need for PWC to continue with its custody responsibilities for special purpose properties within the National Capital Region. Individual user departments of special purpose properties are best able to fulfill the custody roles of planning, budgeting and control. Not only would this relieve PWC of an arbitrater function, it would give program Ministers and their officials the ability and accountability to control priorities for all their property investments on a national basis, rather than having two separate systems - one in the National Capital Region and another in the rest of Canada. Implementation of these changes can be made with minimum effect; it primarily involves changes in appropriations.

The study team is of the opinion that the NCC should be viewed as the custodian of certain federal lands and associated properties in the region as with any other program department. Due to the need for negotiation and integration of plans with two provinces, two regional governments and 27 municipalities, it is logical to assign those roles to an agency like the NCC which has a more arms length status than a government department. Furthermore, there are in PWC custody 'designated properties', such as Parliament and official residences, which have a national interest and are more logically placed in the custody of the NCC in its role of fostering a national capital. Transfer of these properties to the NCC can be made with minimum effort. It will primarily involve changes in appropriations.

The devolution of PWC authority to the program departments and the expansion of the NCC custody role must not be permitted to result in an increase in the already existing overlap and duplication in the National Capital Region. A solution would be to designate PWC as the official service agent for architecture, engineering, real estate and operations and maintenance services for those properties transferred to program departments, and then sell such services back to the custody departments. For all program departments, except the NCC, this would involve minimal change in the practices planned under PWC revenue dependency. For the NCC, this would involve the merger of some 700 to 800 NCC staff in PWC. PWC would then be in the position of rationalizing services in the National Capital Region and applying its contracting out policies.

With this changed relationship with PWC, the current Schedule CI status of the NCC would be inappropriate. It would be preferrable that the NCC be converted to a Schedule B status which will permit it to retain an arms length arrangement with government, yet permit closer integration with PWC. Legislation would be needed to make this change.

OPTIONS

The study team recommends to the Task Force that the government consider:

- transferring the custody responsibility for special purpose properties within the National Capital Region from PWC to program departments at the beginning of the 1986-87 fiscal year;

- transferring the custody of designated properties of national interest in the National Capital Region, such as the Parliament buildings and official residences, from PWC to the NCC at the beginning of the 1986-87 fiscal year;

- designating PWC as the common service organization for providing architectural, engineering, real estate and operations and maintenance services on a full cost recovery basis to the NCC and maintaining its role for providing these services for all program departments in the National Capital Region. PWC should assume responsibility for all NCC staff charged with providing such services and apply its contracting out practices to NCC services; and

- converting the NCC from a Schedule CI to a Schedule B organization.

DESIGN, CONSTRUCTION, OPERATION AND MAINTENANCE SERVICES

BACKGROUND

In this paper, we will be referring to six major functions related to design, construction and operation and maintenance services:

- The preplanning function is the identification of the need, the development and analysis of options and obtaining approval for new or renovated facilities. It also involves the development of performance standards and outlines specifications for facilities;
- The project development function is the overall management of contracting, design, construction (including site project management), cash flow and related activities including final commissioning. (In the federal government this function is called Project Management and this term will be used henceforth in this paper);
- The design function is the preparation of all architectural and engineering drawings and specifications. It also includes the supervision of construction from the design perspective;
- The contracting function is the tendering and engagement of consultants and contractors for the implementation phase of Design, Construction or Operation and Maintenance projects;
- The construction function is the construction of buildings or major renovations to facilities;
- The Operation and Maintenance (O&M) function includes:

  - routine maintenance, including infrastructure repair and minor renovation, usually by construction tradesmen, and cleaning services; and
  - operation, including such activities as fire-fighting/fire protection (MOT and DND), heating plant operation, water and sewage plant operation, power generation, management of building complexes, management of laboratories, etc.

  Usually O&M expenditures are lumped together so that it is difficult to separate resource data between pure operations and routine maintenance.

The Schedule A organizations which employ significant numbers of in-house architectural, engineering and operations and maintenance staff are PWC, DND (including Defence Construction Canada), Transport Air, Parks Canada, Indian Affairs and Northern Development and External Affairs. In addition, the National Capital Commission (NCC), which is a Schedule C1 corporation, employs significiant numbers of in-house property services staff. Several other major custody organizations, such as the RCMP and Correctional Service, make extensive use of PWC as their service agent.

A recent survey carried out by the Interdepartmental Engineering and Architecture Committee (IEAC) indicated there are some 22,000 real property staff employed by the six major departments. Another 1,000 staff are employed by the NCC. The distribution of those 23,000 staff by employee group is as follows:

- Professional (architects, engineers) - 6 per cent or 1,380 persons;
- Technical (draftsmen, operating engineers) - 14 per cent or 3,220 persons;
- Trades (O&M) - 61 per cent or 14,030 persons; and
- Other (Administrative) - 19 per cent or 4,370 persons.

The activities of these staff were divided as follows:

- Corporate Management - 3 per cent or 690 persons;
- Design and Related Functions - 14 per cent or 3,220 persons;
- Operations and Maintenance - 81 per cent or 18,630 persons; and
- Special Projects and Programs - 2 per cent or 460 persons.

The capital projects undertaken by these organizations in 1982-83 were divided:

- Under $250,000 - 90 per cent or 11,129 projects.
- $250,000 and Over - 10 per cent or 1,109 projects.

Annex A contains a breakdown of these statistics. Although these seven organizations do not represent all the architectural, engineering and O&M resources of government, the above distribution is a fair representation.

These resources carry out only a portion of the design and O&M functions of their organizations. The government has been pursuing a contracting out policy for over a decade, so that virtually all construction, 70 per cent of the dollar volume of design and 40 per cent of O&M is now contracted out. Most of the in-house design resources are allocated to supervision of consultants and contractors or conduct of small design projects. Nearly all major design projects are contracted out. Except for DND, Transport Canada (Air) and the NCC, most departments contract out a high percentage of routine maintenance. Almost all operating functions are carried out in-house. Annex A provides rough figures on the percentage of contracted work for the seven major authorities.

Assessments prepared by this study team and detailed elsewhere in this final report, indicate various directions and observations about the services of major property holders. Briefly, these observations are:

- PWC services are overstaffed and PWC should increase its contracting out of O&M services;
- DND should undertake an active program to reduce civilian employees engaged in maintenance through contracting out. Defence Construction Canada (DCC), which acts as the DND contracting and supervising agent, is an effective operation;
- The future role of the design, contracting and O&M staff of Transport Air is in doubt if the government approves our recommendation to transfer airports to local authorities;
- Indian and Northern Affairs has already turned over a high percentage of real property functions to Native groups, and the trend is continuing;
- A significant percentage of Parks Canada staff would be transferred to other jurisdictions if our recommendations for divestiture and devolution are followed. A high percentage of the remaining professional and technical staff would be employed in the restoration of historic sites; and
- There is duplication of effort in the National Capital Region between PWC and the NCC for design, contracting and operation and maintenance.

Various studies over the years have examined the issue of consolidation of real property services under PWC. The argument for consolidation of design, construction and related contracting made by Glassco in 1962 was:

"continuing dispersal of construction activity throughout the government should be reversed and that, to achieve economy and efficiency in the conduct of public business, responsibility for all construction required by civil departments and agencies should be consolidated in a single construction agency."

Other advantages claimed for consolidation were the capacity to equalize the variable workload among in-house design staff, improvement of the dead-end nature of professional careers caused by lack of mobility among separate groups and the improvement of the uneven level of competence among groups.

In 1978, the Senate Committee on National Finance proposed that PWC be responsible for design and construction for all federal facilities. In 1979, the Minister of Public Works proposed the consolidation of design, construction, O&M and contracting. The same year, the Lambert Commission proposed that large real property design and contracting organizations should remain separate but be placed on revolving funds. In 1980, an Inter-Departmental Steering Committee supported the Senate Committee recommendation and provided comments on the implementation stages. No action has been taken subsequently.

There are several arguments presented against total consolidation. Since government has encouraged contracting out, the resources remaining within major property holders are generally performing the Preplanning and Project Management functions. These functions are integrated with the program function of an organization; they are not services which are normally bought by the private sector or other levels of government. Design is carried out in these organizations only to keep technical and professional staff current. This level of activity ensures that the custody organizations retain the capability to act as a 'knowledgeable client'.

OBSERVATIONS

Operation and Maintenance

About 81 per cent of total architectural, engineering and maintenance in-house resources are employed in the O&M function. With the exception of PWC and the NCC, most of these resources are employed on remote/specialized sites -

DND (bases), Transport Canada (airports), Parks Canada (parks and historic sites) and External Affairs (embassies). The study team questions the number of resources allocated to these functions in several of our individual program assessments. The study team recommends to the Task Force that the government consider initiating an A-base review of the number of in-house staff. Furthermore, greater contracting out of these services is warranted. PWC should also move as quickly as possible towards full cost recovery of its O&M services. However, consolidation of all O&M in-house staff under one agency would not achieve significant economies.

Preplanning and Project Management

In line with its analysis, the study team recommends to the Task Force that the government consider strengthening the preplanning and project management functions, which are custody functions, across government and staffing custody organizations at the minimum necessary level to fulfill these functions. It is not necessary for each custody organization to do all such work in-house, they can and should contract to the private sector and/or to PWC for technical assistance. However, the custody organization must sustain a capacity to define and plan its requirements and to maintain program or project control so that program delivery is not impaired. This need increases with the technological complexity of the accommodation and its degree of integration into ongoing operations.

Good construction site project managers are valuable and rare creatures in both the private and public sector. Government has been underutilizing this rare resource by isolating them in individual departments. Moreover, the classification and compensation system of government does not adequately recognize nor compensate the site project management function. Private sector site managers are occasionally used, but the policy is to keep this function in-house in order to retain custodial control. Government personnel regulations make it difficult to compensate private sector site project managers on term assignments at the appropriate level and contracting regulations reduce the ability to contract for an individual to perform the function.

Design

In the words of a former Minister of Public Works to this study team "design professionals in the government are like eunuchs in a harem, they get to see all the action but cannot participate". Some 90 per cent of capital projects are under $250,000 and tend to be designed in-house; the more challenging larger projects tend to be contracted out. The environment has led to distrust between private sector professionals and their government equivalents. From the private sector perspective, there is no single person in charge. Instead, government is seen to manage projects by committees of technical specialists, each one acting as a critic of the private sector work. Government professionals go beyond the knowledgeable client role of representing organization needs and become counter-experts. There is no statistical evidence on the extent to which double-checking takes place, since no time charts are available, but it was a universal complaint of all private sector representatives we interviewed.

A further irritation for private consultants is that government architects and engineers are not required to be licensed, yet they criticize, oversee and approve work of professionally licensed private sector practitioners. The failure of government to insist on professional registration is a policy decision which creates needless friction in the professional relationship and should be changed.

From the perspective of the government project manager, the extra checking and supervision is a requirement created by the contracting system. Unlike the private sector, government contracting has a limited memory; professional firms or construction contractors which have a good track record are not necessarily rehired for further work and those with poor performance are not precluded from bidding. The government has a weak record in penalizing firms for non-performance. Furthermore, the government manager perceives that junior, less qualified members of professional firms are being assigned to government projects to a great extent because there is an assumption that the government will double-check and assume liability for everything.

Also, behind the poor relationship is a selection process which is cumbersome and often political. The natural in-house response is to overstaff to protect the organization.

The end result of accumulated distrust is that contracting out to the private sector does not result in a corresponding reduction of in-house staff; instead the total design cost just keeps increasing. Some additional contracting out should be pursued, but the critical need is for the government to improve and restructure its relationship with the private sector architectural and engineering community. As part of this renewal process, the community should be invited to formally participate in the development of the new processes and policies which we have recommended throughout our report. Another key element of this renewal should be the move towards greater use of design/build and performance specification contracting. Under this approach, the prime architect/engineer will maintain control and accountibility for the design function and will more clearly bear legal liability for performance.

In the view of the study team, it is time to put the architectural and engineering consolidation issue to bed, one way or another. In our judgement the advantages claimed for consolidation of design functions outweigh the problems. Moreover, the dramatic rationalization and reduction outlined earlier in this report would change the dimensions of the argument. The size of the architectural and engineering community would be reducing to a level in which consolidation is essential to retain a critical mass. Only PWC and DND would have major domestic programs. Approximately 300 to 400 staff from various departments would be transferred to PWC under this concept.

In addition to the economics of scale and skill from this consolidation, the new design group would also serve to improve career development for design professionals within government. It would be used as a rotational break for in-house professionals in order to further their career development. This design group would be operated as an optional, full cost recovery service to custody organizations.

Contracting

The management of the contracting function is a custody responsibility. However, for purposes of probity and prudence, there is value in separating the administration of contracting from the custody organization. No better example of the split occurs than in DND where DCC, a Crown corporation, provides contracting services for the department. In the other major real property departments, contracting is undertaken by internal organizations but with separation and controls.

This fragmentation of contracting among several authorities has created some complaints from consultants and contractors about the variation of practices among government departments. The construction industry is less concerned about these problems. Professional firms are much more agitated by the wide variation among departments in the terms and conditions of consultant contracts. The establishment of a 'single window' to deal with the private sector would improve the relationship with the community.

In other parts of this report, the study team recommends that the government consider simplified processes for the selection and awarding of contracts. These processes involve greater use of prequalification lists for architects and engineers and some increased latitude to select other than the lowest tender for construction and operation and maintenance contracts. In both cases, these processes would require a contracting function which is more arms length from the custody organization than present practice and is totally professional in its approach. It would also require an organization which can be seen to be trustworthy, is able to play 'hardball' for non-performance and can act as a broker between custody organizations and consultants and contractors.

Thus, the study team recommends to the Task Force that the contracting function for real property be consolidated under the Minister of Public Works for operation and maintenance, design and construction. This contracting function would be developed, however, with significant delegation to custody organizations, particularly for O&M contracting. The service should be highly regionalized. Special delegation will also be required for External Affairs overseas contracting. The type of arrangements followed by DCC for DND/O&M contracting, including its site supervision services, should serve as a model. Furthermore, the processes should allow the final decision on selection of consultants and contractors to remain with the custody organization.

Conclusions

The full implementation of this consolidation should be selective and gradual. The PWC design and contracting functions have significant organizational problems. It should not be seen that PWC staff are taking over the other groups. Implementation need not be applied the same way across all groups. For example, DCC is an effective organization with a well developed relationship with DND and industry, and it provides a range of services to DND quite different from contracting organizations in PWC or other authorities. DCC should be transferred under the Minister of Public Works but not fundamentally changed for the interim; rather it should be seen as a base for eventually extending its expertise to other PWC clients.

In summary, the government should consider adopting the following principles in the assignment of architectural, engineering and O&M staff resources:

- major custody organizations should retain the minimum necessary managerial and professional resources to fulfill their custody responsibilities for Preplanning and Project Management;
- major custody organizations should retain O&M staff but substantiate them from a zero base; and
- the Minister of Public Works should be responsible for common design and contracting services for federal government real property functions.

The chart shown in Annex B is a summary of the roles and relationships of custody organizations to PWC and to the private sector resulting from this realignment of resources.

OPTIONS

The study team recommends to the Task Force that the government consider:

- assigning responsibility for providing all real property design and contracting functions to the Minister of Public Works. The staff engaged in these functions in other custody organizations, less those required to fulfill the Preplanning and Project Management functions, would be merged with PWC. PWC would retain the independent identity of existing design and contracting organizations until it has undergone management reform of its own organization;

- transferring Defence Construction Canada to the Minister of Public Works as a separate organization;

- maintaining the required in-house staff to fulfill O&M functions with custody organizations, while substantiating the numbers required from a zero base; and

- initiating a program to improve the private and public sector relationship between design professionals by involving the private sector in the reform of government practices and by requiring certification of government professionals.

ANNEX A

**DESIGN, CONSTRUCTION, OPERATION AND MAINTENANCE
STAFF UTILIZATION
MAJOR REAL PROPERTY ORGANIZATIONS**

	PWC	DND	DOT	DINA	PARKS	EXT. AFF.	NCC	TOTAL
Total Staff	4,531	11,698	3,452	387	1,710	234	977	23,009
Distribution by Employee Group								
Professional	12%	3%	5%	34%	8%	12%	6%	6%
Technical	28%	9%	12%	32%	13%	25%	6%	14%
Trades	41%	69%	70%	19%	47%	60%	54%	61%
Other (Admin)	19%	19%	13%	15%	32%	3%	34%	19%
Distribution by Activity								
Corporate	7%	1%	3%	22%	2%	5%	25%	3%
Design and Related Functions	22%	9%	14%	39%	17%	14%	6%	14%
Technical Operations and Maintenance	69%	87%	83%	35%	80%	80%	60%	81%
Research and Development	1%	-	-	1%	1%	-	-	-
Special Projects & Programs	1%	3%	-	3%	-	1%	9%	2%
Distribution of Work Contracted Out								
Design	90%	75%	60%	75%	60%	99%	20%	72%
Construction	99%	90%	95%	90%	75%	100%	95%	93%
Operations and Maintenance	60%	30%	20%	75%	85%	95%	30%	40%
Capital Projects Started or Ongoing - 1982-83								
Under $250,000	5338	513	992	2222	943	12	N/A	10,020
Over $250,000	474	104	227	196	57	51	N/A	1,109

PROPOSED ORGANIZATION MODEL OF DESIGN, CONSTRUCTION, OPERATION AND MAINTENANCE SERVICES

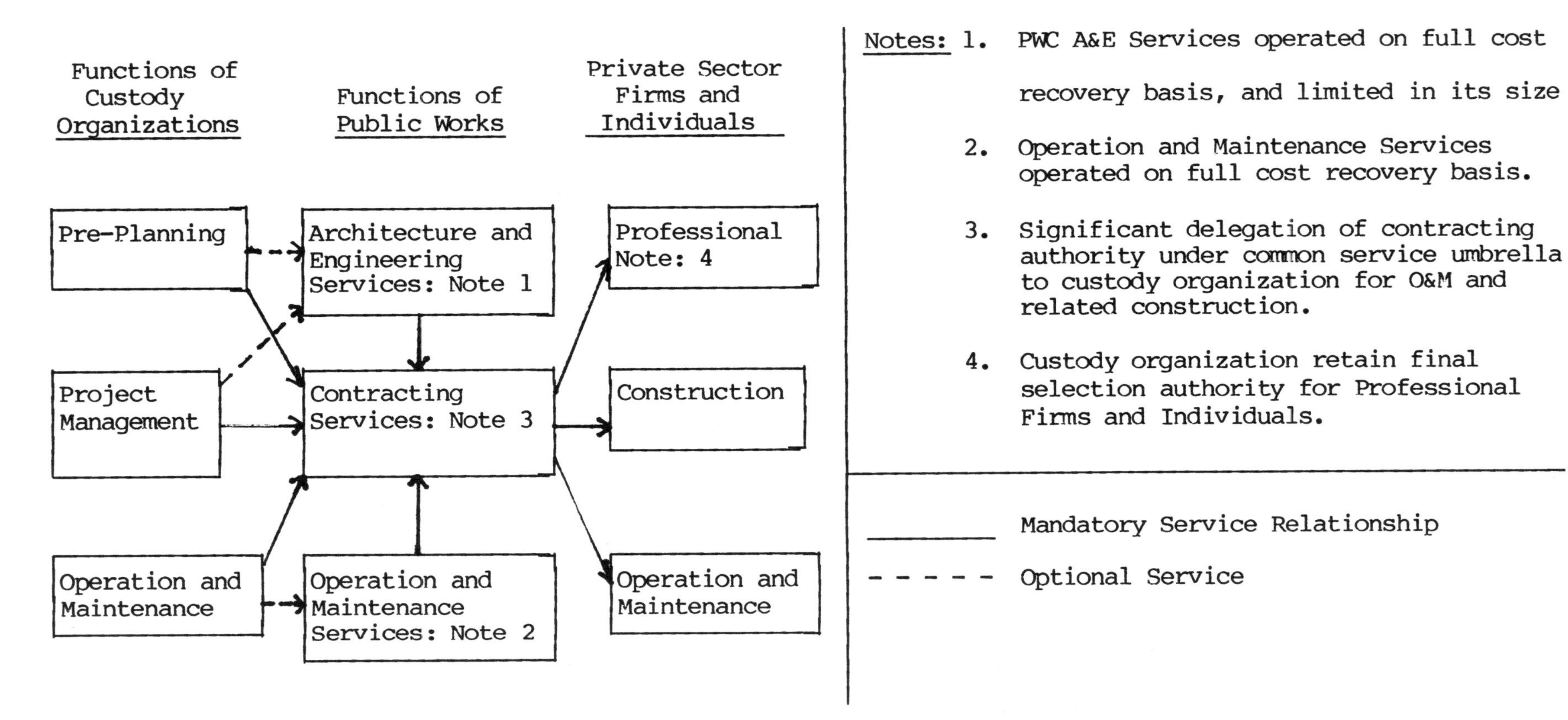

RESPONSIBILITY OF PWC TENANTS

BACKGROUND

Public Works has some 110 tenant organizations. PWC projects that in 1985/86 it will be providing almost 5.865 million square metres of space to its tenants.

Departments and agencies who are tenants of PWC maintain in-house staff in accommodation-related functions. The precise number of these staff is unknown; recent studies have estimated as many as 1,000 person-years among PWC tenants that are dedicated to the accommodation function. These resources are widely dispersed in small cells all over the government and are often integrated with general administrative offices. These staff perform functions such as control of space allocation, minor layout planning, ordering and supervising minor renovations and moves, information reporting and telecommunications services.

Major renovations are handled by PWC and funded from its budget. Other tenant services such as minor alterations are provided by PWC but funded from the budget of tenant departments. Departments currently pay no rent for space and associated maintenance services provided by PWC. Under the proposed concept of revenue dependency, rent would be charged back as an expense to departments.

Satisfaction with PWC as the landlord varies widely. Various surveys of client satisfaction have yielded mixed degrees of approval of PWC services. We did observe several departments which have developed very workable arrangements and are, in general, content with their relationship. Others had a litany of complaints including poor service, lack of response, poor follow-up and an absence of preventive maintenance. It appears that, as the level of sophistication of the tenant in property management improves, so does the PWC/client relationship.

OBSERVATIONS

Friction between PWC and tenant departments can be classified in two basic areas: PWC's perceived role as a control agent, and service delivery. In its relationship with tenant departments, PWC is providing both a landlord service and administering Treasury Board policies. In designing and providing accommodation, PWC has responsibility for providing its client departments with the quality and quantity of space allowed by TB standards and policies. These policies are open to a high degree of subjectivity, thus PWC must go beyond simply obeying TB policies and act as an interpreter.

PWC also has, in theory, the final say on where tenant departments will be located. PWC feels obligated to fill vacant crown-owned and leased space on a priority basis, but tenants argue that their landlord should provide them with space in keeping with their requests and needs and 'end run' PWC by appealing to the Treasury Board staff, Ministers, etc.

This conflict of roles for PWC would become even more pronounced under revenue dependancy. PWC would have to resolve the conflict between maximizing revenues by leasing more space and providing a high level of client service, and at the same time acting as a policy interpreter and tempering property requests. In the study team's view, PWC should cease acting as an interpreter of TB policies and the responsibility be given to the proposed central Real Property Unit.

PWC is responsible for providing a wide range of services to its tenant departments. They include requirements definition, design and construction, acquisition, maintenance and improvements. Many of these services are contracted out to private sector organizations. In virtually all of these functions, PWC acts as a middleman, translating the tenant's requirements to the eventual organization that will perform the task.

Many of the service complaints that we heard revolve around the role and efficiency of the middleman function. There are four basic areas of dissatisfaction:

> **Basic Design Layouts.** Tenant departments in many instances feel more than qualified to develop basic design layouts themselves or to deal directly with third party designers. Most objected to a PWC middleman trying to translate their demands to a third party;
>
> **Tenant Renovations.** Many tenants of PWC felt too far removed from the renovation project and cut off from the process by the middleman function;

Maintenance. PWC maintains buildings either through direct contract, its own staff or as part of a lease arrangement. Tenant departments feel a lack of control when they have to deal through PWC to contact contractors over service problems; and

Management Control and Supervision. The current process produces overlap in resources, with a tenant supervisor overseeing a PWC supervisor who in turn oversees a contractor. In leased space, the landlord's supervisor may also enter the chain.

In the view of the study team there is justification to these comments. In a typical minor improvement, the program manager who occupies a space requiring modification must make a request to his departmental accommodation specialist. This specialist prepares drawings, costs the request and then forwards it to PWC for action. PWC reviews the request, adjusts it if necessary to meet TB standards, may review the change with the tenant, initiates a contracting process to have the work completed and ultimately supervises the work of contractors on-site. The subject program manager who initiated the request is now several steps removed from the contractor who performs the work and is understandably concerned when a minor improvement has taken several months, is being supervised by a third party and has involved three separate organizations. The situation is further complicated in a leased building, when the landlord enters the act, or in a remote location where the middleman can be several hundred miles away.

This process has resulted in duplication in the PWC/tenant relationship. Departments maintain in-house experts, PWC maintains in-house experts, and yet the work is often performed on a contracted out basis. PWC has built considerable expertise in contracting with appropriate firms to carry out necessary accommodation services on behalf of their tenants. The department should continue in the contracting role. Once the contract has been let it is of questionable value to have PWC as the middleman in contract administration or project supervision. Departments that are staffed and equipped to administer their own contracts should be free to do so. To further simplify the process, PWC should negotiate 'standing offer' agreements for design and renovation work so that tenants have easy and quick access to such services.

Departments or agencies that are not staffed or equipped to manage their accommodation should continue to use PWC as a contract administrator and fit-up supervisor.

It is difficult to quantify the exact savings from the arrangement as the reductions will come from partial person years across so many tenant organizations and PWC regions. We estimate the eventual savings to be in the order of magnitude of 200 person-years, or $8.0 million per year.

OPTIONS

The study team recommends to the Task Force that the government consider changing the relationship of PWC and its tenants, with PWC assuming the contracting role for design, renovation and maintenance services but the tenant having the primary role for contract administration and site supervision.

CROWN CORPORATIONS AND REAL PROPERTY

BACKGROUND

The Financial Administration Act (FAA) and Crown Corporations Act divide government organizations according to four schedules, each with different organizational and reporting relationships to government.

> Schedule A organizations are 'regular' departments and agencies subject to the FAA and such personnel legislation as the Public Service Employment Act and Public Service Staff Relations Act.
>
> Schedule B organizations are 'departmental corporations' which are generally subject to the same financial and personnel regulations as Schedule A, but have a more arms-length relationship to government than departments and are legally liable entities. Schedule B corporations have a board or commission structure; an example is the National Museums of Canada.
>
> Schedule CI organizations are Crown corporations set up outside the constraints of the FAA and personnel regulations. Usually, they require Parliamentary appropriations to cover deficits and must receive Ministerial approval for their annual operating and capital expenditure plans. Most Crown corporations are under Schedule CI.
>
> Schedule CII Crown corporations, in theory, do not incur deficits and only require Ministerial approval for annual capital plans. Air Canada and Canadian National are under Schedule CII.

Several CI Crown corporations have been established to manage real property on behalf of government. Two of these, the National Capital Commission (NCC) and Defence Construction Canada (DCC) have been around for many years. DCC was set up in 1951 as the contracting agent for DND construction programs; its status is based upon being able to deal expeditiously and equitably with the design and construction industry in processing contracts. The NCC Schedule CI status is based upon the need for an arms-length relationship from the federal government to negotiate with two provinces, two regional governments and 27 municipalities in the National Capital Region.

Several Crown corporations were set up in more recent years with the apparent objective of avoiding the constraints of government regulations regarding real property. Examples are the Canada Harbour Place Corporation, Canada Lands Company Ltd. (and its subsidiaries, Le Vieux Port du Montréal, Le Vieux Port du Québec and Mirabel Lands) and Canada Museums Construction Corporation (CMCC). As with the NCC and DCC, these corporations receive almost all their funding through Parliamentary appropriations.

Other corporations in the real property business have recently been established due to the strong commercial nature of their purpose. Harbourfront Corporation (Toronto), a Schedule CI, and Canada Ports Corporation, a Schedule CII, are examples.

Two provincial governments have established Crown corporations to manage their property holdings. The British Columbia Building Corporation (BCBC) was established in 1974 and owns building space which it leases back to departments. Most of the BCBC inventory is in office space and 75 per cent of the space is in Vancouver and Victoria. The Société Immoblière du Québec began operations this year and is organized in a similar fashion to BCBC. It also has an inventory concentrated in office space, with 75 per cent in Montreal and Quebec City. Other provinces, most notably Ontario, have considered and rejected the Crown corporation approach.

The concept of a Crown corporation for Public Works Canada has been discussed and studied since the early 1970s. The eventual decision supported by the Auditor General and Lambert Commission was to adopt revolving funds and revenue dependency instead of corporation status. The principal claimed advantages of Crown corporation status for PWC are the freedom to operate separate from government regulations, the discipline of the market and the ability to use retained earnings and private market borrowings to finance capital expenditures instead of depending upon the uncertainty of Parliamentary appropriations. Crown corporation status is also seen, by some, as an administrative vehicle for isolating patronage.

OBSERVATIONS

In the view of the study team the performance of federal Crown corporations in real property has been inconsistent. DCC has been an effective contracting agent for DND. The NCC at times seemed out of control in its acquisitions. CMCC and Canada Lands have rather dubious records while Canada Harbour Place appears well managed. Crown corporation structures are not a panacea for effective management: their success depends upon the extent that market discipline can be imposed and the competence of management.

The Crown corporation issue cannot be isolated within real property management. It has to be viewed in the broader context of government organization. Schedule CI and CII status is intended for use by Crown corporations which combine public policy and commercial purposes and which produce revenues from outside sources. The CI status of corporations whose sole purpose is to serve Schedule A organizations is dubious. The major rationale for such corporations is to evade the structures and regulations which government and Parliament imposes. Conceptually, it would be better to reform the regular system than to create more corporations. Of course, this places even more importance than normal upon the need to simplify and reform the regular system.

In cases such as the NCC and DCC, where an arms-length arrangement from government is desirable but they are not commercial in nature, Schedule B status would be more appropriate than Schedule CI.

OPTIONS

The study team recommends to the Task Force that the government consider reserving Schedule C, Crown corporation status for real property organizations whose primary purpose is commercial. Schedule A and B status would be used for organizations whose primary purpose is to provide real property services to government.

LEGISLATIVE BASE FOR REAL PROPERTY

BACKGROUND

The management of federal real property is governed by numerous statutes, many of which can find their roots prior to Confederation. Originally, most of the property functions of the government fell under the mantle of the Minister of Public Works. The Public Works Act dates from 1867 and despite several minor amendments remains essentially unchanged. Under the Act, PWC is responsible for the "management, charge and direction of federal buildings and properties not under the jurisdiction of other departments" and "the heating, maintenance and keeping in repair of government buildings and any alterations from time-to-time therein and the supplying of furniture or fittings or repairs to those buildings." Due to changes in the roles of other departments and agencies and to the nature of the real property management business, the Public Works Act is an anachronism.

The Minister of Public Works is also responsible for the administration of all or portions of several other statutes and for the fulfillment of a number of specific government mandates related to real property. These statutes include the Bridges Act, the Dry Dock Subsidies Act, the Expropriation Act, the Kingsmere Park Act, the Laurier House Act, the Municipal Grants Act, the Official Residences Act, the Ottawa River Act, the Surplus Crown Assets Act and the Trans-Canada Highway Act.

Over 40 Acts now exist which give other Ministers authority to manage real property. These other statutes fall into two categories: those that indirectly give a Minister real property authority and those that grant specific property management functions. The Parks Act is a good example of a general statement:

> "5.(1) The administration, management and control of the parks shall be under the direction of the Minister."

The Transport Act, on the other hand, is very specific:

> "... the duty so conferred upon the Minister of Public Works, shall be exercised or performed by the Minister of Transport."

It continues, by saying:

> "The Minister shall direct the construction, maintenance and repair of all railways and canals and of all other works appertaining or incident thereto that are constructed or maintained at the expense of Canada and are placed under his management and control."

In a few other cases, such as for External Affairs, there appears to be no specific legislation giving real property authority except for annual Appropriation Acts.

The Financial Administration Act gives Treasury Board its authority in real property. Section 5 states:

> "5.(1) The Treasury Board may act for the Queen's Privy Council for Canada on all matters relating to
>
> a. general administrative policy in the public service of Canada;
>
> b. financial management including estimates, expenditures, ... fee or charges for the provision of services or the use of facilities, rentals, licences, leases, revenues from the disposition of property......; and
>
> c. the review of annual and longer term expenditure plans and programs.... and the determination of priorities with respect thereto."

Several of the options in this report would require legislative changes; these are dealt with in the individual assessment papers. This assessment concerns only the concept and feasibility of umbrella legislation for real property.

OBSERVATIONS

The lack of a single statute governing real property does create some confusion within the system concerning authority and responsibilities. For example, it is not clearly established that real property is in the 'custody' of individual departments and that the ownership resides with the Her Majesty the Queen in right of Canada and thus with the Governor-in-Council. Various reviews of real property have observed on the value of consolidating and improving existing real property legislation. Certainly, the Public Works Act needs an overhaul.

One option is to develop a single statute along the lines of the Financial Administration Act, which would clearly define authorities and responsibilities for real property and simultanously to eliminate and clean-up existing legislation. Our review, including discussions with real property officials and the Department of Justice, indicates that such legislation would require extensive efforts and time to draft and to enact and would produce marginal benefits to the system. The authority and responsibility problems we identified are organizational, not legislative, in nature. Furthermore, some of the details of the legislation would be in doubt for the next two or three years if some of the further studies recommended by this study team are initiated. Thus, the development of comprehensive legislation would have some value but should be assigned low priority.

OPTIONS

The study team recommends to the Task Force that the government consider developing consolidated and comprehensive legislation governing real property management across the government, with a view to enacting the appropriate legislation in 1988.

SECTION 3 - PROPERTY POLICIES AND PRACTICES

INTRODUCTION

The current policies and practices relating to the management of federal real property are often cumbersome, lengthy, and in many instances are crippled by a lack of authority at the centre or delegation to line Ministers. They are a prime cause of inefficiencies in the real property system. To make improvements, the study team recommends to the Task Force that the government consider:

- restating the Federal Land Management principle to give greater emphasis to economic consideration as the purpose of real property management;
- changing the contracting-out policy for real property services by adopting privatization as the norm and in-house services as the exception;
- providing the Real Property Unit with a 'challenge' role for the identification of surplus and underutilized properties; and
- restating the government's commitment to revenue dependency for Public Works and accounting for all real property services on a full cost basis.

BACKGROUND

The policies and practices relating to real property management emanate from the Administrative Policy Branch (APB) of the Treasury Board (TB). APB develops and distributes property management policy and monitors departmental performance against these policies. The various policies and procedures are published in the Administrative Policy Manual and periodically updated.

More than 15 chapters are directly related to real property and topics include acquisition, disposal, use, office accommodation, living accommodation, management of major projects, decision making and cost control. Other important chapters with implications for real property include Common Services and Contract Regulations.

The Auditor General recently commented that the current policy framework is sound. We agree with this statement. Our assessments are more concerned with the practices which have grown around implementing the policies.

OBSERVATIONS

The current umbrella policy on the purpose of real property states:

> "Federal lands should be managed so as to combine the efficient provision of government services and the efficient use of federal real property with the achievement of wider social, economic and environmental objectives."

Since the establishment of this policy in 1975, there has been a bias towards emphasizing the wider objectives, at the expense of the economic use and management of property. While recognizing that wider objectives should exist, the wording of the statement and the related implementation process should be adjusted to place more emphasis on economic considerations.

The concept of Revenue Dependency (RD) for PWC Accommodation and Services has been on the government agenda for 23 years. It is now being implemented, but without a target date or unqualified government commitment. Although we acknowledge that RD is not a panacea for real property ills, we do feel that it will promote discipline within PWC, particularly in the Services Program, will provide a better finanical display of information and will focus PWC/tenant discussion on services and costs.

We suggest to the Task Force that the government consider restating its commitment without qualifications to full revenue dependency for PWC and establish firm deadlines for implementation. The implementation of full revenue dependency for the Services Program should be set for April 1, 1986 and for the Accommodation Program, April 1, 1987.

The current policy is to contract-out where it is more economic than using in-house staff. In real property areas, virtually all construction work is being contracted out, about 70 per cent of design work, and as little as 40 per cent of operations and maintenance work. The actual numbers vary widely by department. For example, DND and Transport contract out only 30 per cent and 20 per cent respectively of their operations and maintenance requirements. There is room for increases in the amount of work being contracted to the private sector, particularly for operations and maintenance.

We agree with the concept behind the current government policy of contracting out work. The current bias, however, is towards performing work with in-house staff. This has been prompted to a large extent by the failure to adequately cost in-house staff, to define 'more economic' and to refine 'lay-off' policies as they relate to public servants. We recommend to the Task Force that the government consider a policy in which contracting out is assumed to be the norm, and in-house resources are justified on the basis of cost-benefit analysis or cost recovery based upon all direct and indirect costs.

Current tendering and selection procedures impact on the timeliness, cost and quality of projects, and create attendant frustration for all parties involved. To be consistent with the new policy, the contracting process for architectural and engineering design consultants would be amended to make use of a central inventory of prequalified consultants, assembled in a representative manner to ensure the inclusion of interests including regions and small business. For smaller jobs, under $500,000 in fees, firms would be selected from the list on a rotational basis, their ability to perform the specific task assessed, and invited to negotiate a price. For larger jobs, the current proposal call process would be retained.

The selection of construction and maintenance contractors based on the acceptance of the lowest bid creates duplication and overlap in the management of projects. In-house managers often distrust the quality of contractors and overstaff their organizations to ensure quality control. There must be greater consideration of relative competence among contractors. The PWC Contracting Service should be given authority and latitude to adopt alternatives to lowest bid selection, under prescribed rules and as part of a visible process.

The current procedures for project approval are time-consuming, costly and operationally ineffective. The level of detail requested by Treasury Board analysts and the number of times a project must be reviewed by the Board are excessive. We recommend that the government consider incorporating project approvals into the annual budget approval process. Line Ministers would be delegated Preliminary Project Approvals and would be delegated higher levels for Effective Project Approvals.

The current process for the identification and disposal of surplus property lacks authority and incentives to ensure "the highest and best use" of federal property. There is little direct cost to a manager for holding idle property and no authority has the power to challenge custody. Opportunity costs are seldom factored into the consideration of future use of a property.

We recommend remedying the current identification/ disposal dilema by giving the Real Property Unit a periodic 'challenge' function over continued use of property, and by initiating new disposal processes and incentives. We also suggest an active disposal program managed by the Real Property Unit and making use of private sector real estate expertise.

REVENUE DEPENDENCY AND ACCOUNTING PRACTICES

BACKGROUND

Since 1962-63, the cost of Public Works Canada (PWC) services provided to government programs have appeared in the Estimates as shadow billings for services received without charge. These shadow billings have been ballpark estimates, as the PWC internal cost allocation systems have been far from accurate. On April 1, 1985, the first stage in the conversion of PWC to full revenue dependency was introduced.

Few subjects in real property have been so debated and discussed as revenue dependency (RD) for the Department of Public Works. In 1962 the Glassco Commission recommended a cost recovery system for PWC space. In the early 1970s, PWC took initial steps towards becoming a revenue dependent Crown Corporation but the initiative was stopped in 1975. In 1976 the Auditor General, and in 1978 the Senate Committee on National Finance, recommended RD for PWC. The Lambert Commission joined the chorus the following year. The Public Accounts Committee has been recommending some form of RD since 1960.

In 1980, the Cabinet approved PWC/RD subject to evaluation of the readiness of policies and systems prior to full implementation. Systems development for RD was incorporated into the PWC/Improved Management Practices and Control (IMPAC) program led by the Office of the Comptroller General. In 1983, the readiness evaluation determined PWC was not in a position to proceed.

The PWC/RD concept is based upon a combination of two revolving funds and separate appropriations. The Accommodation Program revolving fund will charge rental of PWC crown-owned and leased space to its tenants at rates determined by local markets. An imputed capital cost will be established for the existing inventory for purposes of calculating depreciation and subsequent capital projects will be recorded at actual costs. Interest costs will be imputed on the initial capital cost and on subsequent appropriations for capital additions.

The Services Program Revolving Fund will charge for architectural, engineering, real estate and operations and maintenance services provided by PWC to its own

Accommodation Program, other PWC programs and to other government department clients. Business is split about 45 to 55 between PWC and other government departments clients. Billings will be on a time utilization basis, charged at market rates.

Under the approved RD concept, capital will continue to be voted as separate Parliamentary appropriations, as will such other PWC activities as central services delivered on behalf of Treasury Board.

The Services Program Revolving Fund went into operation on April 1, 1985; however, rates are based upon direct salaries, benefits and expenses only. Overhead costs are not included in the formula and market rates have not been established. There is no firm date for PWC to convert to the full revolving fund for services.

Neither is there an official date for PWC to introduce the Accommodation Program Revolving Fund. In the view of the study team it is highly unlikely that in the next year the PWC systems will meet the established evaluation criteria.

About 73 per cent of the real property of the government is not under the control of PWC and in most cases these other programs have similar weaknesses in their accounting practices; namely:

- capital assets are recorded as $1 and no depreciation or interest is included in financial statements;
- unit/cost accounting systems are weak;
- property inventory systems are not accurate; and
- cost information cannot be compared among departments or with private sector rules of thumb.

Under the Office of the Comptroller General/Improved Management Practices and Control program, several departments are improving their cost accounting systems. There is no attempt, however, to standardize reporting for real property programs across government.

There have been other proposals to institute RD concepts for other departments. The Lambert Commission proposed that other major property authorities adopt internal revenue dependent branches for design and construction. In 1979, PWC proposed that all government properties and services be formally placed under the PWC umbrella and then charged back to departments at market rates. Neither proposal was accepted.

OBSERVATIONS

Charging for PWC services has been on the government management agenda for 23 years with much talk, some action and recent progress. Until 1979, the Privy Council Office and Treasury Board Secretariat opposed revenue dependency for a variety of reasons. They preferred to control accommodation costs by placing direct controls upon PWC rather than through decentralized, indirect market mechanisms; they saw revenue dependency as a bureaucratic trap to limit political decision-making through financial systems; they distrusted PWC; and they were concerned that the cost of financial systems would be greater than the benefits of RD.

The 1980 Cabinet decision was a classic example, intentional or otherwise, of killing an idea by approving it with qualifications. It has given the critics of RD five years to argue over the details of readiness, and permitted the internal PWC forces against RD to stall in hope of a decision reversal. Instead of RD becoming an initiative to reform PWC, it has become a vast exercise in financial and information system development. Significantly, in both the United States (General Services Administration) and Britain (Property Services Agency), when government decided to implement a version of RD, it was done quickly. The type of imperfect data PWC has been providing for shadow billing purposes since 1962-63 was used in the initial year, and then the dynamics and pressure of the change provided incentives to improve financial systems.

Often revenue dependency has been oversold by its advocates. It is the study team's view that it is not a panacea for PWC or government accommodation problems. It will not be very effective in controlling the demand of tenants for services. The money tenants will need for services and rental accommodation will, in most cases, come from appropriations and be 'passed through' to PWC. Displaying accurate accommodation costs in departmental estimates is unlikely to improve discipline because such costs are so minor an element of departmental budgets. In the United States, Britain and the two Canadian provinces using Crown corporations to deliver accommodation, control of tenant demands is still exercised by versions of entitlement standards, enforced by central authorities.

RD will also not be flexible enough to allow a free market for tenants to select sites, and therefore choose lower priced accommodation. In response to consumer needs, government policy has been to adopt 'one stop shopping' for many of its services by consolidating departments, in many cities, in federal buildings. The study team contends that this policy should continue. If tenants were to have rights to withdraw from PWC accommodation or freely select from within the PWC portfolio, PWC would need to adopt the unacceptable option of leasing vacant government office space to the private sector.

RD will promote discipline within PWC for the Services Program. It will provide a mechanism for reducing costs towards a private sector equivalent level. After a conversion period, these services should be optional to users.

The discipline of RD on the PWC Accommodation Program will be less direct because 56 per cent of the space to be charged to tenants will be from paid-up inventory, using imputed costs. However, RD will provide a better financial display and it will change, for the better, the tenant/PWC relationship by focussing the discussion on services and costs. It will also make more visible future cases of excess costs in providing accommodation. With the streamlined PWC inventory recommended elsewhere in this report, the most difficult properties for determining market rates have been removed from the PWC inventory. Thus, the implementation of RD for the Accommodation Program will be simplified.

PWC is in the process of developing new financial and operational reporting systems to meet the needs of RD. Most of these systems are required for good cost accounting regardless of whether RD is implemented. The cost of system development should not be a major issue in accessing the RD concept. Furthermore, because PWC has invested so much time and money in these systems, it would not now be practical to adopt the U.S. and British approach of converting to RD immediately. Such a decision would force PWC to create new interim systems, and stop work on its current development efforts.

Implementation of revenue dependency will resolve many of the accounting problems of PWC and its tenants, but it will have no impact on the 73 per cent of government property held by other authorities. Some of these properties, particularly those held by commercial corporations under the Minister of Transport, already have sound private-sector-based accounting systems. If implemented, our recommendations will increase the amount of property under such financial practices.

Nonetheless, the majority of federal property will not fall under the custody of PWC or commercial organizations. These properties (e.g.: defence bases, prisons, national parks) do not have realistic market rates and generally are not subject to alternative highest and best use concepts. We considered the possibility of revising the accounting systems for these properties so that the full cost including depreciation and interest would be formally allocated and reported on by program users. We concluded that although such allocation should be contained in long-range capital planning and individual project analysis, it would have marginal value on a continuing, reporting basis. It would be better to concentrate financial analysis on selected properties than on development of expensive and complex information systems.

On the other hand, the cash accounting systems for many of these properties require improvement. In particular, there is a need for increased commonality among property programs in the intepretation of expenditures (eg: capital vs. Operation and Maintenance) and in reporting of resource utilization.

OPTIONS

The study team recommends to the Task Force that the government consider:

- restating its commitment without qualifications to full revenue dependency for PWC and establishing firm deadlines for implementation. The implementation of full revenue dependency for the Services Program should be set for April 1, 1986 and for the Accommodation Program, April 1, 1987; and

- having the Office of the Comptroller General in conjunction with the proposed Real Property Unit review government-wide systems to ensure development of more common information on real property activities.

CONTRACTING OUT POLICY

BACKGROUND

The current policy of the federal government is to contract out work where it is more economic than using in-house staff. Many of the larger provinces in Canada follow a rigorous policy of contracting out. A debate has been ongoing since the early 1960s and the Glassco Commission as to how much federal work should be done by public servants and what portion should be performed on contract by the private sector. Today's policy was enunciated in 1975 and has been pursued ever since. There are three major labour-intensive functions in the field of real property management subject to contracting out policy: design, construction, and the operation and maintenance of buildings or other facilities.

In design, most major departments (Defence, Transport, DINA, Parks, and PWC) have their own in-house architectural and engineering staff and contract out to the private sector a large portion of these services. A number of other departments and agencies maintain a small in-house professional core (e.g. National Museums Corporation) to be responsible for needs identification and project development and contract with PWC to provide the design service. PWC in turn contracts to the private sector. It has been estimated that 70 per cent of government design work is now contracted out to the private sector. There are no precise numbers on the cost of design services, but our rough calculations of the cost of in-house design work and our discussions with outside authorities indicate that design tends to be more expensive when performed in-house.

The major departments have their own in-house project management staff and other departments use Public Works for some or all of the project management, contracting and supervision services. Regardless of the source, with the exception of military construction units, virtually all federal construction requirements are performed on contract by the private sector.

The major departments arrange for the routine maintenance and operations of their own facilities. Others use PWC as their agent. A high percentage of the current routine maintenance work being performed in federal facilities is being done by private sector contractors. It includes minor repairs, fit-ups and cleaning. The percentage is increasing because contracted services are 25 to 30 per cent less expensive and because of person-year restraints on in-house resources. On the other hand, most operating functions are performed by in-house employees. These tasks are most commonly associated with heating, ventilation, air conditioning and other mechanical systems, fire protection, (Ministry of Transport and Department of National Defence), power generation, etc. Many of these activities are run 24 hours a day, 7 days a week. Operation and Maintenance expenditures are not individually separated in government accounting; however, it is estimated that 40 per cent of combined operating and maintenance work is contracted out. The major exceptions are DND, which does 70 per cent of its operating and maintenance using in-house staff and DOT, 80 per cent in-house.

OBSERVATIONS

In the view of the study team there are several arguments for performing some work in-house:

- it requires a unique skill not readily available;
- the job requires an in-depth knowledge of the specific program area being served;
- the work demands high levels of security;
- it is necessary to maintain an internal core of competence in the subject skill;
- in many locations there is no contractor base; and
- in the National Capital Region, the federal government is such a large percentage of the market, that it creates a private sector monopoly which results in increased costs.

Other arguments stand for contracting work out:

- high degrees of variation in workload make it uneconomic to staff to the peak demand levels;
- it can be more efficient and effective to buy state of the art knowledge than develop it in-house;
- it is not economical to incur the long-term liabilities of in-house employees in skill areas which are of a short-term nature;
- the skills being sought are not the business of the program; and

- it would be advantageous to transfer knowledge in specialized government functions to the private sector to further international trade opportunities.

On the surface, the current contracting-out policy is rational. In actual practice, the definition of 'more economic' is a difficult one. There is no standard method of costing the in-house service. The government does not usually, for example, factor the unfunded liabilities associated with in-house staff (benefits, pensions, leave, etc.) in the make-or-buy decision. It often does not consider associated overhead, such as supervision or transportation to the work site. This has created a structural bias against contracting out.

In the United States recent changes in the process have been designed to favor contracting work out. In-house work is assumed as the exception. Federal agencies have to periodically justify the use of in-house resources. If they cannot demonstrate that they are 10-15 per cent less expensive than contracted services, the agency must turn to a contracting out mode.

Many private sector real property operators resort almost exclusively to contracting out. They most frequently cite the rationale of management focus, saying that: "If its not the business we're in, we contract it out." They acknowledge their areas of expertise and are quick to turn outside of their organization for other skills. We think that with certain exceptions, this is an appropriate model for the federal government.

The current contracting process is a barrier to contracting out. It is cumbersome, lengthy and has many structural barriers, which include:

- the turn around time for contract award is slow and promotes the use of in-house staff;
- the lack of a corporate memory to reuse good performing contractors and exclude bad ones creates distrust and uncertainty in each relationship;
- the practice of accepting only the lowest tender results in inconsistent quality and a subsequent tendency to only trust in-house staff; and
- the lack of, or failure to enforce, penalties for non-performing contractors reduces the reliability of contracted service.

This process has created barriers to further contracting out on smaller projects and duplication and excessive double-checking and criticism by in-house professionals of the work done by private sector contractors. The objective of further contracting out is commendable both for economic and policy reasons, but it cannot be carried out effectively without changes to the contracting process.

Contracting out for design work has reached a relatively high level of 70 per cent. There are some marginal increases in contracting which could be pursued, particularly in a few departments and agencies. Perhaps a target of 80 to 85 per cent contracted out would be ideal. However, as described in other papers of this study team, the real issue of contracted design work is how contract consultants are managed by in-house staff, not the degree of contracting out.

Clearly, the current federal policy on contracting out for operations and maintenance work, premised on the cost of in-house work as a standard, has not set the tone for action. Much of this contracting out has resulted from constraint on person-years, rather than economic considerations. It is the study team's view that what is needed is a public policy decision to contract out as the norm and to use in-house as the exception. As in the United States, the burden of proof should be to justify in-house staff.

Merely setting a policy direction will not be sufficient to significantly change levels of contracting-out for Operations and Maintenance work. While there is no magic level for contracting out, we recommend that mechanisms be put in place whereby departments and agencies establish specific targets and develop specific implementation plans for increasing their contracting out over a three to five year period. A zero base of in-house staff should be the starting point.

As well, to be successful in a contract out scenario, Ministers and officials must be able to contract with qualified individuals in a reasonable amount of time. The existing processes ought to be simplified in line with recommendations elsewhere in this report.

The option of increased contracting out could have an impact on the jobs of existing public servants. This will be alleviated somewhat by an expected high rate of attrition among an aging population. However, in areas where attrition will not suffice, related personnel policies and practices, including employment of effected government staff by successful contractors, will need to be developed.

OPTIONS

For all of these reasons, the study team recommends to the Task Force that the government consider contracting out all property related work, unless it can be proven that in-house staff are operationally essential or more economic. Departments should establish specific targets and implementation programs for increased contracting out starting with a zero-base assumption.

In support of this policy, the government should establish common policies and practices related to full costing of internal services in the make or buy decisions.

PROCESSES FOR PLANNING, APPROVAL AND EXECUTION

BACKGROUND

The acquisition or construction of real property to accommodate federal government departments and agencies is an ongoing, capital intensive activity, subject to complex processes for planning, approval and execution. The type of property being built or acquired covers a wide range of configurations, from general office space to specialized laboratories. Departmental skill at managing the process varies as well. Some organizations have large, well developed in-house staff. Others rely almost exclusively on the services of Public Works.

Planning

Treasury Board (TB) policy requires that departments periodically review land use to ensure:

- the efficient provision for government service;
- the efficient use of government real property; and
- the achievement of wider social, economic and environmental objectives.

In addition, over the past several years TB has instructed departments to table long term capital plans. Although not all plans have been submitted and approved, most departments have made reasonable attempts to comply. In addition to the long range plans, departments submit requests for capital funds on an annual basis through the Multi-Year Operational Plan (MYOP) process. Funds included in the long-range plans are not automatically approved in the MYOP. The MYOP process must by necessity operate within the confines of short-run fiscal considerations.

Departments must also seek approval for funds for individual projects in addition to the MYOP process. Planning documents which accompany these requests for capital funds are expected to include a needs analysis, an impartial assessment of options, realistic capital cost estimates and an analysis of life-cycle costs.

Additional formal processes have also been defined for planning and managing Major Crown Projects (those in excess of $100 million). Presented in Chapter 140 of the Treasury Board Administrative Policy Manual, they include the creation of a planning committee to conduct the analysis and present a preferred option for approval. The options analysis information is, in most cases where there are policy/resource implications, submitted to a Cabinet policy committee. Other cases could be submitted to the Treasury Board under cover of a Treasury Board submission.

Although there have been few real property projects over $100 million processed, the Major Crown Projects process has been applied to projects below that amount.

Project Approval

All projects which exceed departmental delegated authorities must come through Treasury Board for all levels of approval. The delegated authorities of departments to directly contract for design or construction vary widely, based on TB's historical judgments of a department's ability to deliver.

In most projects where the cost estimate exceeds delegated authorities, at least two sequential approvals are required:

The Preliminary Project Approval (PPA); and
The Effective Project Approval (EPA)

Documentation requesting these approvals becomes increasingly lengthy and complex. In the event of overruns, a separate TB submission and approval is required.

The Preliminary Project Approval (PPA) authorizes the department to begin Project Definition and Conceptual Design stages. This is usually the first significant expenditure of funds on a project. At the completion of this phase, application is again made to the Treasury Board Secretariat for the Effective Project Approval. In this instance, the submission includes conceptual design and refined cost estimates for the project. Upon receipt of the Effective Project Approval, work can proceed on working drawings and the execution process begins. Both of these approvals are only approvals to proceed. Individual transactions (e.g. hiring architects, engineers) must also go through an approval routine governed by contract regulations.

At various steps in the approval to proceed process, different classes of estimates are prepared.

Estimate	**Approval**
Class D Estimate: based upon a statement of requirements and an outline of potential solutions. An indication of rough order of magnitude.	**Cabinet:** generally used when approval is sought from a Cabinet policy committee or within a department for approval to proceed with planning.
Class C Estimate: based upon a general description of the end item, construction experience and market conditions. It is generally sufficient for selecting a preferred option and obtaining Preliminary Project Approval.	**Preliminary Project Approval**
Class B Estimate: data which exists after the completion of site investigation and major systems design.	**Effective Project Approval**
Class A Estimate: based upon a complete description of the end item, with working drawings and specifications in hand.	Used as a base for contracting work.

Project Execution

In most projects standard project management processes are followed, usually revolving around a project manager. In PWC projects the manager is usually a staff person from PWC. Some of the larger departments that manage their own property have in-house project managers. Rarely is this function contracted out. In the 1984 Report of the Auditor General, it was concluded that the standard of the project management process was significantly advanced and that a project management organization was usually in place early in the life of a project.

For design work, major departments (Transport, DND, Parks, PWC, and External) can engage architects and engineers directly provided that the amount of the contract falls within its delegated authority. No departments, save PWC, have a design fee limit above $100,000 which would normally accommodate construction project work of approximately $2 million. Public Works Canada has $400,000, which would roughly relate to an $8 million construction project.

The process for selecting architects and engineers varies for different value projects:

- for smaller design contracts, generally below $15,000, the qualifications of several firms are considered at the departmental level and one is requested to perform the work;
- for design contracts between $15,000 and $100,000, a similar process ensues, but the firms on the short list are reviewed by the appropriate Minister before one is invited to perform the work; and
- for design contracts in excess of $100,000 a more formal process is involved. A list of firms is submitted to the appropriate Minister. Three or four firms from this list are selected and invited to attend a briefing and submit formal proposals. From these proposals, one firm will be selected by the Minister and awarded the contract. The proposal call process takes 5 to 9 months to complete and is costly to all parties.

Authority to enter into construction contracts without Treasury Board approval is generally limited to $200,000. Some Ministers have higher limits. For example, the Minister of Environment has $250,000, the Minister of Indian and Northern Affairs, $500,000, Transport, $2.5 million, Public Works Canada, $5 million and the Minister of National Defence, $10 million. Departments can directly award contracts within their limits provided they have two valid tenders and accept the lowest.

Recently, the formal process was considerably changed for both the approval and the contracting process in the Special Recovery Capital Projects Program (SRCPP). This was an accelerated capital project system designed to aid in national economic recovery. Projects under SRCPP were submitted to Ministers as a package. Project inter-relationships and total impacts were clear. There were two key changes to normal processes. The Preliminary Project Approval for each project was delegated to the Minister responsible for SRCPP and transactional authority to enter into contracts was entirely delegated providing that the amount was within the original project estimate and that there was a competitive selection process. At the same time that these authorities were delegated, accountability was strengthened with more stringent performance objectives and reporting requirements.

OBSERVATIONS

It is the view of the study team that long-range planning for real property does not exist uniformly across all federal departments and agencies. Some of the larger property holders have developed fairly detailed plans (for example, Parks, and the Department of National Defence). These plans revolve around the efficient fulfilment of a program requirement and, to a lesser extent, land use efficiency. For all property holders, the cost of contributions to wider economic and social objectives is not easily identifiable, nor is the opportunity cost of alternative land uses. Public Works Canada has been having particular problems producing its plan because of its unique position as arbitrater between departments in the National Capital Region.

Recent surveys of departments and agencies have found varying degrees of concern with the current project approval process. Current procedures are time-consuming, costly and ineffective from an operational perspective. Departmental comments ranged from concerns over the level of technical detail requested by Treasury Board analysts with little real property expertise, to the number of times a project must be reviewed by the Board.

The contract approval process has been criticized on several fronts, mainly centred around lack of delegated authorities from TB and the competitive selection process. Low delegated authorities mean repeated trips to the Board for approvals. Although the results are not yet in on the impacts of decreased central control in SRCPP, it is already evident that a 50 per cent time saving was generated as a result of delegating contracting authorities.

The consultant and contraction selection process has two areas of contention. The practice of selecting design architects/engineers for relatively small projects via proposal call is time-consuming and expensive for both parties. The rigid interpretation of contract regulations leads almost invariably to the acceptance of the lowest bid in construction tender calls, effectively ignoring the relative qualifications of all contractors submitting bids.

FUTURE COURSES

Planning and Project Approvals

Long-range capital plans, annual planning/budgeting and project approvals should be more closely integrated, the study team maintains. Departments should use this process to periodically submit a package of projects for approval as part of the government's operational planning system. The long range plan will present the general thrusts and directions for capital expenditures over the long term. The annual budget will specify which elements of the approved long-term plan come due that year and their estimated cost (probably at a Class C level).

This process should suffice to give the department Preliminary Project Approval for all those projects in that year's plan. There should be no need for individual submissions, provided they are within the estimated project costs and within the limits of the department's transactional authority. The department would return to TB for award of the Effective Project Approval, although it would be advantageous to increase the delegated level for EPA's to Ministers as well.

Execution

There are options available as well in the contracting process as it applies to the execution of projects in both the selection of architects and engineers and construction contractors.

With respect to the engagement of design consultants, the government should establish a formal, centralized inventory of prequalified consultants. The inventory could be designed to accommodate any special interests such as regional equity or small business participation. Consultants would be selected from the list on a rotational basis, their ability to conduct the specific work in question assessed, and then invited to negotiate a price for the work. If a contract cannot be negotiated, the consultants name would remain at the top of the list.

For larger projects, we support the use of proposal calls. This is appropriate where sensitive, costly projects are involved but the 'monumental' nature of the project is not such as to warrant a full design competition. The proposal call threshold is now $100,000 for consultant fees, which would only accommodate projects costing approximately $2 million. The threshold for design fees should be raised to the neighbourhood of $500,000, which effectively accommodates a $10 million project.

By using a rotating list, the consultant selection process will become more neutral and by raising the threshold for proposal calls to $500,000, the selection process will be streamlined and shortened. However, both of these actions will heighten the importance of the development and administration of the prequalification system. In this light, we recommend that representatives of the private sector professions be formally involved in the development and the review of the administration of this system.

Elsewhere in this report, we have suggested that all consultant contracting be centralized under the Minister of Public Works. We think it appropriate that the signing authority for such contracts be raised from the current $400,000 limit to $1,000,000.

The current convention of selecting the lowest bid in every construction and maintenance contract tender is unsatisfactory. The concept of contractor competence should be given greater importance in the decision. The government should provide authority to the PWC Contracting Service, under specific prescribed rules and as part of a very visible process, to choose other than the lowest tender. We do not anticipate that the volume of tenders let to other than the lowest bid will be great, but the avenue must be open.

OPTIONS

The study team recommends to the Task Force that:

- Treasury Board project approval be incorporated into the annual budgeting process and the Preliminary Project Approval should be delegated to line Ministers within the approved budget;

- delegated levels of Effective Project Approvals to line Ministers be increased. At the same time, the threshold for approval of consultant contracts by the Minister of Public Works should be raised from $400,000 to $1,000,000;

- the design contracting process be amended to make use of a central inventory of prequalified consultants. Below the value of $500,000, consultants should be selected from the list on a rotational basis, their ability to perform the specific task assessed and one consultant invited to negotiate a price. For contracts above $500,000, consultants should continue to be invited by public notice to submit proposals;

- a revised contracting process for consultants be developed in conjunction with and periodically reviewed by professional representatives from the private sector; and

- the process for approval of construction contracts be changed to provide authority to the PWC Contracting Service to choose other than the lowest tender under prescribed rules and as part of a visible process.

HIGHEST AND BEST USE OF REAL PROPERTY

BACKGROUND

The Federal Land Management (FLM) principle states that:

> "Federal lands should be managed so as to combine the efficient provision of government services and the efficient use of federal real property with the achievement of wider social, economic and environmental objectives." TBS Administrative Policy Manual 110.2.

Current interpretation of the policy emphasizes achievement of the broader objectives at the expense of the highest and best use of real property.

The Treasury Board Secretariat (TBS) estimates the current value of federal real property to be between $40 billion and $60 billion. The holdings of departments and agencies are reported in the Central Real Property Inventory (CRPI). It provides information on location, holding department, size, original cost and identification of the current occupants. PWC maintains the CRPI but the primary responsibility for inputing data is departmental. The quality of the information is directly dependent on the quality of the input from the department. The inventory is constantly criticized for containing incomplete or inaccurate data.

Public Works Canada, acting on behalf of Treasury Board Secretariat, inventories and reports on properties suitable for alternate uses or disposal using the Area Screening Canada Program (ASCP). ASCP reports have been completed for almost 50 urban areas and work is continuing. In spite of ongoing follow-up from TBS, very few ASCP recommendations have been acted upon. The 1984 Report of the Auditor General stated that of 508 cases where potential for more intensive use of a property had been identified, in no more than 28 cases had the identified potential been realized.

The system effectively lets a manager maintain uneconomic property and funds him to do it. Capital expenditures (for acquisition or major improvement) on real property are accounted for by the government's cash accounting system, and appear in total in the year in which the expense is incurred. Money for Operating and

Maintaining (O&M) real property is also obtained via the annual budgeting process. It is ironic that large O&M expenditure requests receive almost routine approval while relatively small capital programs are vigourously challenged and frequently modified or eliminated.

The federal government does not pay taxes on property or structures that it owns. In most instances, a grant in lieu of taxes is made to the appropriate jurisdiction, often a municipal government. These are statutory payments. With the exception of the National Capital Commission, these grants in lieu of taxes are currently paid by Public Works Canada (PWC), and are not allocated to, nor appear in the estimates of, the occupant department.

The Department of Public Works is responsible for managing or selling real properties declared surplus by federal departments and agencies. A department which considers a piece of real property to be surplus to its needs voluntarily surrenders the property to PWC for eventual disposal or reallocation within the federal government. PWC attempts to dispose of the property itself using in-house staff. In 1983-84, total sales were about $10 million. PWC has been given a disposal target for 1985/86 of $27 million.

The Treasury Board Advisory Committee on Federal Land Management (TBAC/FLM) is charged with the review and advice to TB of all significant real property proposals to ensure their consistency with policy. The committee is not a control mechanism and has no vested authority to enforce decisions. The committee is chaired by a middle level TBS official. PWC sits on TBAC/FLM and it is from this forum that a recommendation for disposal would be put to the Treasury Board. In recent years the volume of recommendations has not been heavy.

The President of the Treasury Board and the Minister of Public Works have recently announced a proactive program for the disposal of surplus property. Treasury Board Secretariat officials have produced rough calculations that estimate the potential market value of saleable property to be in the area of $1.0 billion. In our view, this is an unreasonably high figure but there is certainly significant potential.

OBSERVATIONS

In the view of the study team, the Federal Land Management policy has created a bias towards inaction. Before the 1975 FLM policy, 97 per cent of surplus lands were sold. Since then the policy has required that federal land holdings which are no longer required to meet a department's needs be retained to help achieve broader government objectives. Few properties have been disposed of, even fewer at market rates. Regardless of the intent, the policy has been interpreted so as to emphasize the broader objectives at the expense of economic real property management. While recognizing broader objectives, the policy needs to be restated to emphasize the economic considerations.

There is no incentive for a departmental manager to volunteer properties for sale. There is little cost to the manager for holding the property unless it incurs an inordinate maintenance charge. Grants in lieu of taxes are paid by another body (PWC) and the property is valued for accounting purposes at one dollar. Even if the property is expensive to maintain, the realities of government budgeting make this money easier to obtain than capital funds to replace the facility. When a property is disposed of, the proceeds from the sale can be credited to the resource 'envelope' from which the program is funded. This is of little value to the program as, in the end, if it wishes to recover the funds it must vie for them with any other programs that draw on that envelope.

The current process lacks authority to implement more efficient use or disposal recommendations. Individual departments to a large extent operate their property autonomously and do not view it as part of a government-wide inventory. If a surplus property is suitable for reallocation to some other purpose in the federal government, PWC is charged with considering this in the process of approving a land acquisition request. There have, however, been few instances in recent years where surplus property has met the requirements specifications of a PWC client department. In addition, other levels of government (provincial, municipal) often exert pressure to assume ownership of surplus property, often at less than its market value.

There is no mechanism for considering properties for alternative uses if they have not been formally surrendered as surplus. The benefits that a real property could generate if put to its highest and best use, either in terms of revenues or level of service, are rarely factored into property decisions.

Couple the lack of incentive to a manager to dispose of a property with a lack of authority by central agencies (TBS, PWC) to force a disposal, add a failure to recognize opportunity costs, and it is understandable why there is little action on surplus property identification and disposition. Options for remedying the current disposal inaction involve establishing the authority of a central group to identify surplus property and initiating new disposal processes and incentives. The objective of the strategy should be to instill an attitude among property managers that they hold property on behalf of, and for the benefit of, the overall Government of Canada.

One way to increase central authority is to assign all real property to a central agency and lease parcels to departments for specific uses, for specific periods. As each period expires, a review of the property use could be conducted before a decision to renew is made. This would remove from any department the feeling that they have proprietary rights to any specific property. This would involve a massive paperwork exercise to force change through mechanical means. The government already has central holding of real property, it has lacked the focus to manage it. Thus, we prefer an approach in which individual users hold property, but that the Real Property Unit has a real challenge authority over its use.

To assist with disposal, greater use of private sector expertise should be made. For example, the Province of Ontario uses private realtors for disposal.

OPTIONS

The study team recommends to the Task Force that the government consider:

- assigning to the new Real Property Unit authority to periodically and systematically 'challenge' a department's continued holding of a property and 'expropriate' it if insufficent need is identified;

- establishing a common approach for calculating all costs (including depreciation, interest, taxes) of holding a property in all planning and analysis of highest and best use of individual properties;

- continuing the proactive program of identification and disposal of surplus property and making greater use of private sector realty expertise to assist with disposal; and

- restating the Federal Land Management principle to give greater emphasis to the efficient and economic management of real property.

MANAGEMENT OF ACCOMMODATION STANDARDS

BACKGROUND

Chapter 120 of the Administrative Policy Manual establishes the authorities and standards for the management of accommodation and accommodation services. The policy applies to Schedule A and B organizations with respect to space provided by Public Works Canada and to office accommodations provided by departments with separate authorities. The standards apply to approximately 4.0 million square metres of rentable space, which is 14 per cent of total government building space.

The policy of the government is to provide office space of a quality and quantity equal to the average of major private sector employers. The policy establishes office accommodation space standards using a formula which multiplies the number of persons in an organization by a square metre per person factor, which factor varies according to the average salary of the organization. For example, an organization with an average salary of $20,000 would be allocated 10.0 square metres of usable space per person, and one with $30,000 would be allocated 13.0 square metres per person. This formula is based upon studies which show a correlation between the average salary of an organization and its functional space needs.

By applying the formula, a control standard limit is calculated which becomes the maximum space entitlement for an organization for normal office accommodation, including work station spaces, conference rooms, file and library areas. Specialized facilities such as research laboratories, computer centres and major storage areas are outside the control standard and are controlled individually on a case-by-case basis. Within these macro control standards, individual departments are to develop and implement their own office planning standards.

The Common Service Policy designates PWC as responsible for controlling the use of these standards. When requesting space, PWC tenants are to provide a full accounting of space requirements within this standard and PWC is only to provide such space if the request is within the policy. If the request exceeds the control limit, tenant organizations are to receive prior Treasury Board approval. In addition to this control role, PWC has responsibility for advising

Treasury Board on the nature of the standards and for maintaining an Accommodation Management Information System (AMIS) which records the information used to apply the standards.

The primary responsibility for enforcement of the standards is assigned to each deputy head, who is responsible for establishing reporting systems and auditing plans to monitor departmental space utilization. The Administrative Policy Branch, Treasury Board, monitors compliance through periodic review.

This system or variations of it have been in place since the early 1970s. It has undergone several modifications since that time. It replaced an unofficial flat allocation standard (135 sq. ft or 12.5 square metres per person) which was not being followed. It is ironic that the General Services Administration in the United States has recently adopted 135 sq. ft. as its target for average space utilization.

Reviews by individual departments, Treasury Board, the Auditor General and Public Works Canada, have all revealed that the system has not been observed. Specifically:

- departments occupy on average from 5 per cent to 10 per cent above the standard;
- PWC occasionally provides space to departments above the standards without the required Treasury Board approval; and
- the available data on space occupied, population and average salary required to operate the system is unreliable.

If the various over-occupancy figures are accurate, at an annual equivalent rental value of $150 per square metre, the excess space costs between $30 and $60 million in rent each year.

Three major initiatives are underway to improve space occupancy. Firstly, by September 1985, PWC is committed to produce an updated, improved Accommodation Management Information System. Secondly, PWC is committed to a multi-year space optimization program to recapture excess space. Some 21,000 square metres were recaptured in 1984-85, the 1985-86 target is 30,000 square metres. This program is based upon reducing occupancy levels of selected organizations as they make major accommodation changes.

Thirdly, PWC, Treasury Board Secretariat and tenants are reviewing the standards and are considering major revisions. The proposed concept is based upon two or three levels of flat standards, with approval by Treasury Board of individual departmental allocations.

OBSERVATIONS

It is the view of the study team that the accommodation space standards system has not worked. Tenants claim, with justification, that each time the Treasury Board policies have been modified over the past 12 years, the control limit has effectively been reduced. The result is that a department which was within standards one year, finds itself in non-compliance the next.

Tenants are also aware that the data upon which the standards are based are highly subjective and manipulatible. Space allocations depend upon a series of interpretations of who is an employee and which employees are in which buildings. The decision on space to be included within the control standard as against the special space outside the standard is often judgemental. The organizations charged with reviewing requests for accommodation - Program Branch (program approval and population), Administrative Policy Branch (overall policy compliance) and PWC (technical interpretations) - often do not communicate and/or have different interpretations of the policy.

Many tenant organizations have not fulfilled their roles under the system. Many have not established functional planning guides and standards within their organizations, and if they have, they often do not enforce them.

For many years PWC has considered that enforcing such standards is a control role inconsistent with its service orientation and that Treasury Board should carry out this role. Treasury Board has considered that PWC has the responsibility to abide by government policies and standards and should do so. With these differing attitudes, it is not surprising that enforcement has not been strong. From our perspective, PWC has an unacceptable conflict because the interpretation of accommodation standards is so subjective. PWC is being asked to be a policeman to enforce regulations as well as the judge in interpreting the regulations. The interpretation role belongs with the proposed Real Property Unit.

The end result of the conflicts over interpretation and enforcement of the standards is that all parties, tenants/TBS/PWC, have been playing rigid numbers games with standards, which at their best, are very general and judgemental. The more flexible systems now being developed (described earlier) would appear to be on the right track.

Due to inadequate data on government occupancy, there is no firm evidence that the government is more generous with its office accommodation than the private sector. Various audit observations have noted that occupancy figures are above the control standard, but the system allows for exceeding the control standard with TB approval. All that may be missing in many cases is the appropriate approvals. Thus, the excess space costs of $30 to $60 million are highly unreliable. The real figure is probably closer to the $40 million level.

The costs of 'recapturing' excess space can be considerable. PWC has estimated that for every metre of space recaptured, about 9 metres of space must be renovated. It is difficult to establish an accurate cost per square metres recaptured because such costs are combined with general fit-up of space. Nonetheless, a rough estimate is $300 per square metres which results in a payback period for investments in space recapture of about 2 years.

A major barrier to space recapture is the disruption to the operations of the effected organization. To recapture the estimated excess space in the PWC inventory, about 200,000 individuals will have to be moved. The major organization changes expected in government over the next few years as the result of the work of the Task Force on Program Review, will provide an opportunity to recapture most excess space. However, the PWC program will have to be accelerated to keep pace with the anticipated changes.

OPTIONS

The study team recommends to the Task Force that the government consider:

- revising the Treasury Board guidelines in light of the present review to a system whereby the functional allocation of space of each organization is approved individually rather than the present rigid system based on average salaries;

- assigning interpretation and compliance control of these standards to the proposed Real Property Unit; and

- accelerating PWC space optimization program to recapture excess space.

SECTION 4 - PUBLIC WORKS CANADA

INTRODUCTION

In the study team's opinion, Public Works should become a common service agency and provide real property services and general purpose accommodation to all departments and agencies on a full cost recovery basis. To achieve improved accountability and efficiency, a number of measures could to be taken:

- a streamlining of current operational responsibilities such as: transferring marine and land transportation programs to other levels of government, transferring custody for special purpose buildings in the National Capital Region to program/user departments, transferring responsibility for central government management activities to a new Real Property Unit and reducing the utilization of Crown corporations for social objectives;
- an expanded mandate to deliver real property services to all departments and agencies: these services to include a mandatory contracting service and optional design and operation and maintenance services;
- a reduction of the operational organization through increased contracting out of the majority of the services to the private sector; and
- a revised management structure to focus on accommodation and real property services on a full cost recovery basis.

BACKGROUND

Established by the Public Works Act at the time of Confederation, Public Works Canada (PWC) was originally responsible for all real property and land management of the Government of Canada. This included a wide range of professional and support activities related to buildings, roads, locks, dams, bridges, etc. PWC has seen its responsibilities modified since that time as custody for specific properties were transferred to other designated Ministers in support of the programs for which they were responsible.

After the Royal Commission on Government Organization (Glassco 1962), PWC ceased its involvement in furniture procurement and supply. In the early 1980s, approximately one half of PWC's inventory was transferred to Canada Post upon its conversion to a Crown corporation, which has had a major operational impact on PWC. In the 1970s, after the Treasury Board promulgation of the Federal Land Management Policy, PWC assumed increased responsibilities in support of central management of real property. PWC became a land management advisor to Treasury Board and administrator of a number of programs, with responsibility for the compiling of the Central Real Property Inventory, for the expropriation of land for all departments, agencies and Crown corporations, for the disposal of all surplus land and buildings and for land and real property projects in support of 'broader' objectives.

Currently PWC is the exclusive and mandatory provider of office accommodation for the Government of Canada. Almost 75 per cent of this accommodation is provided free of charge to some 110 federal departments and agencies. PWC also provides special purpose facilities (such as laboratories, museums) in the National Capital Region for which it plans, budgets and carries the costs. In 1984-85 PWC spent about $650 million to operate and lease almost 6 million square metres of accommodation. It also spent $140 million to construct and renovate crown-owned facilities.

PWC provides a range of real property services not only in support of its own accommodation, marine and transportation programs, but to other departments and agencies which do not have appropriate in-house staff to undertake the activities. In fact, over 60 per cent of its architectural and engineering services, 30 per cent of its property maintenance services, 80 per cent of its real estate services and 100 per cent of its dredging services are performed for other departments. Until April 1, 1985, some departments paid for these services while the majority received the services in support of their programs at no charge. After April 1, 1985, all departments will pay direct costs for services and will pay full costs as soon as relevant information systems are developed. PWC has a complement of 8,323 person-years to manage and deliver the services. Even with this level of staff, a high percentage of the services are contracted to the private sector; for example, 90 per cent of the architectural and engineering services are handled by outside consultants.

PWC also continues to operate and construct some highways, bridges, locks, dams and drydocks which do not at this time support government operations but are vestiges of activities originally defined in the 1867 legislation.

OBSERVATIONS

Role and Mandate

It is the study team's view that the Public Works Act is out of date: it does not reflect the present practices of PWC in providing federal government accommodation and real property services to other federal departments and agencies. Commencing with the Royal Commission on Government Organization (Glassco) in 1962, numerous reports and studies have contained extensive recommendations that Public Works should be assigned a substantially streamlined role as a common service agency in support of the management of federal real property. This study team does not differ from this position. In spite of over 25 years of discussion on the need for PWC to commence cost recovery of the goods and services it provides, there continues to be resistance, both within PWC and within central agencies, to get on with the job. Years of discussions and reports and millions of dollars later, the debate still focuses on the control of only 14 per cent of the government's crown-owned accommodation, which is currently in the custody of PWC. The study team recommends that the government amend the Public Works Act to clearly reflect the common service role of the department.

Service Role

PWC provides four major types of services: architectural and engineering services, realty management services, real estate services and dredging services. With 46 separate organizations having their own real property authority, it is a myth that Public Works is the government's real property manager; at best it is only a service agency. Many departments have the authority to provide their own services with in-house staff or to engage PWC services. The proliferation of professional and technical real property services across government has resulted in the quality of real property management across government being very inconsistent. The overlap and duplication between competing agencies, especially now that PWC will begin to charge for its services, undermines the efficiencies possible within government. The study team recommends that architectural, engineering and real estate services and, where operationally feasible (for example the NCC), property maintenance services be consolidated within PWC and provided on a full cost recovery basis to client departments.

Public Works Canada has, just this year, commenced charging 'direct costs' for its services. PWC will eventually be charging fees which are comparable to the private sector. Since PWC's costs tend to exceed market rates, being forced to operate on market norms will impose an efficiency-stimulating discipline on PWC hitherto lacking. PWC currently forecasts a $30-40 million deficit in the first year of totally revenue-dependent operations (some time in the near future). With a possible withdrawal of the Canada Post's requirements, and in order to balance revenues with expenditures, PWC is facing a potential downsizing approaching 3,000 person-years. The study team recommends that PWC streamline its operations by increasing the proportion of work to be contracted out to the private sector and improving the productivity of in-house staff.

Accommodation Role

Public Works provides accommodation to over 110 departments and agencies across the country. Approximately 40 per cent of the space is provided in the National Capital. Since most clients do not pay for space, PWC attempts to satisfy client requirements within a budget authorized by Parliament. Poor client demand forecasting, inadequate information systems and fiscal restraint hinder Public Works' ability to satisfy client requirements.

As clients request space, PWC strives to accommodate them by offering available space already owned by the crown, by leasing space, or planning for the design and construction of new federal buildings or the lease-purchase of them. PWC does not at this time have the systems in place to charge clients for space, either on a direct cost, full cost recovery or market rate basis. Systems are, however, being developed.

Public Works has an impossible combination of roles. PWC is asked to be service oriented to clients and to act as a central control agent. In the National Capital Region, PWC is responsible for managing a capital budget and allocating capital funds to a number of departments which control their own capital budgets elsewhere in the country. Confusion exists between the 'ownership' and service functions across the system, but particularly in the National Capital Region.

The study team suggests that custody (including capital budgets) be transferred from PWC to program departments for all special purpose buildings, and that designated properties (Parliament Buildings and official residences) be transferred from PWC to the National Capital Commission. PWC will be streamlined and its custody role focused upon the general purpose office buildings and the provision of office space. The study team further suggests that all PWC accommodation be charged to client departments on a revenue-dependent basis, and that efficiency indicators be developed to permit comparisons with the private sector.

Central Government Support Role

PWC also currently carries program responsibilities which are not consistent or compatible with its functions as a common service agency. On behalf of the Treasury Board, PWC is responsible for the central management of municipal grants, fire protection, land expropriation, surplus property maintenance and disposal, the Central Real Property Inventory, improved federal land management and management of projects which achieve broader social objectives. The study team recommends that the control of and accountability for programs which are in support of central real property management be consolidated within one Real Property Unit and not be a part of a Common Service Agency.

In support of the 'broader' objectives, PWC has for the last 10 years assumed responsibility for urban redevelopment projects, especially those involving waterfront redevelopment. The federal intervention has too often been in the form of federal ownership of properties (Vieux Port de Montréal) rather than federal subsidies to local authorities. Once the government owns such properties, it acquires long term financial and political liabilities which reduce its flexibility to withdraw. The government has also established subsidiary Crown corporations under the Canada Lands Company Limited to bypass internal regulations in developing these urban projects.

The study team suggests that no further interventions be authorized, and that current urban redevelopment projects (Vieux Port de Québec, Trois Rivières, Welland, Chicoutimi, Toronto, Vancouver) be either sold to the private sector or transferred to local governments. With respect to specific Crown corporations, the study team suggests to the Task Force that the government consider dismantling the Canada Lands Companies and that ways be explored to privatize the Habourfront Corporation or transfer it to another level of government.

Transportation/Marine Support Role

For various reasons, PWC has gradually assumed financial responsibility for the operation of properties which are best run by provincial and local jurisdictions. This is especially true for the 10 dams, one lock, 17 bridges and several roads of which PWC has custody and control. The study team suggests that the government consider negotiating with the relevant provincial and municipal authorities to divest the federal government of future responsibilities in this area.

Management Structure

The many levels of authority, which are a consequence of the size and complexity of Public Works' operations, have resulted in fragmented decision making. There are too many interlocking functional units within PWC, each of which must be satisfied that it has had an opportunity to react to individual proposals. The study teams suggest that PWC should reexamine its organization structure in order to make it more efficient. The objectives of any reorganization strategy should be to preserve the present decentralization of decision-making while increasing the levels of authority. The study team suggests that PWC appoint separate senior officers with clear accountabilities; one for the Services Program, another for the Accommodation Program.

PUBLIC WORKS CANADA - AN INTRODUCTION

The Department of Public Works was constituted in 1867 from an organization which performed similar duties for the former Province of Canada. The current mission of Public Works Canada (PWC) is to manage real property for the Government of Canada and to provide planning, design, construction and realty services to government departments and agencies while contributing to the government's wider social, economic and environmental objectives in relation to that property. This statement does not imply that PWC is the only agency which performs such activities; it is, however, the only major department dedicated solely to the pursuit of this objective. Real property includes land, buildings (occupied or surplus), roads, highways, bridges and marine works such as locks, dams and dry docks.

PWC operates under authority of the Public Works Act R.S.C. 1970 c. P-38, which has changed very little since 1867. The department's primary role is that of a common service organization in the provision of accommodation and services to clients within the requirements of its legislation and the policies and directives of the Treasury Board of Canada.

PWC is expected to obtain the maximum value for money within the context of government-wide requirements as established primarily by the Treasury Board. The department serves as an advisor to the Board on its directives and to clients on their effective use of the services available. The Treasury Board is responsible for issuing directives and guidelines which apply generally or approving specific variations from those directives and guidelines. Departments and agencies are responsible for determining what they need and, to the extent authorized, funding their requirements.

PWC is also responsible for the administration of all or portions of several statutes and for the fulfillment of a number of specific government mandates related to real property. These statutes include the Bridges Act, the Dry Dock Subsidies Act, the Expropriation Act, the Kingsmere Park Act, the Laurier House Act, the Municipal Grants Acts, the Official Residences Act, the Ottawa River Act, the Public Works Act, the Surplus Crown Assets Act and the Trans-Canada Highway Act.

To achieve these goals, PWC undertakes four types of businesses:

Provision of Services

PWC provides a wide range of professional, technical and operational services required by the Government in relation to the acquisition, management, operation and disposal of real property.

The services PWC currently provides and the levels of person years assigned to them in 1984-85 are:

- architectural and engineering services (1,551 PY);
- realty management services (4,776 PY);
- real estate services (281 PY);
- dredging services (277 PY); and
- administrative and corporate services (1,590 PY).

The cost of providing the services in 1984-85 is $180 million.

Provision of Space

Through the Accommodation Programs, PWC provides the full range of office and other forms of accommodation required to support the operations of government.

In 1984-85 PWC spent $767 million to construct, operate, lease and lease-purchase space in order to accommodate some 110 departments and agencies.

Fulfilment of Specific Government Mandates

Through the Government Realty Assets Support Programs, PWC provides a central capability for the government to achieve wider social, economic and environmental objectives related to real property.

PWC spent $393 million to provide grants in lieu of taxes to municipalities, redevelop urban waterfront properties, undertake technological research and development and undertake special projects.

Marine and Land Transportation Support

PWC provides specific locks, dams, dry docks, highways and bridges to facilitate marine and land transportation.

PWC spent almost $100 million in 1984-85 to support these activities.

Figure 1 shows the overall program structure of the department. The programs define the funding structures through which PWC receives its appropriations from Parliament.

Figure 1. Programs of Public Works Canada

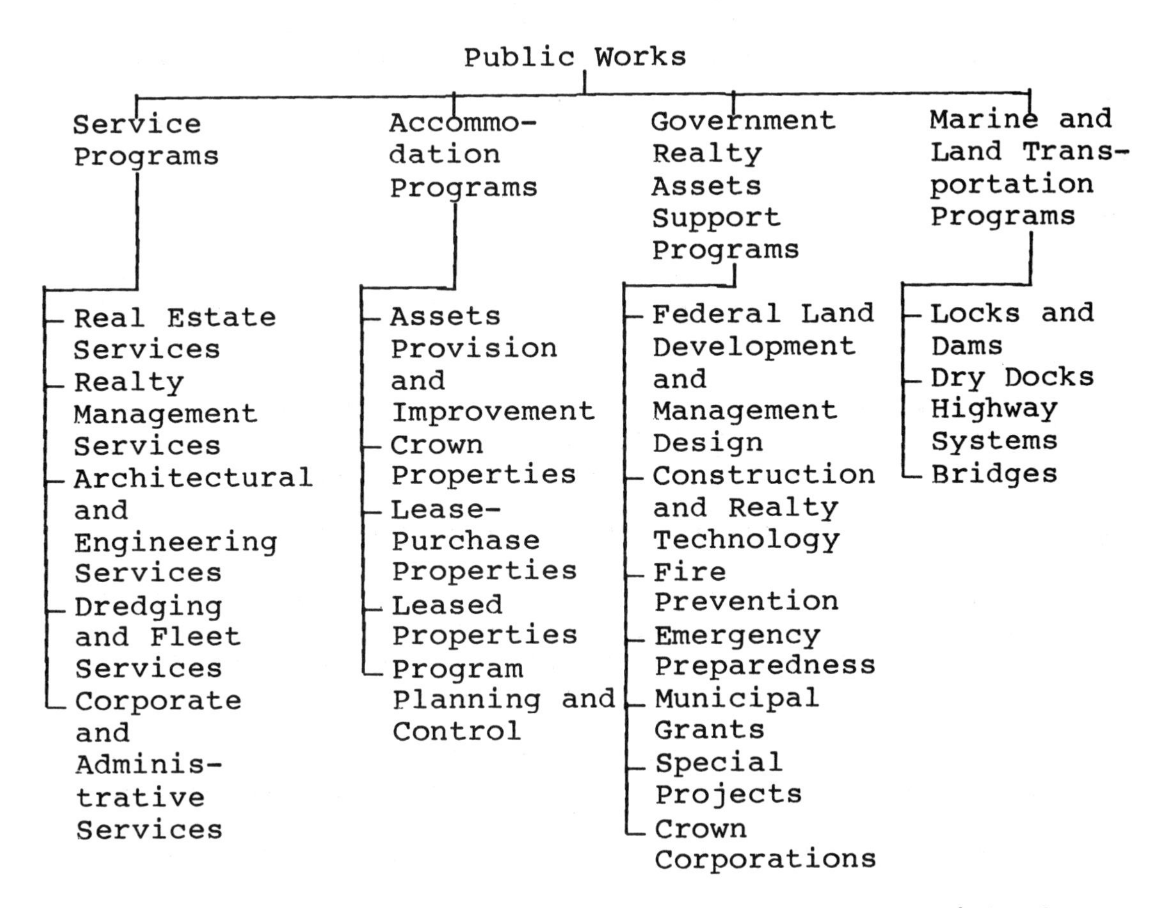

To carry out its responsibilities and accomplish the objectives of its programs, the PWC's organization and operations are highly decentralized into six regional offices located in the five major geographic regions -

Altantic (Halifax), Quebec (Montreal), Ontario (Toronto), Western (Edmonton), Pacific (Vancouver and one for the National Capital Region (Ottawa). The headquarters is in Ottawa.

Approximately 90 per cent of both the 8,791 person-years and the $1.3 billion financial budget are allocated to regions. The regional offices have a substantial degree of autonomy and largely mirror the headquarter's organization.

Figure 2 shows the overall organization structure of the department. One should note the large number of staff reporting directly to the Deputy Minister and the variance of the organizational structure to the program structure. PWC is in the process of undertaking an organizational review to better reflect an accountability framework for its programs. Figure 3 provides an overview of the headquarters and regional matrix organization. Figure 4 provides a crosswalk table between the program structure and the current management structure.

Figure 2. Organization of Public Works Canada

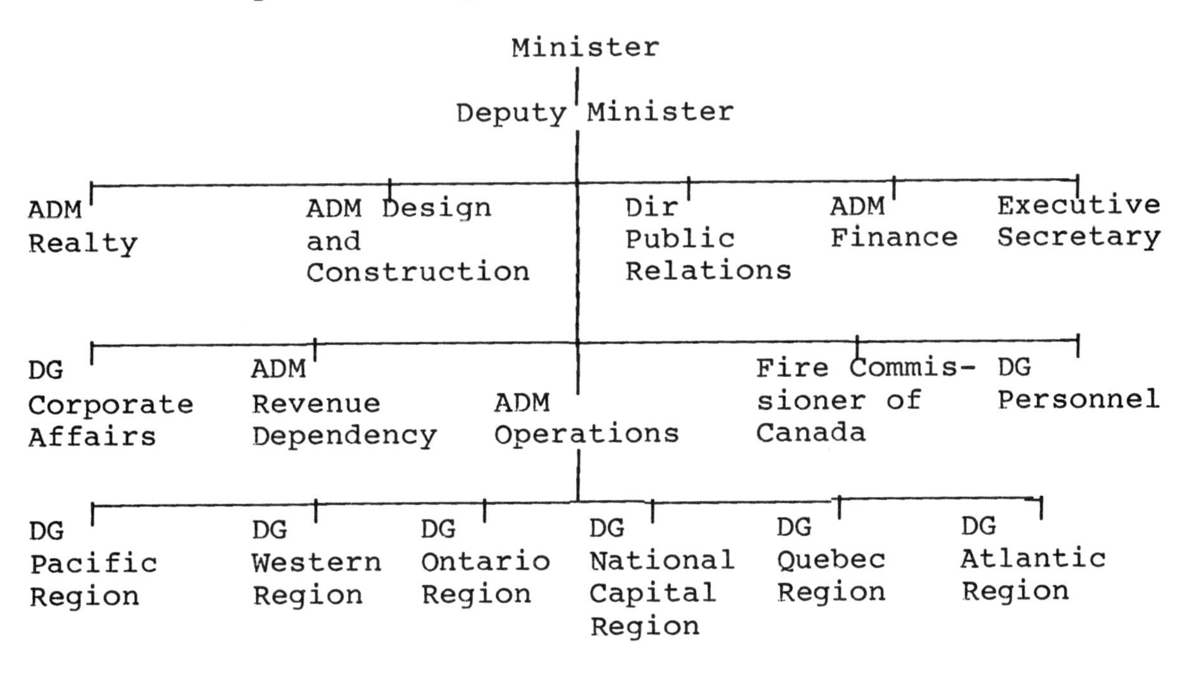

Figure 3. Public Works Canada: A Matrix Organization

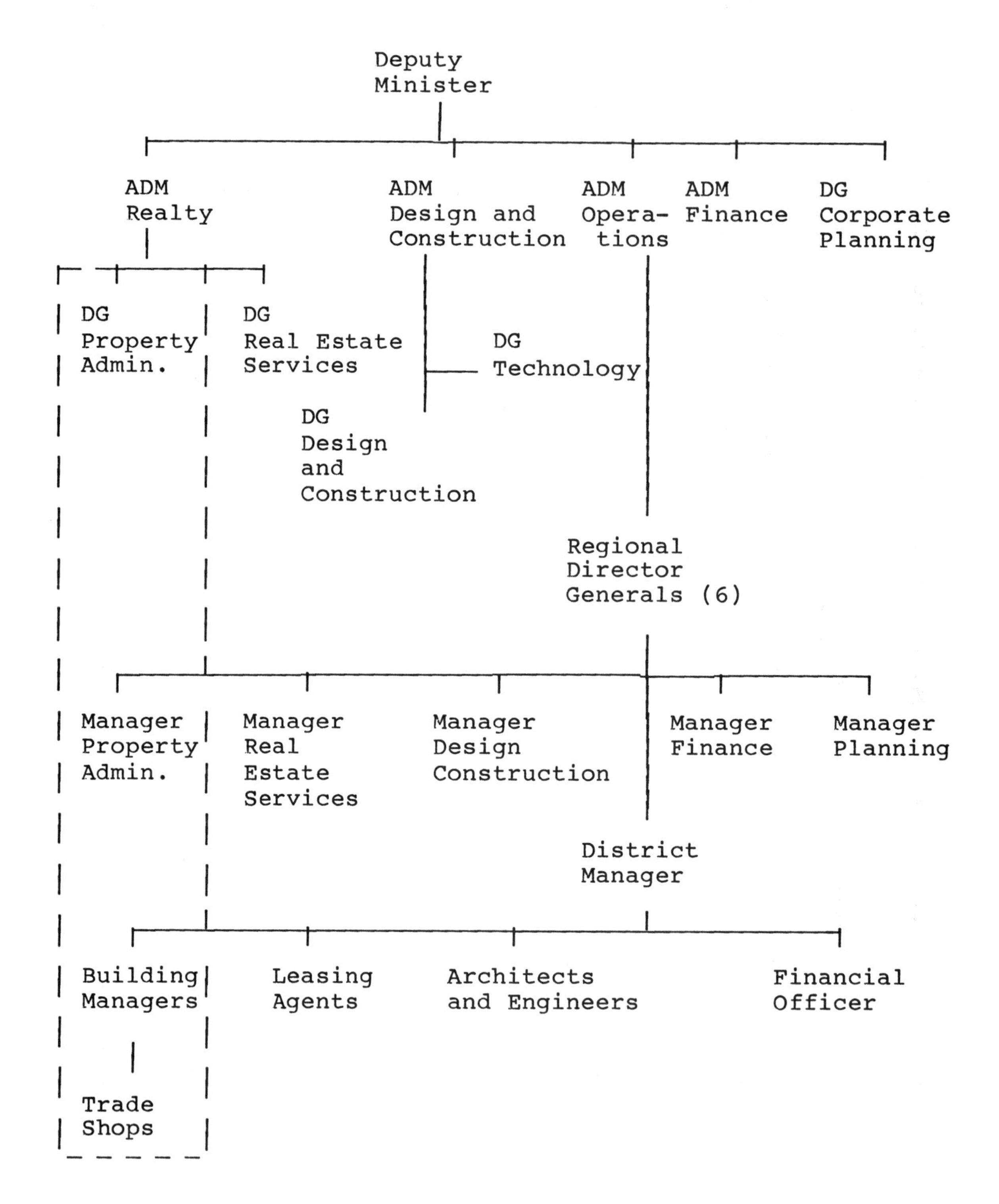

Figure 4. Public Works Canada Management Responsibility for Programs 1985-86

	Services		Accommodation		Government Realty Assets Support		Marine Trans-portation		Land Trans-portation		Total	
	($ 000)	P-Y	($000)	P-Y	($000)	P-Y	($000)	P-Y	($000)	P-Y	($000)	P-Y
Deputy Minister	2,401	44									2,401	44
ADM Corporate Affairs	4,782	67									4,782	67
DG Personnel	6,111	135									6,111	135
ADM Realty	4,183	84	503	13	17,626	2					22,312	99
ADM Revenue Dependency	653	9									653	9
ADM Operations	1,440,685	7418	781,612	117	349,407	59	12,345	4	65,890	2	2,649,939	7600
ADM Design and Construction	16,878	227			6,257	2	69	1	66	1	23,270	231
ADM Finance	26,858	168									26,858	168
Executive Secretary	7,533	158			1,104	20					8,637	178
Director, Public Relations and Information Services	911	13									911	13
Fire Commissioner of Canada					821	14					821	14
	1,510,995		782,115		375,215		12,414		65,956		2,746,695	
Less: Revenue	(1,352,690)	8323	(176,722)								(1,529,412)	
	158,305	8323	605,393	130	375,215	97	12,414	5	65,956	3	1,217,283	8558

SECTION 5 - PWC ACCOMMODATION PROGRAMS

INTRODUCTION

Public Works Canada

In the view of the study team, Public Works Canada (PWC) needs to strengthen the managerial control and accountability of the Accommodation Programs by assigning a senior official to plan, budget and manage government accommodation. PWC's responsibilities should be streamlined by transferring custody and control for all special purpose facilities to the appropriate user departments. PWC could charge rent to client departments which require accommodation in general purpose office buildings to support their programs.

BACKGROUND

The Public Works Accommodation Programs provide the accommodation required for approximately 110 federal departments and agencies. The Accommodation Programs provide mainly general purpose office accommodation, although in the National Capital, Public Works does provide a wide range of special purpose facilities.

Public Works Canada acquires this accommodation through four means: leasing, lease-purchase, crown construction and purchase of existing facilities.

Overall PWC provides almost 6 million square metres of space to its clients. The following figures provide an indication of the amount of space (in thousands of square metres) that PWC provides:

	83/84	84/85	85/86
Crown-owned	3,230	3,253	3,270
Lease-purchase	374	438	464
Leased	1,949	2,088	2,131
TOTAL	5,553	5,779	5,865

PWC manages a portfolio of space in over 2,500 leased premises, 10 lease-purchase buildings and over 1,800 crown-owned buildings.

Although PWC administers the program, the Treasury Board, through its policies and directives, has assumed a managerial role (without a corresponding operational role) over these programs. Treasury Board sets the policies for the amount of space to be authorized, the quality of space to be provided, the location of the accommodation and the amount of money that may be spent on accommdation. Under the common services policy of Treasury Board, departments are directed to use PWC to obtain their office accommodation within Canada. PWC is the sole agent for renting office accommodation from the private sector. In effect, PWC is required to act as an agent of the government (by direction of the Treasury Board) in acquiring and administering 14 per cent of the accommodation requirements of government.

In 1984-85, PWC spent $767 million on the three major categories of its Accommodation Programs:

- For the inventory of Crown-owned accommodation, the Asset Provision and Improvement Program expended $131 million for the construction of new Crown-owned buildings and the renovation of existing facilities and the Crown Properties Program funded $212 million for operating and maintaining 1,821 Crown-owned buildings;
- For the accommodation with an option to purchase, the Lease-Purchase Properties Program funded $83 million in payments on 10 buildings; and
- For the remainder of its space requirements, the Leased Properties Program funded $304 million in rental payments and other occupancy costs for leases obtained from the private sector.

The administrative costs associated with managing these programs, approximately $13 million, are funded in the Accommodation Planning and Control Program.

OBSERVATIONS

The relationship between PWC, its client departments and central agencies is varied and complex: landlord and tenant, owner and builder, monitor and manager, service agency and program agency. The relationship is further confused by the role PWC is expected to perform as an enforcer of accommodation standards promulgated by the Treasury Board, and PWC's own position that a common service philosophy dictates that a 'no control' role is absolutely essential.

Historically, PWC had managerial control over its accommodation programs; however, as PWC control over the program weakened in the face of more powerful clients, Treasury Board commenced to take a role in issuing government-wide policies to overcome the loss of this control. It is no longer clear who manages the accommodation program - Treasury Board, by dictating policies, standards and resource levels, or PWC, who administers the program. The ongoing conflict has resulted in regulations being developed without provision for compliance. While there is no doubt that the primary accountability for compliance must rest with the user/occupant of accommodation, there is no agreement on who the user should report to.

The debate over cost recovery for accommodation to departments has raged for more than 25 years. The development of a simple system to charge rent has been overtaken by incredibly complex and expensive experimental information systems which have seriously handicapped efficient management within PWC.

Part of PWC's inability in the past to assume a more managerially aggressive stance with respect to the efficient and economical provision of accommodation, has been the absence of any one PWC executive who had responsibility, accountability and control of the accommodation programs. The PWC matrix organization, which led to management by committee, has not proven successful. With no one manager in charge, expensive information alternatives were sought, for example the complex system of paying rent. The study team suggests that PWC appoint a senior official to be accountable for the efficient and effective provision of government office accommodation.

Numerous advocates have proposed that federal departments should pay rent for the space they occupy. Some have proposed that accommodation is best provided through a Crown corporation. While some provinces, for example, British Columbia and Quebec, have adopted this model, others who have studied it, such as Ontario, have rejected it. A revenue-dependent mode of accommodation management would impose an efficiency-performance discipline on Public Works and would increase the client department's consciousness of accommodation costs. It would also permit the eventual accummulation of information by department of their total real property expenditures. The study team suggests that PWC proceed as expeditiously as possible to commence charging rent for government accommodation.

PWC's privileged position of being the government's major provider of accommodation has been eroded over the years as more and more departments received authority to have custody and control over their space requirements. At this time, PWC is still the sole provider of federal office accommodation for all departments. However, many departments now plan, construct and maintain special purpose buildings, such as, laboratories and research centres in all regions across Canada except the National Capital Region (NCR). PWC has maintained custody and control of almost all federal accommodation in the NCR. This has led to major client dissatisfaction as PWC has neither the necessary funds, nor authority, to priorize competing interests.

In order to permit federal departments to be accountable for all their special purpose facility requirements, regardless of location, the study team recommends that the user departments, rather than PWC, seek and justify resource requirements in the NCR. By removing this responsibility from PWC, the complexity which has plagued PWC for the last 5 years and has hindered it from completing long term accommodation capital planning will be removed.

Various studies of PWC, performed by people knowledgeable in the Real Estate industry, have all reached similar conclusions, that it is impossible to measure the efficiency of PWC's provision of accommodation. In spite of years of systems improvements, the Auditor General in his 1984 report noted that there was little evidence of building specific performance standards, or norms, to assist in forecasting, evaluating current performance against standards, and analyzing trends. The unit cost system in PWC does not include important elements of building performance such as potential revenues and building condition. As a result, building managers lack the necessary tools to forecast resource requirements, evaluate performance, challenge resource requests, analyze investment alternatives and control the operations and maintenance costs of individual crown-owned properties.

Without this information, there exists no framework within which managers can be expected to manage. This is not to suggest that the operations have been ineffective. On the contrary, it's just that numerous examples of inefficiency have been brought to light over the last few years: high levels of underutilized and vacant office space, excessively expensive in-house cleaning compared to private sector cleaning, excessively expensive leasing arrangements and crown-constructed federal buildings costing substantially more than buildings constructed by the private sector.

There is no framework for the rate at which existing space should be renovated, or the level at which existing space should be maintained. In the absence of a planning framework, PWC continues to request more money. PWC accommodation planning, historically and at present, is simply a bottom-up aggregation of largely unevaluated demands.

In the study team's view PWC should organize its management structure, implement a cost recovery system with performance indicators, improve its information systems and effect a number of efficiency improvement measures. It is anticipated that savings in the order of $50 million annually could be achieved.

ACCOMMODATION - ASSET PROVISION AND IMPROVEMENT

Public Works Canada

OBJECTIVE

To provide new Crown-owned facilities and/or improvements to current Crown-owned facilities and supporting infrastructure, including the infrastructure for lease purchase properties, to meet client requirements.

RESULTS/BENEFICIARIES

New and/or improved facilities including office, warehousing and special purpose space for PWC and other government departments.

AUTHORITY

The Public Works Act, The Expropriation Act, Government Land Purchase Regulations, Government Contracts Regulations, and Common Services Policy.

RESOURCES

	84/85	85/86
Capital	$137M	$136M

PROGRAM DESCRIPTION

This program funds both PWC Crown-owned capital projects and the infrastrucure capital costs of lease-purchase properties. External costs include land and development fees, the costs of construction and other building costs, improvements and building equipment. Internally, the salaries and benefits of professional, technical and operational staff directly involved are charged from the appropriate services program to the individual projects. Each project is specifically approved by Treasury Board and monitored by PWC from inception to post-implementation evaluation. Projects are grouped according to size and type into four categories: major office, small office, special purpose and miscellaneous.

PWC has spent the following amounts (millions of constant 1984-85 dollars) for capital over the last 10-year period:

	Total	New Construction	Renovations
76/77	$421	$371	$ 50
77/78	489	438	51
78/79	361	300	61
79/80	155	127	28
80/81	116	85	31
81/82	145	102	43
82/83	96	64	32
83/84	90	50	40
84/85	146	41	105
85/86	189	105	84

The funds comprising this program provide for approximately 25-30 per cent of the government's total annual real property capital expenditures. (Another 30-35 per cent is funded through other departments but executed by PWC. The remaining 35-45 per cent is carried out by other government departments and agencies without the involvement of PWC).

No person-years are included in the estimates for this activity because the person years are provided by the applicable service program. The salary and benefit costs charged to this planning element for 1984/85 amounted to $8.0 million covering 192 proxy-person years.

Outside the National Capital Region (NCR), funds are provided for general purpose office space, border stations and warehousing. Within the NCR, construction of special purpose structures as well as general purpose office buildings is funded through this program.

OBSERVATIONS

General Purpose Office Buildings

Demand for space frequently exceeds the available funding due to a number of reasons:

- the absence of a reliable, useful inventory of facilities to assist PWC and its clients in

determining the utility of available facilities to meet new demands;
- the absence of a formal, acceptable mechanism to select from or prioritize alternative demands;
- deficiencies in forecasting methods used by PWC and its clients; and
- the inclusion of broader government objectives in the decision process.

In providing accommodation, PWC has to decide whether it should obtain that accommodation by leasing it from others; by leasing it with an option to purchase; by constructing it on federally-owned land; by purchasing previously constructed accommodation from others, or by variations on these main themes. Each situation should be assessed on its own economic merits, including return on investment, potential risk, inflation calculations, project size, flexibility, market conditions, tenure, etc. In the opinion of the study team this should be the approach of PWC. There is, however, a prejudice within PWC in favour of the Crown construct solution. This is due to a number of things such as the composition of the PWC staff; a reaction to the necessity to provide accommodation by leasing in a period of tight capital money and rapid federal growth; and a perceived need for a federal presence or a feeling that wherever possible the Crown should own its own accommodation.

The alternatives to Crown-owned facilities used by PWC have been increased leasing or the lease purchase method of acquisition which spreads out the capital requirement over several years through lease payments and a final capital input after a specified number of years. This has led to a situation in the National Capital Region in which only 55 per cent of the inventory is Crown-owned whereas PWC's ideal is in the range of 75-80 per cent Crown-owned. All things being equal in the public and private sectors, the cost of accommodation should be higher under lease and lease-purchase conditions to accommodate the profit motive of the private sector landlord and developer.

However, Public Works does not deny that federal buildings are more expensive to construct than those built by private industry. Private sector buildings normally are not 'monuments' with attendant costs and cost less to design. Best price contracts can be negotiated and can be completed much faster because decisions can be made at all levels of management (pursuant to delegated authority and responsibility) and the process is much less cumbersome than in government.

Special Purpose Buildings

The present method of capital funding is such that PWC has been given a nearly impossible combination of roles: a service organization to clients requiring special purpose buildings and arbitrater of competing interests for capital funds. Since many departments and agencies which have custody of special purpose properties outside of the National Capital Region already control their own capital budgets, they could also have (but do not have) control of capital expenditures affecting their special purpose properties in the National Capital Region.

OPTIONS

The study team recommends to the Task Force that the government consider:

- providing the custody and control of special purpose buildings in the National Capital Region to the revelevant departments; and

- ensuring that crown construction of general purpose office buildings is limited to circumstances where there is a long-term need for large areas of space.

ACCOMMODATION - CROWN PROPERTIES

Public Works Canada

OBJECTIVE

To provide in the most economic manner, consistent with government policies and directions, accommodation required by federal government departments and agencies.

RESULTS/BENEFICIAIRES

Public Works Canada operates and maintains Crown-owned facilities for the use of other departments and agencies.

AUTHORITY

Public Works Act

RESOURCES (thousands of current dollars)

	84/85	85/86
Operating	$211,517	$215,391
Revenue	$(98,729)	$(98,574)

REAL PROPERTY ASSETS

Number of buildings - 1,821
Amount of Space - 4.5 million square metres

PROGRAM DESCRIPTION

This program provided $211 million of funding in 1984-85 required for the maintenance and operation of government owned buildings. The funds are spent on the provision of on-site supervison, heat, light, power, ventilation, custodial and cleaning service and the carrying out of cyclical maintenance and repair projects.

In 1984-85, Public Works operated some 4,514,700 square metres of federally-owned space.The department had custody of 1,821 buildings located in all 10 provinces and two territories, of which 90 per cent of the space was located in 26 major municipalities. The total number of buildings include 831 residential buildings mainly in the Yukon and Northwest Territories (Yellowknife).

The regional distribution of buildings for which PWC has custody and control is as follows:

	Housing	General Purpose Office & Special Purpose Buildings	Total
Atlantic	72	150	222
Quebec	3	122	125
Ontario	2	92	94
Western	478	116	594
Pacific	262	67	329
National Capital	14	443	457
TOTAL	831	990	1821

Approximately 50 per cent of the space is located in the National Capital Region. In addition to the general purpose office buildings which PWC operates and maintains, PWC is responsible for the custody of special purpose facilities like the Agricultural Experimental Laboratories, the Customs Training College (at Rigaud, Quebec), the Government Conference Centre, etc.

The inventory (in square metres) is divided among the following categories of space:

General Purpose Office Buildings	2,743,100
Special Purpose Buildings*	765,300
Miscellaneous Buildings (housing)	1,006,300
TOTAL	4,514,700

* Warehouses, laboratories, conference centres, training centres, processing plants

PWC has historically been unable to provide a meaningful accounting of the operating and maintenance costs for maintaining this inventory of crown-owned properties. PWC historical expenditures are, of themselves, meaningless since they do not take into account service levels or changes in the mix of space to be maintained year over year (i.e. heating and cleaning of warehouses, offices, courthouses, laboratories). Comparison with data available in the most recent Building Owners and Managers Association (BOMA) guide shows the following comparison between PWC average unit O&M costs and BOMA costs:

	82/83	83/84	84/85	85/86
BOMA (all buildings)	40.84	48.29	45.45	47.27
PWC (all buildings)	39.57	42.83	44.51	44.51

In 1984-85 PWC maintained the following vacant space (in square metres):

Assigned but Unoccupied	71,000
Under Renovation	88,900
Unuseable (basements, etc.)	47,500
% of Inventory	6.4%
TOTAL	207,400

The services of professional, technical and operational personnel required to manage and operate the various buildings are purchased from Public Works Services Program (Realty Management Services, Architectural and Engineering Services and Real Estate Services). This program purchased the services of some 2,600 Public Works service employees to undertake the necessary operations in 1984-85.

OBSERVATIONS

This program has the role of property owner. In the owner role, it has a responsibility to manage the assets, to satisfy the building occupants, minimize costs and preserve the value of the building.

Although PWC has developed internal policies on property management, the Auditor General noted a concern by building managers that reduction in staff and maintenance budgets were causing postponement or reduction of preventive maintenance. This was resulting in potentially higher maintenance and repair costs in the future and the attendant loss of value in the asset.

PWC recognizes that during periods of restraint in the past, that maintenance and cyclical repair funding had to be redirected to other priority areas (for example, payment of costs under escalating clauses of leases). However, the magnitude of the problem is not known because there are no commonly accepted standards for measuring the quality of building maintenance or the condition of a building. A major factor for this is the lack of an adequate cost data base for the Operations and Maintenance of government buildings. The Auditor General noted that of the $214.9 million requested by PWC in 1983-84 for operations, maintenance and cyclical repairs for Crown properties, $113.7 million is not verifiable because documentation linking regional submissions with global averages used in the consolidated corporate submission is missing. The lack of these information systems, which the department is now undertaking to establish, prevent any reasonable comparison with private industry standards and make it difficult for the department to identify and eliminate inefficiencies.

While the Auditor General noted that buildings examined in his audit were, in general, cleaned to the satisfaction of the occupants, PWC has noted difficulties in the quality of service provided by contract cleaning. Part of the problem rests with the tendering process which requires PWC to engage the lowest price tenderer, even if PWC is aware (from past experience) that the quality of service to be provided is substandard.

Nevertheless, PWC is aware that contract cleaning is less costly than employing in-house staff (in the Ottawa area it can be as much as 30 per cent cheaper), and that the potential for savings do exist in the department. These will be realized as attrition and redeployment of staff and other circumstances permit.

Although PWC states that the cost of operating and maintaining PWC's inventory is $211 million, the full cost is actually understated. In the National Capital Region, the department does not undertake in-house, or pay for, grounds keeping services for its facilities. These are provided, at no charge, by the National Capital Commission. Nor does this amount reflect the cost of grants in lieu of municipal taxes, which PWC pays out of other accounts.

The Long Term Policy for Living Accommodation prepared by the Treasury Board Advisory Committee in 1983 proposed the phased devolution of Crown housing to the private market at Whitehorse and Yellowknife because private markets exist in these areas. In the view of the study team PWC should divest itself of residential housing units in all areas where private markets could provide accommodation.

PWC has gradually commenced charging various departments and agencies for the space which it provides. This has come about not as a result of a central government policy, but by accident, in that certain agencies were required to pay for accommodation, as part of the legislation establishing them, for example, the Unemployment Insurance Commission. PWC, although not having cost data per client, ended up providing guess estimates and accepting the payments. PWC now collects $98 million annually from 15 departments and agencies. The remaining 95 departments and agencies receive space at no charge from PWC.

Although there are counterparts to this activity in all property holding departments there is no comparative data among property-holding departments, nor is there a forum for coordination and communication among the government's real property managers. The effectiveness of this activity is dependent upon the calibre of management and operations, state of the inventory and availability of resources to operate and maintain properties to some appropriate standards.

OPTIONS

The study team recommends to the Task Force that the government consider the following three measures:

- PWC to develop an asset-based management system to provide information on expenditures and revenues per building to permit a comparison with private industry standards;

- PWC to proceed to realize savings over time with increased utilization of contract cleaning; and

- PWC to increase contracting out realty management services.

ACCOMMODATION - LEASE-PURCHASE PROPERTIES

Public Works Canada

OBJECTIVE

To obtain, operate and maintain lease-purchase accommodation facilities and supporting infrastructure at Public Works, Treasury Board agreed upon levels of service in order to meet the accommodation requirements of clients.

RESULTS/BENEFICIARIES

Public Works provides clients which are mainly departments, agencies and some Crown corporations of the federal government with the space they require. The crown has the option to purchase the buildings which are being leased.

AUTHORITY

Public Works Act
Treasury Board Financial Administration Act and Treasury Board Contract Regulations
Public Lands Grants Act

RESOURCES (thousands of current dollars)

	84/85	85/86
Operating Expenditures	$83,388	$89,951
Revenues	$ 2,043	$ 3,646

REAL PROPERTY ASSETS

Number of Buildings - 12
Amount of Space - 545,200 square metres

PROGRAM DESCRIPTION

Public Works has, over the last decade, identified space requirements in certain regions of the country and instead of leasing or constructing, sought to have the private sector design and build office buildings which the government would lease with an option to purchase.

The lease-purchase approach generally provides for provision of the space, with an option for the tenant to purchase the property at some time in the future, usually at a predetermined price. The lease normally is based on a net rental, with the tenant being responsible for all operating costs.

The lease-purchase option was available and had been used by the private sector for over 20 years before PWC adopted it to acquire space in Ottawa/Hull in 1974. A list of the 12 approved Lease/Purchase Projects is provided in Annex A.

OBSERVATIONS

Ownership gives the government the strongest levers over the control and management of the overall cost, disposition and security of its accommodation. Generally, ownership also provides the best opportunity for the government to maximize the achievement of other real property-related socioeconomic goals in target communities, such as federal presence and visibility.

Usually ownership is obtained through government financing of accommodation capital projects (whether for new or existing buildings) as part of its borrowing requirements and the issue of government bonds.

Given the increasing constraints of capital expenditures, since the mid 1970s the government, through Public Works, has used lease-purchase as an alternative to crown construct or leasing for accommodation acquisition.

For long-term accommodation requirements, the government policy permits the use of the lease-purchase method of acquisition depending on a review of the merits on a case-by-case basis. Comparative analysis at the moment of investment decision should demonstrate that the lease-purchase mode of space acquisition compares favourably to either the Crown-owned or lease options.

The policy also specifies that Public Works may use lease-purchase as a supplemental means to crown finance in moving towards a higher crown-owned to lease ratio of the office inventory (including the existing inventory).

The design-build method of project delivery negotiated with a developer in the lease-purchase is a form of acquisition which effectively combines private sector expertise, enterprise and speed of implementation with the Crown's need to assure quality and cost control over its accommodation acquisition and management.

The benefits of a particular lease-purchase may result from one or a combination of the following factors:

a. The equivalent of a Crown-owned acquisition at a cash flow equivalent to or less than lease and the avoidance of an initial large capital outlay;
b. A more economic product: analysis immediately prior to the issue of a tender call or analysis of responses to a tender call should show a lease-purchase to be less costly than a crown-owned option; and
c. The excerise of leverage to realize mixed use urban development schemes through the government's lease-purchase commitment to occupy space in such projects.

Conversely, lease-purchase may be less advantageous to the government in the following situations:

a. At a future time, when the government could become 'locked in' to lease-purchase when leasing is substantially less expensive;
b. When a potential lease-purchase project may be more expensive than crown construct or crown purchase alternatives;
c. When the use of lease-purchase may limit competition to developers who have the necessary understanding, skills and resources to handle lease-purchase projects (although the development industry is gradually adapting to the government's lease-purchase practices); and
d. When the nature of the proposed project may demand full crown control of the specification, design and construction, which can best be secured through crown-owned construction.

The recent Auditor General's Report has criticized this method of property acquisition for being more costly than

Crown construct. Because a private developer's borrowing power is less than the Crown's, the AG suggests that the financing costs of lease-purchase acquisitions are considerably higher than those of other Crown-financed acquisitions. The private sector would reply that it is able to finance on the strength of the federal government's covenants under a lease-purchase agreement and thus obtain financing at the same cost as the government. The Auditor General's Report also raised concerns that PWC does not disclose its contingent liability to Parliament.

Various factors have led to PWC failing to observe precautions taken as a regular course in all other projects for the acquisition of space. The intense demand for space by the federal government, political desires for federal presence, a lack of capital funds, a desire to control architectural design, (especially in the National Capital), and a PWC desire to fix costs during an inflationary leasing period, all have led to lease-purchase agreements, some of which have committed PWC to pay rents for the space involved beyond the prevailing private sector level. For example, L'Esplanade Laurier building was fully occupied on October 1975, the total rental cost upon occupancy was $10.13 a sq. ft. compared to the prevailing market rental rate of $8.65. However, in 1985 the same building costs around $13.00 per sq. ft. compared to comparable leases at $26.00 per sq. ft.

OPTIONS

The study team is of the view that PWC should consider lease-purchase agreements for the provision of accommodation in future only on condition that the rental rate pursuant to any lease-purchase agreement (together with the cost of amortization of any final payment) is competitive with both the general market rate for straight leases and the amortization of full costs of crown constructed properties. The current policy requiring Treasury Board to review each lease-purchase proposal on its merits should continue.

ANNEX A

LEASE-PURCHASE PROJECTS

Building	000M2	In Service Year	Agreement Completed	Capital Costs-1 ($000)	Annual Lease Purchase Payments - 2 ($000)	Present Value Payment-3 ($000)
Esplanade Laurier, Ottawa, Ont.	80.7	1975	2010		5,849	60,337
Place du Centre, Hull, Qué.	36.0	1977	2012		3,020	23,283
C.D. Howes, 240 Sparks, Ottawa, Ont.	96.0	1977	2012	34,100	6,100	47,600
Terrasses Chaudière, Hull, Qué.	138.0	1977	2012	14,800	16,838	144,156
Guy Favreau, Montréal, Qué.	53.1	1983	2018	107,600	11,228	87,600
Shediac, N.B.	6.8	1982	1982			
Yarmouth, N.S.	3.9	1983	1983			
Charlottetown, P.E.I.	12.8	1984	2019	8,567	2,243	15,600
Cornwall, Ont.	6.7	1984	2019	4,000	1,412	9,600
Chatham, N.B.	5.7	1985	2020	881	625	4,940
Scarborough, Ont.	35.5	1985	2020	6,800	5,202	42,800
Edmonton, Alberta	70.0	1987	2022	7,500	13,200	105,000

NOTES:

1. Capital costs refer to the initial development costs of a specific project and include such items as land cost, legal costs, costs of a podium where applicable, etc. and these are financed through the PWC Asset Provision Program.

2. Annual lease-purchase payment refers to the negotiated rental costs for a specific lease purchase project over the life of the lease (typically 35 years) at the current financing rate of the day.

3. Present value of payments refers to the discounted sum of annual lease-purchase payments and a final payment, if the option to purchase is exercised, at the applicable interest rate, on the date of the first payment.

ACCOMMODATION - LEASED PROPERTIES

Public Works Canada

OBJECTIVE

To lease, operate and maintain facilities to meet the accommodation requirements of clients.

RESULTS/BENEFICIARIES

PWC leases space from third parties, manages it to Public Works/Treasury Board approved plans, standards, levels of quality, service and cost which meet the needs of client departments and agencies.

The beneficiaries are the departments and agencies of the federal government within the context of the Treasury Board's Common Services Policy.

AUTHORITY

Public Works Act, Financial Administration Act and Treasury Board Government Contract Regulations.

RESOURCES (thousands of current dollars)

	84/85	85/86
Operating Expenditures	$304,662	$319,902
Revenue	$ 65,445	$ 74,502

REAL PROPERTY ASSETS

Leased Space - 2.1 million square metres
Estimated Number of Buildings - 2,500

PROGRAM DESCRIPTION

The program encompasses the activities necessary to obtain and manage leased space (2,131,300 square metres in 1985/86), to Treasury Board/PWC standards and agreed on levels of service, to meet specific client accommodation requirements. The type of property which is leased includes office space, special purpose space (laboratories, computer areas, conference centres, warehouses, processing plants, etc.) and miscellaneous space.

The leasing program provides all funds required for the payment of annual contract rents and escalation, operations and maintenance for net leases and fit-up costs totalling $305 million in 1984/85, of which $130 million is spent on leases in the National Capital Region.

The program is delivered by regional and district staff based on the requirements identified by various government departments and agencies.

OBSERVATIONS

The recent Auditor General's Report identifies serious weaknesses in this program resulting from an inadequate definition of client needs, the lack of planning systems and disregard for Treasury Board and departmental directives.

In the absence of a long-term capital plan encompassing an overall accommodation framework, this program has been demand driven and over-reactionary, which has resulted in a significant growth in leasing costs. The lack of a lease management/planning system has resulted in problems meeting client requirements and lost opportunities for most favourable lease renewal rates. It should be noted that a particular problem exists in planning for new space. Demand is usually driven by other government department's program needs, some of which are approved by Treasury Board. The information is often poorly communicated to PWC.

Public Works 'designates' space to various client departments who do not, for a variety of reasons, occupy it for prolonged periods of time. PWC cannot assign the vacant space to anyone else. Mechanisms are not in place to resolve disputes in this regard. Designated but unoccupied space practices cause excess space and unnecessary expenditures.

The Auditor General has commented that PWC has not complied with the Government Contract Regulations governing tendering. The AG noted that only 7 per cent of 1,200 leases were tendered. However, over 400 of these were leases which had expired and were renegotiated at favourable rates and another 400 were leases which sought additional adjacent space to already leased premises.

In an effort to comply to the letter of the law, the department is now attempting to tender all leasing requirements (even if all that is required is some small extra space by one department on the same floor of the building it already occupies). As a result, major costly delays in meeting client requirements for space are being experienced.

The government's policy to locate in the downtown 'core' of urban areas (especially in the nation's capital) as opposed to outside the core, has swung back and forth over the last two decades. In the 1950-60s, Public Works accommodated clients in the periphery; in the 1970s it leased and lease-purchased in the core. In 1983 the government again adopted a policy to move to the periphery of urban areas unless departments could substantiate a need to have their presence in the urban core. It appears that much of the new and renewed leasing activity continues to remain in the downtown cores.

In principle, leasing should generally be used only to provide additional flexibility, or to meet short-term or small scale requirements. For example, La Société Immobilière du Québec has established an objective of providing space from a 90 per cent owned and 10 per cent leased inventory. In the National Capital Region, the actual ratio of leased office space to Crown-owned is 32 per cent leased to 68 per cent Crown-owned (i.e. directly or through lease-purchase agreements). For all types of space in the National Capital Region, the ratio is 28 per cent leased and 72 per cent crown-owned.

Recently, PWC has developed a plan and may seek approval to decrease dependence upon leases to a level of 25 per cent over a period of 10 years. To achieve this ratio, an additional expenditure of about $475 million would be required for new Crown construction; this would result in savings of approximately $200 million in terminated leases over the same period.

OPTIONS

The study team recommends to the Task Force that the government consider:

- providing clear policy guidance to departments and agencies on the future occupancy of "core" downtown accommodation versus less expensive accommodation outside of core areas;

- reducing its dependence on costly leases in urban areas for major departments (Transport and National Defence) by developing ownership through crown construct or lease-purchase alternatives when these alternatives are clearly cost effective; and

- reviewing its current Government Contract Regulations with respect to tendering for leases, to ensure that it has the flexibility to both lease space on a timely and cost effective basis while respecting prudence and probity.

ACCOMMODATION - PLANNING AND CONTROL

Public Works Canada

OBJECTIVE

To manage the overall Public Works accomodation portfolio including the development, monitoring, and control of acquisition, improvement and operating plans and the development of individual project plans and submissions in order to meet the accomodation requirements of approved clients.

RESULTS/BENEFICIARIES

Outputs include approved accomodation plans and strategies for PWC controlled properties, approved projects, a portfolio of assets at approved standards of quality, safety, utility, efficiency and economy and reduction in marketable vacant space for government departments and agencies.

AUTHORITY

The Public Works Act

RESOURCES (millions of current dollars)

	84/85	85/86
Operating Expenditures	$13	$19
Person-Years	130	130

PROGRAM DESCRIPTION

Public Works utilizes 130 person-years to manage its accommodation inventory. It conducts studies to determine accommodation requirements, develops policies and plans respecting capital asset acquisition and utilization designed to optimize long-term benefits. Funds related to refit projects and forced client moves are provided within this program.

The group is intended to function as a real property investor, who, in assessing market (government) demands, attempts to put together a portfolio of assets which will minimize long-term costs.

Public Works strives to determine how much space is required by all departments and agencies in the National Capital, and mainly how much office space is required across the rest of the country. The department then attempts to determine how to acquire the necessary space based on the amount of budget it expects to be able to obtain from Parliament. The decision is then taken as to how much Crown construction should occur, what level of leasing is required and what projects could justify a lease-purchase approach to acquisition. This group then also determines the optimum level of maintenance and operations for existing Crown-owned buildings and enters into contracts, either with the private sector or Public Work's services arm, to obtain the necessary maintenance, cleaning and property management services.

This program also provides the funding required to conduct space optimization studies and the funds necessary to reorganize the office accommodation of client departments to achieve greater efficiency of space utilization.

OBSERVATIONS

The recent findings of the Auditor General indicate that, in PWC there was little evidence of building-specific performance standards, or norms, to assist in forecasting and evaluating current performance against these standards and analysing trends. The unit cost system in PWC does not include important elements of building performance such as potential revenues and building condition. As a result, PWC property managers lack the necessary tools to forecast resource requirements, evaluate performance, challenge resource requests, analyze investment alternatives and control the operations and maintenance costs of individual Crown-owned properties.

The relationship between Public Works and its client departments is varied and complex: landlord and tenant, owner and builder, monitor and manager, service agency, program agency and control agency. PWC perceives itself to be in a no-win situation in its relation with both clients and control agencies. PWC is unable to provide all of the space clients demand during the course of any fiscal year. Nevertheless, in striving to satisfy clients' needs, PWC spends more annually than is authorized in the Main Estimates.

Both Treasury Board (TB) and PWC assume some responsibility for accommodation standards and guidelines impacting on the quantity and quality of space and services. There are numerous regulations, many of them developed by TB with no enforcement mechanisms, yet with the expectations of voluntary compliance by departments and monitoring by PWC. This vacuum has resulted in a lack of real property management focus and missed opportunities for improved efficiencies and economies. For example, although Treasury Board has issued a policy not to locate departments in the expensive downtown areas of cities when there were no strong operational reasons for so doing, the implementation of the policy, in the absence of an enforcement authority, has been less than successful.

There are no clear lines of responsibility and accountability in the current PWC organizational structure to plan and control PWC accommodation programs (crown-owned operations, capital construction, leasing and lease-purchase). Currently, the same Assistant Deputy Minister who identifies the type of real property services required and enters into agreements to purchase these services, is also in the business of selling the services. The matrix management organization does not work. PWC has too many competing groups trying to control and plan the accommodation programs (There are at least three groups in PWC headquarters planning accommodation operations, plus various units in the regions).

PWC finds itself in a conflicting role when it tries to deal with the question: can it provide space to satisfy clients at the same time as controlling the amount of space in order to satisfy Treasury Board regulations? Mechanisms do not yet exist to clearly define the roles and mandates of both PWC and TB; as a result a vacuum is created and neither clients nor central agencies are satisfied with PWC's performance.

The accommodation inventory is too diverse to be managed as one integral entity. Different and smaller functional product line units need to be created. For example, office space management and special purpose space management should be segregated for planning and control and other management purposes. Product line divisions need to be implemented and an adequate inventory control system for each product line has to be developed.

Public Works carries a high a ratio of unoccupied space. Greater attention must be paid to managing vacant space in terms of recording of vacant space by product line. PWC should identify alternative uses for vacant space. PWC often hides behind the practice of assigning space to a department and allowing it to remain unoccupied for far too long. The Treasury Board policy for departments to report 'unoccupied' space needs to be more vigorously enforced.

Public Works is not in a position to know how much space clients will require or how much they have been authorized to obtain. PWC needs to develop a mechanism to find out what type of space its clients will require, how much and when. Without this data, planning will continue to remain a mystery. Both TBS and client departments should be actively involved. Although TB approval of person-years per department is one planning tool and another macro planning tool is the overall growth of the public service (½ per cent per annum) is another, neither of these is a substitute for a good client requirement forecasting process.

The amount of space which Public Works leases continues to grow and costs have escalated at a rate faster than the costs of operating Crown-owned accommodation. PWC should seek clarification of the government's preference to own or to lease from the private sector, especially in the National Capital Region and other major municipalities.

Since most departments do not pay for their accommodation, they strive to have Public Works locate them in expensive downtown office highrises. PWC should seek TB guidance about which departments need to be located in urban cores, especially Ottawa, and which ones can operate well outside of the downtown core areas. Factors would include service to the public as well as inter-departmental considerations.

Public Works annually exceeds the Main Estimates authorized by Parliament. PWC must develop planning and control capabilities to operate within established budget levels. To date, PWC has spent whatever was required to keep clients relatively satisfied. In many years the total exceeded the amount which Parliament had originally voted. Treasury Board has been unable to restrict the department's expenditure growth.

Too many departments request more new accommodation than Public Works' annual capital budget can possibly handle. A long-term plan will help focus competing interests. The transfer of budgetary control for special purpose facilities in the National Capital Region to program departments will also help resolve some of the conflicts faced by PWC. Even so, PWC must develop a long-range capital plan so that the projects displayed to Parliament (through Main Estimates) will bear some resemblance to not only what PWC will be spending to construct, but also how much it will spend (cash flow management). Capital projects identified in the Part III Main Estimates include both approved projects and PWC's wish lists and the annual cash forecasts are often inflated.

Although PWC charges some clients 'market' rates, it has a great deal of difficulty in defining market comparable data for its accommodation portfolio. Some clients, for example, the Post Office, are charged 'direct' costs, even though PWC doesn't have a cost accounting system which would identify these costs.

OPTIONS

The study team recommends to the Task Force that the government consider:

- defining the accommodation role and mandate of Public Works with respect to client departments and central agencies, specifically with respect to the question of the 'service' role versus the 'control' role;

- reorganizing PWC's management structure to establish a framework for accountability for the Accommodation Program; and

- developing a strategy to accommodate in downtown core areas only those deparments which have an undisputable operational requirement to be located there.

SECTION 6 PWC SERVICES PROGRAM

INTRODUCTION

PWC should become the government's common service agency for real property services in more than just name. Architectural, engineering and real estate services across government should be centralized within PWC. PWC should significantly increase the degree of contracting out and continue with its move to revenue dependency. The Government Contracting Regulations require streamlining and simplification to improve effectiveness and efficiency.

BACKGROUND

The Public Works Act assigns to the Minister of Public Works the responsibility for providing engineering and architectural services and directing the construction, maintenance and repair of public works placed under his management and control.

The extent of control has substantially decreased since the legislation was promulgated in 1867. The PWC Services Programs are subject to a variety of Treasury Board policies and regulations, including the Common Services Policy, the Government Contracts Regulations, Public Land Leasing and Licencing Regulations, Public Works Leasing Regulations and the Government Land Purchase Regulations. Additional statutory authorities are contained in the Expropriation Act, the Surplus Crown Assets Act, the Public Land Grants Act, and the Adjustment of Accounts Act.

The Services Program provides a wide range of professional, technical, operational and managerial services in the areas of Real Estate Services, Realty Management Services, Architectural and Engineering Services and Dredging and Fleet Services (see Annex A), to other programs of PWC, other government departments and departmental corporations (Section A and B of the Financial Administration Act),

Schedule C Crown Corporations by agreement and other organizations outside of the federal government which qualify. A Corporate and Administrative Services section provides executive management and administrative services as well as policy direction to all PWC programs.

Approximately $1.5 billion and 8,300 person-years (PYs) are utilized in the delivery of these services. Of the total expenditures, $1.1 billion represent disbursements made on behalf of clients, including outside contracts, which are to be recovered in full from the appropriate programs. Approximately 50 per cent of the remaining $400 million, the internal costs, are to be recovered under the system of direct cost charging to all clients implemented April 1, 1985.

Except for Dredging and Fleet Services, headquarter's staff for each service report to Assistant Deputy Ministers who have responsibility for setting standards and norms. Dredging and Fleet and all regional service staff report, through Regional Directors General, to the ADM Operations, who functions as an owner/manager/developer of Accommodation Programs as well as the owner of the service organizations from which the services are purchased. Some 7,400 of the 8,300 person-years in the Services Program are allocated to this executive.

OBSERVATIONS

The person-years and expenditures within PWC represent only about one third of the total federal in-house capacity for these services. Except for dredging and fleet services, several other government departments and agencies, notably the NCC, DND, DOT, Parks, retain person-years dedicated to the provision of real property maintenance, architectural, engineering and real estate services. Over one half of PWC services are provided to departments and agencies that have custody and control of their real property.

This study team has elsewhere suggested a reorganization of PWC to clearly separate its two remaining functions - custody and management of general purpose facilities and provision of architectural, engineering, and property management services to itself and its clients. Within the services function, greater efficiency and effectiveness can be achieved by centralizing from across government specialized and technically sophisticated services - architectural and engineering - under a reorganized PWC. User departments for their part should be prevented from duplicating PWC expertise on their staff and should seek instead to be informed clients, that is, clients who can clearly state their needs to PWC and can work cooperatively with PWC in the process of meeting those needs. It is not necessary for user departments to have their own realty development personnel to fulfill this obligation.

In the view of the study team there is an overabundance of in-house capacity and far too little use of contracting out for these services. As a result, when work volumes are low, departmental productivity is low. Even when services are contracted out, PY levels are not reduced. Instead, they are spent in excess supervision and second-guessing of the work of the consultants. PWC has estimated that under the present circumstances the first year of full revenue dependency could produce a deficit of $30-40 million. While it appears that in these services in particular, a level of in-house capacity is desirable, the study team recommends that PWC should be required to reach a contracting out level approximating 80 per cent. Double and triple supervision of other professionals should be discontinued. The government should utilize the same legal recourses for non-satisfactory performance as is used by the private sector.

Most, if not all, property maintenance skills can be purchased externally and at times at less cost. PWC continues to utilize approximately 2,000 person-years in support of cleaning services. PWC has advised that in the National Capital Region, the private sector is able to provide cleaning services for up to 30 per cent less than PWC in-house staff, although it is of a lower quality.

The maintenance expertise required in-house is that for negotiation and administration of satisfactory contracts. The custodians of property for each department should decide whether to retain staff for property maintenance within its department or contract out - unlike the recommended procedures for architectural and engineering services. The managers of PWC's accommodation program and the NCC will be required to utilize the PWC services group for their property maintenance requirements.

There is an inherent conflict of interest when the purchaser of the services happens also to be the major provider of the in-house capability, as is the case with the ADM Operations. The separation of custody and service roles within PWC would ameliorate the condition. Therefore, the study team recommends that one senior official be designated to manage the PWC Services Program, another the Accommodation Program.

The largest, single, external client for maintenance services, Canada Post Corporation, has threatened not to extend its agreement with PWC. Such a move would have a major impact on PWC as it represents approximately 1,400 person-years, or 30 per cent of the current person-year allocation to realty management services. Regionally, it represents 30 per cent of the Atlantic, 35 per cent of the Quebec, 65 per cent of the Ontario, 50 per cent of the West and 45 per cent of the Pacific regions' person-years levels. CPC seeks numerous concessions and subsidies from PWC in order to continue its contract. The study team recommends that PWC prepare contingency plans and organizational alternatives in the event of a withdrawal of requirement by the Canada Post Corporation.

The Government Contracts Regulations and other regulations provide barriers to efficient contracting out procedures for all services. Regulations governing contracting out require simplification if the process is to be conducted efficiently. The present procedures with the objective of ensuring probity are imprudently expensive. The study team recommends that greater use be made of standing orders, pre-approved supplier lists, limited tender or no tender where conditions warrant.

If PWC increased its contracting out for all services, especially its cleaning services, decreased its staff levels to reduce its deficit and if Canada Post decided to terminate its service agreement, PWC could see a downsizing of up to 3,000 person-years. PWC recognizes that it will need to reduce its projected $40 million annual deficit over the next 5 years through staff reductions and improved efficiencies.

ANNEX A

ACTIVITIES OF THE SERVICES PROGRAM

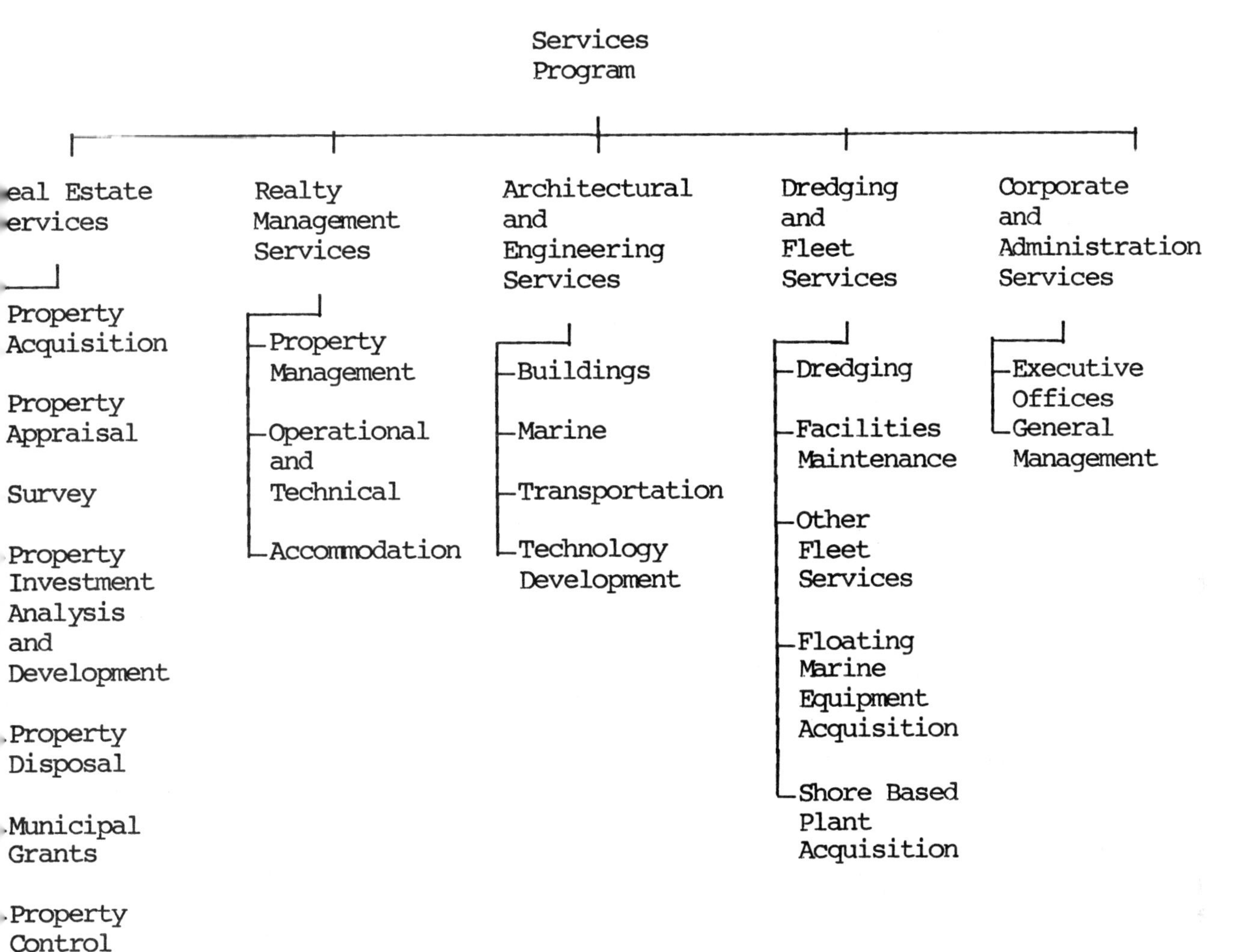

ARCHITECTURAL AND ENGINEERING SERVICES

Public Works Canada

OBJECTIVE

To provide client departments and agencies and other PWC programs those professional and technical and related advisory services for the design, construction and project management of buildings, marine and transportation facilities, and technology development.

RESULTS/BENEFICIARIES

Public Works undertakes professional and technical services in the areas of project management, construction management, operational and asset management. It also develops standards relating to the above services for some 110 federal departments and agencies.

AUTHORITY

Public Works Act.

RESOURCES (thousands of current dollars)

	84/85	85/86
Operating Expenditures	$73,594	$77,255
Revenue	$34,379	$52,997
Person-Years	1,551	1,499

PROGRAM DESCRIPTION

Public Works has the capacity to provide a full scope of architectural and engineering services for the complete range of built work projects: buildings (offices, laboratories, warehouses, heritage buildings) marine works (dams, locks) and land transportation projects, (bridges highways). The traditional disciplines engaged in the department are: architectural, engineering (mechanical, electrical, civil-roads, bridges, municipal, marine - structural), urban planning, landscape architecture, interior design specialists, etc. The range of services they provide are: project management, cost control, schedule control, quality control, planning, design, construction contract administration, advice, program management and research and development.

Utilizing these skills, the department also engages in a variety of special services and support. For example:

a. **Technical Services.** The department undertakes technical studies and investigations in a large number of fields, such as solar energy, heritage preservation, energy research and development, ureaformaldahyde foam installations, etc.;

b. **Technical Support.** The department develops standards, guidelines, directives and training programs as well as monitors quality control;

c. **General Support.** The department supports its professional and technical staff with a large number of administrative, planning and management staff; and

d. **Energy Core Activities.** PWC undertakes energy conservation measures to reduce the high costs of heating and cooling government buildings.

In summary, the Architectural and Engineering functions can be classified in five categories utilizing person-years as follows:

Built Work Services	1,018
Technical Services	227
Technical Support	85
General Support	243
Energy Core Activities	97
* **TOTAL**	1,670

* Because departmental data bases are not well established, the above data provides an order of magnitude based on 1982-83 figures.

Of this total of 1,670 person-years providing architectural and engineering services, 34 per cent, or 570 person-years, are professional staff; the remainder are technical and support staff.

A detailed distribution by region, using the five categories above is attached as Annex A.

An examination of the largest category, the provision of built work services, reveals the following general approach in the department for the provision of planning, design and construction contract administration:

a. **Built Work Buildings**

Minor Works (property administration):
Planning, design and construction contract administration (P-D-C) done mainly in-house.

Projects $100K to $1M:
Planning done in-house; and
Design and construction contract administration done 35 per cent in-house.

Projects $1M plus:
Planning done in-house; and
Design and construction contract administration done mainly by outside consultants.

b. **Built Works Marine**

Minor Works:
P-D-C done mainly in-house.

Projects $300K to $1M:
P-D-C done mainly in-house.

Projects $1M plus:
Planning done in-house; and
Design and construction contract administration done mainly by outside consultants.

c. **Built Works Transportation**

All Projects:
P-D-C done in-house.

The Architectural and Engineering group in PWC undertook approximately $670 million worth of construction projects for other departments and agencies in 1984-85 and $260 million of construction and operations on behalf of the department's own programs (accommodation, government realty assets support, marine and land transportation). The value of work done for other departments is normally about $250 million, the 1984-85 increase was due to the introduction of the Special Recovery Capital Projects Program.

Approximately 90 per cent of the architectural and engineering services for the $930 million total of the construction projects undertaken by PWC are contracted out to the private sector. The remainder are implemented in-house.

The organization in 1984-85 consisted of approximately 240 person-years in Headquarters organized into the following units:

Buildings Directorate (17 PY) -
provides specialized professional services to regions and other client departments.

Environmental Design Directorate (18 PY) -
provides landscape architectural, urban design and heritage architecture resources to regions.

Marine (28 PY) -
develops standards and guidelines and undertake project design and management activities.

Transportation (19 PY) -
develops standards and guidelines and undertake project design and management activities.

Consultant Services (9 PY) -
support management in selection of consultants.

Engineering Technology (33 PY) -
provides design expertise for all product lines.

Architectural and Building Sciences (32 PY) -
provide diagnostic and problem solving expertise for buildings.

Project Management Technology (23 PY) -
provides in-house expertise for cost planning, scheduling, claims, negotiations, etc., related to building construction.

Science and Technology Development (40 PY) -
develops government and national master specifications, material standards and testing.

Solar Programs Office (24 PY) -
manages the purchase and use of a solar heating program across all departments.

Urea Formaldehyde Foam Installation (UFFI) Initiative (2 PY) -
provides UFFI research.

Special Services (14 PY) -
support all product lines.

Total 259 PYs (1982-83 data base)

The organization in 1984-85 utilized 1,299 person-years in the six regions, distributed generally as follows:

National Capital Region		207
Atlantic		295
Quebec		203
Ontario		192
Western		263
Pacific		251
TOTAL	(1982-83 data base)	1411*

* See also Annex A for further description of activities by region.

OBSERVATIONS

Public Works, for years, has had difficulty in quantifying and rationalizing the type of activities it is engaged in. Its professional and technical services cover a very broad spectrum of services. The Time Recording and Performance Measurement System, which was to support planning and operational control, as well as monitoring and resource utilization control, has continued to reveal major deficiencies. In short, the department is unable to provide a clear statement justifying the level of staff required to undertake projects, either on behalf of PWC or other government departments.

In addition, until recently, PWC has been unable to provide any indicators of comparability for its performance with that of the private sector.

PWC commenced to charge its clients the direct costs for services provided on April 1, 1985. It has estimated that it will require a $24 million subsidy to cover its other operating expenses (indirect costs and overhead).

Since the data bases described above are so weak, PWC management has difficulty evaluating efficiency and performance and in determining the minimum complement of staff required to handle a construction program that has variable funding levels. PWC also has problems in establishing the right mix of professional and technical staff and, given the decreasing mobility of staff, having them available in the proper location. PWC is involved in many areas of expertise (docks, bridges, roadways, municipal works, etc.) which has made it difficult to develop efficiency norms in all areas.

A preliminary review of PWC's delivery methodology for built works projects indicates that a very high level of high quality project management exists, not only for in-house planning, design and construction contract administration, but also for projects undertaken by external consultants. PWC uses its own professional and technical expertise to support the project manager, as part of a matrix organization, in order to provide what it identifies as additional "Value for Money". The costs of these additional services could be as high as 3 per cent of the total construction costs. In short, PWC places very little reliance on the private sector. Interviews with developers and consultants indicated that the private sector people were unanimously concerned and frustrated over the number of necessary PWC attendees at every meeting and the lack of authority to settle issues there and then, and the attendant time delays occasioned as outstanding matters were referred to a higher level.

PWC undertakes four other categories of services: Technical Services, Technical Support, General Support and the Energy Core function. Over 650 person-years are not associated with the direct delivery of construction projects. There are numerous services in these categories which are discretionary and for which PWC has the ability to either eliminate areas of overlap (research and development) or reduce excess capacity (administrative-overhead).

A comparison of PWC's activity to that of the British Columbia Building Corporation (BCBC), a provincial Crown corporation, highlights the following differences:

- the political controls governing the employment of consultants and the awarding of construction contracts is extensive within the federal government;

- there is a greater reliance on the private sector performance by BCBC. (Less utilization of in-house expertise to assist the project manager in double checking the work of the private sector which results in at least a 1 per cent reduction in total project costs.);
- although planning is done in-house, all design and construction activities are contracted out in BCBC; Public Works utilizes over 750 person-years for design and construction contract administration; and
- BCBC is not engaged in architectural and engineering services related to marine and land transportation projects.

A comparison of Public Works' treatment of variation in project workload to that of the private sector indicates that architectural and engineering firms are understaffed by 10-15 per cent during normal times. Troughs in workload are handled by salary cuts, reduced working hours and layoffs in the private sector. This is not the case in Public Works.

There is very little research and development undertaken by the private sector as this activity is usually non-revenue generating. Research is undertaken by the National Research Council and universities. The private sector has limited formal training programs or knowledge transfer plans. Public Works, on the other hand, utilizes up to 300 person-years for these types of activities.

In summary, the management of the architectural and engineering program of PWC has come under criticism by the Auditor General. Concern continues to be expressed, in all sectors, that the department is unable to account for or justify the high level of staff in this area. It is well known that the private sector has extensive capacity to perform the same services as offered through Public Works in-house expertise.

The growing number of architectural and engineering service units across departments and departmental comments point to a level of dissatisfaction with the services provided by PWC (both in the area of overdesigning and overbuilding and in the timeliness of product delivery).

By moving to a 'fee for service' basis, however, PWC has taken a first step in identifying a chargeable client and the 'direct costs' of providing services. PWC has been unable at this time to develop a rate structure which is acceptable to all parties for charging fees which are comparable to those in the private sector.

Given the monopoly privilege provided to Public Works under the government's Common Service Policy and given that Public Works is proposing to build in some of its higher costs (for example, up to 3 per cent of construction costs for added-value, costs of its matrix management and expertise and doing business in a government environment), the issues therefore become:

- whether the government requires a dedicated in-house staff;
- what the size of the staff should be;
- who should determine the staffing (a central agency or the forces of supply and demand, as dictated by the competitive process); or
- how the staff should be organized.

Added to this dilemma is the fact that even though Public Works is designated as the government's architectural and engineering arm, there exist another 30 departments, agencies and crown corporations which possess to varying degrees their own professional and technical services. Some concerns were expressed about the inappropriateness of constraining Public Works through a charging system for architectural and engineering services, while similar services in other departments would continue without the same discipline and would compete with Public Works.

Since the government is such a large owner of real property, there is a requirement to maintain a core of professional and technical expertise, if for no other reason than the protection of the investment. There is, at this time within PWC, an excess capacity of professional and technical staff.

There remain at least three areas which require resolution within PWC:

- what types of services should be available?
- what level of resources are required? and
- how should the services be delivered?

a. **Types of Services:**

PWC could have on staff a core of people with expertise in the whole range of architecture and engineering services for all product lines (buildings, marine and land structures); or

PWC could specialize only in the area of accommodation, divesting itself of expertise in highway, road, bridge, dams, docks, etc., construction. This expertise would reside in other departments, such as Transport, or in the private sector.

b. **Levels of Resources:**

The level of resources required by PWC will be determined by the size of its client's requirements. PWC could provide services to all departments of government, or it could provide services to only those which do not yet have the capacity to provide their own.

c. **Delivery of Services:**

The government has the option of requiring departments to use the services of the department of Public Works within a monopoly, or it can permit departments to engage PWC or other qualified private sector companies. The services which Public Works provides could be organized either within the framework of a department or a Crown corporation (which is not required to abide within the Government's Contract Regulations).

OPTIONS

Common Services Policy

Assuming no change in the mandate of Public Works, the alternatives for the delivery of Public Works architectural and engineering services include the following:

Option 1 - No Monopoly

The department could continue on its road towards self-sufficiency by operating on a fee structure based on full cost recovery basis. However, rather than the Treasury Board attempting to establish (and thereafter, arbitrate) a rate structure within a monopolicy environment, departments would be free to negotiate a price with Public Works or purchase the services directly from the Private Sector.

Option 2 - Monopoly

The department has embarked on a revenue dependent mode of operation which in future will permit it to define both revenues and expenditures and to operate within revenue. The long term implications of this exercise is an eventual reduction in size. The fee schedule would be approved (and disputes arbitrated) by the Treasury Board. As a common service agency, client departments would not be able to secure private sector expertise without employing Public Works first.

Level of Service

Should the government wish to rationalize the architectural and engineering services across government, then the following alternatives can impact on this program:

Option 1 - Full Services - Government Wide

The department could be directed to either provide architectural and engineering services (or purchase them from the private sector) for all construction activity in the Government of Canada. This could be achieved in either a common service (monopoly) environment, or a consulting (competitive with private sector) environment.

Option 2 - Specialized Services

The department could be directed to reduce its in-house expertise in built work buildings, eliminate its capabilities in marine and land transportation projects (by transferring them to other departments, such as Transport Canada), eliminate its research and development activities, and reduce its training and overhead.

Based on these considerations, the study team recommends to the Task Force that the government consider:

- authorizing the Minister of Public Works to be a central contracting authority for all private sector architectural and engineering services required by federal departments and agencies;

- designating PWC as a common service organization for providing departments architectural and engineering services on a full cost-recovery basis; and

- decreasing in-house strength of architectural and engineering services by increasingly contracting out to the private sector.

ANNEX A

Public Works - Architectural and Engineering Services Distribution of Workload (1982-83)

Architectural and Engineering services varies by classification of built work and the distribution of person-years varies across all regions. The following data is from the 1982-83 time recording system.

	HQ	NCR	ATL	QUE	ONT	WES	PAC	TOT
Built Works Buildings - Project Services: Planning, Design & Construction Contract Administration for - Projects $100K - /1M - Projects $1M+	10	73	104	107	96	95	57	542
Built Works Marine - Project Services: Planning, Design & Construction Contract Administration for - Minor Works - Project $300K - $1M - Projects $1M+	13	9	77	53	36	9	52	249
Built Works Transportation - all projects	0	2	40	0	2	84	99	227
Technical Services - Advisory Services - Solar Energy R&D, UFFI, Technical Studies, Investigations	96	40	22	4	24	38	13	227
Technical Support - Knowledge Transfer - Technical Procedural Standards Guidelines Quality Control	65	2	6	2	8	1	2	86
General Support - Administation & Consultant Selection Planning	75	43	34	22	24	23	21	242
Energy Core - Energy Analysis & Building Retrofits	0	38	12	15	12	13	7	97
TOTAL person-years	259	207	295	203	192	263	251	1670
Number of Offices	1	1	14	6	26	26	15	89

ANNEX B

Public Works - Architectural and Engineering Services
Level of Service Provided to Clients (1985-86)

Client	Client Capital Budgets ($ millions)	PWC Service Level (PYs)
PWC Accommodation	138	161
PWC Other Programs:		
Marine	5	102
Transportation	40	141
Government Support	13	54
Other Government Departments	672	760
TOTAL	868 M	1218 PY

ANNEX C

Public Works - Architectural and Engineers Services
Built-Work Project Data (1982-83)

	HQ	NCR	ATL	QUE	ONT	WES	PAC	TOT
Built Work Buildings								
- person-years used for Project Management		16	40	43	15	9	14	137
- Project Planning Design & Construction	10	57	64	64	81	86	43	405
TOTAL (person-years)	10	73	104	107	96	95	57	543
% Time Spent In-house on Projects*		78%	65%	65%	85%	90%	89%	73%*
Total Expenditures on Capital-Built Work Building Projects ($million)		$24	$49	$83	$26	$55	$27	$265
Number of Built Work Building Projects Undertaken		1,070	511	568	1,196	924	274	4,539

* Despite the large amount of time spent planning and designing projects, the department attests that 90 per cent of the works which are built are actually designed and completed by private sector consultants. It therefore appears that much of the department's time is spent either on projects which never get built and/or on duplicating work being commissioned to the private sector.

REALTY MANAGEMENT SERVICES

Public Works Canada

OBJECTIVE

To provide departments, agencies and other programs of the department with those realty management and related advisory services required for the management, operation and maintenance of real property.

RESULTS/BENEFICIARIES

The results include standards, guidelines and policies, tenant services, accommodation and space optimization strategies, operational services such as heating and cleaning, technical services such as electrical, plumbing and structural and leasing of space to and for other government departments and agencies, and programs of PWC itself.

AUTHORITY

The Public Works Act

RESOURCES (thousands of current dollars)

	84/85	85/86
Operating Expenditures	$355,575	$420,339
Capital Expenditures	$ 760	$ 760
Revenues	$325,055	$379,465
Person-Years	4,876	4,733

PROGRAM DESCRIPTION

This service is responsible for the operation and maintenance of over 8,319,000 square metres of space. The major client is the Public Works Canada Accommodation Program followed by the Canada Post Corporation under a specific management agreement. Management agreements exist also with other government departments, for example, the RCMP, Via Rail and the Unemployment Insurance Commission.

Approximately 28 per cent of the gross (including expenditures disbursements on behalf of clients) and 57 per cent of the person-years of the Services Program are utilized in this service element.

	Estimates 84/85		**Estimates 85/86**	
	Expenditures (000)	**PY**	**Expenditures (000)**	**PY**
Realty Management Services	153,984	4,783	161,673	4,640
Program Support	6,895	93	7,022	93
Sub Total	160,879	4,876	168,695	4,733
Disbursements on behalf of clients	195,456	-	252,404	-
TOTAL	356,335	4,876	421,099	4,733

Services are categorized as four types:

a. **Property Management:** those required to meet acceptable standards of effectiveness, efficiency and economy; the development of strategies and policies for efficient management; the implementation of other federal government programs such as energy conservation, federal identity, accessibility for the handicapped; the administration of tenant occupancy agreements and other service agreements related to various tenant services.

b. **Operational and Technical:** those required to operate, maintain and protect existing accommodation to acceptable standards of cleanliness, utility and efficiency: the development of strategies and policies together with technical advice to ensure new accommodation is planned and built to acceptable operating standards.

c. **Accommodation:** leasing, letting and marketing expertise including the development of recommended rental rates and fee schedules; the implementation of space optimization programs; the development of accommodation strategies, the implemenation of various services such as parking, retail outlets, housing, moving and conference facilities; the preparation and maintenance of a Facilities Inventory System; advisory services to central agencies and other government departments on the subject of accommodation.

d. **Program Support:** the provision of administrative and management support staff.

Revenues earned from these activities include recoveries of salaries and benefits and disbursements made on behalf of clients.

Revenues and Recoveries by Source ($000)

	Forecast 84/85		Estimates 85/86	
	$	PY	$	PY
Canada Post Corporation	126,691	712	126,408	712
Other Government Departments and Agencies	7,886	13	59,879	197
Other Public Works Canada Programs:				
- Government Realty Assets Support	27,071	433	21,638	431
- Accommodation	152,144	2,784	171,540	2,664
TOTAL	313,792	3,942	379,465	4,004
Percentage of Cost Recovery	88.4%		90.2%	
Percentage of Person-Years Chargeable		80.8%		84.6%

Person-years in 1985/86 are estimated at 4,733, a reduction of 143 or 3 per cent over 1984-85. Departmental costs are estimated at $169 million, an increase of $5 million or 3 per cent. Disbursements on behalf of clients will increase by $61 million to $252 million or 3 per cent.

Disbursements are recovered totally but without an administration fee. In 1985-86 the department implemented direct cost charging to all clients, other than Canada Post Corporation, where the management agreement provides for the recovery of a fee for overhead in addition to direct costs. Direct cost charging will increase revenues (other than recoveries of disbursements) by $4.8 million, some $350 thousand less than the related cost increase.

The program is delivered through regional and field offices with a functional group resident at headquarters. In 1985-86, 30 PYs and $1.5 million are assigned to the ADM Realty, with the remaining 4,703 PYs and $420 million allocated to the ADM Operations.

OBSERVATIONS

As with other planning elements related to services, assessments are difficult because previous years lacked consistency in the method of charging and the clients charged. Chargeable time has been estimated on an incomplete historical data base. The method of charging is scheduled to proceed to market rate or revenue dependency in the fiscal year 1986-87 although several reports indicate PWC may not be ready to implement the procedure at that time. Private sector comparisons on specific costs are not possible in many cases because they are defined and accounted for differently.

It is clear that some 4,733 PYs costing $164.2 million will be utilized in this activity in 1985-86.

Canada Post Corporation, the department's largest single client accounted for approximately 30 per cent of the 1984-85 PYs and $32.5 million of salary and other personnel costs. In 1985-86, the estimates are 28.4 per cent and $34 million. The corporation may terminate the agreement upon two year's notice with respect to the labor element. Presently PWC is recovering the direct costs and a small element of overhead.

Regionally, the CPC contract is distributed, with respect to PY's, as follows:

Region	% of PYs
NCR	less than 1
Atlantic	30
Quebec	35
Ontario	65
West	50
Pacific	45

No major decreases in PYs are estimated up to fiscal 1987-88 and no major alternative client can be identified for these services. As well, the possibilities for contracting out the services presently provided by these PYs have not been fully exhausted.

Canada Post Corporation has indicated displeasure with the level of service presently provided and the level of operating costs. CPC management has taken advantage of the importance of their business volume to obtain concessions and exemptions from the original agreement. PWC should begin negotiations with CPC to take over the operations including the transfer of all dedicated PYs in PWC. Failing that, a revised agreement with a definite term (say five or six years) should be negotiated, during which time PWC will convert services of present PYs to contract and reduce the overall PWC PYs by approximately 1,400 (700 related to properties in the custody of CPC and 700 related to properties in support of CPC but in the custody of PWC).

OPTIONS

The study team recommends to the Task Force that the government consider:

- increasing significantly the degree of contracting out of PWC's property management and maintenance services;

- moving towards revenue dependency for PWC's realty management services with the earliest possible implementation; and

- developing a contingency plan for PWC's organizational restructuring in the event of termination of service requirements by Canada Post.

REAL ESTATE SERVICES

Public Works Canada

OBJECTIVE

To provide departments, agencies and other programs of the department with those real estate and related advisory services required for the evaluation, survey, acquisition, development and disposal of real property.

RESULTS/BENEFICIARIES

The results include property inventories (CRPI), appraisals, surveys, market studies, grant administration services, acquisitions of various types and disposals of various types for PWC itself, other government departments and agencies and Crown Corporations.

AUTHORITY

The Public Works Act.

RESOURCES (thousands of current dollars)

	84/85	85/86
Operating Expenses	$23,421	$29,374
Revenues	$14,740	$23,033
Person-Years	281	276

PROGRAM DESCRIPTION

Business volumes by activity type are of the following magnitude:

Business Volumes

	Actual 83/84	Forecast 84/85	Estimate 85/86
Number of Acquisitions	599	965	880
Number of Evaluations	1,486	1,816	1,288
Number of Surveys	997	1,042	1,014
Number of Disposals	541	524	549
Number of Municipal Grant Applications	2,889	3,000	3,267
TOTAL Number of Projects	6,512	7,347	6,998

Acquisition includes expropriation, purchase, lease and property transfers and exchanges. Appraisals are performed on properties designated for acquisition, disposal or to be leased. Surveys include those for properties to be acquired and disposed of, topographical and hydrographical, airport zonings and building surveys under condominium and air rights legislation. Evaluations include standard investment analysis, feasibility studies, cost/benefit analysis, land use studies, market surveys, Federal Land Management studies, Area Screening studies, and Asset Management studies. Disposal includes the services related to lettings, exchange, transfer, granting of licences and demolition of structure as well as disposal by sale. Municipal grants include the services required for the determination and payment of grants on behalf of other government departments and agencies, Crown corporations and the Department of External Affairs as well as for its own account.

Additionally, this planning element is responsible for: property control - the maintenance of the CRPI, program support - management and administrative, performance information/resource justification - reporting on the activities listed.

Surveys and appraisals are frequently contracted out whereas other activities are generally performed in-house.

Revenues earned from these activities include recoveries of salaries and benefits and disbursements made on behalf of clients.

Revenues and Recoveries by Source (\$000)

	Forecast 84/85		Estimate 85/86	
	$	PY	$	PY
Other Departments and Agencies	228	5	8,931	79
Other Public Works Canada Programs:				
- Government Realty Assets Support	13,408	76	12,961	76
- Accomodation	1,104	27	1,141	27
TOTAL	14,740	108	23,033	182
Percentage of Cost Recovery	62.9%		78.4%	
Percentage of Person-Years Chargeable	38.4%		65.9%	

The significant increase in 1985-86 is due to additional disbursements of \$4.9 million and an increase in recovery of salary and benefit costs of \$3.4 million. In 1985-86, \$15,256,000 of the total recoveries of \$23,033,000 represent recovery of disbursements made on behalf of clients, the remaining \$7,777,000 is for salaries, benefits and Operations and Maintenance. The anticipated salary and benefits increase will result from implementation of direct cost charging for all services to all clients.

The program is delivered through regional and field offices. In 1985-86, estimated person-years total 276 with expenditures (excluding disbursements on behalf of clients) of \$14,118,000. Of this, 54 PYs and \$2,689,000 have been allocated to the ADM Realty. The remaining 222 PYs and \$11,429,000 have been assigned to the ADM Operations.

OBSERVATIONS

Assessment of this planning element is difficult because past and present actual data does not reflect consistency in either the method of charging for services or in the charging of all services to all departments. Estimates for the future are based on incomplete past data on chargeable hours because a comprehensive system of time reporting was not in place.

What is known is that the internal cost of providing these services in 1985-86 will be \$14,118,000, an increase of 8 per cent over 1984-85 forecast. The issue is what the services ought to cost if performed efficiently. It has been suggested in various studies that to determine the latter, comparisons to the private sector are appropriate. There is an assumption here that the private sector performs these services efficiently. Certainly, survivors in the private sector do perform them at a pre-tax profit of between 10-15 per cent of revenues.

The implementation of direct cost charging is the first step taken by the department leading ultimately to market-rate charging or revenue dependency in fiscal year 1986/87. It will take some two years after that to determine if the department can attain the level of efficiency exhibited by the private sector and this under monopoly conditions. In the interim, direct cost charging is estimated to produce a recovery in 1985-86 of 55 per cent of internal costs compared to 33 per cent in 1984-85 and the charging out of 66 per cent of the 276 PYs.

As noted, 54 PYs and $2,689,000 are allocated to the ADM Realty with the remaining to the ADM Operations. The allocations to the ADM Realty are essentially headquarter costs associated with the setting of policies and standards. Most of the ADM Operations allocation is in the regions. Firstly, this amount for the establishment of policy appears excessive. Secondly, this type of allocation appears to result in the duplication of efforts as both allocations become involved in the provision of the same services to the same clients.

OPTIONS

The study team recommends to the Task Force that the government consider:

- continuing the move to revenue dependency under non-mandatory conditions for real estate services with the earliest possible implementation;

- decreasing PWC's in-house staff engaged in property appraisal, acquisition, development and disposal services through increased contracting out to the private sector; and

- rationalizing PWC's method of charging for real estate services and re-assess the number of head office personnel needed to manage its service functions.

DREDGING AND FLEET SERVICES

Public Works Canada

OBJECTIVE

To provide dredging services on a 'contracted out' basis, providing for maximum use of private sector dredging capacity wherever it is more effective and less expensive or using Public Works Canada Dredging Fleet.

AUTHORITY

Appropriation Act.

DESCRIPTION

The federal government undertakes dredging activity in all regions of Canada. Program responsibility for dredging rests with the various Marine Directorates and Corporations of Transport Canada, with the Department of Fisheries and Oceans and with the Parks Branch of Environment Canada. The implementing agency is Public Works which undertakes the work by contract with the private sector or by use of its own dredging fleet.

The department provides dredging services with the in-house fleet and personnel only where required, to avoid monopoly situations, to minimize mobilization costs, to provide rapid response, and to deliver services to the client in the most efficient and effective manner. Specifically, the project must have one or more of the following characteristics:

a. requires a special type of dredge;
b. is in an area inaccessible to private sector equipment;
c. is continuous and requires unique machinery;
d. is small;
e. is remote and/or dangerous;
f. is urgent;
g. has unique material to be dredged or geophysical conditions;
h. has broad range of material to be dredged.

BENEFICIARIES

Dredging companies, federal government departments (Transport Canada, Department of Fisheries and Oceans) federal government agencies (Ports Canada, St. Lawrence Seaway Authority), port and channel users, cargo owners, and shippers.

EXPENDITURES (millions of current dollars)

	83/84	84/85	85/86	86/87	87/88
Salaries	9.7	10.6	11.3	11.3	11.3
Other O&M	6.5	5.3	6.2	6.2	6.2
Capital	1.4	-	5.5	10.1	12.5
Grants & Contributions		0.1	-	-	-
TOTAL	17.6	16.0	23.0	27.6	30.0
Revenues	7.0	7.3	17.5	17.5	17.5
Person-years	277	277	277	277	277

The cost of Canadian government maintenance dredging in 1983-84 was $41.1 million allocated among Public Works ($17 million), Transport Canada ($19 million), and Fisheries and Oceans ($6 million). Percentage distribution of expenditures, by region, was:

Atlantic	33	West	18
Quebec	14	Pacific	35

Total revenue is 1983-84 was $7.0 million. User fees cover all of the $1.8 million dredging costs at major ports and the St. Lawrence Seaway, as well as a portion of the $6.89 million dredging costs incurred at commission harbours, public harbours and Heritage Canals. There is no revenue generated from dredging in commercial waterways or small craft harbours.

OBSERVATIONS

Ports Canada has 15 harbour authorities and its dredging of harbour facilities which excludes main channels, has normally been contracted to the private sector without

PWC involvement. The Harbours and Ports Directorate of Transport Canada presently funds most public dredging at the nine Great Lakes and Pacific Commission harbours with dredges provided by PWC. The Directorate also manages dredging at the 50 public harbours using PWC technical services, some PWC dredges and some private sector dredges. Dredging of 1400 small craft harbours is carried out with $6 million in PWC dredging fleet services. The Canadian Coast Guard uses PWC dredging services for its 15 main channels and 30 port entrances. The St. Lawrence Seaway Authority contracts out all its dredging requirements and Parks Canada contracts with PWC for its infrequent dredging needs.

In the late 1970s PWC managed 85 per cent of the federal government dredging and PWC equipment was used for 60 per cent of the work. By 1982-83, PWC was managing 60 per cent of total government dredging activity, 70 per cent of which was done with PWC equipment.

The demand for dredging services is growing with the introduction of larger ships requiring greater drafts. Additional costs of $16 million annually are identified for small craft harbours and $6 million annually for commercial waterways.

PWC, as the implementing agency, maintains that a basic fleet capacity is required and that funds for fleet upgrading are needed.

ASSESSMENT

With PWC functioning solely as an implementation agent for dredging, and several departments and agencies having dredging needs, there is a requirement to define exactly who has responsibility for what. An interdepartmental committee was formed to deal with this and other related problems and their report "Government of Canada Dredging" will be released shortly.

Dredging services will always be in demand, particularly when the user does not pay. As noted above, dredging costs will increase significantly if all demands are met. In order to induce some discipline on demand, a user pay concept could be developed. Administratively, the user fees for dredging should be integrated with a broad base of other charges for shipping services to avoid a shift of commercial shipping to U.S. harbours.

The level of service -- how deep should channels be and should they be this deep all the time -- defines dredging requirements. While these have been defined and costed within Transport Canada, the Department of Fisheries and Oceans has not yet introduced a harbour classification system and associated level of service concept.

The Auditor General has been critical of PWC dredging in the areas of criteria for use, cost accounting, and cost sharing for the dredging fleet.

According to existing government policy, Canadian dredging can only be done with Canadian registered, built or modified dredges. At present, dredges account for a very small portion of the Canadian shipbuilding industry and hence, this non-tariff barrier is of little significance to the domestic shipbuilding and repair industry. Removal of this restriction might stimulate competition in the Canadian dredging industry. It is not anticipated that an identical barrier that prohibits Canadian dredges from working in the United States will be lifted for some time.

OPTIONS*

Implement immediately the following recommendations from the "Government of Canada Dredging Policy" report.

a. Jurisdiction:

1. Agencies with territorially defined mandate have full authority for dredging, e.g. Parks Canada.

2. Agencies with functionally defined mandates have full authority for dredging, e.g. TC Harbours and Ports Directorate for harbour facilities; Canadian Coast Guard for main channels; DFO for small craft harbours.

* **Note** - The Study Team on Real Property Management supports the above observations and options prepared by the Study Team on Services and Subsidies to Business.

b. User Fees:

1. Adopt user fee principles for waterway users.
2. Fees should be integrated with all other marine services changes.

c. Level of Service:

1. DFO should complete categorization of harbours.
2. The level of service associated with each category of DFO Harbours should be approved by Treasury Board.

d. Accelerated Private Sector Involvement:

1. PWC establish early target dates whereby one half to two thirds of PWC managed dredging volume be let to the private sector.
2. PWC dredging fleet be limited to those required to meet exceptional dredging requirements

No capital acquisition should take place for PWC dredges until the impact of the recommendations can be evaluated.

The impact of removal of the non-tariff barrier protecting Canadian dredging should be studied. If there is any indication that this would stimulate competition in the dredging business, PWC should immediately begin to reduce their fleet, starting with the vessels in the Gulf of St. Lawrence.

The potential savings from implementation of the above options are the proposed acquisition program to replace or refurbish the existing $100 million fleet as well as additional revenue of some $20 million from user fees.

CORPORATE AND ADMINISTRATIVE SERVICES

Public Works Canada

OBJECTIVE

To provide executive and general management, policy direction and administrative services for all departmental programs.

RESULTS/BENEFICIARIES

The provision of administrative and personnel services, management and financial information services, strategic and operational planning and control, consultative and evaluative studies.

The beneficiaries are other programs within the Department of Public Works.

AUTHORITY

The Public Works Act

RESOURCES (thousands of current dollars)

	84/85	85/86
Operating Expenses	$81,702	$81,604
Revenues	$ 886	$ 1,039
Person-Years	1,590	1,538

PROGRAM DESCRIPTION

Corporate and administrative costs include the cost of operating the offices of the Deputy Minister, the Assistant Deputy Ministers, the Executive Secretary, the Directors General and the Regional Directors General.

In 1985-86 expenses and person-years are:

	$000s	PY
Deputy Minister	2,401	44
Executive Secretary	7,533	158
Director General, Corporate Affairs	4,782	67
Assistant Deputy Minister, Finance	26,858	168
Director General, Personnel	6,111	135
Director, Public Relations	911	13
Assistant Deputy Minister Revenue Dependency	653	9
Assistant Deputy Minister, Operations	32,355	944
TOTAL	81,604	1,538

The three sub-activities identified by the department are the executive offices, responsible for ensuring the direction of the department towards the achievement of its goals; general management services, including policy formation and implementation, planning and control, financial and other management and administrative services; performance information/resource justification, responsible for the introduction and follow-up of a new Operational Plan Framework, the implementation of a revised accountability structure, the implementation of a computerized Financial Management System, corporate and operational performance reporting and the development of signed agreements with all the internal clients utilizing the services of this program.

Revenues are recoveries of salary costs of staff dedicated to the administrative support of specific projects funded by clients.

Two ratios have been established to measure efficiency: corporate and administrative costs as a percentage of gross departmental expenditures and corporate and administrative person-years as a percentage of departmental person-years. For 1985-86, these ratios are 2.8 per cent and 18.0 per cent respectively.

OBSERVATIONS

It is difficult to assess the value of the ratios as measures of efficiency. The private sector, for example, tends to use a ratio of administrative costs to gross revenues for operations and capitalized administrative costs as a percentage of total project costs for capital projects. The definition of costs varies between the sectors.

Costs in the range of $80 to $85 million appear excessive and the need for reduction has been recognized by the department. In a revenue dependent system, contributions to overhead from other services will have to cover the cost of providing corporate and administrative support to these services.

OPTIONS

The study team recommends to the Task Force that the government consider:

- moving PWC's to a common service organization and to revenue dependency under non-mandatory conditions with the earliest possible implementation; and

- rationalizing PWC's method of charging for services and reducing the number of head office and overall corporate and administrative personnel needed to manage its service functions.

SECTION 7 - PWC CENTRAL GOVERNMENT SUPPORT PROGRAMS

INTRODUCTION

Federal land management is not the responsibility of PWC. PWC serves as an adviser to Treasury Board and an administrator of various programs in support of central real property management. Program operations should be transferred to the proposed Real Property Unit, which could have management responsibility. Property ownership either directly or through Crown corporations is not the most economical or efficient means of achieving broader social objectives and in the view of the study team the government should consider discontinuing this function.

BACKGROUND

Originally, the whole property function of the government was the responsibility of the Department of Public Works (PWC). By the early sixties, real property operations were being carried on by several departments. It had become accepted that various departments or agencies could acquire custody of land provided they received approval for the expenditure.

As the largest holder of real estate in Canada, the federal government, through the acquisition and disposition of its property, had influenced the physical layout of many cities and towns. During the sixties and seventies, the government launched a series of initiatives to better organize its real property management: the Central Real Property Inventory System was established under the custody of PWC, the Expropriation Act was amended in 1970 to give PWC the sole responsibility to act in the expropriation of land required by federal departments and agencies, and in 1975 Treasury Board (TB) established a Treasury Board Advisory Committee on Federal Land Management (TBAC/FLM) to coordinate and direct the implementation of a new policy.

The Treasury Board policy stated that "Federal lands should be managed so as to combine the efficient provision of government services with the achievement of wider social, economic and environmental objectives". The responsibility of PWC was to provide professional land management advice and service to departments and agencies in the planning of real property requirements. The policy applied within

Canada to all departments and agencies listed in Schedules A, B and C of the Financial Administration Act, with the exception of Indian lands, national parks and territorial lands. Proprietary corporations (formerly Schedule D, now Schedule C-II) were encouraged to follow the policy.

The TB policy also instructed all departments and agencies "to report to PWC any real property holdings which were no longer required to meet their operating needs". These holdings would be transferred to PWC, which would act as a holding agency until some decision about an end use had been made by the TBAC/FLM.

In the late 1970s, and with the demise of the Ministry of State for Urban Affairs (MSUA), PWC became more actively involved in land planning and development, not only in providing advice but in taking over projects commenced by MSUA. PWC took over the Toronto Harbourfront Corporation in 1979 and used the Public Works Lands Company to manage the 3,000 expropriated properties around the Mirabel Airport (Quebec).

In the 1980s, PWC became a vehicle to undertake land management and development under the umbrella of achieving wider social, economic and environmental objectives in a number of urban waterfront redevelopment projects. In order to balance the activities at Toronto Harbourfront, the government engaged in similar projects on the waterfronts at Montreal, Quebec City , Chicoutimi and Trois Rivieres. To bypass existing property regulations governing PWC, the Public Works Lands Company (established 1956) was converted into the Canada Lands Company Limited (1981) and subsidiary corporations were spun off from the parent body (which continues to remain a shell company): Canada Lands Company (Mirabel) Limited, Canada Lands Company (Le Vieux Port de Montreal) Limited, Canada Lands Company (Le Vieux Port de Québec) Limited, Canada Harbour Place Corporation and Canada Museums Construction Corporation. Although the parent company controls the majority of shares of the latter two subsidiaries, the voting shares have been passed to the Minister of Transport and the Minister of Communications respectively to oversee the construction of the Canadian Pavilion at Expo'86 in Vancouver and the National Gallery and the National Museum of Man in Ottawa and Hull.

Also in the early 1980s, PWC assumed on behalf of the government at large central responsibilities for payment of grants in lieu of taxes to municipalities and various special projects - access to federal buildings for the handicapped, solar energy conversions and asbestos removal from federal buildings, and preparations for emergency planning in accommodation and construction.

OBSERVATIONS

The federal land management policy added a major dimension to the work of PWC - that of an advisor to Treasury Board and all departments and agencies, and as an administrator on behalf of the government. It was the federal land management policy, with its emphasis on managing land in such a way that it contributes to the achievement of "broader" objectives than the accommodation of government services, that gave PWC a new mandate and Treasury Board a new role.

Although PWC assumed greater responsibilities in the areas of acquisition and disposal of properties, management of the central real property inventory, municipal grants, fire protection and urban redevelopment, it was not the master of its own house. The Treasury Board assumed the de facto role of the central manager of real property by issuing policies, circulars and directives which superseded those of PWC. The Treasury Board did not assume operational responsibilities for implementing its policies or ensuring their compliance. From the outset, the respective roles and responsibilities of the two agencies were not clarified. PWC was an administrator, but not an operational arm of the Treasury Board, because the Treasury Board was not involved in the day-to-day management of the operations. There was a void.

The programs under PWC, in support of the central management of government, are administered in isolation. Grants in lieu of taxes are being paid (over $250M annually) on a routine basis without reviewing the implications or levers available for federal-provincial relations; the Central Real Property Inventory is being maintained but there exists no one manager in PWC or in the Treasury Board Secretariat with authority to take managerial advantage of the information; area screening studies are prepared by PWC for the TBAC/FLM, however, of the 508 recommendations made over the last 10 years to make better use of underutilized properties, only 28 have been acted on.

Although the disposal practices of surplus property are reported on in detail by the study team in a separate report, one should note that before the 1975 Treasury Board policy on Federal Land Management, 97 per cent of surplus lands were sold. After 1975, the TB policy stated that federal land holdings which are no longer required to meet the operating needs of particular departments and agencies will normally be retained in federal ownership to help achieve broader government objectives. Few properties were sold, fewer at market rates. For 10 years, no one agency or manager was responsible for reviewing the impact of these policies. The study team suggests to the Task Force that the government consider combining the managerial and operational responsibilities, currently unsatisfactorily shared between the Treasury Board Secretariat and PWC, into one central Real Property Unit.

The federal policy of increasing ownership and the achievement of broader objectives, especially the "social" objectives, have resulted in major expenditures to support urban waterfront redevelopment. Since the federal government eliminated the Ministry of State for Urban Affairs in 1978, PWC has spent hundreds of millions of dollars acquiring, developing and operating such projects. Although the study team does not question the federal government's authority to be involved in regional development, it does question the prevailing philosophy that the federal government must own and operate public, residential, commercial and recreational facilities in mixed-use urban areas.

Ownership and various sundry agreements (for air rights, designated property uses, etc.) create long term liabilities for the federal government in areas which the federal government may not need to have proprietary interests. For example, although the federal and provincial governments agreed that the Canadian Pavilion at Expo'86 (cost $100M) would be transformed into a Trade and Convention Centre and transferred to the City of Vancouver; the city, not a party to the negotiations, has declined to accept the facility.

The establishment and use of numerous Crown corporations to bypass government contract regulations and various employment practices which are followed by PWC and all federal departments point to a serious need to review current regulations governing real property management and restrictions on federal departments and agencies. When authorized exceptions to the rules become the norm, one needs to amend the rules to reflect the new authorized norm. The study team questions the need for a Crown corporation to operate and dispose of surplus peripheral property around the Mirabel airport, when the responsibilities have been carried out by PWC during various periods since the lands were expropriated.

The study team recommends to the Task Force that the federal government consider ceasing further urban redevelopment through PWC or through Crown corporations and seek to divest itself of ownership in existing redevelopment projects. The study team further recommends that future urban subsidies be provided through grants and contributions through the Department of Regional Industrial Expansion.

Should these measures be implemented, we judge that annual savings of $10M can be achieved from curtailing the operations of Crown corporations, a cost avoidance of over $200M over the next 5 years due to not proceeding with future urban redevelopment projects, and revenues of up to $150M over the next 3 years from the disposal of federal holdings in urban waterfront projects.

ACTIVITIES OF THE CENTRAL GOVERNMENT SUPPORT PROGRAMS

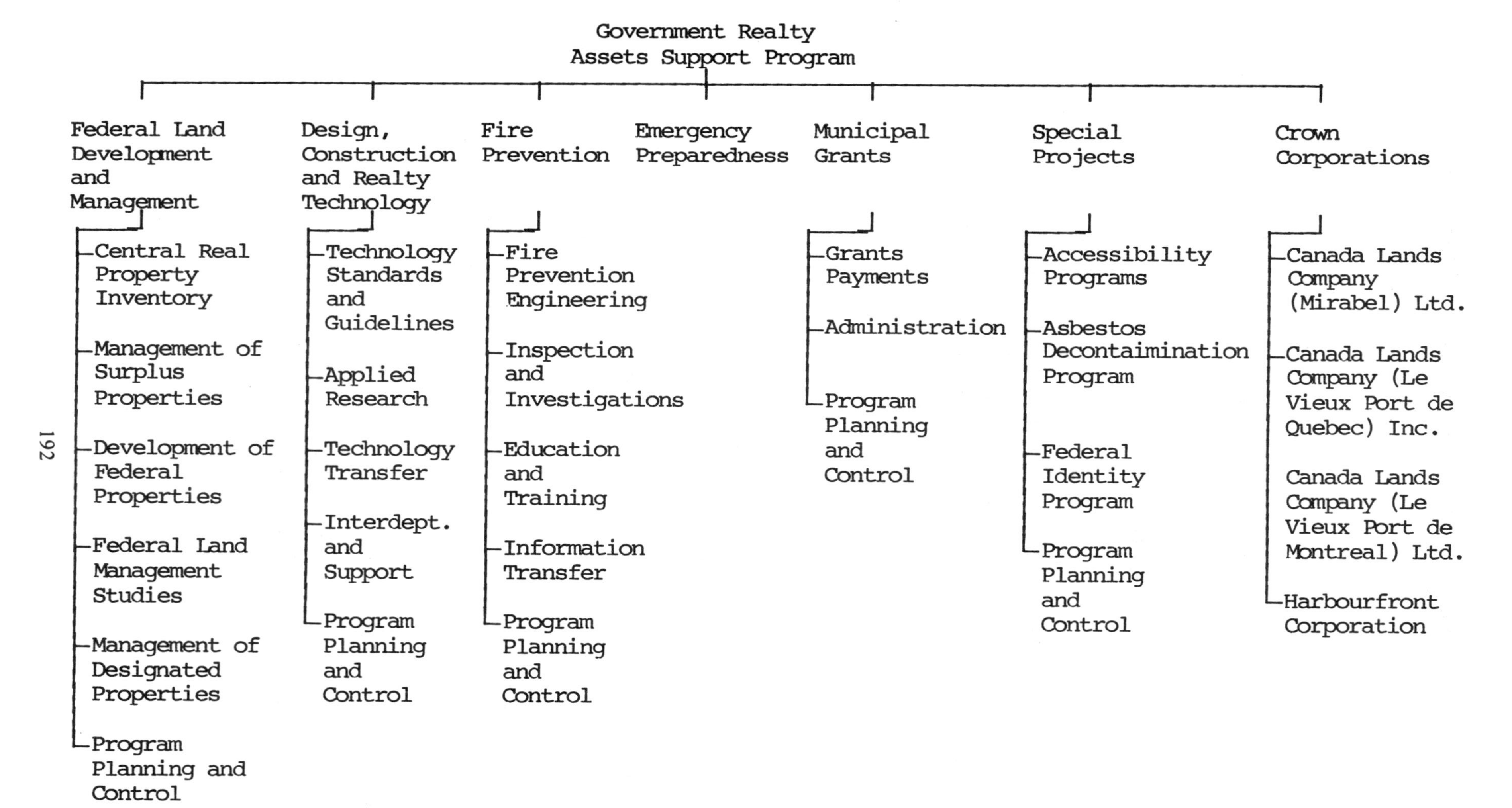

FEDERAL LAND MANAGEMENT AND DEVELOPMENT

Public Works Canada

OBJECTIVE

To provide the government with an advisory and implementation capability related to federal lands and holdings.

RESULTS/BENEFICIARIES

Public Works provides a service to the government by coordinating the management and disposal of various federal properties which are no longer required by the government, and by acting as an agent for the Treasury Board. It also provides social and economic benefits to various municipalities through urban redevelopment projects.

AUTHORITY

Public Works Act (Section 9)
Kingsmere Park Act
Laurier House Act
Official Residence Act
Surplus Crown Assets Act
Public Lands Grants Act

RESOURCES (thousands of current dollars)

	84/85	**85/86**
Operating Expenditures	$38,656	$37,181
Capital Expenditures	$11,518	$8,512
Transfer Payments	$13,783	$8,246
Person-Years	2	2

PROGRAM DESCRIPTION

Through PWC's Federal Land Development and Management program, the government has provided an advisory and administration capability which support the management of federal lands and holdings. The program has the following six activities:

Central Real Property Inventory. At an annual cost of $350K, the department manages the Central Real Property Inventory, which is the inventory record of property owned and leased on behalf of the Crown by all federal departments and agencies. The information is provided by the various departments owning property, and it is estimated that approximately 97 per cent of the holdings are in the inventory.

Management of Surplus Properties. The department spent $4.3 million managing and maintaining surplus properties in 1984. This figure does not include the costs of grants in lieu of municipal taxes. Properties are declared surplus by either PWC or other departments. Public Works maintains these properties from the time they are declared surplus until disposition. The revenues from the sale of these properties in 1984 was $7 million.

Development of Federal Properties. The department undertakes planning associated with developing and disposing of surplus and underutilized properties, at such locations as Welland Canal ($1 million), and waterfront properties at Trois Rivieres ($5 million). The department provides funds necessary to further the socio-economic objectives of the "Federal Land Management Policy" along with the contributions to municipalities and provinces under Economic and Regional Development agreements, for example, payments for projects in the cities of Sault Ste. Marie ($4.6 million) and Moncton ($2.9 million).

Federal Land Management Studies. This includes the activities associated with the support of the Treasury Board Advisory Committee on Federal Land Management (TBAC/FLM), more specifically land use and socio-economic impact studies associated with the acquisition, disposal and re-utilization of properties. These studies are presented as Area Screening Canada reports or Federal land Management (FLM) reviews.

Management of Designated Properties. The department acquires, operates and maintains properties specifically designated to it by the government, e.g. Official Residences ($3.2 million), Goose Bay ($22 million), Parliament Buildings and Grounds ($5.3 million), Recreational Association Centre ($.75 million) and others ($2 million) for a total cost in 1984-85 of $33.5 million.

In summary, the program spent the following sums in 1984-85 to implement the above activities:

Central Real Property Inventory	$ .35 million
Management of Surplus Properties	4.32 million
Development of Federal Properties	28.55 million
Federal Land Management Studies	.77 million
Management of Designated Properties	33.57 million
TOTAL	$67.56 million

The services required to run this program are purchased from either the Public Works Services Program (approximately 473 person-years and $16 million in salaries and operating costs) or from contracting out to the private sector. The operating expenditures are $37 million, 69 per cent of this program, while capital expenditures amount to 16 per cent or $8.5 million.

OBSERVATIONS

PWC, in a number of areas, provides a service to the Treasury Board by providing assistance in the government-wide role of managing real property. The Central Real Property Inventory (CRPI) is maintained by Public Works for Treasury Board. The information includes location, holding department, size, original cost and identification of occupants. Given the limited information available, the data base has limited managerial use to either individual departments or a central agency for planning or managing purposes. The CRPI should be made more flexible to make it a management tool.

PWC, also on behalf of Treasury Board, carries out studies on properties that have potential for improved use. PWC reports these to the Treasury Board Advisory Committee on Federal Land Management (a committee of officials chaired by the TB secretariat). These reports are the only government-wide consolidation of information on the potential for improved use of government real property. The reports do not contain the economic implications of continued under-utilization.

In the view of the study team there appears to be a major vacuum in the decision-making process affecting real property management. Neither PWC, nor the TBAC/FLM advisory committee, have been able to have an impact on achieving results to improve property utilization. Since the reports were started in 1978, over 508 cases were identified where potential for more intensive use exists. To date, in no more than 28 cases has the identified potential been realized.

PWC, from time to time, has been directed by the government to assume responsibilities for running programs or projects which fall in between the mandates of other departments or agencies. For example, as a result of decreasing activities in the early 1970s at the Goose Bay Labrador airport (a Second World War aircraft staging base for overseas military operations), Public Works was requested to assume surplus properties no longer required by National Defence or Transport Canada. It has cost PWC over $20 million and 300 person-years annually to maintain these 400 buildings while a long-term plan was being developed. A long-term plan now proposes that Public Works upgrade and operate the facilities to continue to provide jobs and prop up the community. Does the government really require all three departments managing pieces of a small community?

PWC also provides contributions annually to the Public Service Recreational Association Centre. These subsidies benefit only members living in Ottawa and are not part of any collective agreement or special benefit to the public service community.

With the elimination of the Ministry of State for Urban Affairs in 1978, PWC assumed responsibility for some of the urban waterfront redevelopment projects. Over the last 7 years, PWC has become increasingly involved in subsidizing certain communities by either directly undertaking or spinning off crown corporations to complete waterfront re-development projects at such sites as Quebec City, Montreal, Chicoutimi, Welland, St. John, etc. Is the mandate of the department to support government operations, or to support regional and economic development? Should the department of Regional Industrial and Economic Expansion play a lead role, or should all real property activities be part of the Public Works mandate? PWC was requested a number of years ago to prepare a policy framework for Cabinet consideration of this matter; the issue remains outstanding.

PWC also manages a number of symbolic and heritage properties in the national capital (Parliament Buildings, War Memorials, etc.). There continues to be an overlap of responsibilities related to the real property management activities of these properties between PWC and the National Capital Commission. Does the government really require two property managers for the same properties, with Public Works providing facilities maintenance and the Commission controlling building design and providing grounds maintenance? These properties have been designated by PWC as falling outside of their accommodation mandate. They are, however, integral components to the federal plans of the National Capital Commission.

The main issues impacting on the multitude of activities in this program are related to the role and mandate of the department:

- Is PWC a control agent of the Treasury Board or a service agent for clinets?
- Should PWC be the government's replacement of the former Ministry of State for Urban Affairs or a provider of government accommodation?
- Should PWC be a subsidy granting vehicle to achieve regional, economic and social development objectives or an efficient provider of service to government operations?

The Treasury Board could define more clearly the service role of PWC, as a service agent of Treasury Board; and clarify its own role in the area of real property management. On the other hand, the government could remove the operational responsibilities from PWC and place them clearly within the mandate of the Treasury Board Secretariat, or within a central real property agency.

Should the government wish PWC to continue to operate a wide range of special properties, then the responsibilities currently exercised by the Canada Lands Companies could be returned to PWC, from where they were originally developed. On the other hand, the government could also remove from PWC the management of special properties and the mandate to support regional and economic development, and limit PWC's mandate to the accommodation of government operations. Future support for regional and economic development could be handled via grants and subsidies to the appropriate levels of government or to the private sector, rather than through ownership and direct project delivery by PWC.

OPTIONS

The study team recommends to the Task Force that the government consider the following measures:

- the management of PWC activities in support of central property management, such as the Central Real Property Inventory and the Federal Land Management Studies, be transferred to a central real property agency;

- PWC to cease making contributions to the Public Service Recreational Association;

- responsibility for custody, management and funding at Goose Bay, Labrador be transferred to a program department (for example to the Department of National Defence, or the Department of Regional and Industrial Expansion); PWC to provide services on a cost recovery basis;

- responsibility for the custody and funding of designated properties in the NCR, such as Parliament Buildings and official residences, be transferred to the National Capital Commission; PWC to undertake to provide services to the NCC;

- a moratorium be established on further expenditures related to urban redevelopment until the government completes a policy review for Cabinet consideration of the federal role in urban development and the level of funding to be provided; and

- programs undertaken in support of broader social, economic or environmental objectives be achieved by departments other than PWC and through funding vehicles other than property ownership.

HARBOURFRONT CORPORATION

Public Works Canada

OBJECTIVES

To develop Harbourfront as Toronto's central urban waterfront, preserve and develop it as a public place while achieving corporate financial self-sufficiency.

RESULTS/BENEFICIARIES

The creation of an environment containing residential, retail and office space in a park and public walkway setting.

AUTHORITY

Letters Patent issued July 14, 1978 under the Business Corporations Act of Ontario.
Included as Schedule C, Part I SC 1983-84 c.31.
Minister of Public Works is the designated Minister responsible under Order-In-Council PC 1980-1622 (June 13, 1980).

RESOURCES (thousands of current dollars)

	84/85	85/86
Operating Expenditures	$8,855	$10,084
Capital Expenditures	$23,093	$6,291
Revenues	$8,039	$9,893

PROGRAM DESCRIPTION

In 1972 the federal government announced its intention to acquire central waterfront property in Toronto and to open it up for public use. From 1972 to 1976 a number of departments attempted to propose redevelopment plans, however no consensus could be reached.

In 1976 using a numbered Ontario corporation purchased during expropriation, the Harbourfront Corporation was established by the federal government, having local representation on the Board of Directors.

By 1979 a Development Framework had been approved by the federal government, by 1980 a "management agreement" had been entered into between the Minister of Public Works and the Harbourfront Corporation and by 1981 all four levels of government had agreed to and approved an ambitious redevelopment plan.

The plan anticipates the complete rejuvenation of the 92-acre assembly into a mix of housing, commercial and institutional facilities, parks, marinas and public walkways. When the development is complete (around 1991) the waterfront will house a mix of offices, hotels, retail complexes, apartments, condominiums, preserved and restored historic buildings, theatres, concert halls, restaurants and recreational opportunities. It is anticipated that over $500 million worth of private sector development (primarily in 3,500 housing units and 150,000 square metres of office and retail space) will be attracted to the site.

In addition to the original costs of the expropriations, approximately $50 million, the federal government has also provided approximately $50 million for infrastructure develop and $8 million for the operations of the corporation.

Based upon investments and revenues generated from build rentals, parking lots and social and cultural activities, the Corporation anticipates becoming self-sufficient (that is operating without federal appropriations) in 1986-87, a year ahead of schedule.

The organization is kept small by contracting out the management of most of the various entertainment, cultural and artistic projects undertaken. A total of $3.9 million was spent in 1984-85 for personnel costs. The total operating costs in1984-85 were $8.8 million and the total capital expenditures $23 million (exclusive of private sector developments).

OBSERVATIONS

According to a headline in the Globe and Mail (March 11, 1984) "Harbourfront sets standard for private sector with an upfront investment of approximately $100 million from federal funds, the private sector will spend $500 million in the area. By 1991 the financial spin-off from Harbourfront is estimated at $89 million in municipal revenue and realty and business taxes and $103 million in provincial and federal income tax. The project will have created 43,000 permanent jobs on the site. Currently, about 2.5 million people visit the site annually.

The project has already successfully transformed derelict warehouses, grain elevators and railway tracks to a number of recreational and commercial uses. By 1991 it will also be home for 5,000 to 10,000 people.

The Corporation provides an effective instrument for the planning of a redevelopment requiring the cooperation and approval of all levels of government. The Corporation is also capable of planning, developing and delivering the appropriate land use solutions more expeditiously than the normal departmental process and of handling intergovernmental consultations and public/private sector negotiations successfully.

Given that Harbourfront Corporation's mandate was primarily land redevelopment, there is some question as to its role in funding cultural and recreational activities. However, it is partly as a result of drawing in the visitors to the site, that the Corporation has been also been able to attract developers who are willing to invest in the projects.

The Corporation will apparently become financially self-sufficient in 1986-87. It is currently a Schedule C-I Corporation under the Financial Administration Act. The Corporation would like to receive greater autonomy for decision-making and has asked to become a Schedule C-II "commercial" corporation.

Given that the Corporation will no longer require direct appropriations of any substance, there are some advantages to the Corporation to operate more independently as a "commercial" corporation.

Given also that the present "Management Agreement" between the Minister of Public Works and the Corporation expires in June 1987, a new agreement should be negotiated as soon as possible to assist in the achievement of the Harbourfront's goals.

The land which the corporation manages is not owned by the Corporation, it is owned by Her Majesty with the Minister of

Public Works having custodial responsibilities. The proceeds of any land sold to private developers goes to the Consolidated Revenue Fund and the Corporation receives interest payments on an amount equal to the proceeds of sales, which helps to finance a portion of its operating expenses. The revenues of any long term land leases (99 years) are utilized by the Corporation towards the costs of its operations. Some concerns exist that this method of financing the operations of the Corporation are in fact federal subsidies which are not explicitly approved by Parliament.

The Corporation is non-profit oriented in that excess revenues are applied to infrastructure improvements, operations and cultural activities.

Currently, Harbourfront has no authority to enter into agreements, for example with the City of Toronto, without specific authorization of the Minister of Public Works. The Corporation has no authority to borrow, yet as a developer of land and manager of property, there are many circumstances when it would be of benefit for the Corporation to obtain private financing. The Corporation does not have the authority to provide loans, which it would wish to do particularly in the form of tenant improvement allowances under lease agreements.

Given that the objectives of the Corporation will have been met within the next 5 years, and that a structure will be required to administer the lands and agreements in perpetuity, there are possibilities that the Corporation could be privatized and removed from the federal inventory.

At issue are any continuing requirements of federal presence and visibility in the Toronto area; the desire of government and the method of obtaining some agreed-to return on the initial $100 million investment; the impact of privatization on the "non-profit" status of the corporation and on the legal agreements entered into with the private sector.

Possible alternatives include the sale of shares in the Corporation to the people of Metropolitan Toronto, or to transfer the Corporation to the Regional Municipality of Metropolitan Toronto or the Government of Ontario.

OPTIONS

The study team recommends to the Task Force that the government consider developing a policy framework for federal involvement in urban waterfront redevelopment, and that the Minister of Public Works be requested to recommend alternatives for the government's divestiture of Harbourfront Corporation to the private sector or another level of government.

CANADA LANDS COMPANY LIMITED

Public Works Canada

OBJECTIVE

To make payments to certain subsidiary Crown Corporations pursuant to agreements approved by the Governor in Council. The subsidiary corporations of the Canada Lands Company Limited are:

Canada Lands Company (Mirabel) Ltd.;
Canada Lands Company (Le Vieux-Port de Québec) Inc.; and
Canada Lands Company (Le Vieux-Port de Montréal) Ltd.

RESULTS

Payments to subsidiary Crown Corporations to meet the approved operating and capital funding required for each subsidiary corporation to fulfill its responsibilities as described in the Program Description below.

AUTHORITY

Letters Patent issued March 7, 1956 under Part I of the Companies Act, 1934 Schedule C-I as a Parent Corporation under the Financial Administration Act, SC 1983-84, C.31. Minister of Public Works designated as the appropriate Minister by Order-in-Council P.C. 1984-132 (19 January 1984).

Each subsidiary corporation is incorporated under the Canada Business Corporations Act.

RESOURCES (thousands of current dollars)

	84/85	85/86
Operating Expenditures	$68,866	$11,423

PROGRAM DESCRIPTION

Canada Lands Company Limited

Originally incorporated in 1956 as the Public Works Lands Company to hold certain leasehold interests in one property in London, England and two properties on Indian reserves in Canada, the name and mandate of this company were amended in 1981. CLCL has power to acquire, purchase, lease, hold, improve, manage, exchange, sell or dispose of real or personal property. The Board of Directors, made up of senior officials of Public Works Canada, are responsible to the Minister of Public Works. The company is a parent corporation with no budget of its own. It has three subsidiary corporations.

The subsidiary corporations must conform to the following restrictions: they cannot create subsidiaries without Treasury Board (TB) approval; cannot borrow money or issue securities, mortgages, hypothecations or other property charges without TB approval; regulations of the subsidiary corporations are approved by the shareholder and the president and the executive vice-president are named by the shareholder. Although the shareholder is the Canada Lands Company Limited, one can read this as the Minister of Public Works. One should also note that the subsidiary corporations do not own land. The lands are "owned" by the Minister of Public Works (in right of Her Majesty) who has entered into separate 5-year property administration and management agreements with each of the subsidiary corporations. None of the subsidiary corporations are authorized to retain revenues; revenues are returned to the government's Consolidated Revenue Fund and the subsidiary corporations' financial requirements are provided by appropriations.

Canada Lands Company (Mirabel) Ltd.

The expropriation of the 38,850 hectares (96,000 acres) of land and the management of the 36,420 hectares of peripheral lands around the Mirabel Quebec Airport was originally the responsibility of the Department of Public Works. In 1978, the management of the lands was conferred upon a Board of Directors using the Public Works Lands Company (now Canada Lands Company Limited by change of name). In 1979, the Board was disbanded and the responsibilities returned to the Department of Public

Works. In 1981, the responsibilities were transferred to Canada Lands Company (Mirabel) Ltd. (CLCML). Whose the mandate is to manage the surrounding lands of Mirabel Airport and to dispose of the properties. Senior officials of Public Works Canada are represented on the Board of Directors.

To date CLCML has sold over 542 properties covering a surface area of 2,750 hectares. It still has under its jurisdiction responsibility for leasing and maintaining:

696 residential properties;
617 agricultural properties;
144 commercial properties; and
356 forestry properties.

A recent announcement by the Minister of Public Works indicates that further land sales can proceed, namely:

348 residences;
250 agricultural properties;
70 commercial establishments; and
175 forestry properties.

CLCML anticipates that between 1985/88, it should be able to achieve sales of $46 million. It also estimates it will require operating expenses of $17 million over the same 3-year period.

Canada Lands Company (Le Vieux-Port de Québec) Ltd.

This corporation was established in 1981 to implement the development master plan for Le Vieux-Port de Québec approved by the government in November, 1980. It is responsible for administering, managing, promoting and operating the land and its developments. Within the context of broader government objectives, it is to contribute to regional economic development through the establishment of office buildings, the addition of recreational and touristic facilities, new shops and businesses.

To achieve its cultural objective, this corporation is to preserve the heritage aspect of the area by promotion of the site in its historical perspective, renovating and improving the utility of its components and by providing an interpretation centre.

Canada Lands Company (Le Vieux-Port de Montréal) Ltd.

This company, also incorporated in 1981, is mandated to develop and promote the development of Le Vieux-Port de Montréal lands by putting into place the infrastructure, equipment and services needed. Similar to the Toronto Harbourfront and Le Vieux-Port de Québec projects, it is to invest in the redevelopment or construction of revenue producing buildings directly and through agreements with the private sector and other levels of government. Finally, it is to administer, manage and maintain these Crown properties. No master plan has yet been approved by the government, although $55 million has been spent on the project since 1981.

OBSERVATIONS

Canada Lands Company Limited

Except for creating and holding the shares of the subsidiary companies, this corporation appears to be inactive. No funding is provided nor person-years allocated.

Canada Lands Company (Mirabel) Ltd.

Assessments of the whole question of Mirabel have been carried out by the Canadian press, other levels of governm-ent and the private sector for many years. This corporation deals only with the management and disposal of the peripheral lands. In short, the government of the day, in order to protect its air rights, expropriated too much land.

Large sums of money have been spent on the construction of the infrastructure required for industrial development of the area. Since the market for industrial development of these lands depends largely on the amount of traffic gener-ated by the airport, which has proved to be much less than forecast, these expenditures appear to have been a waste of money. Even if a reasonable level of traffic were generated, the infrastructure would require significant additional outlays to overcome the deterioration resulting from a lack of maintenance.

The government, through the Minister of Public Works, has recently signed an agreement to undertake the second phase of the sale of these lands to the original owners or present tenants or general public, in that order. Qualifications have been placed on market and there is a requirement for unanimous agreement on the valuation of each property segment by a committee made up of a representative of the buyers and a representative of the sellers (government). These factors make it unlikely that a rapid, satisfactory sale will take place.

Canada Lands Company (Le Vieux-Port de Québec) Ltd.

Le Vieux-Port de Québec, which neighbours the historic site of old Quebec, contains an area of 33 hectares (72 acres) adjacent to the St. Lawrence River. The original total cost of the project, approved in 1981 and to be completed by 1987, was $60 million, consisting of $43 million capital construction and $12 million operating expenses. The corporation was mandated to structure its investments so that by 1987 the annual revenues would be equal to the annual operating costs of the corporation; in other words a break-even operation before debt service.

With 2 years still to go on its mandate, the corporation has spent to date $94 million, of which $78 million has been on capital and $16 million on operations. Not only is the corporation nowhere near its self-sufficiency target (it can generate an annual income of $2 million) but it is seeking another $55 million for the 5-year period 1985-1990 (another $21 million in capital and $34 million for operations). In spite of the large outlay of funds, primarily to create a focal recreation spot in Quebec, and in spite of publicity and events supporting the 300th Anniversary of Jacques Cartier's landing at Quebec in 1984 (for example, the arrival of the tall ships), le "Vieux-Port de Québec" site has been abandoned by both the merchants and the public. The corporation recognizes that its investment decisions and predictions were based on optimistic assumptions.

As noted, completion of the development master plan resulted in appropriations of approximately $35 million more than compared to the original estimate of approximately $60 million - a significant under-estimation by anyone's definition. The latest revised total estimated cost is $150 million, which will require a further outlay of $55 million, if approved. One must ask at what stage an owner/investor chooses to cut his losses.

Revenues have been much lower than anticipated due largely to the fact that very little private sector development has accompanied the government initiative and also the general economic conditions. Although this corporation plans future negotiations for private sector involvement, the likelihood of self-sufficiency for the corporation within the next 5 years appears again grossly over-estimated.

Canada Lands Company (Le Vieux-Port de Montréal) Ltd.

Interviews were declined by the president of the corporation. Although this corporation was established in 1981, the government has never approved the master redevelopment plan. The lack of approval stems from two reasons: the corporation has had difficulty in acquiring property from other federal agencies and therefore has had difficulty in preparing a total financial plan, and several preliminary ambitious cost estimates exceeded $150 million, which was well in excess of available federal funding. In 1984-85, a total of $31.2 million was spent on the site, the majority ($29 million) under the Special Recovery Capital Projects Program. In 1985-86, only $1.5 million has been authorized for operating expenses pending a review of the master plan.

To-date $55 million has been spent on administration and construction of piers, parkland, landscaping, some infrastructure and an administrative building. A comprehensive audit, taking value for money into consideration, would be a welcomed initiative.

The corporation has recently proposed a 5-year corporate plan which calls for the approval of Le Vieux-Port de Montréal project's master plan. It seeks approval of a further expenditure of $186 million between 1985-1990, consisting of $168 million for capital construction and $18 million for operating expenditures. Over the same period it anticipates the generation of a total of $9 million of revenue from its investments.

Given the physical location of Le Vieux-Port de Montréal and the attraction of Old Montreal, this corporation may have a slight edge in avoiding the same failures and inabilities of attracting private sector investment as faced by its sister corporation -- Le Vieux-Port de Québec. Considering the economic climate, it is doubtful that this corporation will ever produce sufficient annual revenues to offset its annual operating expenses. One must question the economic wisdom of proceeding under these circumstances.

General

Each of the Vieux-Port corporations is involved in urban and industrial development and cultural and recreational activities - activities which are not in support of providing accommodation for government operations and for which the Minister of Public Works has no clear mandate.

OPTIONS

In view of these observations, the study team recommends to the Task Force that the government consider the following measures:

Mirabel

Changing the agreement between the Canada Lands Company (Mirabel) Ltd. and the group representing the expropriated parties in order to clarify the establishment of "market value" and the mechanism for resolving disputes.

The Canada Lands Company (Mirabel) Ltd. be wound up as soon as possible and the responsibility for the disposal of surplus properties be transferred to the Department of Public Works.

Le Vieux-Port de Québec/Le Vieux-Port de Montréal

Establishing a policy framework which curtails federal involvement in urban redevelopment projects through direct property ownership and through crown corporations.

In the interim, a moratorium be placed on additional capital outlays required by the Canada Lands Company (Le Vieux-Port de Montréal) Ltd. and the Canada Lands Company (Le Vieux-Port de Québec) Ltd.

In order to provide greater control over the activities performed, the Canada Lands subsidiary corporations be wound up and the properties brought back into the normal PWC departmental framework for disposal.

CANADA HARBOUR PLACE CORPORATION

Public Works Canada

OBJECTIVE

To design and construct in Vancouver, B.C. a facility at Pier B.C. to include a Canadian Host Pavilion for Expo '86, to organize and operate the participation of the Government of Canada as exhibitor and host nation for Expo '86 at Pier B.C. and to transform the Pavilion into a Trade and Convention Centre to be transferred to the City of Vancouver for one dollar.

RESULTS/BENEFICIARIES

An awareness of Canadian accomplishments/capabilities; industrial and market development for Canadian manufacturers; international liaison with systems operators and regulators in transportation and communications.

The beneficiaries will be the Canadian and foreign visitors to EXPO'86:

- business, professional and academic interests related to the transportation and communication industries both Canadian and foreign, including manufacturers, systems operators and government regulators;
- provincial and corporate participants in EXPO'86; and
- federal departments and agencies contributing to the Canadian Pavilion and other forms of federal presence at EXPO'86.

AUTHORITY

CHPC was incorporated under the Canada Business Corporations Act in June 1982 as a subsidiary of the Canada Lands Company Limited, a federal crown corporation reporting to the Minister of Public Works. On December 20, 1984, CHPC was added (as a parent crown corporation) to Part 1 of Schedule C of the Financial Administration Act. There are three shares issued and outstanding, all held by the Minister of Transport in right of Her Majesty the Queen.

RESOURCES (thousands of current dollars)

	84/85	85/86
Operating Expenditures	$11,392	$44,080
Capital Expenditures	$46,924	$39,748
Person-Years	75	75

PROGRAM DESCRIPTION

Canada Harbour Place Corporation, which now reports to the Minister of Transport, is responsible for implementing the terms of the federal agreement with the Province of British Columbia to participate in EXPO'86 which include:

- the design, construction, operation and managment by CHPC of a permanent facility named CANADA PLACE on the waterfront of Vancouver and a Canadian Pavilion, within Canada Place, and its subsequent conversion to a Trade and Convention Centre; and
- the establishment of the federal presence at EXPO'86 and the planning for the provision of essential federal services in British Columbia during the period of EXPO'86 (May 2 to October 13, 1986).

CHPC has been mandated to meet federal obligations under the 1928 Convention Governing International Expositions. It will undertake to realize the federal obligations to the Government of British Columbia pursuant to the April 1982 Federal-Provincial Agreement. CHPC will also serve as a coordinating agency to ensure that federal departments and agencies in the Vancouver area meet the expected increase in workload caused by EXPO visitors and activities. In order to demonstrate Canada's commitment to increased trade and economic development with countries in the Pacific Rim, CHPC will present in the Canadian government's host pavilion demonstrations of Canadian transportation and communications achievements and cultural accomplishments.

OBSERVATIONS

The "Canada Place" site will include the following facilities: parking for 770 cars, a cruise ship terminal, the Canadian Pavilion, a World Trade Centre Office Complex, a CN Imax Theatre, a Pan Pacific Hotel, and various public amenities (restaurants, gift shops, outdoor amphitheatre, and public places).

The total estimated project expenditures by CHPC on Canada Place is $227 million. The cost of constructing the Canadian Pavilion is $85 million, the cost of transforming it into a trade and convention centre after expo '86 is estimated at $15 million. CHPC will construct a cruise-ship terminal on behalf of and funded by the Vancouver Port Corporation at a cost of $23 million. CHPC has agreed to loose space in the Canadian Pavilion to Teleglobe for approximately $220 thousand, in which Teleglobe will construct at its expense a theatre, estimated to cost $4.5 million. Canadian National is providing another $5 million to CHPC to sponsor an IMAX film and theatre.

Although the Canada Place site (with the Canadian Pavilion) is not on the Expo '86 site (located at False Creek, about a mile away), the two are linked by road and a light rapid transit system. Coordination between federal departments and agencies contributing exhibits to the Canadian Pavilon and the Expo 86 Board of Management is handled by CHPC.

The Canadian Pavilion is to be transformed into a Trade and Convention Centre after Expo 86. Both the province and the federal government had reached agreement that the Trade and Convention Centre would be transferred to the City of Vancouver. The city, however, was not a signatory to the agreement and has publicly declined to accept the offer.

Identification of an operator for the Trade and Convention Centre is a major unresolved issue. Discussions are proceeding with the City of Vancouver, Provincial officials and private concerns with a view towards establishing a new corporation which would lease the centre from CHPC. Full financial responsibility for operation would become that of this new corporation.

Work is proceeding well on all phases of construction. Minor issues need to be resolved such as whether CHPC or Expo 86 will pick up the costs of operating transportation systems between the two sites (estimated at $1.5 million), and the provision of cafeteria, fast food and merchandizing services to Canada Place (estimated at $2 million).

The mandate of the corporation expires on December 31, 1988 before which time the responsible Minister is to make a recommendation to the Governor-in-Council, taking into consideration any liabilities and obligations incurred by the corporation. The Minister should ensure that these liabilities are kept to a minimum and are such that they are transferrable to other levels of government. CHPC managment are directing the affairs of the corporation in such a manner that, should CHPC need to continue, a very small staff could manage its operations.

OPTIONS

The study team recommends to the Task Force that the government consider:

- securing an operator for the Trade and Convention Centre at the Canada Harbour Place; and

- developing a plan to ensure that a recommendation can be made to the Governor-in-Council after Expo '86 to divest the federal government of real property at the Canada Place site and to dissolve the Canada Harbour Place Corporation.

DESIGN CONSTRUCTION AND REALTY TECHNOLOGY

Public Works Canada

OBJECTIVE

To provide technical advice, resource and implementation support including technological improvements and standards development, to the government as a whole in relation to the design, construction, maintenance and operation of real property.

RESULTS/BENEFICIARIES

The development and transfer to the private sector of improvements in technology and standards, through research studies, reports, training courses, seminars and technical support services.

AUTHORITY

Public Works Act.

RESOURCES (thousands of current dollars)

	84/85	85/86
Operating Expenditures	$6,569	$6,257
Person-Years	2	2

PROGRAM DESCRIPTION

This unit of PWC identifies the research requirements of program managers in various departments, as well as Public Works' program managers, and arranges for the purchase of these research services from the appropriate Public Works service agency (either Architectural and Engineering Services or Real Estate Services). The unit also develops methods to pass on the new technology or the new standards to the private sector. Approximately $6 million is spent and 140 person-years are used within Public Works to undertake the research projects.

This activity is intended to focus on the application of the technology to the government's real property assets, to keep abreast of technological changes and improved methods and techniques in order to solve problems such as energy conservation, quality of air in the workplace, etc.

For example, in the area of indoor air quality research, the department determines the effects of outgassing on air quality and attempts to prevent such problems by incorporating the knowledge gained into design procedures.

The work is done mainly in headquarters. The exact number of employees will fluctuate according to workload and available funding.

OBSERVATIONS

The Auditor General has expressed his concern that the activities of Headquarters Technology were not being utilized by the department's main client - its own regional operators. The Auditor General also noted that there is a lack of clarity as to PWC's role and relationship in the use of technological services.

The effectiveness of this activity has varied substantially. There are various instances of success - the development of energy conservation techniques, the Government Master Specifications and thermographic testing. Overall, the efficiency and effectiveness of this program have never been measured, and no reports are available on the success, failure, or costs of most of the various research and development projects.

Research activities related to real property are also carried out by the Division of Building Research of the National Research Council, and are funded by the Natural Science and Engineering Research Council and the Canada Mortgage and Housing Corporation. Technological research is also carried out at Canadian universities, as well as within the private sector. While the research undertaken at these facilities is more theoretical, PWC research is more applied and in support of efficient asset operations.

Much of the research coordination is undertaken by the Canadian Committee on Building Research (a National Research

Council associate committee which is oriented towards building science and technology).

The major issue is whether the government requires a dedicated in-house knowledge capacity for research and development, or whether these activities can be undertaken more efficiently outside of the government.

The private sector is generally considered insufficiently involved, both in terms of funding and the establishment of research priorities. One proposal would be to amalgamate the NRC's Division of Building Research and Public Works' Technology Branch and create an industry institute, with the private sector responsible for management and funding. For example, in 1979 the federal government's Forest Products Laboratory was privatized as "Forintek". At the present time, the federal government provides about 60 per cent of the funds, with the rest coming from five provincial governments and major companies. Roughly two thirds of Forintek's Board of Directors are from the private sector.

Another option considered was for PWC to contract out the pure research and development activities to the National Research Council; however, the NRC does only pure research and does not provide advice relating to applications and operations. PWC could also examine contracting out the work to private industry and to the universities.

OPTIONS

The study team recommends to the Task Force that the government consider consolidating the various research and development capabilities within the federal government and creating a jointly funded (private sector - provincial - federal) Building Research Institute which would maximize industry involvement in funding and management.

FIRE PROTECTION

Public Works Canada

OBJECTIVE

To provide for fire protection, inspection and investigation on the federal governments' owned and controlled properties, and contribute to the knowledge base and the competence of public and private agencies in the field of fire protection in Canada.

RESULTS/BENEFICIARIES

Results include the setting of fire protection standards for use in the public and private sectors, the inspection of federally owned and controlled properties for compliance with the standards set, the preparation and production of training courses and materials and the preparation and publication of statistical and analytic information. Beneficiaries include Public Works Canada and its clients and other government departments.

AUTHORITY

The legal mandate is found in Government Property Fire Protection Regulations (PC 1960-50/1499) (SOR 72-479), Section 2(a), which designates the Minister of Public Works as the minister responsible and Section 2(b) which identifies the Fire Commissioner of Canada (FCC) as the officer designated by the Minister to administer the regulations. The regulations are ancillary to the Financial Administration Act. Other legal documents include the Fire Losses Replacement Account Act and the Fire Losses Replacement Regulations.

RESOURCES (thousands of current dollars)

	84/85	85/86
Operating Expenses	$3,515	$4,004
Capital Expenditures	$ 19	$ 21
Person-Years	63	69

PROGRAM DESCRIPTION

Properties included in the mandate comprise 19.1 million square metres of land and buildings. Excluded from the mandate are DND bases, DOT Airport Crash Fire Fighting and government ships.

At headquarters, this element is composed of the Fire Commissioner and four directors - fire protection engineering, inspection and investigations, fire prevention programs and special projects - together with support staff. Approximately 13 PY and $800,000 are allocated to the Fire Commissioner. These are utilized primarily in standard setting for construction, equipment and materials; designing of training programs and materials; review and approval of building plans and in the preparation of statistical data for publication.

Since the fire fighting services provided by municipalities are utilized, the remaining 50 PY's and related costs of $2,700,000, assigned to the ADM Operations, are used for inspections, investigations and training.

OBSERVATIONS

A recent program evaluation report (October, 1984) concluded that both the private and federal sector fire protection requirements are based on similar codes and standards and at similar costs.

In the private sector, self-insurance is the exception rather than the rule, and is normally limited to the size of the deductible amount. Since the quality of loss prevention facilities is a major consideration in the establishment of the cost of coverage, insurance companies employ the services of loss prevention consultants who evaluate these facilities prior to construction completion and monitor them on a regular basis. In general, the codes are considered minimum standards and acceptable coverage rates frequently demand additional requirements. Reliance is not placed on the inspection services provided by municipal and provincial authorities.

The mandate of the Fire Commissioner of Canada is a dual role: that of the enforcer of a code aimed primarily at the preservation of life, and that of the loss prevention consultant advising on acceptable levels of risk to the preservation of property, its cost and revenue streams.

It was noted that although the FCC carries out the inspections normally performed by municipal authorities, no deductions are made from grants in-lieu of taxes. The municipalities claim that the services are available to the federal government whether or not utilized. The FCC indicated, however, that municipal authorities have been reluctant to assume the inspection responsibility when asked.

Given the environment of self-insurance, the services of the FCC are essential. It is unlikely that the services could be purchased more economically from the private sector.

There is the possibility of some savings through reductions in grants in-lieu of taxes for inspection services not performed by the appropriate municipalities.

OPTIONS

The study team recommends to the Task Force that the government consider transferring the functions of the Fire Commissioner of Canada as a regulatory body on behalf of all federal property, to the proposed central Real Property Unit.

EMERGENCY PREPAREDNESS

Public Works Canada

OBJECTIVE

To provide plans and arrangements for the control and regulation of engineering and construction resources, for protection of the population against the wartime effects of radioactive fallout and of other weapons, and for timely departmental emergency response (peacetime emergencies and war), as well as to provide emergency government facilities.

RESULTS/BENEFICIARIES

PWC prepares plans and procedures to handle emergencies in support of the Canadian public.

AUTHORITY

The Governor-in-Council approved the Emergency Planning Order (P.C. 1981-1305) on 21 May, 1981.

RESOURCES (thousands of current dollars)

	84/85	85/86
Operating Expenditures	$600	$1,104
Person-Years	7	20

PROGRAM DESCRIPTION

PWC is responsible for: the development and maintenance of plans and preparations for establishing and operating a national emergency construction agency to control and regulate construction and allocation of engineering and construction resources throughout Canada; the development of plans and arrangements, in collobration with the appropriate provincial minister to protect the population from the wartime effects of radioactive fallout and other weapon effects by identifying government buildings that could be used as shelters; the provision and maintenance of emergency government facilities for the Continuity of Government program; and the development and maintenance of readiness plans that will enable the department to carry out its emergency responsibilities in peace and war.

The program is delivered by the Directorate of Emergency Preparedness with 7 person-years at headquarters. An additional 13 person-years have been approved for 1985-86 and it is proposed to staff Regional Emergency Planning Officers in each of the six PWC regions.

OBSERVATIONS

The provinces have responsibility for emergency planning and managing in peace time and these capabilities would exist in wartime.

The Emergency Planning Canada Organization under the Department of National Defence has responsibility for coordinating the emergency planning activities of 10 departments, and Public Works is one of them. The National Emergency Agency for Construction, which Public Works would be responsible for directing and controlling in wartime, would be under a Central Emergency Organization.

It appears that the Emergency Preparedness organization in Public Works is currently authorized to carry too large a staff in 1985-86 (20 person-years) to only develop and update the small part of the Emergency Plan for which PWC is responsible. No savings are projected as no staffing has yet taken place.

There are a number of activities within PWC which the department undertakes on behalf of the government in the role of a central real property manager. PWC is not, however, organized to easily achieve its responsibilities. It is proposed that the management of real property across the government should reside in one central agency which is authorized to manage programs. As a minimum, PWC should appoint one senior officer to assume responsibility for all activities which are in support of the government's broader objectives impacting on real property.

OPTIONS

The study team recommends to the Task Force that the government consider transferring the responsibilities for planning and purchasing services from PWC related to emergency preparedness to the proposed central Real Property Unit.

MUNICIPAL GRANTS

Public Works Canada

OBJECTIVE

To make grants to taxing authorities in lieu of taxes in respect of federal property pursuant to applicable legislation.

RESULTS/BENEFICIARIES

Public Works pays grants, in lieu of taxes to 3,140 municipalities and the Province of New Brunswick .

AUTHORITY

Municipal Grants Act.

RESOURCES (thousands of current dollars)

	84/85	85/86
Operating Expenditures	$259,898	$287,971
Person-Years	40	40

PROGRAM DESCRIPTION

Grants are paid to municipalities in lieu of taxes on federal property. These payments are designed to compensate the municipalities for services provided to federal property and to prevent a loss of revenue to the municipalities where real property is owned by the government. The payments are made in response to the local or provincial assessors who discover and value all real property subject to grants in lieu of taxes and who apply to the federal government for a municipal grant.

PWC makes payments on behalf of most properties owned by Her Majesty. PWC also performs a property valuation and grant calculation service for properties owned by other agencies which have separate authority to pay their own grants in lieu of taxes: Canada Post Corporation, Royal

Canadian Mint, National Research Council, Canadian Arsenals Limited, Canada Ports Corporation, National Battlefield Commission, and External Affairs in respect of foreign diplomatic and consular properties in Canada. The National Capital Commission has its own program and its own staff and does all the work in-house.

The program is delivered by 5 person-years at headquarters and 35 in the regions. A Municipal Grants Review Committee was established in November 1983, based on the Pollock Report recommendations, to assess any municipality's appeal against departmental decisions related to grants in lieu of taxes. The committee is composed of a chairperson and two other members, one individual being from the private sector. To date, two appeals have been made. Generally 5 per cent of the municipal assessments are challenged by Public Works.

Approximately 50 per cent of the applications are finalized within 50 days in accordance with the time parameter defined in the act. The remaining applications relate to large government holdings for which payments are made by installments or in total following confirmation and evaluation of properties listed in the application.

No tax reductions are made by the municipalities for the government's provision of its own services, i.e. fire inspection, utility services on DND bases, etc. The municipalities claim that they do provide these services. As long as the federal government wants to play the role of a good corporate citizen, as it has decided to do since 1950, it will continue to pay grants in lieu of municipal taxes. A review should be undertaken to focus on areas of duplication of payment and federal self-servicing.

A number of Crown corporations pay their own grants, but utilize the services of the Department of Public Works in reviewing the assessments. The National Capital Commission has its own program and employees whereas the Department of Public Works has employees in the National Capital Region who could provide the service without additional personnel resources. A letter from the Deputy Minister of Public Works to the National Capital Commission recently offered the services for $10,000.00 a year. The offer was refused by the National Capital Commission on the grounds that Municipal Grants Assessments are the basis for their asset management system.

The Assessment Review Committee established in late 1983 could become more busy if PWC decides to challenge more of the municipal assessments, particularly in major urban centres. It is well known that there are some weaknesses in municipal assessments of federal property.

It is to be noted that neither PWC nor other federal departments include Municipal Grants as part of their operating costs of buildings or their land holdings. Furthermore, the estimated $50 million in municipal grants paid on behalf of Canada Post are not charged to the Post Office. When departments are not aware of what expenditures are made on property under their custody and control, there are few incentives or reasons to improve utilization or declare property surplus.

PWC is able to provide real estate appraisal services for the purposes of grants in lieu of taxes on a fee basis to a greater number of departments, agencies and crown corporations. It has commenced to make its services known to these agencies.

An estimated $50 million is paid annually for grants in lieu of taxes on behalf of Canada Post, which is not charged to Canada Post and could be considered as a hidden subsidy. Canada Post replies that they do not pay for the grants in lieu of taxes because of a trade-off for services that they supply free of charge to the government.

Although PWC manages this program, there is no evidence of broader real property management. The grants represent a significant potential lever in negotiating real property transactions with municipalities. They would be valuable in broader federal-provincial relations which deal with the transfer of federal real property (bridges, roads, dams, etc.) to the other levels of government. While PWC could provide a service, the overall responsibility for Municipal Grants should reside with a central agency responsible for real property management.

OPTIONS

The study team recommends to the Task Force that the government consider transferring the responsibility for the management and funding of grants in lieu of taxes on behalf of all federal departments and agencies to the proposed central Real Property Unit; PWC should be engaged to provide the service.

As taxes are a normal operating cost associated with real property ownership, grants in lieu of taxes should be reflected in the total costs of the property management function of each department and agency which has custody of federal property.

The Canada Post Corporation, which is currently receiving an indirect $50 million subsidy by not paying grants in lieu of taxes on its assets, should assume this responsibility.

SPECIAL PROJECTS

Public Works Canada

OBJECTIVE

To undertake, solely or jointly with other departments, those projects, as directed, which have a significant impact on the design, construction, maintenance or operation of real property.

RESULTS/BENEFICIARIES

Results and beneficiaries depend upon the specific projects in place. Current projects include accessibility for the handicapped, asbestos decontamination and federal identity. Planning and control is provided for each project.

AUTHORITY

The Public Works Act.

RESOURCES (thousands of current dollars)

	84/85	85/86
Operating Expenses	$ 565	$ 104
Capital Expenditures	$6,500	$4,300
Person-Years	2	2

PROGRAM DESCRIPTION

The projects are usually of a highly specialized and unique nature. Generated externally, the projects are assigned to the department for implementation.

The accessibility program, undertaken in 1981, involves the use of a barrier free design standard for buildings to provide access to the handicapped to all public buildings. In 1985-86, expenditures of $3,002,000 will be made to complete the necessary alterations of Crown-owned and leased buildings.

In 1985-86, $100,000 will be spent to complete the removal of asbestos in several remaining buildings containing spray-applied asbestos insulation.

The 4-year Federal Identity Program, to install Canada Wordmark signs on all government-occupied facilities as a method of fulfilling federal visual image objectives, is to spend $1,212,000 in 1985-86.

Program planning and control, utilizing 2 person-years, will require $90,000 to supply the support services.

OBSERVATIONS

These projects are usually directed by Cabinet in order to achieve the "broader social objectives" of government. Once a project has been defined, requirements can be forecast and controlled. Potential new projects cannot be anticipated; therefore, planning resources for this planning element as a whole is difficult.

Certain projects have been transferred to other departments where this has been considered more appropriate, e.g. the Solar Program to the Department of Energy Mines and Resources.

Government-wide policies established by the Treasury Board or Cabinet should be directed for implementation to a central real property agency with services to be purchased from PWC.

OPTIONS

The study team recommends to the Task Force that the government consider transferring the responsiblity for management of and budgeting for special real property related projects, in support of broader social objectives, to either a program department or to the proposed central Real Property Unit; PWC, as a common service agency would be able to provide a services on a cost recovery basis.

SECTION 8 - PWC MARINE AND HIGHWAY PROGRAMS

INTRODUCTION

To achieve a true common service agency status, PWC should transfer program responsibility for these facilities to other federal departments which have a lead role in the area and to the relevant provincial and municipal governments under whose jurisdiction these facilities more appropriately fall.

BACKGROUND

There is a fascinating story behind every marine and highway facility still operated by PWC. Whether a highway, dry dock, bridge, lock or dam, there was at some point in time a decision taken by some other agency to transfer it to PWC. For example, the Alexandra Interprovincial Bridge (behind the Parliament Buildings) was constructed between 1878 and 1901 for the Pontiac Pacific Junction Railway Co. Several agreements were entered into in the past between the different railway companies, the City of Ottawa, and the Dominion Government related to the use and maintenance of the bridge. The most recent was an agreement, dated July 26, 1966, between the Canadian Pacific Railway Co. and the National Capital Commission which transferred ownership of the bridge to the NCC. On August 1, 1966, the NCC sent a letter to PWC transferring ownership and operation to PWC. Since then, PWC has been maintaining the bridge. The centre lane was abandoned for train use in 1966 and PWC rehabilitated it to carry highway traffic in 1967 as part of a PWC major upgrading of the bridge.

Another example is the Northwest Highway System (some 2000 kilometres of roadway) which comprise the Alaska Highway (except the first 133 kilometres north of Dawson Creek which was taken over by B.C. in 1962) and the Haines Road from Haines Junction, Y.T. to the B.C.-Alaska border. The Alaska highway was originally constructed in 1942 by the United States government as a defence route to Alaska. In 1946, the U.S. Army transferred responsibility of the Canadian portion of the highway system to the Canadian Department of National Defence. In 1964, National Defence transferred it over to PWC.

The result of these and similar stories is that PWC spent $95 million in 1984-85 on the maintenance and operation of:

- Northwest Highway System and the upgrading of the Trans Canada Highway through the National Parks ($81 million);
- seventeen bridges: five international, seven interprovincial and five intraprovincial ($1.5 million);
- One lock and 10 dams on the Ottawa, French and Red Rivers ($2.2 million); and
- dry docks located at Lauzon, P.Q., Selkirk, Manitoba and Esquimalt, B.C. ($11 million).

OBSERVATIONS

PWC is not the sole or even major federal department or agency in marine and highway programs. The Department of Indian and Northern Affairs has policy and program responsibility for federal roads and highways north of 60 degrees; Transport Canada has responsibility for overall federal highway policy and for funding highways with regional-economic considerations; Parks Canada has responsibility for the maintenance of the Trans Canada Highway through its parks; the St. Lawrence Seaway Authority has the responsibility for the operation and maintenance of the Jacques Cartier and Champlain bridges. A recent major policy paper on the federal roles and responsibilities in highways totally excluded PWC.

Bridges and highways (the Trans Canada Highway running through the National Parks) by their location and nature form only a portion of the adjoining transportation networks. These over-all networks are generally under the jurisdiction of provincial or municipal authorities. The study team recommends that the custody and control of PWC bridges and highways be transferred to more appropriate levels of government. Any negotiations for transfer should take into account the requirements of the end user; for example, a transfer of the B.C. - Yukon highway should ensure that the B.C. portion is adequately maintained to permit passage to the Yukon portion.

There is a changing requirement for maintenance of water levels (locks and dams) where the major beneficiaries are no longer the pulp and paper companies floating timber, but hydro-electric companies, users of pleasure craft and downstream land-owners. The role of the federal government in these activities is questionable. The study team recommends to the Task Force that the government consider transferring responsibility for the lock and dams to provincial jurisdictions.

The dry dock industry is not likely to be internationally competitive again. Since it services mobile assets, increased costs of operation cannot be passed on to the user. The Canadian problem is acute and PWC-owned facilities will never generate sufficient revenue to be self-sufficient. While PWC dry docks are all used, there are also privately owned dry docks in each area that are under-utilized. The study team supports the suggestion of the Study Team on Services and Subsidies to Business that the Dry Dock Subsidies Act be repealed and that the government extricate itself from the dry dock business.

In 1980, the then Prime Minister directed the Public Works Minister to divest the department of further responsibility for the Marine and Highway Programs. However, to date there is no evidence of any progress. The reasons are either a lack of commitment from PWC or a lack of political will, or a combination of both. The study team suggests that the government consider transferring all facilities in support of Marine and Highway Transportation Programs to other levels of government.

In the view of the study team there is a need to clarify PWC's role and mandate as a common service agency in support of accommodation and real property services. In order to achieve this mandate a streamlining of its operations, by divesting itself from program responsibilities such as marine and highway programs, is required. Should a continued major delay be anticipated in the transfer of highways and bridges, the study team suggests that the program responsibility be transferred to Transport Canada. PWC in the interim could provide Transport Canada a "service" agent function which would be more in keeping with its role as a service agency rather than a program manager.

If transfers to other levels of government are successful, the government could anticipate annual savings of up to $95 million, depending on the terms and conditions of the transfers.

DRY DOCKS

Public Works Canada

OBJECTIVE

To acquire, construct, reconstruct, operate and maintain certain dry docks and to make contributions under the Dry Dock Subsidies Act. To ensure that competitive and accessible ship repair facilities are available.

AUTHORITY

The Dry Dock Subsidy Act; Appropriation Act.

DESCRIPTION

This program currently maintains and operates Crown owned dry docks at Lauzon Quebec, Selkirk Manitoba, and Esquimalt British Columbia. There is one principal user for each of the facilities at Lauzon (Davie Shipping), Selkirk (Purvis), and Esquimalt (Burrard-Yarrows), with a fee for service being authorized by Order in Council.

BENEFICIARIES

Shipbuilders, shipping companies, ship repair contractors.

EXPENDITURES (millions of current dollars)

	83/84	84/85	85/86	86/87	87/88
Other O&M	4.8	4.5	5.6	4.2	4.2
Capital	2.1	7.4	3.9	.1	.1
Grants & Contributions	.2	.2	.2	.2	.2
TOTAL	7.1	12.1	9.7	4.5	4.5
Revenues	1.0	1.0	1.0	1.0	1.0

OBSERVATIONS

As a result of government policy in the late 1960s and early 1970s, the federal government got into the dry dock business using various program instruments. Public Works became the custodian for these facilities.

By the late 1970s the Canadian shipbuilding industry was in decline, and Canadian dry docks became marginally competitive. Public Works has since made attempts, most strongly in Lauzon, to divest themselves of the dry docks. They have not increased the fee structure since 1971, in order to further subsidize the beneficiaries, and this was cited by the Auditor General as inappropriate.

Two large additional dry docks have been built in Canada with significant government assistance. The Burrards dock on the west coast recently won a U.S. Navy contract and so it has found some niche in the market where it is competitive. The Halifax Industries dry dock is in receivership but ownership could revert to the province.

The Dry Dock Subsidies Act has been used only once to construct a dry dock in Montreal owned and operated, with an on-going subsidy, by Versatile-Vickers.

The dry dock industry is not likely to be internationally competitive again. Since it services mobile assets, increased costs of operation cannot be passed on to the user. The Canadian problem is acute and the PWC owned facilities will never generate sufficient revenues to be self sufficient.

ASSESSMENT

Privatization of the dry docks in Selkirk and Esquimalt could be pursued. It is anticipated that Burrard-Yarrows or another current part time user of the facility would purchase Esquimalt and Purris would likely buy the Selkirk dry dock.

The sale of the Lauzon facility was attempted once, but collapsed because Davie could not pay the property taxes. While the financial position of Davie has improved somewhat, the sale of the Lauzon dry dock will likely require municipal agreement in order to forgive the property taxes that Davie, as the new dry dock owner, would have to pay.

Further assistance to dry docks under the Subsidies Act is not justified. The payment is very small and its removal would have little impact.

Revenue from the docks could certainly be increased, given the fact that the fees structure has not changed since 1971. However, these facilities cannot hope to reach a break even point under federal government ownership.

While the PWC dry docks are all used, there are also privately owned dry docks in each area that are under-utilized.

OPTIONS

The Study Team on Real Property Management supports the observations and options presented by the Study Team on Services and Subsidies to Business that:

- the Dry Dock Subsidies Act should be repealed. This would generate a small savings in government expenditures and would have not impact on the dry dock operated by Versatile-Vickers;

- negotiations should commence on the sale of the Selkirk and Esquimalt facilities. In order to ensure that these are concluded in an expeditious manner a fee structure which will yield a break-even point should be put in place immediately. Also, the potential buyer should be advised that the federal government will close the dry dock if the sale is not consummated; and

- with respect to the Lauzon facility, negotiations should be opened with Davie Shipping so that the federal government may divest itself of this facility as soon as possible.

LOCKS AND DAMS

Public Works Canada

OBJECTIVE

To regulate water levels and flows required for safe navigation and other purposes on certain rivers through the establishment of the required water levels, construction, reconstruction, operation and maintenance of certain locks and dams.

RESULTS/BENEFICIAIRIES

The operation of locks and dams to maintain water levels, where the major beneficiaries are no longer solely commercial users but hydro electric companies, users of pleasure craft and downstream land owners.

AUTHORITY

Public Works Act (s.9.1)

RESOURCES (in thousands of current dollars)

	84/85	85/86
Operating Expenditures	$1,355	$1,359
Capital	$ 845	$1,053
Person-Years	5	5

PROGRAM DESCRIPTION

PWC provides for the operation and maintenance of lock and dam facilities located on the Ottawa, French and Red Rivers. The work includes dredging, construction and other maintenance efforts in order to control the level and flow of water and thereby support navigation along these waterways by facilitating the passage of commercial vessels, pleasure craft and forest products. PWC contributes to other government department's objectives through maintenance of appropriate water levels for navigation, hydro electricity production, logging operations and other similar purposes. It is an activity which PWC has been involved in for over 70 years.

Of the total expenditures in 1984-85, $1.3 million is for the operation and maintenance of the locks and dams, $0.8 million is for capital expenditures. Of these costs, $1.0 million is for the program to engage the services of 28 additional person-years provided by PWC's Services Program.

In 1985-86, PWC will be operating 10 water level control facilities: seven on the Ottawa River, two on the French River and one on the Red River, which control the level and flow of water. PWC controls one lock complex, the St. Andrews lock in Manitoba. It is PWC's intention to ensure that the operating costs in 1985-86 remain within the average costs over the past 5 years.

The operations of the locks and dams are carried out in three regions: National Capital, Ontario and Western.

OBSERVATIONS

The level of Public Work's activities in the Marine Program have diminished considerably over the past few years, as program responsibilities formerly carried out by Public Works were transferred to Program Departments (Transportation, Fisheries and Oceans, etc.).

There are currently a number of other departments and agencies which have custody and operate locks and dams: Parks Canada, Welland Canal Authority, St. Lawrence Seaway Authority, etc., and the Department of Environment administers the Ottawa River Act. Despite various negotiations and executive direction that PWC divest itself of marine program responsibilities, PWC has had difficulty in finding willing clients, either in or out of the federal government. Yet there are numerous beneficiaries; for example, the Ontario and Quebec Hydro companies, who do not pay for the benefits derived from the Ottawa River water level controls.

PWC's marine activities (program responsibility for water level control, dry docks, locks and dams) are being considered for possible transfer to other jurisdictions, either within the federal government or where relevant, to provincial governments or the private sector. Discussions are currently underway with the Province of Quebec regarding the possibility of transferring some two dams to the Province, which it currently leases. Quebec would like to see them rebuilt, at a cost of $4-6M, before any transfer is agreed to.

OPTIONS

The study team recommends to the Task Force that the government consider negotiating the transfer of responsibility for the operations of all locks and dams to the appropriate provincial governments.

HIGHWAY SYSTEMS

Public Works Canada

OBJECTIVE

To support the federal government's transportation plans, policies and economic and social development goals, through the construction, reconstruction and maintenance, to agreed standards, of designated highway systems and to undertake improvements of the Trans Canada Highway through the National Parks.

RESULTS/BENEFICIARIES

Public Works provides new and improved sections of highways. The beneficiaries are all the users of the Alaska Highway and Haines Road and those of the Trans Canada Highway through the National Parks.

AUTHORITY

Public Works Act (S.9 and S.12). Trans Canada Highway Act (S.8).

RESOURCES (thousand of current dollars)

	84/85	85/86
Operating Expenses	$26,480	$22,906
Capital Expenditures	$58,210	$40,403
Person-Years	3	3

PROGRAM DESCRIPTION

The legislation gives PWC the authority to provide for the construction of such highways within National Parks as form part of a Trans Canada Highway. They empower the Minister with the management, charge and direction of roads and bridges. They also make him responsible for administering the federal portion of shared-cost road transportation projects for which Public Works has been made responsible. The major activities in the Highway Systems program are the reconstruction of the Northwest Highway (66 kilometres in 1984-85), and the Banff Trans Canada Highway (6 kilometres in 1984-85) and the maintenance of (2,100 kilometres) the Northwest Highway System (Alaska Highway and Haines Road) and capital improvements to the Trans Canada Highway through the National Parks. Maintenance of the Trans Canada Highway in the parks is the responsibility of Parks Canada. This program also maintains the bridges which are an integral part of these highways.

The Yukon Territorial Government, under an agreement with the Department of Public Works, carries out maintenance on the Yukon portion of the Alaska Highway and the Haines Road. Although PWC has budgetary responsibility and pays for maintenance work on the British Columbia portion of the Alaska Highway, PWC contracts out both maintenance and new construction.

The manager responsible is the Assistant Deputy Minister Operations through the Regional Directors General and the Regional Managers Design and Construction. The Assistant Deputy Minister Design and Construction provides functional management including the development of policies and standards and must be consulted on relevant issues. Of the 119 person-years, nine are at headquarters with the Transportation Directorate under the Assistant Deputy Minister Design and Construction. There are 46 person-years in the Western Region and 64 in the Pacific Region. The regional positions include nine engineers, six draftsmen, 61 engineering support staff, 15 general labour, and two clerks.

OBSERVATIONS

The operational outputs of the program are the reconstructed and maintained sections of highway. The standard of the Trans-Canada Highway (TCH) was decided upon at the time of construction, through agreement of the applicable province and the Minister of Public Works Canada. The minimum arterial road standards of the Roads and Transportation Association of Canada (RTAC) have been adopted for the Northwest Highway System. However, reconstruction to this standard only takes place as traffic volumes make the projects economically efficient, or where justified by reduced maintenance costs, subject to availability of funds and Treasury Board/Cabinet approval. Capital improvements to the TCH in National Parks are made on a similar basis. At present it is inferred that road users are generally satisfied with the standard of highways provided for both the Northwest Highway System and the TCH, given the lack of formal complaints or representation from organized interest groups, i.e. truckers associations.

This program successfully achieves its intended effects related to improved/maintained transit times, unit costs of transport, reliable service, accident rates, and energy usage rates. Socio-economic effects in the case of the NWHS relate to relief of isolation, tourism and supply to the resource development areas of northern British Columbia and Yukon. It should be noted that the highway is not used extensively for transporting resources mined in the north.

The major issues involving this program stem from basic questions of objectives and mandate, and arise mainly from a lack of clarity surrounding federal highway policy. The federal policy on highways was last articulated in 1974. At that time, three departments were given responsibility for highways in the federal area: Department of Indian and Northern Affairs has policy and program responsibility for federal roads and highways north of 60 degrees; Transport Canada has responsibility for overall federal highway policy; and Department of Regional Industrial Expansion was given responsibility for federal funding for highways with regional-economic considerations. The Department of Regional Industrial Expansion's responsibilities have since been assumed by Transport Canada. The role of Public Works Canada in this area was not defined, despite its responsibiltiy for the NWHS and the TCH in the National Parks. It should be noted as well that on-going TCH maintenance is the responsibility of Parks Canada.

Superimposed on these federal departmental relationships are the federal/provincial jurisdictional questions. Highways in general are a provincial responsiblity. There does not appear to be any satisfactory reason for the NWHS to continue to be an exception, other than the difficulties which have been encountered in attempting devolution to the Province of British Columbia.

In the study team's view there is one alternative to the status quo. The option is to transfer the program responsibility to the respective Provinces and Territories. Should there be an interim period, it may be appropriate, in order to clarify the PWC's mandate, to remove any highway program responsibility from Public Works Canada, Indian and Northern Affairs and Parks Canada by transferring it to Transport Canada.

Transport Canada has responsibility for overall federal highway policy and for funding in support of regional economic objectives. An interim transfer from PWC to Transport Canada would remove all program responsiblity for highways from Public Works and transform PWC into a "service" agent for the government departments involved with federal highways. The service role would be more in keeping with a streamlined Public Works.

OPTIONS

For the reasons outlined above, the study team recommends to the Task Force that the government consider negotiating transfer of the custody and control of the highway system from PWC to the provincial governments.

In the interim, Transport Canada should assume custody and control of all federal highways.

BRIDGES AND OTHER ENGINEERING WORKS

Public Works Canada

OBJECTIVE

To support the federal government's transporatation plans, policies and economic and social development objectives through the construction, reconstruction, operation and maintenance of certain designated bridges and other engineering works.

RESULTS/BENEFICIARIES

PWC owns and operates bridges for use by commercial transport companies and the local general population. In the case of the New Westminster Bridge, the beneficiaries are the railway companies, exporting industries and the Port of Vancouver.

AUTHORITY

Public Works Act

RESOURCES (thousands of current dollars)

	84/85	85/86
Operating Expenses	$2,417	$2,426
Revenue	$1,269	$2,675

PROGRAM DESCRIPTION

Public Works has responsibility for a total of 17 bridges: five international, seven interprovincial and five intraprovincial bridges.

International

Bridge Location	Province	City
Edmunston, Madawaska	N.B.	Edmunston
Clair-Fort Kent	N.B.	Clair
Ste-Croix-Vanceboco	N.B.	Ste-Croix
St. Léonard-Vanceboco	N.B.	St. Léonard
St. Stephen-Calais	N.B.	St. Stephen

Interprovincial

Perley	Ont./Qué.	Hawksbury
Alexandra	Ont./Qué.	Ottawa-Hull
Chaudière	Ont./Qué.	Ottawa-Hull
Macdonald-Cartier	Ont./Qué.	Ottawa-Hull
Allumette	Ont./Qué.	Pembrooke
Rapide des Joachins	Ont./Qué.	Roolphton
Campbellton-Cross Point	N.B./Qué.	Campbellton

Intraprovincial

Laurier Avenue	Ont.	Ottawa
Burlington Canal	Ont.	Burlington
Plaza	Ont.	Ottawa
Lasalle Causeway	Ont.	Kingston
New Westminster	B.C.	Vancouver

"Other engineering works" include stand-alone sewer systems, water mains, etc. No works of this type is presently being operated or constructed.

The cost of the program in 1984-85 was $2.7 million, the revenues for 1984-85 were $1.3 million from the tolls on the New Westminster Railway Bridge.

The manager responsible for this program is the Assistant Deputy Minister Operations through the Regional Directors General. The Assistant Deputy Minister Design and Construction provides functional management including the development of policies and standards and must be consulted on relevant issues. Capital projects and major maintenance projects are contracted out. However, $1.1 million of the total expenditures are fees paid for services provided by the PWC Services Program.

OBSERVATIONS

The bridges, by their location and nature, form only a portion of the adjoining transportation networks. These networks are generally under the jurisdicition of other levels of government. The effectiveness of these facilities clearly relates to their role within the larger network of which they are a part, normally an essential part. There would appear, in some cases, to be potential to transfer facilities to the provinces or their municipalities. Such transfer would reduce the program cost in terms of person-years and maintenance dollars.

It is difficult to substantiate the need in the Transportation Directorate at Headquarters for three bridge engineers, five design engineers and their technical support under the Assistant Deputy Minister Design and Construction since they are exclusively used on highway bridges. Given the size of the program and the already existing expertise in the private sector for design and construction of highway bridges, there is no need to maintain the in-house capacity.

There are three possible alternatives to the status quo:

a. PWC could contract out to the private sector or other levels of government, the operation and maintenance of bridges;

b. PWC could transfer custody and control of the bridges to the provinces or municipalities; or

c. PWC could adopt a user-fee principle for all bridges and then decide to operate itself or contract out. For example, the tariff for the New Westminster Bridge (the only toll bridge) is $1.95 per railway car and the operating expenditures amount to $4.11 per car. A request to Treasury Board is being made to increase the tariff.

OPTIONS

The study team recommends to the Task Force that the government consider negotiating the transfer of ownership of the 17 bridges to either the provincial or municipal governments.

In the interim, PWC should increase revenue generation by increasing tolls on existing bridges or developing proposals for new cost recovery mechanisms.

SECTION 9 - NATIONAL CAPITAL COMMISSION

INTRODUCTION

In the view of the study team the NCC should retain its role as the federal planner for the National Capital Region, however, as a more streamlined branch of government, as a Departmental corporation, not a Crown corporation. While assuming new responsibilites such as custody of the major symbolic buildings in the area (e.g. Parliament), it should divest itself of all operating and maintenance functions and purchase these from a consolidated Public Works service agency. It should also transfer custody of roads and bridges to the local municipalities and undertake a review to rationalize its real property holdings.

BACKGROUND

The challenge facing the National Capital Commission (NCC) is to create a symbol of Canada's strength and unity, the spiritual home of its nationhood, and the face it shows the world. These are lofty and expensive ideals currently costing the taxpayers $100 million a year (without the significant capital outlays for land acquisitions which occurred up to 1980).

Since 1857 when Queen Victoria selected Ottawa as the Capital of the Province of Canada, as the seat of government, people have sought ways to have it reflect vitality, dynamism and dreams for the future, indeed the soul of Canadians. A series of commissions have tried their hand at beautifying Ottawa, starting with the Ottawa Improvement Commission in 1899, the Federal Plan Commission in 1913, the Federal District Commission in 1927, and finally the National Capital Commission in 1958.

The adoption of the National Capital Act in 1958 was based on the recommendations of a Joint Parliamentary Committee which supported the implementation of a master plan for the nation's capital prepared by Jacques Gréber, a famous French architect. The main recommendations of the Gréber Plan included five points: railway relocation, extension of the parkway network, decentralization of federal office complexes, creation of a greenbelt, and enlargement of Gatineau Park.

Twenty-five years later the Gréber Plan has been substantially completed, and the National Capital Commission is an agency in search of a new master plan. It has grown from a planning commission to a large property manager. Most of its annual expenditures go to operating and maintaining the 48,200 hectares of property it owns, or about 10 per cent of the total area of the National Capital Region. The commission undertakes the maintenance of 80 kilometres of roadways, 54 bridges, 668 hectares of parks, 100 kilometres of bicycle paths, 1,300 residential, commercial and agricultural properties, numerous parking lots and flower beds, three golf courses, and the exterior grounds of all federal government buildings throughout the capital region. The estimated replacement value of the real property owned by the commission is $350 million.

The following data provides an overview of the financial expenditures of the commission for 1984-85 and 1985-86:

	Operating Expenditures $(million)		Person-Years	
	84/85	**85/86**	**84/85**	**85/86**
Planning Design and Construction: federal land use planning, contributions for inter-provincial transit and cost-shared agreements for roadways, bridges and heritage buildings	34	25	87	87
Property Operations and Maintenance: maintenance and renovations of bridges, parking lots, buildings, roadways, grounds of federal government buildings and grants-in-lieu of taxes	57	53	614	630
Recreation and Culture: information and tourist activities, Canada Day, Gatineau Park, Winterlude	8	7	101	84

Administration: administrative overhead, finance, personnel and material management services	16	16	203	199
TOTAL	107	94	1,005	1,000

OBSERVATIONS

Role and Mandate

Over the last 25 years, the National Capital Commission has been invaluable in transforming Ottawa-Hull into a capital of which the nation can be justly proud. In the absence of a master plan at the local levels, it had filled a major void, using its powers of expropriation and property acquisition to achieve its master plan - the Gréber Plan. The NCC recognizes that it has implemented the major elements of the plan: it now focuses on minor improvements and on public cultural, recreational and tourist activities to make the capital more accessible to Canadians. Many of these activities overlap with those of the local and regional authorities.

In the 1970s, significant changes in local government took place. Two new regional governments - the Regional Municipality of Ottawa-Carleton and the Outaouais Regional Community - were established to coordinate the 27 municipalities within the boundaries served also by the National Capital Commission. Both regional governments exercise extensive authority over property with respect to planning and development and both have prepared official plans which reflect local aspirations. Although a coordination role still exists for the NCC, it has diminished substantially with the creation of responsible and representative regional authorities.

There is a great deal of overlap and duplication in the National Capital Region between the NCC and Public Works Canada (PWC). PWC has custody of all of the significant and symbolic buildings in the region (Parliament, Governor General's Residence, etc.). PWC has extensive property management, architectural, engineering, and real estate services in support of the federal government's requirements in Ottawa-Hull. The NCC's operations are considerably smaller than PWC's in the area.

It is the view of the study team that the NCC could be folded into PWC. Yet the NCC does provide a valuable coordinating role with the regional and local governments. The NCC is almost totally dependent upon appropriations, therefore there is little rationale for it to continue as a full arms-length Crown corporation (Schedule C-I). The study team recommends to the Task Force that the government consider rescheduling the NCC from a Schedule B of the Financial Administration Act to a Departmental Corporation.

There are also a number of operational initiatives which can now be undertaken to help streamline the real property management activities of the federal government in the National Capital Region.

Operational Improvements

While not challenging the role of the NCC in federal planning, we question the continued requirement for ownership of certain types of property. Recognizing that property acquisition may be necessary to achieve certain planning objectives, the prevailing attitude within the NCC overplays its significance.

The commission has, in the past, pursued an aggressive policy of land acquisition, which was curtailed only by a Cabinet-directed moratorium on further property acquisitions 5 years ago. The study team recommends to the Task Force that the government consider undertaking any new acquisition or land assembly in the context of a renewed and streamlined NCC mandate.

Ownership begets more ownership which results in ever increasing development and operating expenses. We question the continuing need for the NCC to own and operate roads, bridges and bicycle paths. Having achieved the transportation or recreational objective, the study team recommends that the government consider transferring these facilities to the local municipalities. The NCC holds a vast amount of properties in anticipation of the requirements of the next 100 years - three golf courses, greenbelt lands, etc. The study team suggests that the government review the short and long term objectives of land ownership and the future requirements and provide clear direction to the NCC. Other forms of leverage, which ensure that NCC objectives can be achieved, could be provided to the NCC by continuing the authority to issue grants in lieu of taxes to municipalities for all federal properties in the National Capital Region.

The Gatineau Park has a mixture of potential uses; as a wilderness retreat in an urban environment, as a recreational area and as a federal land bank for future requirements. It contains the residences of the Speaker of the House of Commons and the summer residences of the Prime Minister and the Governor General. As part of a review of federal land requirements, the study team suggests that the NCC retain custody of land required for future federal plans and transfer the responsibility to preserve the natural park environment to Parks Canada.

The NCC also has levers, other than property ownership, to achieve its planning objectives. It has had some success using contribution agreements and joint-funding projects. Unfortunately, in the view of the study team it has shown some disregard for the public purse by entering into open-ended agreements (for example, a 50 per cent cost-shared road construction agreement with the Province of Quebec with no ceiling or time frame).

There exists tremendous potential for the NCC to develop mixed land uses, encourage private sector development and make full use of private sector funding while promoting the broader objectives of a long term plan. The study team recommends that the NCC take advantage of its unique authorities and resources to strive towards increased revenue generation.

It is the study team's view that the NCC should focus its major role on the custody of symbolic facilities, for example the Parliament Buildings, the Governor General's and other official residences. The competition and overlap between the Department of Public Works and the NCC should be brought to an end. The study team suggests that these designated buildings should be transferred to the custody of the NCC.

Almost half of the NCC resources are directed to operations and maintenance, mainly with in-house staff. The study team recommends the transfer of these operational human resources to the Department of Public Works, which will be tasked with providing central real property services, on a fee basis, to all departments and agencies in the National Capital Region. The NCC would be directed to purchase its services from PWC.

By streamlining the operations, reducing marginal property holdings best owned and operated by local governments, reducing its large administrative apparatus, focusing on federal planning and increasing revenue generation, the study team judges that the NCC should be able to reduce its net dependence on appropriations by at least $25 million annually.

PLANNING, DESIGN AND CONSTRUCTION

National Capital Commission

OBJECTIVE

To plan and develop, from a national perspective, those elements of the physical and spatial character of the Capital of Canada which contribute to its aesthetics, symbolism and functional effectiveness.

RESULTS/BENEFICIARIES

The National Capital Commission provides planning studies, architectural and engineering services and project management for construction projects which benefit the citizens and tourists of the area.

AUTHORITY

National Capital Commission Act, 1958

RESOURCES (thousands of current dollars)

	84/85	85/86
Operating Expenditures	$34,189	$25,114
Person-Years	87	87

PROGRAM DESCRIPTION

The National Capital Commission (NCC) utilizes 87 person-years and spends approximately 25 per cent of its budget annually preparing studies and federal land use plans and undertaking minor construction in the Ottawa-Hull area. The plans include a master plan for the Parliamentary Precinct and a plan for the Inner Core of the region. NCC makes contributions (approximately $1.8 million) for Interprovincial Transit between Ottawa and Hull. NCC also provides architectural, landscape and engineering services for approximately 100 construction projects valued at approximately $10-15 million annually. It also enters into a number of cost-sharing projects with the provinces and municipalities (e.g. Québec roadways, bridges, etc.)

and spends approximately $15-20 million annually on these projects.

The program is delivered in Ottawa-Hull and the number of person-years allocated to each activity follow:

Planning	30
Design	41
Construction	16
TOTAL	87

OBSERVATIONS

The legislation in 1958 was adopted in order to resolve a number of property coordination problems - the elimination of the railway lines from downtown Ottawa and the implementation of a coordinated federal plan for the area. Since the establishment of the NCC, other coordinating bodies have been added to the government of the area - the introduction of the Regional Municipality of Ottawa-Carleton and the Communauté regionale of l'Outaouais. Despite the growth of regional governments, there continues to be a need for a senior coordinating agency in the National Capital Region that would prepare and implement a long-range master plan for the area utilizing the real property holdings of the federal government.

NCC maintains a small core staff of professionals to undertake planning, design and construction. The majority of the work is contracted out to the private sector. The NCC's use of professional achitectural and engineering services overlap with the capabilities of the National Capital Region office of Public Works Canada. As a result, NCC competes with the Department of Public Works for the employment of in-house staff resources and in the engagement of professional staff from the private sector.

While a number of federal departments plan, design and construct built works in the Nation's Capital, only the NCC has the legislative authority to grant final approval for building designs and land use in the area.

NCC also overlaps and competes with Public Works for the ownership of federal land in the region. Only the National Research Council (which owns and manages its laboratories), National Defence (which has two airbases) and

Transport Canada (which owns and operates the Ottawa airport) have been excluded from the coordination role assigned to Public Works Canada on behalf of the federal government.

NCC in the past, had undertaken an aggressive policy of land purchases which was only curtailed by a Cabinet-directed moratorium on further property acquisitions. Properties are guarded jealously and difficulties have been encountered in realizing broader government objectives when the two major federal property owners in Ottawa-Hull have been unable to reach agreement on the exchange, sale or disposal of property.

There are various alternatives for the delivery of this program. While retaining the responsibilities for federal land use planning with NCC, the government could consolidate title of all real property in the National Capital Region with one agency responsible for property ownership. On the other hand, there is some merit to maintaining the status quo concerning land acquisition ownership and architectural and engineering services, on the grounds NCC needs to be able to own property to influence regional planning and needs a small professional staff to oversee planning and design approvals.

Although there is a tendency in the NCC to rely heavily on property ownership to influence local and regional planning, there are other alternatives which could be used, such as the withholding of grants, especially those in lieu of municipal taxes.

OPTIONS

The study team recommends to the Task Force that the government consider amalgamating NCC's architectural and engineering services with those of Public Works Canada.

REAL ASSET MANAGEMENT

National Capital Commission

OBJECTIVE

To manage and develop the real property holdings of the National Capital Commission and to maintain and conserve federal land in the region.

RESULTS/BENEFICIARIES

The National Capital Commission provides a beautiful, well-maintained environment for the citizens and tourists of the area.

AUTHORITY

National Capital Commission Act, 1958

RESOURCES (thousands of current dollars)

	84/85	85/86
Operating Expenditures	$57,186	$53,314
Revenue	$ 3,245	$ 8,430
Person-Years	614	630

REAL PROPERTY ASSETS

Land Holding - 48,200 hectares
Number of Buildings - 1,300
Estimated Value of Assets - $352M

PROGRAM DESCRIPTION

The National Capital Commission (NCC) is a major land owner in the National Capital Region with holdings of some 48,200 hectares of property or about 10 per cent of the total land area. The portfolio consists of parkways, large wilderness and rural properties, many of the major parks within the urban core, revenue producing properties, as well as buildings of significant historical and architectural interest.

NCC used a total of 613 person-years and spent approximately $50 million in 1984-85 to undertake property administration, property development, pay grants-in-lieu of taxes and acquire property.

NCC undertakes the maintenance of 80 kilometres of roadways, 54 bridges, parking lots, 668 hectares of parks, 100 kilometres of recreational pathways, flower beds and the exterior grounds of all federal government buildings throughout the National Capital Region. This includes the maintenance services required for a number of public activities (such as skating on the Canal and facilities for Canada Day).

NCC undertakes a number of property restoration projects and joint property development ventures with the private sector. It pays its own grants-in-lieu of taxes, costing some $10 million annually and owns and leases over 1,300 properties, of which 200 are commercial, 113 are agricultural or rural and 700 are residential. Work also continues on tile-drainage of the NCC's farmlands. NCC also has an in-house capacity to undertake surveying and mapping.

The following highlights the distribution of human resources associated with this program:

	Person-Years	
	84/85	**85/86**
Operations and Maintenance	521	541
Property Development	3	3
Property Services	7	3
Realty Operations	64	62
Surveys and Mapping	18	16
TOTAL	613	625

All of the activities are managed in the National Capital Region by three Branches: the Property Branch handles property development, property services, realty operations and surveys and mapping. The Development Branch handles property maintenance and the Public Activities Branch handles the maintenance of the Gatineau Park and other public activities.

OBSERVATIONS

In the view of the study team there is a great deal of overlap and duplication in the National Capital Region (NCR) between the Department of Public Works and the National Capital Commission. Both are in competition as property owners and both are interested and/or involved in the maintenance and operation of a number of federally owned buildings. Specifically, NCC is interested in integrating the various symbolic institutions (Parliament buildings) etc. into its long range plans for improving the attractiveness of the capital. For example, while Public Works owns and is responsible for the building structures on Parliament Hill, NCC undertakes the grounds upkeep, provides visitor information and tours, has developed a "light and sound" show on the premises and is currently developing plans for a Parliamentary Precinct.

NCC undertakes real estate activities comparable to those performed by the Department of Public Works, such as leasing properties. For example, in downtown Ottawa one side of a street is owned by Public Works, the other is owned by the NCC and different regulations and leasing practices are employed by these two organizations in the competition for clients.

Public Works provides a common service and pays grants-in-lieu of taxes for most federal holdings in the capital. NCC has recently refused to take advantage of an offer by Public Works to provide these services for a nominal fee.

As a result of a long-standing, unwritten understanding, NCC provides an indirect subsidy to Public Works and all other federal organizations which own property in the NCR. It provides grounds maintenance around all federal buildings at no cost to the owners.

Both Public Works and NCC are empowered to acquire and dispose of land and both have engaged expert staff to undertake the responsibility.

Over 50 per cent of the total NCC staff are engaged in property maintenance. Only recently has the NCC commenced to take advantage of the services available in the private sector, as a result of restrictions imposed upon its continuing growth. NCC undertakes road and public walkway snow clearances using its own in-house personnel and equipment, along streets which it owns, whereas the streets which border and intersect them are maintained by the municipalities. NCC agrees that there are areas of maintenance which could be contracted to the municipalities.

NCC currently has a portfolio of properties which are normally owned and operated by local municipalities, such as roads, bridges and parks. Having established them and achieved their acceptance into local city plans, there remains little reason for the NCC to continue to own and operate them. These facilities should be transferred to the appropriate local authorities.

The actions of NCC are very similar to independent municipal governments, (constructing roads, bridges, bicycle paths, etc.) at times without the cooperation or consent of the elected municipal governments which are accountable to the people of Ottawa-Hull. Various NCC roadways do not contain entry or exit ramps and are not integrated with regional plans and requirements. This approach has resulted in the expenditure of $6 million between 1978-1984 to construct 5.5 kilometres of a roadway known as the "Eastern Parkway" which has never been opened.

Public Works operates a number of special facilities in the National Capital Region which are not part of their normal accommodation portfolio (war memorials, official residences, parliamentary buildings). The NCC should be charged with the custody of these symbolic facilities which could be considered an integral component of their plan to promote the symbols of the Nation's Capital.

To eliminate the current overlap and duplication and improve efficiencies related to real property management in the NCR, there are two options. The NCC could transfer to PWC the custody and maintenance of all its federally-owned properties, or responsibility for the management of all special property in the NCR could continue to be held by the NCC (with transfers of such special properties now held by PWC to NCC) with PWC providing all the necessary realty management services.

OPTIONS

The study team recommends to the Task Force that the government consider the following re-alignment of real property management in the National Capital Region:

- the custody and control of the symbolic, designated buildings (such as Parliament, Official Residences) be transferred from PWC to the National Capital Commission. These flagships should be the cornerstone of the NCC property holdings;

- NCC to transfer ownership of all property that is not central to the NCC mission such as roads, bridges, bicycle paths, to the relevant local municipalities; and

- all real property services required by the NCC be purchased from PWC.

SECTION 10 - MARINE PROGRAMS

INTRODUCTION

The federal government has a proliferation of harbour and port infrastructure. It has resulted from over a century of incremental growth based on often loosely defined notions of "socio-economic" benefits; and upon an imperative by successive governments to disperse and perpetuate federal presence. This infrastructure is largely inefficient, costly to administer, of arguable economic benefit, and is politically difficult to dismantle. Breaking this pattern will require rationalization based upon principles of:

- withdrawing from operations more properly or better handled by other levels of government;
- disposal of assets to the private sector where there are short or long term gains to be made; and
- the management of remaining infrastructure within the following regime:
  - maximum local/regional autonomy,
  - full financial self-sufficiency, and
  - levels of service driven by the market.

BACKGROUND

Marine programs of the federal government involve a massive investment in real property infrastructure. This investment comprises over 2,500 ports and harbours (exclusive of naval installations), the St. Lawrence Seaway, bridges, canals, and other diverse and dispersed assets. These are delivered by several organizations.

In summary, real property administered by these marine programs has been conservatively estimated as having a current replacement value of some $ 8 to 10 billion. Total annual expenditures of $540 million are reduced by $340 million of revenues for an annual cost to the government of $200 million. Approximately 3,500 person-years are employed in real property related activities.

The Department of Transport has responsibility for some 325 wharves, ports and harbours, administered at an annual cost of $380 million. Annual revenues are in the order of $260 million. Approximately 2,000 person-years are employed in the administration and operation of the ports.

The Canadian Coast Guard expends approximately $36 million annually and employs some 215 person-years in the administration and operation of real property related to its operations.

The St. Lawrence Seaway Authority expends approximately $83 million annually on the St. Lawrence Seaway and its bridges, recovering approximately $78 million. It employs some 1,200 person-years.

The Department of Fisheries and Oceans administers over 1,400 fishing harbours and over 800 recreational harbours at an annual cost of $45 million, recovering only $2.5 million in revenues. Some 114 person-years are employed in this activity.

A more detailed tabulation of the above is appended as Table 1 of this overview.

Real property of these programs is administered and controlled on behalf of the Crown primarily by two ministers: the Minister of Transport and the Minister of Fisheries.

The Minister of Transport is responsible for the provision and administration of the majority of this infrastructure as follows:

- The Canada Ports Corporation (CPC) administers directly or through wholly owned subsidiary local ports corporations (LPC), 15 ports on the east and west coasts and on the Great Lakes. The CPC ports handle approximately 60 per cent of total marine traffic.

- The nine harbours in Ontario and British Columbia are administered by independent, largely autonomous Harbour Commissions (HC) reporting directly to the Minister under the terms of three separate acts of parliament. The HC harbours handle approximately 20 per cent of total marine traffic.

- The Department of Transport directly administers a further 301 public harbours through its Harbours and Ports Directorate (HPD) in all regions of the country. These HPD harbours handle approximately 20 per cent of total marine traffic.

- The Canadian Coast Guard (CCG) has a substantial investment in CCG bases, property related to navigational aids and marine traffic management, and the Canso Canal in Nova Scotia.

- The St. Lawrence Seaway Authority operates the Canadian portion of the St. Lawrence Seaway, two international bridges and, through a wholly owned subsidiary, it operates the Jacques Cartier and Champlain Bridges and part of the Bonaventure Autoroute in Montreal.

The Minister of Fisheries, through the Small Craft Harbours Directorate of the Department of Fisheries and Oceans (DFO) operates some 2,232 fishing and recreational harbours across the country.

OBSERVATIONS

The federal government provides, operates and maintains infrastructure which should be the responsibility of other governments:

- The Jacques Cartier and Champlain Bridges cost the Government of Canada over $5 million annually and should be controlled, operated and paid for by the Governments of Quebec and/or Montreal.

- The Government of Canada operates ferry wharves and terminals which form part of provincial highway systems.

- The Canadian Coast Guard operates the Canso Canal, whose existence is necessitated only by the Canso Causeway, a provincial highway.

Cost recovery practices are not generally in accordance with levels of service provided. Moreover, charging policy varies from department to department, region to region, and in accordance with explicit or implicit subsidization of special groups of users:

- little or no attempt is made in any of the programs to recover capital costs of infrastructure with the exception of the nine Harbour Commission harbours and 15 Canada Ports Corporation ports;

- charges in DOT Public Harbours and in DFO Small Craft Harbours are predicated on the recovery of only a small percentage of annual operating costs;

- recreational harbours of DFO generally charge tariffs significantly lower than those levied by corresponding private marina operators;

- fishing harbours of DFO have fee exemptions for Atlantic, Prairies and Northwest Territories fishermen based on criteria related to the need to subsidize an industry;

- no charges are made for the operation of the Canso Canal to either the provincial department of highways or to the canal users in spite of the tolls levied on the causeway users (highway and rail) by the province; and

- tolls on the Champlain Bridge (unchanged since 1962), are only about 50 per cent of those needed to cover annual operating costs of the two bridges and the autoroute in Montreal.

In the view of the study team the federal government is in businesses it should not be in:

- DFO provides 10 per cent of Canada's recreational berths at subsidized rates, which discourages private sector investment in adjacent areas.

- Notwithstanding a long history of public ownership both in Canada and other industrial nations, there is a strong case to be made for increasing private sector participation in DOT ports and harbours.

There are several hundred ports and harbours surplus to either commercial traffic needs or for support to isolated communities:

- of the 325 DOT ports and harbours, fewer than 50 account for more than 80 per cent of all commercial traffic; and

- of the 1,400 DFO fishing harbours more than 450 "Class D" harbours are inactive and recognized as surplus.

There is an overwhelming urge to centralize and systematize. This urge should be resisted. Of the organizations we have observed, those which have the following attributes are the most successful:

- clear objectives focused on efficient use of capital;

- an arms length relationship with the political and bureaucratic processes of Ottawa represented by local management responsive to local and regional needs, accountable to local "boards";

- management decisions which are driven by the regional or local market forces rather than those imposed by a central hierarchy in response to some notion of "national needs"; and

- access to and a history of use of private sources of capital, under business-like conditions, and as a corollary, no entrenched history of access to the public treasury.

In short, and in the view of the study team, regional businesses should be run as such. In our view, the organizations which best fulfill the above conditions are the nine independent Harbour Commissions. To the extent that the federal government remains in the harbours business, this form of management is recommended.

Ironically, in spite of efforts to centralize the management of ports and harbours, the federal government has perpetuated the existence of three separate organizations managing commercial harbours (i.e. Harbours Commissions, Canada Ports Corporation, Public Harbour of DOT). The end result has often been wasteful internal competition and the dispersal of limited investment funds to too many facilities.

In summary, the study team recommends to the Task Force that the government consider the following options:

- sell or cede to the provinces those assets which should normally form part of the provincially mandated programs (e.g. intra-provincial highways and bridges);

- maintain a small number of DOT and DFO harbours which are required to support otherwise isolated communities. The federal government should immediately develop restrictive criteria to approve such facilities, clearly identify the qualifying harbours, and fund them and account for them as a social subsidy;

- all DOT, CPC and HC ports and harbours remaining be sold at the best prices achievable through the most appropriate mechanism (e.g. outright sale, share participation in CPC or a subsidiary etc.);

- all DOT, CPC, and HC ports and harbours which cannot be sold initially be subject to a regime of full financial self-sufficiency, classified as Harbour Commissions. Those which cannot be self-sufficient should be closed or otherwise divested;

- all DFO recreational harbours be sold as soon as possible at the highest price achievable;

- all "Class D" fishing harbours of DFO be officially declared surplus, turned over to the requisite disposal agency and disposed of in the prescribed manner;

- from a purely real property management perspective, all remaining DFO fishing harbours be subject to a regime of full financial self-sufficiency. Those which cannot be sustained by user fees should be closed or otherwise divested; and

- toll structures on other marine program infrastructure, not sold or divested to the provinces (e.g. the St. Lawrence Seaway, international bridges) be maintained to ensure full financial self-sufficiency.

TABLE 1

OVERVIEW - MARINE PROGRAMS - REAL PROPERTY

Fiscal Year 1984/85 Resource Summary

	Capital ($000)	Operating ($000)	Total ($000)	Revenue ($000)	PYs	Number of Facilities
DOT Harbours and Ports						
Canada Ports Corporation	95,600	169,400	265,000	213,700	1520	15
Harbour Commissions	13,000	28,100	41,100	40,600	350	9
Public Harbours	40,500	33,800	74,300	7,200	93	301
Total Harbours/Ports	149,100	231,300	380,400	261,500	1963	325
DOT Canadian Coast Guard	22,000	13,700	35,700	—	215	
St. Lawrence Seaway Authority (SLSA)						
St. Lawrence Seaway	5,200	64,300	69,500	69,900	1081	
Associated Bridges	---	13,300	13,300	8,400	113	
Total SLSA	5,200	77,600	82,800	78,300	1194	
DFO Small Craft Harbours	25,100	19,300	44,400	2,600	114	2232
TOTAL MARINE PROGRAMS	201,400	341,900	543,300	342,400	3486	

Notes - Depreciation for fixed assets of Crown corporations included above and items not requiring cash outlay are not included above to allow consistent treatment under Government of Canada accounting practices. All figures have been rounded to the nearest $100 thousand. Amounts reported above do not include Special Recovery Capital Projects Program (SRCPP) expenditures, nor the expenditures by the CCG on dredging of channels and waterways.

CANADA PORTS CORPORATION

Transport Canada

OBJECTIVE

The provision of an efficient national ports system to facilitate Canada's trade objectives.

RESULTS/BENEFICIARIES

Designation of a crown corporation comprising fifteen financially self-sufficient commercial ports located on the east and west coasts and along the St. Lawrence river.

International freight shippers handling export/import flows for the Canadian market and the communities in which the ports are located are the principal beneficiaries.

AUTHORITY

Canada Ports Corporation Act - 1983

RESOURCES (thousands of current dollars)

	84	85
Operating Expense (excluding deprec. of $21,000 and $24,700)	$169,300	$178,100
Capital Expenditures	$95,600	$118,300
Revenues (excluding interest income)	$213,700	$226,600

REAL PROPERTY ASSETS

	84
Estimated Replacement Value	$1.0 billion
Number of - locations	15
- properties	155

PROGRAM DESCRIPTION

Canada Ports Corporation (CPC) is a Schedule C Crown Corporation responsible for the operation of 15 ports. Five of the ports are local port corporations under CPC and the other 10 ports are classed as divisions.

CPC is responsible to Parliament through the Minister of Transport. Each of the corporations has a board of directors whose members are nominated by the Minister and appointed by Order-in-Council. Likewise, the Chairman, Vice-Chairman and President/Chief Executive Officer are appointed by Order-in-Council following recommendation of the Minister in consultation with the Boards of Directors. The General Managers of the local port corporations are appointed by their respective Boards of Directors.

Membership of the CPC board is between 11-17 while the subsidiary boards are 5-7.

The ports provide a full range of maritime services for cargo and passengers. All operations are on a fully commercial basis. The principal activities are handling of grain and container traffic. Montreal has the second largest container traffic volume on the east coast (New York is first). A small amount of US bound containers is routed through Montreal. CPC has little or no influence on overall market conditions or economics.

CPC operates on a calendar year and maintains its financial records in accordance with generally accepted accounting principals. As a consequence, references and tabulations of financial data in this memorandum are not always compatible with the terms and definitions used in the regular accounts of the federal government.

		84 (Millions)			
Corporate Ports	**Employees**	**Revenue**		**Income(1)**	
Vancouver	227	$99.4		16.8	
Montreal	681	66.9		20.6	
Halifax	148	15.1		3.3	
Quebec City	99	15.6		5.7	
Prince Rupert	12	10.8		1.2	
TOTAL - Corporate		207.0	85%	47.6	92%

Division Ports					
Saint John	116	13.5		0.2	
Churchill	28	5.4		(1.1)	
Prescott	24	4.3		2.0	
St. John's	18	2.9		0.9	
Trois Rivieres	9	3.3		1.4	
Colborne	25	2.1		0.2	
Sept Iles	9	1.4		(0.3)	
Chicoutimi	6	1.8		0.9	
Belledune	-	0.3		-	
Bais des Ha!Ha!	-	0.2		0.1	
Total - Divisions		35.2	15%	4.3	8%
Corporate Headquarters	118	-		-	
TOTAL	1,520	242.2	100%	51.9	100%

(1) **Note** - Additional details are provided in Appendix A and B.

CPC ports are intended to be financially self-supporting. Fees and rates are established on a fully commercial basis and cover all operating expenses, depreciation and interest. Cash flow must be sufficient to repay principal of any debt.

Real property assets are the major component of the CPC program with a book value of about $654 million (FY 1984). The assets include:

Ship berths
Wharves
Terminals
Roads and rail lines
Grain elevators
Utilities
Buildings - warehouse, service, administration.

Since much of the CPC port facilities are leased out on a net basis, the lessee is responsible for the costs of operating the assets. Major maintenance of property operated by CPC is contracted out.

The overall direction of the 15 ports is provided by the Ottawa headquarters. Staff at HQ was 118 in December 1984 (this was recently reduced to 97).

Planned real property capital spending for FY'85 is $118 million (all provided from internally generated funds). This includes expenditures at Montreal for railway upgrading and additions to the container operation.

There are varying degrees of competition between CPC ports, and Harbour Commission and other federal ports. The financial arrangements vary between CPC/Commission and other ports (self-suficiency vs. deficits funded through appropriation). It would appear that the 'Other' ports may be using their access to the federal government's cheque book as a means of undercutting rates and attracting traffic from CPC and Harbour Commission ports.

The investment banking firm of Levesque Beaubien Inc. (LB Inc.) studied the possiblities of privatizing CPC as a whole with a more detailed examination of the Port of Quebec. In their report to the Treasury Board they concluded that neither CPC nor Quebec City Port could be currently sold in the public investment market except at a very attractive (to the buyer) price i.e. substantial discount from book value.

LB Inc. considered the availability of surplus properties at the various CPC ports. It was their opinion that there were no major unused or underused properties from which CPC might raise significant amounts of cash through sale of the properties. This conclusion was contrary to the popular opinions regarding 'large amounts of surplus property' amongst CPC ports. Vancouver may be an exception as they do hold vacant land for which they have no immediate requirements.

CPC and its local ports corporations hold about $280 million in short and long term investments. The securities are mainly treasury bills and long-term bonds issued by the federal government.

Some operating savings are possible through further major reductions of headquarters staff. Sale of the ports or a public equity issue might raise $100 million or more.

OBSERVATIONS

There are no statutory requirements for the federal government to own ports. This gives the government the opportunity to divest all or any of the 15 ports of CPC. By aggressively pursuing sale of some or all of the ports to private investors, the federal government could theoretically realize a substantial one-time amount of cash.

The LB Inc. evaluation cites CPC's lack of a track record as a distinct disadvantage in any attempt to fully or partially privatize CPC through a public share offering. A 'track record' will only help if the financial results in the proving period are satisfactory. There is no assurance under current market conditions that CPC will show improved results in the future. If the results were unsatisfactory, the future price could easily be lower than what might be obtained now.

In the view of the study team the federal government could take over (probably as dividends) the $280 million of current short and long term investments of CPC. Such an action would have no net effect on the funds available since the bills and bonds are a liability of the federal government. However, the investments are intended to finance future real property and other business requirements. One way or another, the federal government will provide the cash through redemption of the bills and bonds or respond to CPC with capital appropriations. It is mainly a matter of timing for the alternatives.

Irrational competition between the various categories of ports makes little sense. Instead, consideration might be given to closing the least efficient of competing CPC, Harbour Commission or major public harbour ports in order to enhance the results of the surviving ports and avoid future government operating and capital appropriations to the discontinued ports. This action would likely also enhance the market value of the surviving ports.

OPTIONS

The study team recommends to the Task Force that the government consider:

- closing the least efficient of competing CPC ports

and undertake to sell the remaining individual ports; and

- any CPC ports which cannot be sold should be reclassified as Harbour Commission ports and administered in the same manner as the present Harbour Commissions.

Note - A majority of CPC ports are already partially 'privatized' through leasing out of port activities to private sector operators. Sale of the Crown properties would be a natural extension of the existing condition.

APPENDIX A

CANADA PORTS CORPORATION
Year Ended Dec 31, 1984
(Millions)

LOCAL PORT CORPORATIONS AND CONSOLIDATED	Vancouver	Montreal	Halifax	Quebec	Prince Rupert	TOTAL CORPORATE	TOTAL (1) DIVISIONS	TOTAL CPC
FINANCIAL CONDITION								
Assets								
Cash & investments	38.9	106.7	11.9	37.1	5.9	200.5	78.1	278.6
Other	14.6	10.8	2.9	5.5	0.8	34.6	8.3	42.9
Fixed	167.5	119.6	43.4	41.0	72.9	444.4	136.9	581.3
TOTAL ASSETS	221.0	237.1	58.2	83.6	79.6	679.5	223.3	902.8
Liabilities								
Other	14.0	20.0	5.5	3.9	1.9	45.3	15.3	60.6
Long-Term loans - Govt. Can.	108.4	239.2	30.5	-	87.6	465.7	122.6	588.3
TOTAL LIABILITIES	122.4	259.2	36.0	3.9	89.5	511.0	137.9	648.9
NET EQUITY (DEFICIT)	98.6	(22.1)	22.2	79.7	(9.9)	168.5	85.4	253.9
OPERATING RESULTS								
Operating revenue	94.8	56.7	14.0	11.6	9.4	186.5	27.2	213.7
Interest income	4.6	10.2	1.1	4.0	0.6	20.5	8.0	28.5
TOTAL REVENUE	99.4	66.9	15.1	15.6	10.0	207.0	35.2	242.2
Operating & Maintenance	77.7	39.5	10.4	8.3	8.0	143.9	20.8	164.7
Depreciation	4.5	6.3	1.4	1.6	0.8	14.6	6.4	21.0
Interest expense	0.4	0.5	-	-	-	0.9	3.7	4.6
TOTAL EXPENSE	82.6	46.3	11.8	9.9	8.8	159.4	30.9	190.3
NET INCOME	16.8	20.6	3.3	5.7	1.2	47.6	4.3	51.9

(1) See Appendix B

APPENDIX B

CANADA PORTS CORPORATION
Year Ended Dec 31, 1984
(Millions)

PORT DIVISIONS

	Saint John	Churchill	Prescott	St. John's	Trois Rivieres	Colborne	Sept Iles	Chicoutimi	Belldune	Baie des Ha!Ha!	**TOTAL DIVISIONS**
FINANCIAL CONDITION											
Assets											
Cash & investments	11.0	8.6	18.6	6.2	10.9	7.0	5.1	9.3	0.9	0.5	78.1
Other	2.2	0.6	0.8	0.3	0.4	0.3	0.9	2.6	0.2	-	8.3
Fixed	88.0	10.9	4.6	8.2	12.3	2.8	4.4	4.4	1.3	-	136.9
TOTAL ASSETS	101.2	20.1	24.0	14.7	23.6	10.1	10.4	16.3	2.4	0.5	223.3
Liabilities											
Other	5.2	0.6	0.4	0.8	0.5	0.3	3.0	4.4	0.1	-	15.3
Long-term loans - Goverment	95.7	17.1	-	1.9	-	-	3.8	0.9	3.2	-	122.6
TOTAL LIABILITIES	100.9	17.7	0.4	2.7	0.5	0.3	6.8	5.3	3.3	-	137.9
NET EQUITY (DEFICIT)	0.3	2.4	23.6	12.0	23.1	9.8	3.6	11.0	(0.9)	0.5	85.4
OPERATING RESULTS											
Operating revenue	12.3	4.5	2.3	2.3	2.2	1.4	1.0	0.9	0.2	0.1	27.2
Interest Income	1.2	0.9	2.0	0.6	1.1	0.7	0.4	0.9	0.1	0.1	8.0
TOTAL REVENUE	13.5	5.4	4.3	2.9	3.3	2.1	1.4	1.8	0.3	0.2	35.2
Operating and Maintenance	7.3	5.4	1.9	1.4	1.5	1.5	0.9	0.7	0.1	0.1	20.8
Depreciation	2.7	1.1	0.4	0.4	0.4	0.4	0.8	0.1	0.1	-	6.4
Interest expense	3.3	-	-	0.2	-	-	-	0.1	0.1	-	3.7
TOTAL EXPENSE	13.3	6.5	2.3	2.0	1.9	1.9	1.7	0.9	0.3	0.1	30.9
NET INCOME (LOSS)	0.2	(1.1)	2.0	0.9	1.4	0.2	(0.3)	0.9	-	0.1	4.3

HARBOUR COMMISSIONS

Transport Canada

OBJECTIVE

To provide Harbour Commissions (HC) with a high degree of autonomy for the management and operation of the ports for which they are established, consistent with the responsibility of the Minister to ensure the integrity and efficiency of the national ports system and the optimum deployment of resources.

RESULTS/BENEFICIARIES

The designation of nine ports as Harbour Commissions, five in Ontario and four in British Columbia.

Shippers, a wide variety of industries, fishermen, recreational boaters and surrounding communities are the beneficiaries of Harbour Commissions and their respective ports. The Canadian taxpayer also benefits from the financial independence (from the federal government) of these ports.

AUTHORITY

Harbour Commissions Act, 1964
Toronto Harbour Commissions Act, 1911
Hamilton Harbour Commissions Act, 1912
Other: British Columbia Six Harbours Agreement and the Ontario Harbours Agreement.

RESOURCES **December 31, 1983(1)**
($millions)

REAL PROPERTY

	Net Book Value	Capital Expend.	Revenue	Net Income(2)
Toronto (1911)	$75.8	$0.7	$11.6	$(2.4)
Hamilton (1912)	22.2	8.3	4.2	(0.5)
Thunder Bay (1958)	16.6	0.3	2.2	0.5
Oshawa (1964)	3.2	0.1	0.5	0.1
Windsor (1957)	2.3	0.2	0.4	0.1
	120.1	9.6	18.9	(2.2)
Fraser (1913)	22.9	1.8	6.1	3.9
Nanaimo (1960)	10.8	1.2	5.1	1.0
Port Alberni (1947)	5.3	0.3	2.7	0.6
North Fraser (1913)	3.0	0.1	2.8	0.5
	42.0	3.4	16.7	6.0
TOTAL	162.1	13.0	35.6	3.8

(1) Toronto amounts are for fiscal year ended Mar 31, 1984.
(2) Net income - after depreciation and without income tax.

Employees - 358

Note - Additional details are provided in Appendix A.

REAL PROPERTY ASSETS

Replacement value of real property (excluding land) is estimated in the range of $300-400 million.

PROGRAM DESCRIPTION

The Harbour Commissions have a long history with four established in the early 1900s and the last in 1964. The enabling acts refer to a "port system". The Commission ports are in reality independent bodies rather than a system.

In conjunction with the establishment in 1983 of the new Canada Ports Corporation and reaffirmation of the national ports system, the then Minister of Transport declared that "Each of these ports (Harbour Commission) ... operates with a high degree of autonomy and has minimal administrative structure at the federal level."

A majority of members on each board are appointed by the federal government. The remainder are appointed by the local community. Toronto is the exception where the municipality appoints the majority. Six of the Commissions each have five members and the other three commissions each have three members.

Several of the ports dedicate a major part of their real property to a single user (Port Alberni - MacMillan Bloedel Ltd.) or industry (Thunder Bay - grain).

In keeping with the mandate of self-sufficiency and an objective of a high degree of management and operating autonomy, the nine ports maintain their financial records in accordance with generally accepted accounting policies. This is not necessarily consistent with the standards followed by other departments within the federal government.

Each Harbour Commission's financial results and budgets are presented annually to the Minister (Transport) but they do not form part of the federal accounts. The Commissions may obtain financing through public (Treasury Board) or private sources. All funds in excess of the operational and capital requirements (as determined by the Commission and approved by the Minister) of each Commission are to be transferred annually to the federal treasury. Toronto and Hamilton surpluses are transferably only to the respective municipalities.

All Harbour Commissions are generally adhering to market forces in determining the revenues generated from the real property which they control.

There is a high level of contracting out through lease of real property to private operators and the use of outside services for O&M expenditures.

The ports have a history of financial self-sufficiency, including capital expenditures. The 1983 returns on equity ranged from 2 per cent to 13 per cent. Toronto is currently in a loss position but anticipates an early return to profitability.

The Harbour Commission federal administrative structure is minimal (2 PYs). The "lean" management structure is also generally evident in the organization of individual Commissions which typically operate with a small number of employees.

Most of the Commissions insure their real property against liability and physical damage. This may be contrary to the general policies of the federal government to self-insure (1983 insurance premium expense was approximately $275,000).

OBSERVATIONS

A review of the statutes suggests that there is no legal obligation for the federal government to own and operate ports.

The Commission ports are meeting their objectives of financial independence. The very high degree of local management autonomy and almost total absence of departmental supervision and administration and overhead expense appear to be the key conditions for this success.

The nine ports are each largely self financing and are likely to meet future capital requirements through internally generated funds and accessing private financing.

There is only a fine line to distinguish between "public" and "private" in the management of the Harbour Commissions' operations. "Privatization" of management would be a relatively simple matter. However, the ports' return on equity is generally below the return of a comparable investment in the private sector.

There are varying degrees of competition between Canada Ports Corporation (CPC), Harbour Commissions and other federal ports. Canada Ports Corporation/Harbour Commissions are required to be financially self-supporting. Other federal ports do not have this requirement and their deficits are covered through appropriations. This condition can lead to price-cutting to gain traffic without regard to the bottom line of the other ports. Such action is irrational since it tends to benefit only the shipper and not the competing ports.

Most of the Commission ports appear to be financially viable and could be divested to the private sector. The potential value will reflect the return which can be expected. This suggests that the selling prices will generally be less than book value. Nevertheless, the federal government in conjunction with the other levels of government having a vested interest in the individual ports could probably realize a substantial amount of cash through sale of the ports -- perhaps $100 million or more.

There are compelling argument to maintain the status quo if sale of the Commission ports is not deemed appropriate. The apparent success of the Commission ports suggests extension of the concept to other federal ports and similar commercial or near commercial operations/programs.

OPTIONS

Based on these considerations, the study team recommends to the Task Force that the government consider:

- closing the least efficient of competing ports and selling the federal interest in as many as possible of the Harbour Commission ports; and

- any which cannot be sold should continue to operate under the status quo.

APPENDIX A

HARBOUR COMMISSIONS
Year Ended Dec. 31, 1983 (1)
(Millions)

FINANCIAL CONDITION	Fraser	Hamilton	Nanaimo	North Fraser	Oshawa	Port Alberni	Thunder Bay	Toronto	Windsor	Total
Assets										
Cash & S&T investments	8.0	9.2	4.9	1.4	0.4	2.3	2.9	-	0.2	29.3
Other	1.4	1.3	0..9	0.2	0.1	0.1	0.4	1.9	0.2	6.5
Fixed	23.0	23.8	12.6	3.4	3.4	5.5	16.9	77.9	2.3	168.8
TOTAL ASSETS	32.4	34.3	18.4	5.0	3.9	7.9	20.2	79.8	2.7	204.6
Liabilities										
Short term loans	-	-	-	-	-	-	-	32.8	0.3	33.1
Other	0.8	0.6	0.5	0.4	0.1	0.2	0.2	1.3	-	4.1
Long-term loans - government	-	1.2	-	-	-	1.0	0.3	-	-	2.5
TOTAL LIABILITIES	0.8	1.8	0.5	0.4	0.1	1.2	0.5	34.1	0.3	39.7
NET EQUITY	31.6	32.5	17.9	4.6	3.8	6.7	19.7	45.7	2.4	164.9
OPERATING RESULTS										
Operating Revenue	5.9	3.4	4.6	2.6	0.5	2.5	1.9	11.6	0.4	33.4
Interest Income	0.2	0.8	0.5	0.2	-	0.2	0.3	-	-	2.2
TOTAL REVENUE	6.1	4.2	5.1	2.8	0.5	2.7	2.2	11.6	0.4	35.6
Operating and Maintenance	1.2	3.6	3.3	2.2	0.3	1.7	1.4	10.0	0.3	24.0
Depreciation	1.0	1.0	0.8	0.1	0.1	0.3	0.3	0.6	-	4.2
Interest expense	-	0.1	-	-	-	0.1	-	3.4	-	3.6
TOTAL EXPENSE	2.2	4.7	4.1	2.3	0.4	2.1	1.7	14.0	0.3	31.8
NET INCOME	3.9	(0.5)(2)	1.0	0.5	0.1	0.6	0.5	(2.4)(2)	0.1	3.8

(1) Toronto - Fiscal year ended March 31, 1985.
(2) Excludes extraordinary gains on sale of land - Hamilton $5.0M; Toronto $1.4M.

PUBLIC HARBOURS

Transport Canada

OBJECTIVE

To develop, administer, and maintain designated harbours and port facilities, in order to meet commercial shipping needs and to support a safe and efficient national marine transportation system.

RESULTS/BENEFICIARIES

The Crown owns real property in 301 public harbours consisting of wharves, harbours and ferry terminals serving commercial shipping in all regions of Canada.

Principal beneficiaries include:

- ship operators, national and international; and
- communities adjacent to harbour facilities and the industries using these harbours to transship their products.

AUTHORITY

Public Harbours and Port Facilities Act; Public Land Grants Act; Public Works Act (Section 35); Canada Shipping Act; British Columbia Six Harbours Agreement; Ontario Harbours Agreement.

RESOURCES (thousands of current dollars)

	84/85	85/86
Operating Expenses	33,800	40,400
Capital	40,000	31,000
Revenues	7,200	9,000
Person-Years	93	93
Fees-of-Office Appointees	350	350

REAL PROPERTY ASSETS

Three hundred and one public harbours comprising land, wharves, sheds, storage areas and associated marine civil works, improved channels and water lots. The ports are not generally highly mechanized. Total current replacement value is estimated at approximately $1 billion.

PROGRAM DESCRIPTION

At the time of Confederation, the federal government gained title to several public harbours then existing. These were increased under the terms of union when subsequent provinces joined Confederation. Additionally, the Public Harbours and Port Facilities Act empowers the Governor-in-Council to proclaim as a "Public Harbour" ... "any area covered by water within the jurisdiction of Parliament".

The proclamation of a "Public Harbour" gives the Minister of Transport certain rights and obligations within the proclaimed boundaries relating mainly to the control of the water surface including the right to levy harbour dues. With the exception of Ontario and British Columbia, ownership of harbour beds is in many cases still subject to federal/provincial negotiation. Federal ownership of harbour beds, adjacent land and infrastructure is not a prerequisite for proclamation. (There are 30 public harbours in which the Crown does not own property). However, the Department of Justice has advised DOT that improvements and works should only be constructed where title has been secured by the federal government.

The program objective has been expanded into several sub-objectives relating to accessibility, cost recovery and productivity. However, one sub-objective has been added: "to support achievement of objectives that relate to national, regional, and urban social and economic development and to industrial, environmental, energy, and other policies." which allows the development and perpetuation of facilities which cannot be justified or supported under strict adherence to the mandate of efficiency, and full cost recovery pertaining to transportation needs.

Public harbours in which the Crown owns property are located as shown in Table 1 with regional expenditures and employment data.

TABLE 1

(Source HPD estimates provided by DOT [Marine])

Region	HPD(1) Ports (No.)	Person-Years (No.)	O&M (incl. sal.) ($000)	Revenues ($000)	Capital Expend. ($000)
HQ (NCR)	---	35	2,668	---	1,500
Newfoundland	60	9	3,068	643	5,850
Maritimes	43	18	5,478	1,801	17,980
Laurentian	63	13	10,978	1,723	3,558
Central	32	9	6,931	1,589	8,126
Western	103	9	4,694	1,447	3,572
TOTAL	301	93(2)	33,817	7,203	40,586

Notes (1) Harbours and Ports Directorate (HPD) Public Harbours in which the Crown owns property.

(2) In addition to the 93 person-years, there are approximately 350 "fee of office" ministerial appointees serving as local harbourmasters or wharfingers, paid on a commission basis out of port revenues. Average remuneration is small (approximately $2,000 annually) and is included in the above consolidation of revenues and expenses.

The smallest of these ports have limited traffic and exist only to provide access to isolated communities. The larger ports are somewhat more active and account for some 20 per cent of the national maritime tonnage. Thirty to forty HPD ports account for the majority of this traffic.

Property consists generally of wharves, sheds, storage areas, and associated marine civil works and improved channels and water lots. The ports are not highly mechanized and generally do not accommodate larger deep draft vessels.

Current estimated replacement value of HPD ports by region is as follows:

Newfoundland - $214 million
Maritimes - $191 million
Laurentian - $493 million
Central - $145 million
Western - $129 million

The total estimated replacement value is currently $1,172 million.

Capital expenditures over the next three fiscal years are planned at approximately $110 million broken out as follows. (Not as yet approved by Treasury Board):

Newfoundland - $25 million
Maritimes - $35 million
Laurentian - $33 million
Central - $17 million
Western - $0.1 million

The HPD operates from an Ottawa Headquarters through five regions. In each region, a Regional Director General has a small management and technical staff and in some cases of larger ports a local public servant port manager. The Directors General report to a Deputy Marine Administrator in Ottawa. Functional direction is provided by the Ottawa based Director General Harbours and Ports Directorate. The Regional Directors General are also tasked with regional direction of the Coast Guard, for which they report to the Commissioner of the Canadian Coast Guard.

The HPD has undertaken and maintains regional port master plans to guide investment decisions. While some updating of these plans is required, they represent a reasonable foundation for the management of HPD facilities. However, many investments have been dictated by successive governments in response to needs apart from strictly marine transport requirements.

There are no set standards for the design or provision of port infrastructure related to levels of service criteria. Design and construction is carried out by Public Works under the terms of General Service Agreement and the private sector, with HPD in-house personnel involved only in the definition of requirements and actions consistent with good program control.

Direct services such as cargo handling are not provided. Operations and maintenance activities are carried out primarily by Public Works and usually on their behalf by private contractors.

The current fee structure recovers only about 20 per cent of O&M costs. The HPD has proposed revisions of the fee structure to recover an increased portion of O&M costs; the increases to be phased in over 5 years. Eighty-five per cent of current revenues is generated by the 34 top revenue generating ports (about 12 per cent of all HPD ports).

Local management of HPD ports is entrusted largely to ministerial appointed fees-of-office wharfingers and harbourmasters. While this appears to be economical, it is being examined against the requirements to strengthen local management capabilities, especially in the more active ports, and in the context of guaranteeing levels of service consistent with higher cost recovery and as dictated by the marketplace.

OBSERVATIONS

In the view of the study team the HPD does a creditable job within a framework of objectives which cannot all be met simultaneously.

The HPD port infrastructure represents a large investment in real property. The investment and maintenance decisions can all be justified on the basis of at least one of the operational objectives. There is some evidence that until recently, at least, decisions have been based largely on support of socio-economic policy - but without the opportunity to undertake the requisite economic benefit/cost analysis; and have often been in conflict with the objectives of operating an efficient transportation network.

The result has been a very visible network of federal facilities clearly identified with and strongly protected by local interests, but subject to a national management structure which may not be appropriate.

Each HPD port represents generally a relatively small investment in federal presence and requires generally only small annual appropriations for its operation.

It is the view of the study team, however, that the system as a whole is not an efficient response to marine and broader transportation management:

- in many cases the original need for an HPD port provided in the absence of access to other modes of transportation, has been overtaken by the provision of road and/or rail infrastructure;

- industries have come and gone in areas for which an HPD port was provided for a specific purpose;

- patterns for shipping have changed - larger ships calling at major ports now bypass the HPD ports for access to ports having the capability of faster handling of cargoes. HPD ports now depend on the smaller, less efficient vessels which can withstand longer cargo transhipment times;

- upgrading and investment in modern capital intensive transhipment facilities and capacity to handle larger deeper draft vessels is impossible without rationalization and concentration of the investment in fewer ports. This, in turn, is fraught with political difficulty - which ports should be chosen for improvement?;

- current cost recovery for HPD ports is inconsistent with cost recovery in major ports of the CPC and the Harbour Commissions. Only about 20 per cent of annual operating costs are recovered; but more important, in areas where HPD ports are close to the major ports, these price differentials may be leading to unproductive competition, thereby reducing the viability of the major ports concerned;

- current cost recovery policies in HPD ports may well be leading to demands for levels of infrastructure which would be reduced if users were subject to cost-recovery more in line with levels of investment and services provided;

- facilities are now being provided outside the federal mandate. For example, ferry wharves in support of provincial ferry operations;

- facilities are now being managed by HPD which would be more appropriately managed by other departments. For example, harbours primarily serving fishermen and recreational boaters which could be managed by Department of Fisheries and Oceans (DFO) under DFO criteria; and

- facilities are often provided and maintained at standards not related to levels of service required and determined by the marketplace.

In the master plans (1981-82) some 42 HPD facilities have been identified as surplus to need (to be disposed of, or transferred to appropriate other federal or provincial jurisdictions). If the master plans were to be updated and focused on an objective of rationalization, further surplus ports would probably be identified. Approximately 100 of the public harbours are currently justified only because of community isolation.

A large portion of repairs and maintenance expenditure is devoted to maintaining existing infrastructure for its own sake as opposed to maintaining an appropriate level of service. If local management were responsible for operating each, within a regime of financial self-sufficiency, in the marketplace, this would not happen.

Several options are open to the government. All are based upon the following principles:

- divest those ports now serving provincially mandated programs (e.g. ferry terminals) and/or operations of ferry operators (e.g. CN Marine);

- identify and separately account for those ports required solely to support otherwise isolated communities, primarily in Newfoundland, Quebec, and British Columbia;

- sell off at the highest price achievable all remaining ports where possible; and

- manage the remainder under a regime of full financial self sufficiency as automomous Harbour-Commissions until sold.

The impacts of applying the above principles are summarized below:

Financial. Benefits will be longer term, relating primarily to increased system efficiency; to the reduction of future expenditures in surplus properties when disposed of ($20-$40 million over the next 5 to 10 years); and increased revenues ($10-$15 million annually as a conservative estimate).

Social. Minimal, as ports required to meet social criteria will be maintained albeit at minimum levels of service.

Legislative. Minor - tariff increases can be established by Order-in-Council. Regulations relating to charges for services to provincial ferry operations require review/amendment if these facilities cannot be transferred.

GATT. Should the strategy involve an effective transfer of subsidy from that implied by a subsidized port to a more direct industrial subsidy, difficulties may arise.

Federal/Provincial. Reluctance by provinces to accept responsibility for property or costs now federally provided or subsidized.

Economic. Short-term adjustment to revised tariffs which make up only a small amount of total shipping costs (1 to 2 per cent). Longer term positive impact due to increased system (ships/ports) efficiency. Diversion of traffic to non-Canadian ports unlikely to be significant.

Personnel. Strengthened local management of ports may require permanent port managers in certain ports where fees-of-office appointees now manage the port, but levels would be controlled by the necessity to recover all costs from users, as determined by the local Harbour-Commissioners in a market driven environment.

OPTIONS

The study team recommends to the Task Force that the government consider adopting a ports policy based on:

- divestiture of infrastructure to provinces and municipalities where the assets are in direct support of provincial operations, and transfer of fishing harbours to DFO;

- direct federal ownership and/or funding only for those harbours required to maintain otherwise isolated communities, and which cannot be financially self-sufficient;

- sale of other public harbours at the best price achievable; and

- closure of the remainder or management of those not sold as autonomous Harbour Commissions under a regime of full financial self-sufficiency until sold, closed, or otherwise divested.

APPENDIX A

PROGRAM RESOURCE SUMMARY
($000)

	83/84	84/85	85/86	86/87	87/88
Total Expenditures	66,100	73,800	51,400	41,400	40,400
Revenues	7,400	7,200	9,000	11,000	13,000
Salaries	3,100	3,800	3,400	3,400	3,400
Other O&M	32,000	30,000	37,000	36,000	35,000
Grants and Contributions	---	---	---	---	---
Capital	31,000	40,000	11,000	2,000	2,000
Person-Years	91	93	90	90	90
Fee-of-Service Appointees	350	350	350	350	350

This table is based on estimates provided by HPD on Multi-Year Operational Plans and is not consistent with data previously provided by DOT for this review. (In particular, capital for future years is significantly lower than DOT estimates provided).

CANADIAN COAST GUARD

Transport Canada

OBJECTIVE

The Canadian Coast Guard (CCG) operates within the overall objectives set for the Marine Transportation Program:

> "to attend to the development and operation of a safe and efficient national marine transportation system that contributes to the achievement of government objectives and to operate specific elements of this system."

RESULTS/BENEFICIARIES

Real property is employed in the operations of Coast Guard Bases which support search and rescue, icebreaking, navigational aids, communications and vessel traffic management and environmental regulatory activities.

Principal beneficiaries include the national and international shipping community, Canadian ports, harbours and the communities and industries they serve and the Canadian public at large through the facilitation of trade and commerce, and mitigation of ship source pollution of Canadian waters.

AUTHORITY

There are eight principal acts dealing with the Coast Guard's responsibilities:

- National Transportation Act
- Canada Shipping Act
- Navigable Waters Protection Act
- Arctic Waters Pollution Prevention Act
- Pilotage Act
- Government Harbours and Piers Act
- Water Carriage of Goods Act
- Government Vessels Discipline Act

The legislative and regulatory base is complex, and adjustments to Coast Guard program elements should only be undertaken with the input of legal specialists from the Departments of Justice and External Affairs.

RESOURCES (thousands of current dollars)

	84/85	85/86
Operating Expenses	$13,700	$13,700
Capital Expenditures	22,000	22,000
Revenues	---	---
Person-Years	215	215

Note - The CCG does not specifically account for real property expenses as they form only a minute proportion of the total budget. The above figures are considered to be conservative and order of magnitude only.

REAL PROPERTY ASSETS

Real property holdings are diverse, geographically dispersed and large in terms of value. The holdings range from major bases to single radio beacons on a small plot of land or rock outcrop. Real property is currently estimated to have an approximate replacement value of approximately $800 million to $1 billion.

PROGRAM DESCRIPTION

Real property is provided in support of six separate activities. Each is described below in terms of its property holdings.

Direction and Administration

The CCG operates 11 major support bases from St. John's, Newfoundland to Prince Rupert, B.C., which provide workshops office accommodations, yard operations space, stores facilities, and ship husbandry/wharf facilities to support operations outlines in all other planning elements. There are 12 smaller sub and sub-sub-bases which similarly provide such services on a more limited scale. Land, water lots, wharves, and office/shop buildings are controlled by the CCG in its ownership role. In addition, each of five Regional Headquarters plus the Coast Guard national Headquarters at Ottawa occupy office accommodation leased from the private sector or provided through Public Works Canada. Most District bases/sub-bases support helicopter operations on a limited scale, though in four cases helicopter hangars and service facilities owned by the Coast Guard are physically located on nearby civil or military airports for safety reasons and ease of operation.

Estimated Replacement Value: $275,000,000

Aids to Navigation

Conventional Aids

There are approximately 7,500 land based aids of which 272 are major light and fog alarm stations. Each of the 7,500 fixed aids requires purchase, lease or other arrangement for use of a small piece of real property (often only 6x6 metres), plus additional access easements, clearing rights, etc. Most sites are in isolated locations, often inaccessible by any means other than helicopter or small vessel.

Radio Aids

Most minor electronic aids (racons and beacons) are co-located with other fixed aids equipment. Approximately 20 sites in isolated locations require separate real property arrangements - land for a small building and radio antenna. Four Loran "C" sites and four Decca transmitter sites require somewhat larger facilities; typically, 20 to 50 hectares, along with one or more equipment buildings, and in some sites, one to four dwellings for station personnel.

Sounding and Dredging

Ship channels, whether improved by dredging or in their natural state, are not considered as, or inventories as "real property" though they often are the result of significant capital investment and require regular O&M expenditure. Other real property aspects include a number of training works, groins and other marine structures, plus the hydraulics test and development facility in Lasalle, Montreal consisting of one building and associated land.

Estimated Replacement Value: $560,000,000 (including Canso Canal and other marine works)

Ship Movement Systems and Services

There are two separate sub-activities:

a. Vessel Traffic Services - provision of vessel traffic information on ships in harbours, channels and other areas. Property consists of offices, remote radar/VHF sites and some housing for CCG operators.

b. Communications Services - consisting of a national network of CCG radio stations both manned and remote controlled. There are approximately 35 sites across Canada, 15 of which are independent, typically transmitter/received sites with some housing in remote areas. Each site usually requires a dedicated operations building, two or more remote sites with property and small equipment buildings.

Estimated Replacement Value: $65,000,000

Icebreaking, Arctic and Other Ship Support

Real property aspects of this activity are reported under Direction and Administration.

Marine Search and Rescue (SAR)

Major CCG SAR vessels operate from Coast Guard bases described under Direction and Administration. Inshore rescue boats operate from existing government wharves. Real property is restricted to "lifesaving stations". Generally, these consist of a trailer or house, a boat house or storage shed, a wharf and sometimes a fuel tank and/or a helicopter landing pad.

Estimated Replacement Value: $2,500,000

Regulatory Pollution Control

This activity operates from the Coast Guard bases described under "Direction and Administration", though there are approximately 20 remote sites across Canada consisting of a small piece of property and storage building near critical marine locations designed to house stand-by emergency response equipment. There is also one test, evaluation and repair centre.

Estimated Replacement Value: $4,000,000

Canadian Coast Guard services are delivered through an organization structure consisting of an Ottawa Headquarters, five Regional Headquarters and 11 Districts within five Regions.

The Regional Directors General report to the Commissioner, CCG for CCG matters, and directly to a Deputy Marine Transportation Administrator for other Marine programs carried out in their regions.

Real property management functions per se are not identified in the CCG organization either at Headquarters or in the Regions. This reflects the CCG position that "Coast Guard does not operate real property ... Rather real property assets are one of the resources required ... in direct program delivery."

From discussions with CCG managers and examination of DOT (Marine) documents, it appears that Regional real property matters are dealt with in cooperation with regional Ports and Harbours managers. The first level where distinct property functions and personnel are identified is at the district and/or base level.

Relatively few CCG staff are dedicated to real property management and the total person-years expended reflect those dedicated persons plus a small portion of those persons who undertake property management functions as part of wider duties.

Until 1982, CCG carried out major design and construction work through direct contracting with private sector architectural and engineering firms. Since 1982, all major projects are handled through Public Works Canada under the aegis of a general service agreement.

The CCG maintains a small dispersed in-house capability to provide program user interface with Public Works Canada and Public Works Canada contractors. These individuals usually have other management functions in addition to their property related functions. Capital dredging is carried out by Public Works Canada on a cost recoverable basis on behalf of the CCG.

The CCG maintains a small work force at each District Base which is normally associated with minor maintenance, particularly with respect to unmanned or remote locations. Major maintenance is undertaken by contract. Maintenance dredging is carried out by Public Works Canada on a cost-recoverable basis on behalf of the CCG.

Other than general policy direction provided by the resource allocation process and general departmental and central agency policies, no distinct property related policies and procedures are evident.

The CCG is currently attempting to develop a capital investment plan for CCG real property. This is in its early definitional phase and cannot be assessed.

Property management information per se does not exist in any distinct form, and current CCG management information systems do not highlight real property resource allocation, condition, or performance. The data provided for this review were developed based upon estimates provided by CCG regions, districts and bases, and should be regarded as order-of-magnitude only.

OBSERVATIONS

Real property acquisition, operation, and management is large in absolute terms, but is a relatively minor component of all CCG operations.

With the exception of offices and other general purpose structures on CCG bases, most real property assets are highly program specific, specialized structures, many of which are in remote relatively inaccessible locations.

Whether or not there is property surplus to requirements cannot be assessed without a detailed program review of CCG operations. None has been explicitly identified by the CCG, although a Program Evaluation of Ship

Movement Systems and Services (Vessel Traffic Services) is reportedly now in its final stages. Their current initiative to develop a base and Navigation Aids capital investment plan may identify surplus or obsolete real property assets. However, the value of this property for purposes other than its current use (e.g. beacons, lighthouses, civil marine works) is questionable.

The present system of contracting for major work and carrying out with in-house resources minor works and work of a nature critical to ongoing provision of the safety services offers a reasonable mix between internal and external resources used for O&M tasks.

The CCG maintains in-house technical expertise only for minor capital projects. Since 1982, major work has been handled by Public Works Canada under the terms of a General Service Agreement (GSA) and Specific Service Agreements (SSAs) for each project. This approach is judged appropriate.

Real property is not the subject of specific managerial policies and procedures, and property related information is basically non-existent. The absence of information relates to planning requirements (investment plans, inventories, condition surveys); and to performance of existing assets (in terms of current costs, personnel, contracted repairs, utilities, etc.)

The CCG recovers revenues only associated with the rental of government owned housing under Treasury Board guidelines and generally in cooperation with CMHC which establishes appropriate rental rates.

No costs associated with the operation of Canso Canal, dredging of channels and harbour approaches and the other navigation aids is undertaken.

Cost recovery for dredging is the subject of several studies including Dredging and Fleet Services, reviews of the Real Property Study Team, and of the Services and Subsidies to Business Study Team, and a recent Treasury Board sponsored report "Government of Canada Dredging Policy Report".

This review supports the findings of the Study Team on Services and Subsidies to Business which are included as Appendix A to this report.

Cost recovery for other navigational aids, search and rescue, and ships movement services, including their real property components is a subject beyond the scope of this assessment. However, a summary of a recent paper comparing other maritime nations' practices is appended for reference at Appendix B. Essentially, most of the nations observed do not recover capital or operating costs for these services outside harbour boundaries. This is generally consistent with Canada's current policies.

We have also examined recent DOT studies of the potential diversion to US ports of existing maritime transport should "full cost recovery" of CCG provided services be undertaken. A full analysis of these matters would be more appropriately examined by the Study Team on Transportation.

The only major issue revolves around the recovery of costs for CCG services related to real property.

In the view of the study team, cost recovery for CCG property cannot be discussed independently of broader transportation policy issues in both a national and an international context. However, there are two areas which should be assessed for increased cost recovery:

a. Cost recovery from other department, agencies, and private sector beneficiaries for sounding and dredging services (see Appendix A). The allocation of costs closer to end-users might well derive efficiencies through greater discretion in the levels of service demanded;

b. Recovery of the costs of operating the Canso Canal estimated by the CCG at $750,000 annually;

c. According to DOT officials, the Canso Canal was constructed only to allow ships passage through previously navigable waterways when those waterways were blocked by the Canso Causeway. The costs of both the causeway and the canal were substantially borne by the federal government. The causeway provides road and rail passage, subject to tolls collected by the Nova Scotia Department of Highways;

d. The canal was operated without charge under the terms of a 21-year agreement with the province, which is now apparently extended on a year to year basis; and

e. There may now be an opportunity to cede the canal to the province, allocate the costs of the canal to the province or to charge tolls to users.

The issues raised here are similar to those arising from federal ownership and operation of the Jacques Cartier and Champlain Bridges in Montreal. (St. Lawrence Seaway and Associated Bridges Program). Essentially the operation of the canal is directly in support of a provincial highway.

The adoption of one of the approaches outlined above regarding the canal could result in savings of $0.5 to $1 million annually.

OPTIONS

The study team recommends to the Task Force that the government consider:

- commencing negotiations with the Province of Nova Scotia to cede the Canso Canal to that province; and

- implementing cost recovery for dredging services now provided without charge by the CCG.

TABLE 1

CANADIAN COAST GUARD - REAL PROPERTY RESOURCE SUMMARY

(based on estimates provided by DOT Marine Administration)
All Costs/Values in 1985 Dollars

Region	Bases & Sub-Bases (No.)	Other Properties (No.)	Replace-ment Value ($000)	PY (No.)	Salaries ($000)	Other O&M ($000)	Capital 1984/85 ($000)	Remarks
Newfoundland	2	687	95,000	37	1,050	1,000	1,160	
Maritimes	3	1,203	188,000	48	1,920	1,600	3,650	
Laurentian	2	639	208,000	48	1,550	1,500	2,710	
Central	6	1,813	147,000	41	1,205	1,200	10,600	
Western	10	3,126	266,000	38	1,460	1,100	3,620	
Headquarters	1*	NIL	800	3	145	N/A[1]	221	*Test
TOTAL	24	7,468	904,800	215	7,330	6,400	21,961	

Notes - 1. Other O&M does not include the costs of 134 separate properties which are leased from the private sector or provided by DPW having an estimated annual rental value of $12.8 million.

2. Annual O&M Costs do not include sounding and dredging costs of $18,000,000 not directly related to CCG property.

3. Capital Expenditures for the three years FY 81/82 to 83/84 inclusive = $40.2 million.
Capital Expenditures forecast for the three years FY 85/86 to 87/88 inclusive = $65.2 million

4. Annual revenues of approximately $350,000 accrue from the rental of 150 houses to Coast Guard employees.

APPENDIX A

DREDGING AND FLEET SERVICES

Public Works Canada

OBJECTIVE

To provide dredging services on a "contracted out" basis, providing for maximum use of private sector dredging capacity wherever it is more effective and less expensive or using Public Works Canada Dredging Fleet.

AUTHORITY

Appropriation Act.

DESCRIPTION

The federal government undertakes dredging activity in all regions of Canada. Program responsibility for dredging rests with the various Marine Directorates and Corporations of Transport Canada, with the Department of Fisheries and Oceans and with the Parks Branch of Environment Canada. The implementing agency is Public Works Canada which undertakes the work by contract with the private sector or by use of its own dredging fleet.

Public Works Canada provides dredging services with the in-house fleet and personnel only where required, to avoid monopoly situations, to minimize mobilization costs, to provide rapid response, and to deliver services to the client in the most efficient and effective manner. Specifically, the project must have one or more of the following characteristics:

a. requires a special type of dredge;
b. is in an area inaccessible to private sector equipment;
c. is continuous and requires unique machinery;
d. is small;
e. is remote and/or dangerous;
f. is urgent;
g. has unique material to be dredged or geophysical conditions;
h. has broad range of material to be dredged.

BENEFICIARIES

Dredging companies, federal government departments (TC,DFO) federal government agencies (Ports Canada, St. Lawrence Seaway Authority), port and channel users, cargo owners, and shippers.

EXPENDITURES (millions of current dollars)

	83/84	84/85	85/86	86/87	87/88
Salaries	9.7	10.6	11.3	11.3	11.3
Other O&M	6.5	5.3	6.2	6.2	6.2
Capital	1.4	-	5.5	10.1	12.5
Grants & Contributions	-	0.1	-	-	-
TOTAL	17.6	16.0	23.0	27.6	30.0
Revenues	7.0	7.3	17.5	17.5	17.5
Person Years	277	277	277	277	277

The cost of Canadian government maintenance dredging in 1983-84 was $41.1 million allocated among Public Works Canada ($17 million), Transport Canada ($19 million), and Fisheries and Oceans ($6 million). Percentage distribution of expenditures, by region, was:

Atlantic	33	West	18
Quebec	14	Pacific	35

Total revenue is 1983-84 was $7.0 million. User fees cover all of the $1.8 million dredging costs at major ports and the St. Lawrence Seaway, as well as a portion of the $6.89 million dredging costs incurred at commission harbours, public harbours and heritage canals. There is no revenue generated from dredging in commercial waterways or small craft harbours.

OBSERVATIONS

Ports Canada has 15 harbour authorities and its dredging of harbour facilities which excludes main channels, has normally been contracted to the private sector without Public Works Canada involvement. The Harbours and Ports

Directorate of Transport Canada presently funds most public dredging at the nine Great Lakes and Pacific Commission harbours with dredges provided by Public Works Canada. The Directorate also manages dredging at the 50 public harbours using Public Works Canada technical services, some Public Works Canada dredges and some private sector dredges. Dredging of 1400 small craft harbours is carried out with $6 million in Public Works Canada dredging fleet services. The Canadian Coast Guard uses Public Works Canada dredging services for its 15 main channels and 30 port entrances. The St. Lawrence Seaway Authority contracts out all its dredging requirements and Parks Canada contracts with Public Works Canada for its infrequent dredging needs.

In the late 1970s Public Works Canada managed 85 per cent of the federal government dredging and Public Works Canada equipment was used for 60 per cent of the work. By 1982/83, PWC was managing 60 per cent of total government dredging activity, 70 per cent of which was done with Public Works Canada equipment.

The demand for dredging services is growing with the introduction of larger ships requiring greater drafts. Additional costs of $16 million annually are identified for small craft harbours and $6 million annually for commercial waterways.

Public Works Canada, as the implementing agency, maintains that a basic fleet capacity is required and that funds for fleet upgrading are needed.

ASSESSMENT

With Public Works Canada functioning solely as an implementation agent for dredging, and several departments and agencies having dredging needs, there is a requirement to define exactly who has responsibility for what. An interdepartmental committee was formed to deal with this and other related problems and their report "Government of Canada Dredging" will be released shortly.

Dredging services will always be in demand, particularly when the user does not pay. As noted above, dredging costs will increase significantly if all demands are met. In order to induce some discipline on demand, a user pay concept could be developed. Administratively, the user fees for dredging should be integrated with a broad base of other charges for shipping services to avoid a shift of commercial shipping to US harbours.

The level of service ...how deep should channels be and should they be this deep all the time... defines dredging requirements. While these have been defined and costed within TC, DFO has not yet introduced a harbour classification system and associated level of service concept.

The Auditor General has been critical of Public Works Canada dredging in the areas of criteria for use, cost accounting, and cost sharing for the dredging fleet.

According to existing government policy, Canadian dredging can only be done with Canadian registered, built or modified dredges. At present, dredges account for a very small portion of the Canadian shipbuilding industry and hence, this non-tariff barrier is of little significance to the domestic shipbuilding and repair industry. Removal of this restriction might stimulate competition in the Canadian dredging industry. It is not anticipated that an identical barrier that prohibits Canadian dredges from working in the US will be lifted for some time.

OPTIONS

The study team recommends to the Task Force that the government consider implementing the following recommendations from the "Government of Canada Dredging Policy" report.

a. Jurisdiction

1. Agencies with territorially defined mandate have full authority for dredging e.g. Parks Canada.

2. Agencies with functionally defined mandates have full authority for dredging e.g. TC Harbours and Ports Directorate for harbour facilities; Canadian Coast Guard for main channels; DFO for small craft harbours.

b.	User Fees	1.	Adopt user fee principles for waterway users.
		2.	Fees should be integrated with all other marine services changes.
c.	Level of Service	1.	DFO should complete categorization of harbours.
		2.	The level of service associated with each category of DFO Harbours should be approved by Treasury Board.
d.	Accelerated Private Sector Involvement	1.	Public Works Canada establish early target dates whereby one-half to two-thirds of Public Works Canada managed dredging volume be let to the private sector.
		2.	Public Works Canada dredging fleet be limited to those required to meet exceptional dredging requirements.

No capital acquisition should take place for Public Works Canada dredges until the impact of the recommendations can be evaluated.

The impact of removal of the non-tariff barrier protecting Canadian dredging should be studied. If there is any indication that this would stimulate competition in the dredging business, Public Works Canada should immediately begin to reduce their fleet, starting with the vessels in the Gulf of St. Lawrence.

The potential savings from implementation of the above alternative are the proposed acquisition program to replace or refurbish the existing $100 million fleet as well as additional revenue of some $20 million from user fees.

APPENDIX B

COMPARISON OF CHARGING POLICIES FOR MARITIME SERVICES BY OTHER MARITIME NATIONS

COSTS COVERED BY GOVERNMENT FOR EUROPEAN PORTS INFRASTRUCTURES

COUNTRY	Investment						Maintenance					
	Maritime Access Channels	Light, Buoys and navigational aids		Sea Locks and Exterior Breakwaters		Docks, quays reclaimed land etc.	Maritime access channels	Lights, Buoys and navigational aids		Sea Locks and navigational aids		Docks, quays reclaimed land etc.
		Outside Port	Inside Port	Locks	Breakwaters			Outside port	Inside port	Locks	Break-waters	
Belgium	100%	100%	Variable	100%	10%	60 - 100%	100%	100%	Variable	Variable	-	Variable
Denmark	-	100%	-	-	-	-	-	100%	-	-	-	-
West Germany	100%	100%	100%	100%	10%	100%	100%	100%	100%	100%	100%	100%
France Autonomous	80%	100%	60 - 80%	80%	8%	60%	80%	100%	100%	100%	100%	-
Non-Autonomous	100%	100%	100%	100%	10%	100%	100%	100%	100%	100%	100%	Variable
Ireland	-	-	-	-	-	-	-	-	-	-	-	-
Italy Autonomous	Variable	100%	100%	-	Variable	Variable	Variable	100%	100%	-	Variable	Variable
State	100%	100%	100%	-	Over 30%	100%	100%	100%	100%	-	100%	100%
Netherlands "Havenbedrijven"	Over 65%	100%	Variable	Over 65%	Over 65%	-	100%	100%	Variable	100%	100%	-
"Havenschappen"	100%	100%	Variable	Variable	Variable	Variable	100%	100%	Variable	Variable	Variable	Variable
Great Britain	-	-	-	-	-	-	-	-	-	-	-	-
Greece	Variable	100%	Variable	-	10%	Variable	Variable	100%	Variable	-	100%	Variable

Source: EEC Transport Commission - 1982 Figure

ST. LAWRENCE SEAWAY AND ASSOCIATED BRIDGES

PART A - INTRODUCTION

The St. Lawrence Seaway Authority (SLSA) is a Schedule "C" (Part 1) Crown corporation which operates the Canadian section of the St. Lawrence Seaway and the Canadian span of the Thousand Islands Bridge. Two wholly owned subsidiary corporations are as follows:

a. The Seaway International Bridge Corporation, Ltd., which operates and maintains the Seaway International Bridge between Cornwall, Ontario and Roosevelt Town, New York on behalf of the SLSA and its United States counterpart, the St. Lawrence Seaway Development Corporation; and

b. The Jacques Cartier and Champlain Bridges Incorporated which operates and maintains the Jacques Cartier and Champlain Bridges including a portion of the Bonaventure Autoroute in Montréal, Québec.

For ease of reference, the remainder of this report is structured in two parts:

Part B - The St. Lawrence Seaway; and
Part C - Bridges.

PART B - THE ST. LAWRENCE SEAWAY

OBJECTIVE

The St. Lawrence Seaway Authority was incorporated to construct, operate, and maintain a deep waterway between the Port of Montreal and Lake Erie:

- to ensure safe and efficient movement of marine traffic and protection of the environment;
- to recover the associated cost so as to operate on a self-sufficient basis; and
- to assess the need for improvements of the Seaway System and plan their implementation as required.

RESULTS/BENEFICIARIES

The Seaway provides access to inland ports by national and international shippers which would otherwise have access to ports only downstream from Montreal. The result is increased efficiency of commodity transport primarily of grain, iron ore, coal, and petroleum products and manufactured goods, and enhanced opportunity for Canadian export trade.

Principal beneficiaries include national and international shippers and the communities, producers, and industries whose products are transported.

AUTHORITY

The St. Lawrence Seaway Act.

RESOURCES (thousands of current dollars)

	84/85*	85/86*
Operating Revenue	63,000	63,600
Operating Expenses	72,600	78,500
Income (Loss) from Operations	(9,600)	(14,900)
Other Income (Investment)	7,000	5,800
Net Income (Loss)	(2,600)	(9,100)
Add Depreciation and Items not requiring Cash Outlay	8,800	10,600
Funds Provided from Operations	6,200	1,500
Capital Expenditures	4,600	6,000
Cash Flow (excludes changes in working capital)	1,600	(4,500)

Persons Employed: 1,050

* Statements for the year ending March 31, 1985 are not yet available. The above figures are based on the unaudited financial statements, March 31, 1985, and the 1985-86 Government Estimates.

REAL PROPERTY ASSETS

Real property includes canals, locks, adjacent land and buildings in Ontario and Québec and road and railway bridges spanning canals in the Montréal and Welland Canal areas. Some land for future development is held in the Montréal, Cornwall and Welland Canal areas.

Cost of construction was approximately $750 million. Estimates of current replacement value range from $5 to $10 billion.

PROGRAM DESCRIPTION

Real property consists primarily of canals, locks and marine channels, bridges, tunnels and service roads directly associated with the Seaway, unserviced land abutting the Seaway and a small number of office buildings, maintenance and stores buildings. Details, by region, of infrastructure are provided at Appendix A.

In addition, the SLSA owns some 2,212 hectares of land: in the Cornwall area (182 hectares); adjacent to the Welland Canal (1,925 hectares), being held for future development, primarily for the expansion of the Welland Canal System and for the previous disposal of excavation materials at the time of construction; and in Melocheville, Québec (105 hectares) being held for future development. The SLSA is now actively investigating the possibility of selling some of this land to realize ongoing reductions in municipal grant payments, and to avoid potential exposure to liability/damage claims.

The SLSA is organized into two regions: Eastern Region from Montréal to Lake Ontario; Western Region - the Welland Canal. The Eastern Region comprises five Canadian locks and associated infrastructure and land. The Western Region comprises eight locks and associated infrastructure and land. Property management is controlled from its Cornwall headquarters through two separate regional managers in St. Lambert, Québec and St. Catherines, Ontario. A small corporate head office is located in Ottawa.

A staff of engineers is maintained in-house to meet normal annual workload for capital acquisition with private sector consultants retained directly for specialist support. All design and construction of major works is contracted out to the private sector. Capital dredging is carried out by private sector operators, under contract.

The majority of routine operations and maintenance is carried out by in-house staff. However, most cyclical overhaul and restoration work, and rehabilitation and modification work (major and special maintenance) is carried out under contract. Repair and maintenance of railway bridges is undertaken by railway personnel. Maintenance dredging is carried out by private sector operators, under contract. The current collective agreement between SLSA and its employees precludes contracting any work now undertaken by in-house personnel.

Of the real property revenues reported above for 1984/85, the vast majority ($59.6 million) are tolls levied on ships' passage, with land rentals and licenses providing $3.4 million; a large portion of this revenue accrues from the transportation of water for Ontario Hydro ($1.3 million).

Forecast capital expenditures for fiscal years 1985/86 to 1987/88 are approximately $12 million. Capital expenditures in the three fiscal years ending in 1984/85 were $18.7 million; in 1984/85 some $3 million in capital was provided to the SLSA from the Special Recovery Capital Projects Program. Generally, capital funds are internally generated.

The SLSA leases office space for its Ottawa head office at an annual cost of $110,000.

OBSERVATIONS

With the exception of a minor amount of office space and service buildings, the infrastructure is of a highly specialized marine engineering nature, integral to the operation of the seaway.

Revenues accrue mainly from the Canadian share of shipping tolls which are by policy at a level "to ensure self-sufficiency". From an examination of the latest annual reports, this "self-sufficiency" has been restricted to recovery of operating costs alone excluding depreciation. The costs of construction orginally provided as a loan by the Canadian government was converted to equity on April 1,

1977, by Parliamentary appropriation. Unpaid interest of $210 million remains on the books and the SLSA is seeking approval from Parliament to have this unpaid interest forgiven. From an examination of the most recent 5-year corporate plan, the SLSA will not return to operating "break-even" until at least 1990. During the intervening period, Parliamentary appropriations will be avoided by virtue of the current reserves which are sufficient to cover planned capital improvements and forecast negative cash flow from operations to 1990-91.

The setting of tolls is a complex process involving both the United States and Canadian governments and consideration of the diversion from inland ports to coastal ports/land transportation modes should tolls exceed certain levels. The Canadian share of tolls has recently been renegotiated with the United States and raised to 73 per cent from 70 per cent of total tolls levied.

Divestiture of the whole or parts of the current infrastructure of this strategic waterway is judged inappropriate even if a private organization could be found to assume the government's contributed capital plus deferred interest (approximately $850 million) while living within a toll structure which probably cannot be raised beyond the level required to provide operating break-even.

Potential efficiencies from increased contracting out are probably marginal, and the net economic benefit of transferring work in small communities from employees to private companies (who would likely hire these displaced employees) is probably nil. Manpower has been reduced by approximately 13 per cent since 1978/79 coincident with the lower traffic levels and seasonal employment policies are in place to promote efficient mobilization of human resources.

The current toll structure provides some $60 million in revenues. The tolls are structured in such a way that certain commodities, notably grain are given a preferential treatment. Elasticity of toll structure/commodity traffic is difficult to assess. However, when tolls were re-imposed on the Welland Canal, traffic patterns did not change from pre-toll levels. A diversion of United States grain shipments to Mississippi carriers possibly relates more to temporary over-capacity of barges on the Mississippi and this traffic is again rising on the seaway.

The commodity tolls are a very small proportion of total shipping charges and there appears to be room to raise these tolls and rationalize them to remove preferential treatment.

A 15 to 25 per cent increase in tolls and/or shipping volume would provide some $9 - 15 million annually and is required to permit continuing self-sufficiency.

Increases in land rental rates might derive marginal benefits to the St. Lawrence Seaway Authority as a whole. (A doubling of rentals would provide some $800,000.) There would be socio-political implications of increasing the financial burden on farmers at this time (the land is largely leased for agricultural purposes).

Divestiture of lands being held for future development might provide some cash inflow but if covenants were placed on this land to ensure its availability in the event of seaway expansion, values would be depressed.

OPTIONS

The study team recommends to the Task Force that the government consider reviewing current costs and toll structures to ensure full operating self-sufficiency including costs of interest and depreciation.

PART C - BRIDGES

I. THE THOUSAND ISLANDS BRIDGE

OBJECTIVE

To operate the Canadian span of the Thousand Islands Bridge as a financially self-sufficient asset.

RESULTS/BENEFICIARIES

The Canadian span serves international private and commercial vehicle traffic.

AUTHORITY

The St. Lawrence Seaway Act and Order in Council PC 1976-2407.

RESOURCES (thousands of current dollars)

	84/85	85/86
Revenue	900	730
Operating Expenses	450	490
Surplus	450	240
Capital Expenditures	---	---

PROGRAM DESCRIPTION

The bridge was completed in 1936 by an American company. Ownership of the Canadian span passed to the federal government via a series of agreements with the original owners and the Province of Ontario in 1976. Administrtion and control of the structure was entrusted to the SLSA in 1976 pursuant to an order-in-council (PC 1976-2407). The span, associated lands and buildings were transferred at no cost to the federal government. Since that time some $1.5 million in capital improvements have been made by the SLSA.

The SLSA has entered into a management agreement with the Thousand Islands Bridge Authority (United States entity) to operate and manage the Canadian span in return for 35 per cent of net operating revenues. Provision of capital funds required from time to time is arranged by separate agreement of the two parties.

The objective is to operate the span as a financially self sufficient asset. Capital expenditures of approximately $6 million (Canadian share), are forecast for fiscal year (FY) 1985/86 to FY 1987/88. In FY 1983/84, net income from operations was approximately $185 million and retained earnings from 1976 to 1984 were $1.4 million. No person-years are allocated to the bridge.

Approximately five hectares of land are surplus to requirement and their transfer to Parks Canada is under active consideration.

OBSERVATIONS

To divest or to contract management of the Canadian span as a separate entity might have marginal economic benefit to a Canadian firm; but the splitting into two operations of essentially one asset would probably have a negative impact on overall efficiency and on the current positive income flow to Canada. Moreover, there is effectively a quid pro quo in that Canada operates the Seaway International Bridge. (Section II following.)

The asset has been financially self-sufficient to date. However, the 5-year business plan shows that a major capital investment of $6 million will be required in 1987-88. This expenditure is required to redeck the span. The SLSA sees no alternative at this time but to seek a $5 million Parliamentary Appropriation to assist the funding of this rehabilitation.

The current toll structure is on the basis of parity of the United States and Canadian dollar - payment may be made in either currency without conversion. There is a potential for unauditable windfalls to either or both of the American management company and its toll collectors. A toll structure based upon the United States/Canada exchange differential would mitigate this potential to the benefit of Canada and is supported by this review team.

The current management agreement requires the SLSA to pay a management fee of 30 per cent of its share of the operating surplus with a minimum $60,000 fee and no maximum or sliding scale. This appears to be generous to the management company.

There is some potential to gain further revenues from the operation of a duty free shop adjacent to the Canadian span. This is being investigated.

Opportunities exist to increase tolls to a level more consistent with full financial self-sufficiency, and to renegotiate the management agreement in 1986/87. Toll increases must be approved by both parties and by their respective governments.

OPTIONS

The study team recommends to the Task Force that the government consider:

- having the SLSA develop, with its United States counterpart, a revised toll structure recognizing the United States/Canadian dollar exchange differential, and tolls be raised to the levels required to maintain full financial self-sufficiency;

- the Thousand Islands Bridge Authority management agreement be renegotiated with a view of lowering and restructuring the management fee chargeable to the SLSA; and

- the SLSA expedite the implementation of other revenue generating functions (e.g. duty free shop) where feasible.

II. THE SEAWAY INTERNATIONAL BRIDGE

OBJECTIVE

To operate the Canadian and American portions of the International Toll Bridge while recovering operating and maintenance costs and provide for amortization of the costs of the Canadian span.

RESULTS/BENEFICIARIES

This International Toll Bridge serves private and commercial vehicle traffic.

AUTHORITY

The St. Lawrence Seaway Act.

RESOURCES (thousands of current dollars)

	84/85	85/86
Revenue	1,500	1,500
Operating Expenses	1,200	1,300
Surplus	300	200
Capital	---	---
Person-Years	24	24

PROGRAM DESCRIPTION

The Seaway International Bridge Corporation Ltd. owns the north span and the substructure of the south span of this International Toll Bridge and operates and manages both spans on behalf of itself and the United States counterpart of the SLSA (a reversal of the United States management of the Thousand Islands Bridge described previously). Bridge traffic is similar to the Thousand Islands Bridge being passenger and commercial vehicles.

Completed in 1962, total cost of the Canadian assets at that time was $11.5 million. The objective of the corporation is to recover operating and maintenance costs and to return annual surpluses to its parent, the SLSA, to amortize the capital and interest costs of the North span; then to the United States entity to offset amortization of the cost of the United States span; the balance if any, is divided equally between both parties.

To date, payments have been made only to the SLSA, representing, from a Canadian perspective, self-sufficiency. In 1983/84, revenues of $1.4 million and expenses of $1.1 million were recorded, deriving an operating surplus of $300,000. Similar results are projected for the year ending March 31, 1985. Forecast capital expenditures to FY 1987/88 amount to approximately $140,000.

All design construction and maintenance work is contracted to the private sector. There are 24 person-years involved in management and toll collections.

The last toll increase was 4 years ago. North American Indians are given free passage which reduces potential revenues by some $1 million. This was a condition agreed to when land on Cornwall Island was expropriated for the bridge. This special subsidy is an inappropriate charge against a transportation operation and if continued should be funded by an annual contribution from Indian and Northern Affairs. A record is kept of passages and passes are issued. Thus the control of such a contribution is facilitated.

OPTIONS

The study team recommends to the Task Force that the government consider having the Department of Indian Affairs and Northern Development reimburse the corporation for the foregone revenues represented by free passage for Indians.

III. THE JACQUES CARTIER AND CHAMPLAIN BRIDGES

OBJECTIVE

To provide the public with a safe and efficient transit over the Jacques Cartier Bridge, the Champlain Bridge and a portion of the Bonaventure Autoroute in Montréal, Québec... while making every effort to make the bridge self financing.

RESULTS/BENEFICIARIES

The bridges and autoroute serve private and commercial vehicle traffic in the Montréal area.

AUTHORITY

St. Lawrence Seaway Act and Orders in Council PC 1978-3129, and PC 1979-1187. As a result of Cabinet Decision 336-76-RD dated August 5, 1976, administration and control of the bridges and a 10-kilometre section of the Bonaventure Autoroute, were transferred to the Jacques Cartier and Champlain Bridges Inc., the creation which was approved by Treasury Board Minute 759687, September 17, 1978.

RESOURCES (thousands of current dollars)

	84/85	85/86
Revenue	6,500	6,500
Operating Expenses	11,900	11,900
Surplus (Deficit)	(5,400)	(5,400)
Deduct Items not requiring Cash Outlay	1,200	1,200
Funds Required for Operations	4,200	4,200
Capital Expenditures	150	90
Person-Years	89	89

PROGRAM DESCRIPTION

The federal ownership and management of these assets have been the subject of complex and protracted negotiations with Québec and the municipalities over a period of 25 to 30 years.

The assets at time of construction cost:

autoroute	$14.73 million
bridges	$58.55 million
land	$ 3.79 million
TOTAL	$77.07 million

Current annual operating costs total $11.9 million including salaries of toll collectors, policing, and road maintenance. Capital expenditures are minimal and are incurred only to replace worn-out equipment and infrastructure. A total of 89 person-years are employed including management, operation, toll collections, and policemen.

Annual revenues amount to $6.5 million of which $5.9 million are toll receipts on the Champlain Bridge alone. The annual operating shortfall of $5.4 million is appropriated through DOT Vote 30 (1984/85).

Tolls on the Jacques Cartier Bridge were removed in 1962 by an agreement with Québec who would then take over the bridge. Upon removal of the tolls, the province demurred and ownership remained federal.

Tolls on the Champlain Bridge have not been raised since 1962. An initiative to do so in 1982 was effectively prevented by the imposition of the "6 and 5 Program" in 1982. (It was impractical to raise a 25 cent toll by only 1.5 cents).

The autoroute and bridges are maintained, serviced and policed by the corporation. Grants in lieu of taxes to Montreal are reduced by only $13,000 annually in compensation, to their current level of $62,000.

Québec has recently adopted a policy of removing tolls on provincially controlled autoroutes.

OBSERVATIONS

Several issues are raised by these assets: the fundamental issue is - should the federal government be involved in direct administration control and ownership of assets which are part of a municipal/provincial road network? If so, what conditions should apply? If the federal government maintains ownership, can tolls be maintained or raised given the province's intention to remove tolls on provincial highway infrastructure? And finally, can the objective of self-sufficiency of these assets ever be realized - that is to what level can tolls be raised?

The corporation is not financially self-sufficient even from a perspective of meeting operating costs. Amortization of original cost, financing charges and achievement of a return on investment are not being achieved.

Maintenance of and increase in the toll structure in view of the province's recent policy would raise the potential of "negative" federal presence.

The Québec government would probably be reluctant to assume ownership (even at no initial cost) of a losing proposition.

OPTIONS

Nevertheless, the study team recommends to the Task Force that the government consider the following options:

a. Transfer to the province/municipality of the assets, "as is" to achieve jurisdictional consistency - annual savings of $4-5 million operating and removal of future capital expenditures by the federal government;

b. As per Option 1 but negotiate one time payment to offset necessary capital rehabilitation. The one time payment cannot be estimated at this time. Annual operating savings as per Option 1;

c. As per Option 2 but negotiate a limited timeframe (1-5 years say) operating subsidy. Annual operating savings as per Option 2, after the expiry of the subsidy period; and

d. Raise tolls on Champlain Bridge to cover the operating deficit (would require approximately 100 per cent increase in tolls) to 50 cents for passenger vehicles.

Implications are generally as follows:

- federal provincial relations;

- legislative and/or regulatory amendments (except for toll increase);

- possible negative reaction by users and their elected representatives to large toll increase; and

- effect of establishing a precedent for similar federal involvement in provincial transportation infrastructure (e.g. ferry wharves in eastern provinces, the St. John, N.B. Harbour Bridge).

The study team further recommends to the Task Force that the federal government consider negotiating with the Quebec government to cede the bridges and autoroute to the province or the municipality.

St. Lawrence Seaway Authority Infrastructure

Region	Province	Buildings	Bridges/Tunnels	Locks	Canals/Channels
Eastern	Quebec	Administration Maintenance Store	Lift Spans Victoria Bridge Cote Ste. Catherine Bridge Mercier Bridge (South part) 2 CPR Lift spans Beuharnois Tunnel St. Louis and Valleyfield Highway Bridge	2 Locks on Beauharnois Canal 2 Locks on South Shore Canal	Beauharnois Canal South Shore Canal
Eastern	Quebec/ Ontario				Lake St. Francis Navigation Channel
Eastern	Ontario	Ottawa Head Office (leased from PWC) Cornwall Headquarters Offices, Maintenance, Toll Plaza, Customs and Immigration Building	1 Bascule Bridge at Lock 7	Iroquois Lock	St. Lawrence River Navigation Channel*
Western	Ontario	Administration and Maintenance Complex at St. Catherines	11 Bridges/canal crossings on Welland Canal	8 Locks on Welland Canal	Welland Canal

* **Note** - Lake/River Beds owned by provinces. Channel maintained by SLSA.

SMALL CRAFT HARBOURS

Department of Fisheries and Oceans

OBJECTIVE

The Small Craft Harbours (SCH) program objective is to provide, maintain and manage, consistent with fisheries policy, regional harbour systems to accommodate the commercial fishing fleets and to assist in the provision, maintenance and management of recreational harbours.

RESULTS/BENEFICIARIES

There are 2,232 fishing and recreational harbours in all regions of the country serving:

- approximately 70,000 fishermen;
- approximately 1,000 communities and the commercial fishing industry in those and other communities landing and processing some $2 billion worth of fish products annually; and
- recreational boaters and sports fishermen providing approximately 10 per cent of all recreational berths available to the public.

AUTHORITY

The Fishing and Recreational Harbours Act.

RESOURCES (thousands of current dollars)

	84/85	85/86
Operating Expenses	18,300	18,300
Capital Expenditures	25,100	24,200
Revenue	2,500	4,500
Person-Years	114	114
Fees-of-Office Appointments	300	300

REAL PROPERTY ASSETS

	Number of Harbours	Approximate Replacement Value ($ million)
Newfoundland	435	500
Gulf	342	500
Scotia-Fundy	393	400
Quebec	388	250
Ontario	388	300
Western	84	15
Pacific	202	350
TOTAL	2,232	$2,315

PROGRAM DESCRIPTION

Small Craft Harbours is responsible for the maintenance and operation of 1,410 fishing and 822 recreational harbours and wharves. This work activity has two functions: Harbour Maintenance; and Harbour Operations. Harbour Maintenance services include: breakwater protection, dredging of harbours, provision of wharves and launching facilities, installation of operational services (light and power, water, storage, etc.). Harbour Operations involve the day-to-day operation of individual harbours (collection of revenue, traffic control, garbage removal, security, etc.).

Harbours are classified in categories A, B, C, and D depending upon the vessel activity. Services listed above are provided in varying degrees to each class of harbour. For example, whereas Class A harbours are normally provided a full range of services and full-time on-site management, Class C harbours are provided minimal services. Class D harbours are virtually inactive and could be declared surplus. Small Craft Harbours has developed criteria for harbour classification as well as Harbour Condition Guidelines which specify the criteria for each level of service.

The distribution of harbours by the above classification is shown as follows:

TABLE 1
SMALL CRAFT HARBOURS

Region	Number of Harbours by Class				
	A	B	C	D	Total
Newfoundland	30	82	164	159	435
Gulf	22	79	159	82	342
Scotia-Fundy	16	46	187	144	393
Quebec	10	27	314	37	388
Ontario	50	81	236	21	388
Western		15	61	8	84
Pacific	28	29	132	13	202
TOTAL	156	359	1,253	464	2,232

Harbours vary from those where only a launching ramp is provided to those where there is a full range of harbour facilities: breakwaters, dredging, wharves, launching ramps, slipways, electrical services, waterlines, parking lots, storage etc.

Of the total 2,232 small craft harbours, 1,981 are administered directly by DFO and 251 are currently operated by municipalities to which these harbours have been leased.

Annual expenditures are focused on A and B Class harbours and are distributed among classes of harbours as shown in Table 2. However, recent increases have been directed to Class C harbours. Recreational harbours annual expenditures are approximately $1.6 million operating and $850 thousand capital (exclusive of salaries).

TABLE 2
EXPENDITURE BY SCH CLASS

Fiscal Year	Harbour Class			
	A	B	C	D
80/81	52%	29%	15%	4%
81/82	47%	35%	15%	3%
82/83	50%	30%	17%	3%
83/84	53%	22%	23%	2%
84/85	51%	27%	21%	1%

A regional resource distribution is shown in Table 3:

TABLE 3
SMALL CRAFT HARBOURS
Regional Distribution of Resources 1984/85
(includes Special Recovery Capital Projects
Capital Funding of approximately
$55 million) (Source DFO estimates,
March 22,1985)

($000)

Region	PYs	Revenues	O&M	Capital	Contrib.	Total Expend.
Newfoundland	10	63	2,100	10,125	-	8,339
Gulf	10	210	3,057	15,934	-	12,094
Scotia-Fundy	12	143	3,571	18,546	-	16,946
Quebec	7	21	2,436	16,579	1,396	14,132
Ontario(1)	15	600	2,081	14,947	-	13,227
Western	2	15	558	352	-	318
Pacific	43	1,500	3,513	5,882	-	3,761
Headquarters (2)	18	-	2,044	700	-	34,974
TOTAL	117	2,552	19,360	83,065	1,396	103,791

Notes - 1 PYs include three provided under Employment Related Initiatives ending March 31, 1985.

2 Headquarters O&M and Capital consist of essential maintenance and capital project funds which are released to regions upon project approval.

The SCH program is administered through seven Regional DFO offices by Regional Directors who have a line relationship to the Regional Director General for Fisheries Management. Strong functional direction is provided to the regions through a headquarters Small Craft Harbours' Director-General. Unlike most other activities in the department, SCH funds are controlled through headquarters.

The SCH administers and operates harbours in the following ways:

a. through use of staff located in regional offices for relatively inactive harbours where on-site harbour management is not warranted;

b. through on-site Harbour Managers (fees of office harbour managers and a small number of Harbour Manager PYs); and

c. through leasing of harbours to municipalities. The breakdown is as outlined in Table 4.

TABLE 4
SCH ADMINISTRATION

Region	Harbours Administered by Regional Staff	Harbours with On-Site Harbours Managers	Harbours Operated by Municipal Leases
Newfoundland	416	17	2
Gulf	211	130	1
Scotia-Fundy	288	92	13
Quebec	327	2	59
Ontario	147	91	150
Western	73	4	7
Pacific	116	67	19
TOTAL	1,578	403*	251

* Thirty DFO employees in Pacific Region, and approximately 300 fees-of-office appointees manage 403 harbours.

Services such as vessel loading and unloading are not provided. SCH activities relate solely to the operation and maintenance of real property.

Harbour maintenance is carried out by PWC under a general service agreement, primarily by contract with the private sector.

Levels of capital funding generally reflect maintenance of current facilities through major rehabilitation rather than the investment in new plant.

An exception to normal funding levels occurred during the Special Recovery Capital Projects Program by which some $150 million was invested primarily in areas designated by the government to promote economic recovery.

Projects are closely controlled by headquarters and funds are advanced to the regions only upon approval of specific projects. Work is undertaken by PWC largely by contract with the private sector.

The SCH program derives revenues from two main sources: berthage fees and monies collected through leases/licences.

By regulation, berthage fees are collected from commercial fishing vessels based on a fee per vessel metre. Under the regulations, commercial fishing vessels of all sizes are subject to berthage fees in British Columbia and Ontario, while commercial fishing vessels under 13.5 metres (45 feet) are exempt from fees in Quebec and Atlantic Canada. All commercial fishing vessels are exempt from berthage fees in the Prairie Provinces and the Territories. The regulations also specify higher berthage fees for recreational vessels - no exemptions apply to these vessels. However, berthage fees are generally well below those charged by private marina operators.

The second area of revenue generation stems from monies collected through leases and licences which presently account for about 44 per cent of total SCH revenues. Lease rentals are established at 10 per cent of the appraised value in the case of land and waterlot leases. A rental of 15 per cent of the gross revenues is charged in the case of management leases which are primarily with municipalities. The majority of licence charges for installations such as hoists, gas pumps, hydro-lines, bait sheds, etc., fall into the $35 to $100 per annum range.

Simply stated, the policy for collection of fees at commercial fishing harbours is to recover a portion of the program's operating and maintenance costs. In the case of recreational harbours, the department intends to pursue a more vigorous cost recovery policy in the future with the objective of staying within the local market structure. SCH has proposed an increase in berthage rates, effective April 1, 1985, with a view to recovering more of the cost of providing harbour facilities and services. These proposals are now under Ministerial review.

TABLE 5
PROJECTED REGIONAL REVENUE - FISCAL YEAR 1984/85

Region	Revenue from Leases/Licences ($000)	Revenue from Berthage ($000)	Total Revenue ($000)
Newfoundland	43	20	63
Gulf	160	50	210
Scotia-Fundy	93	50	143
Quebec	10	11	21
Ontario	511	89	600
Western	8	7	15
Pacific	300	1,200	1,500
TOTAL	1,125	1,427	2,552

The SCH program is subject to considerable pressure to provide and maintain facilites in response to locally perceived needs. The scope of current operations is largely in response to perceived socio-economic needs as seen from relatively isolated perspectives.

In response to this environment, funding decisions are highly centralized to ensure system efficiency factors are considered in following directions and developing alternatives. The harbour classification system, proposed levels of services criteria and the SCH information system have been developed to assist managers in their advisory service to Ministers.

The department is now proposing a central assets management group to report to the Deputy Minister to further focus efforts in achieving the efficiency of all assets held by DFO.

OBSERVATIONS

Small Craft Fishing Harbours are an integral part of the overall Fisheries programs which are currently under review. Moreover, especially on the East and West Coasts, the whole question of regional industrial development and alternative employment provides a complex socio-economic context in which alternatives should be judged.

Nonetheless, the disposal of of surplus fishing harbours and of recreational harbours should be considered independently of the socio-economic context.

As indicated previously, Small Craft Harbours has slotted harbours into Classes A, B, C and D, based on vessel activity at each harbour. Of these harbours, 464 (20 per cent of all SCH harbours) fall into the Class D category and are virtually inactive. Over the years, some of these types of harbours have been identified surplus but the majority remain on inventory.

In deciding if such properties should now be declared surplus, several factors should be taken into consideration:

- The market value for these Class D harbours is minimal because they are mostly located in small remote communities where alternate uses for them are virtually non-existent. To date, no interest has been shown by anyone in acquiring these harbours. Additionally, most of the communities involved would not have the financial capability to adapt these harbours to other uses.

- In many instances, waterlots were transferred from provinces to the federal government by Orders-in-Council. Many OIC's contain a reversionary clause stipulating that the property must be returned to the province in its original state if the property ceases to be used for the purpose intended (i.e. harbour usage) or be returned in a reasonable state of repair.

- Whether or not harbours were transferred to the government by OIC, considerable expenditure could be required to return the structure to an acceptable state or remove it completely to avoid future liability.

- Given the above and using a DFO estimated average cost of $50,000 per harbour for removal, the cost to government to divest itself of these harbours could be in the $20 million range. (Specific harbours could cost as much as $1,000,000 to remove).

The study team question the need to continue those SCH operations directed primarily to recreational harbours. SCH contributes only 10 per cent of such berths, and cost recovery policies have until recently represented an element of unfair competition with marina operators and have discouraged private investment. Of the 822 recreational harbours, some 251 have been leased to municipalities who presumably can operate them within a market based fee structure. This practice should be extended in cases where outright divestiture cannot take place. In the interim, cost-recovery should be based on full recovery of market level berthage and other fees. DFO has proposed new tariffs which effectively triple recreational fees commencing in FY 1985-86. These proposals are currently under Ministerial review.

In the case of Commercial Fishing Harbours, SCH serves over 80 per cent of all commercial fishing vessels and thus establishes its rates unilaterally in a monopoly-type market. Fee increases must be considered with due regard to their socio-economic impacts. Much of the fishing fleet is composed of marginally economic small inshore fishing vessels using harbours dispersed geographically. In those regions where fee exemptions apply, most fishermen have become accustomed to this exemption. The expectation is that this will continue - for example, in Atlantic Canada, approximately 95 per cent of all commercial fishing vessels are presently exempt from berthage charges because they are less than 13.5 metres in length.

A regime of full financial self-sufficiency will remove the effective regional subsidies now provided by tariff exemptions. In our view, if a subsidy is required, it should be provided as such, under criteria relating directly to those normally associated with subsidy programs.

DPW provides all design and construction related services to SCH, including pre-engineering studies. DFO considers that better targeting of funds and control of projects could be achieved by increased in-house capability in these areas. This would be achieved at the cost of increasing DFO resources by some 40 person-years, and approximately $1,500,000 in salary costs. Unless a corresponding decrease in DPW resources were linked to this proposal, we doubt its value in terms of cost-effectiveness.

The provision of on-site management is required if only to collect fees. The use of fees-of-office appointees appears to be an efficient response to this requirement. In view of increased fees being proposed, DFO should review its agreements to ensure that increased "commissions" do not disproportionately reduce the value of increased fees.

A number of options are highlighted for consideration by the government as follows:

> Divestiture of all recreational harbours. In the short term, market value leases to provinces and municipalities would be extended beyond the 251 harbours now leased. In the longer term, these leases would be terminated and the harbours ceded to municipalities or private operators at the highest price achievable in the market. Remaining harbours should be closed where no provincial, municipal or private operator is prepared to purchase and operate.
>
> Divestiture all remaining Class D harbours. The plan should quantify the capital costs required and the O&M offsets available, if necessary on a harbour by harbour basis. This will prevent inaction due to overgeneralization of cost penalties caused by a global analysis based on rough estimates.
>
> Review of fisheries harbour fee schedules with regard to regional and vessel size exemptions which now represent a sizeable subsidy. New fee schedules would ideally reflect the full cost of the level of service provided. While this would have clear implications for marginal fisherman, it would also have the effect of moderating demands for higher levels of service in marginal harbours and focus on the advantages of rationalization of the SCH system.

A number of impacts would be experienced by adoption of one or more of these options:

> **Financial.** Recovery of total O&M costs and/or reduction in future O&M costs of some $15-20 million annually. Reduced capital expenditures relating to ongoing rehabilitation and major maintenance of up to $25 million annually depending on eventual inventory after divestiture of recreational and Class D harbours.
>
> **Socio-Economic.** Decisions regarding fishing harbours other than Class D fishing harbours should be taken in the context of broader regional and industrial issues regarding the future of the fishing industry.

GATT. Removal of a "hidden" subsidy and its replacement with a more direct subsidy might have trade implications, particularly with the United States.

Regional. Newfoundland, Maritimes, Prairies and Territorial opposition to removal of SCH exemptions for affected fishermen; and difficulty in transferring assets to provinces where private operators show no interest.

OPTIONS

The study team recommends to the Task Force that the government consider:

- selling recreational harbours at the highest price achievable;

- declaring Class D harbours officially surplus and to be disposed of in the prescribed manner;

- implementing a policy of full financial self-sufficiency for remaining fisheries harbours, as part of plans for rationalization of the fishing industry;

- disposing of all fisheries harbours which cannot meet financial self-sufficiency criteria unless such a harbour is required to support an otherwise isolated community; and

- separate funding for fisheries harbours judged essential for support of an otherwise isolated community, as a social subsidy.

SECTION 11 - AIR TRANSPORTATION PROGRAM

INTRODUCTION

The federal government has taken upon itself to be all things to all people in the ownership and/or operation of what is essentially a commercial business - 154 airports. It has done this by fiat and not because of legislation: there is none which requires the federal government to own or operate airports. As well, it has left little room for the customers (passengers) or suppliers (airlines, etc.) or communities to have a meaningful voice in determining what is needed and how it will be provided. In order to correct the situation, action should be taken which will:

- eliminate to the maximum extent the federal government's real property involvement in airports by transferring responsibility for airport operations and finance to a local authority; and
- maintain federal government regulatory control and financial responsibility for national and international air navigation, aviation safety and security and other applicable international agreements.

BACKGROUND

The Air Transport program represents a major cost to the Canadian taxpayer. For those activities with real property, operating expenses (FY 84/85) were about $850 million against revenues of $650 million, leaving an operating deficit of $200 million. Capital expenditures of more than $400 million brought the total appropriation for the year to over $600 million. The program involves more than 10,000 person-years including 4,700 for airport operations and administration and 5,900 dealing with air navigation. The real property dedicated to these endeavors has an estimated replacement value of approximately $7.5 billion.

The federal government entered the airport 'business' in 1927 when it built two civil airports at St. Hubert and Rimouski, Quebec.

Federal airports then blossomed during the 1930s depression with 50 being constructed as unemployment relief projects.

Nearly all airports, regardless of ownership, were mobilized by the federal government at the start of World War II and large sums of federal monies were spent on enlargement and modifications. At the end of the war, a number of municipalities declined to take their airports back, leaving the operating and financial responsibilities with the senior government.

The federal role has been one of ever increasing operational, regulatory and financial involvement. Ownership, operation, regulation and subsidization cover virtually all licensed airports, from those with only minimal scheduled service to the country's busiest.

There are over 1,200 airports in Canada of which almost 600 are licensed airports, including 154 owned by the federal government. Transport Canada operates 103 of the 154 and this group accounts for over 90 per cent of the total passenger traffic. Twenty-three principal airports were in the Self-Supporting Airports Revolving Fund, while all other airports in which Transport Canada had an ownership or financial involvement were classified as financially dependent airports.

OBSERVATIONS

The existing federal government management structure has three distinct levels of authority over federally operated airports. This creates work duplication and puts excessive overhead on the airports.

The community or region which the airport serves has no meaningful input in the management process.

The "national transportation system" is a key term in the existing operation of Canadian airports. This has led to the notion of national standards which are enshrined in the present operations. It is an attempt to establish uniform standards for facilities and services across the country. There is little recognition of the varying expectations of the numerous localities in which the airports are situated or their ability to pay.

The existence of national labour agreements creates rigidities in pay and work practices which limit the individual airport's opportunities to effectively manage and control its costs - illustrating again the need to recognize local conditions.

Airports are a dynamic enterprise and should be in a position to take timely action to meet their individual opportunities and problems. The public service environment and government organizational and administrative structure does not accommodate this need.

A further 'local vs. national' issue is the matter of aircraft landing fees. Centrally determined national fee schedules may not be responsive to local costs. This is a potential opportunity for additional revenues.

The airport revenue administration has a long history of a two-tier landing fee structure with domestic flights paying lower fees than international. There is no significant difference in the related costs and the two-tier arrangement must be viewed as a subsidy to domestic air transportation. If a subsidy is intended, it should be identified as such rather than disguised in lower airport revenues. At present, the "subsidy" is in excess of $20 million annually.

Under current arrangements, site revenues (excluding Air Transportation Tax) at virtually all Transport Canada airports do not cover operating costs. The resulting deficit is federally funded. This support is made partially through the (implicit) allocation of the Air Transportation Tax and the rest through appropriations. The Air Transportation Tax is special in that the revenues are earmarked for the Air Program in Transport Canada.

Presently, a major portion (roughly 40 per cent) of total revenues at the airports is deemed to be derived from the allocation of the Air Transportation Tax. While this air tax is a critical source of airport revenue, the fact that airports have no control over the levying of the tax represents a continuing threat to real financial self-sufficiency or independence.

In the short term, a mechanism to cross-subsidize the low traffic volume airports from the revenues of the high traffic volume airports is necessary. This cross-subsidization can be provided through allocation of the Air Transportation Tax such that a bigger per capita (enplaning/deplaning passenger) share of tax is given to the low traffic volume airports.

In the view of the study team, an explicit allocation formula defined by legislation is necessary for effective financial planning by airports; however, this should be only an interim measure to assist airports in achieving full financial independence.

The goal should be full user-pay. Airports should set landing and general terminal fees (and other such as a "head fee") in accordance with market forces.

Airports which serve remote and isolated communities or have very low traffic volume, may not be able to reach financial self-sufficiency. If there are compelling reasons to keep these airports operating, the costs should be borne by the local/regional community or recognized as a social subsidy.

The United States levies a ticket tax similar to Canada. However, the resulting revenue is used by the federal government (Federal Aviation Administration) to fund discretionary capital projects on a shared cost basis, and to offset air navigation and aviation safety costs which are borne entirely by the federal government.

Airport lands are not presently being fully used for generation of revenues. This may in part be due to limiting their use to aviation or transportation related purposes. If the rules or practices were relaxed (without in any way compromising safety and security) extra revenue could likely be generated.

Airports are capital intensive operations which must respond to market demand for facilities. Capital expenditures over the next 3 years for the 154 airports will approach $700 million. Because the airports currently compete with a wide variety of other programs for federal government capital appropriations, they face a high degree of uncertainty and unnecessary delay in capital projects. Greater flexibility in tapping sources of capital (i.e. private markets) would allow the projects to be tested in the market place and substantially reduce the uncertainties and delays.

The idea of financial self-sufficiency (revenues exceeding operating and financial costs and capital expenditures) led to the concept of an airport revolving fund in which several airports could be grouped and the group would be self-sufficient (winners carrying losers).

A grouping of 23 of the principal airports was previously thought to be capable of meeting the role of financial independence. Most recently it has been estimated that under the present form of organization and operation, this same group would require appropriations in excess of one billion dollars from the federal treasury over the next 10 years - that is clearly not self-sufficient or independent.

The Airport Revolving Funds have proved to be largely an accounting exercise. It has been necessary to change the participating units in the funds in order to meet the previously established bottom line. This is seen in the demise of the group of 23 and creation of the group of nine selected airports. The revolving fund does not address the real issue of how each airport can attain the desired status of financial independence.

An examination of the approach by other western countries to local or regional control of airport operations, reveals a major degree of "decentralization". Canada is notable by the extent to which it has centralized airport ownership and operations. In general, other countries vest a high level of operating and financial autonomy in local authorities. Central government financial involvement ranges from zero to capital cost-sharing programs. The management, operations and finance are largely modelled on private sector commercial principles.

Financial self-sufficiency for commercial airports is a reality viz. an overwhelming majority of United States commercial airports. In Canada, the Edmonton Municipal Airport (EMA) stands out as a very clear example of a non-federal government airport which is financially self-sufficient. This airport does not receive any part of the Federal Air Transportation Tax. EMA covers all operating, debt and capital costs through direct revenues at the airport. It receives no subsidies from the City of Edmonton. Instead, the airport contributes upwards of $2 million annually to the city.

The actions which are described below would represent a very significant change in the federal government's role. Implementation of the change would likely require extensive involvement by the major interest groups at each airport, e.g. all levels of government, airline industry, users, unions, etc. There are multiple courses of action which could be taken to achieve the objective. It is imperative that the objective not be altered as a result of transitional or intermediate steps.

In view of its analysis, the study team recommends to the Task Force that the government consider making a fundamental change in airport policy from ownership and centralized public service operation to one of non-federal ownership and operation.

In the short term, the federal government should consider, through legislation, a weighted allocation and payment to airports of the Air Transportation Tax. The eventual disposition of the tax should be addressed by the Transportation Task Force.

All airports would be locally managed and where possible, locally owned or under local custody, with each airport entity required to be financially self-sufficient (covering all operating costs, debt service and capital expenditures). The experience with Harbour Commissions is a clear indication that this objective is attainable.

Financial self-sufficiency would not be attainable immediately for many airports, but the goal should be set and steps taken to begin the process.

Airports which cannot be expected to reach financial self-sufficiency within a reasonable time would be re-examined. If there are compelling reasons to keep any of these airports operating, the costs should be borne by the local/regional community or recognized as a social subsidy.

It all comes down to recognizing that airports are an integral part of the local or regional financial, commercial and social infrastructure. If they are to be truly successful they must be responsive to local conditions and opportunities and not constrained by a central government. Local management should determine how revenues are to be secured and what costs are incurred.

SELF-SUPPORTING AIRPORTS

Transport Canada

OBJECTIVE

To develop and operate those international and national airports included in the Self-Supporting Airports Revolving Fund (ARF) in a financially self-sufficient mode.

RESULTS/BENEFICIARIES

Twenty-three principal airports (comprising the Revolving Fund, 1979-85) across Canada (see Appendix A) - eight international, nine national, six regional, all owned and operated by Transport Canada. These airports handle 86 per cent of all passenger traffic in Canada.

The major clients/users are the domestic and international air carriers as well as the general aviation community. The major beneficiaries are the travelling public, the business community (especially tourism, cargo and mail), and other aviation related industries.

AUTHORITY

BNA Act
National Transportation Act
Aeronautics Act

These define the specific responsibility of the federal government as follows:

a. provision for aviation safety and aviation services;

b. provision of air navigation services and for the integration of air navigation facilities and services with airport development; and

c. facilitation of the inter-provincial movement of people and goods.

The Aeronautics Act gives the Minister the authority to construct and maintain all government aerodromes and air stations, where he so designates.

RESOURCES (millions of current dollars)

	84/85
Operating Expenses (excl. depreciation)	$355
Capital Expenditures	
- real property	$115
- other (est.)	$ 20
Revenue (incl.air tax)	$415
Person-Years (at airports)	2,535

REAL PROPERTY ASSETS

Estimated Real Property Replacement Value: $4.1 billion

Inventory	**No.**	**Area (000s)sq.m.**
Air Terminal Buildings	25	657
Runways	61	8,151
Taxiways	216	3,713
Aprons	85	4,582

For further details, see Appendix A

Over the next three fiscal years about $384 million in real property capital expenditures (not necessarily approved) will be required at these 23 airports.

PROGRAM DESCRIPTION

The Administrator of the Canadian Air Transport Administration (CATA) has vested the Regional Administrators (RA) with line responsibility for delivering the Air Program and the Assistant Administrator, Airports and Construction Services (AAA) with the functional authority for the airports program (planning elements Self-Supporting Airports and Financially Dependent Airports).

The AAA has several functional directors in the areas of airports security and services, airport facilities, marketing, etc. At the regional level, the RA delegates delivery of the airports program to a Regional Director (Airports and Properties) and a Director (Engineering and Architecture).

The following breakdown summarizes the regional and NHQ Person-Year resources in support of the total airports activity:

	Program Management and Administration	**Design, Construction and Technical**	**Total**
Atlantic	67	71	138
Quebec	67	76	143
Ontario	70	57	127
Central	75	56	131
Western	94	66	160
Pacific	69	62	131
NCR (HQ)	333	63	396
	775	451	1,226

The design, construction and technical people spend 15 to 25 per cent of their time on the real property aspects of the air navigational services activity.

Most of the salary costs associated with the 1,226 PYs, along with a smaller portion of other management overhead, are recovered from the Self-Supporting Airports.

Airport real property assets are as follows:

a. Terminal buildings (includes automobile parking facilities, loading bridges, heating plants etc.);
b. Air traffic, terminal control and flight information facilities;
c. Airport roads, bridges and tunnels;
d. Runways, taxiways, aprons and airfield lighting;
e. Utilities; and
f. Lands (serviced and unserviced).

An airport operates primarily in a commercial environment. To facilitate a more commercial operation with recovery of costs and improved management accountability, these 23 airports comprised the Airport Revolving Fund as restructured on 1 April, 1979. This new fund had a statutory drawing authority of $80 million. In addition, $650 million in outstanding loans were deleted with the passing of the Adjustment of Accounts Act in 1980.

Real property revenues are derived from landing and general terminal fees, space letting, concessions, parking and land rental. The Air Transportation tax is presently a major source of revenue. It is collected by Revenue Canada and 74 per cent is allocated to the Revolving Fund and then to each of the 23 airports based on the relative number of passengers taking off and landing at each airport. This portion of the tax represents about 40 per cent of the total revenues credited to the Revolving Fund.

The direct O&M expenditures which are charged to the Revolving Fund for the 23 airports are in support of the following on-site services:

a. Policing and security;
b. Crash, firefighting and rescue for all aircraft emergencies;
c. Terminal services, including the processing of passengers and baggage, and apron control systems;
d. Water, power, gas, steam, sewage treatment facilities;
e. Maintenance of all facilities; and
f. Property management, marketing, contract administration, finance, etc.

The 23 airports in the Revolving Fund are forecast to show consolidated results for FY 84/85 as follows:

		($ millions)
Revenue (including air tax)		**415**
Expenses		
Direct O&M	191	
Air terminal control	85	
Management overhead	54	
Grants in lieu of taxes	23	
Interest and depreciation	64	417
NET PROFIT (loss)		(2)

See Appendix B for details by airport.

The cash requirements of the same 23 airports for FY 84/85 are estimated as follows:

	($ millions)
Cash from operations	
Depreciation	63
Operating loss	(2)
	61
Capital expenditures (net of SCRPP funding of $27)	108
Net requirements	47

HISTORY OF AIRPORT DEVELOPMENT

The federal government's first involvement in air operations, was under the Air Board Act of 1919. This act provided for the "acquisition of aerodromes (for) the provision of emergency landing grounds". Terminal landing grounds for urban areas were to be provided by the inhabitants of those areas, with the air administration to "determine the essentials of good aerodromes ... and advise municipalities as to the selection and upkeep of grounds".

The federal government built its first two civil airports in 1927 at St. Hubert and Rimouski, Que. These were under exceptional circumstances: St. Hubert was constructed to support a system of Empire Air Communications under international agreement and Rimouski was built as a critical east-west link for experimental air mail services.

This was followed by a major policy decision in 1928 by the federal government to develop the Trans-Canada Airway to provide freight and passenger services from coast to coast. This marked the beginning of growing government involvement in the construction and operation of airports.

In 1929, the airport-capital assistance policy was instituted to provide grants to municipal airports towards the cost of installing lights. During the depression of the 1930s, 50 new federal airports and landing fields were built under the Unemployment Relief Project.

Several other grants were instituted in the mid-1930s to assist municipalities and the provincial governments to upgrade runways, navigational facilities and terminals.

In 1937, the federal government reluctantly purchased Uplands airport, enlarged it and finally operated it for Trans-Canada Airway requirements. This breached the existing policy that the operation of urban airports was a municipal responsibility, and the next year saw North Bay and London being developed federally.

In 1939, the municipal airports were taken over by the federal government for war purposes. They were leased for the duration of the war, enlarged and modified as required. After the war, most leased airports were returned to the municipalities. Some municipalities refused to accept the airports and where these were on the Trans-Canada Airway routes, the Department of Transport continued to operate them.

The department continued to encourage municipal operation of airports in order to enlist the backing of the municipal authorities and the local people. In 1946, Transport introduced an operating subsidy to muncipalities to encourage airport development. In 1958, the department extended its subsidy policy, but also accepted responsibility for the construction, operation and maintenance of mainline airports (those with at least scheduled DC3 service). Halifax and Edmonton were two major airports built during this period.

Into the 1960s, although the policy was still to encourage municipal airport operation, the choice before the communities was to operate the airports directly with some federal subsidies, or to have them run federally at substantial financial gain to the communities. The results were inevitable.

In summary, the federal government has taken on itself an overwhelming role in the ownership and operation of airports through appropriations, not by legislation. The government has done this without a clear definition of its objectives.

There are currently over 1,200 airports in Canada, of which almost 600 are licensed. The federal government owns 154 airports and operates 103 of these (of which 23 are the principal airports covered by this report). The remaining airports are operated by provincial and municipal governments, municipal commissions and others (including DND, DIAND, Flying Clubs, etc.). Airports operated by

Transport Canada account for over 90 per cent of the total passenger volume.

OBSERVATIONS

The concept of an Airports Revolving Fund (ARF) arose from the idea of financial self-sufficiency as a group. The ARF comprising the 23 airports was established in 1979 and was thought to be capable of being self-sufficient as a group. However, in June 1984, it was forecast that the cash requirement of the Revolving Fund would exceed the $80 million statutory drawing authority by about $95 million in 1984/85 (the current forecast is that the drawing authority will not be exceeded, at least for 1984/85).

For the period 1985/95, it was estimated that the total appropriations for the 23 airports would have been in excess of $1.3 billion (clearly not self-supporting).

Effective 1 April 1985, a restructured Airports Revolving Fund was set up to cover the nine major hub airports:

- Calgary
- Dorval (Montreal)
- Edmonton
- Halifax
- Mirabel (Montreal)
- Ottawa
- Toronto
- Vancouver
- Winnipeg

It was also recognized that taken individually, several of these nine airports would not be self-sustaining without annual appropriations (for capital expenditures and compensation for activities of a non-commercial nature[1]).

The change in the ARF may resolve the administrative problem but of itself, it does not address the increasing need under the current operating arrangements for annual appropriations to meet the cash requirements for airports.

Several features of the current management structure makes it very difficult to reduce costs. These are discussed below:

---

1 items such as landing fees for state/military aircraft and lower domestic landing fees.

a. The CATA organization to support this planning element has three primary organizational levels: the airport level, the Regional headquarters level (830 PY) and the Ottawa headquarters level (396 PY). The Task Force on Airport Management[2], concluded that the present management overhead created duplication of work and put excessive overhead on the airports. It estimated that a "reduction of 70 per cent" in this overhead was possible if a simplified organizational structure with full local autonomy were implemented.

   The removal of the principal airports from the federal government system would eliminate the need for checks, balances and controls which are prevalent in the federal bureaucracy.

   The study team in its interviews continually received complaints about five to six levels of authority for almost every item, the lower four levels having the ability to say no, but not yes, and if any one of these lower levels denied approval, that was the end of the process.

b. Central planning for airports provides a more uniform level of service, irrespective of the operating costs and the ability of the airports to afford it. Level of service is defined more on a national standards basis and less on the basis of the user's ability to pay or his need.

   A more aggressive approach towards user pay is preferable as it would include a process for direct user involvement in decisions on airport operating and capital expenditures. This would provide the necessary counterbalance in determining the appropriate level of service and level of capital expenditures.

c. Labour agreements negotiated on a national basis for all Transport Canada employees apply at very large and at very small sites. As a result, high labour costs and high levels of specialization are imposed on very small sites. This hampers the

---

2 There were a number of reports, dated 1979-81, which were produced by the Task Force on Airport Management, reporting to the Air Administrator (See footnote 3).

ability of local airports to attain cost-efficiencies. (For example, the study team found that at airports not operated by Transport Canada, firemen can be used extensively for duties other than as firemen.)

d. The direct public service operation does not create a financial environment in which the incentives exist to increase revenues and minimize costs. An airport operates primarily in a commercial environment and to minimize costs the airport must be able to react to opportunities or problems without undue delay.

On the one hand, airport managers are burdened by an increasing flow of paper; on the other, timely decisions cannot be taken because of delays in the approval process.

The study team also heard many complaints about having to order equipment, etc. from the standard equipment list, and it did not always fit the need and took an agonizingly long time to get; but with the necessary authority, the appropriate equipment for the job could have been acquired in one or two weeks at little or no additional cost - possibly even a saving.

The study team was impressed with the enthusiasum expressed by many airport managers as to what they could do if they were not burdened with the paper flow and the delay and restraints imposed by central management.

So long as on-site airport management is not challenged to be self-supporting, the need for ever increasing federal funding will continue.

Under current arrangements, site revenues (excluding the Air Transportation Tax) at virtually all Canadian airports do not cover operating costs and continued federal government support will be necessary. This support is made partially through the (implicit) allocation of the Air Transportation Tax and the rest through appropriations. The Air Transportation Tax is special in that the revenues are earmarked for the Air Program in Transport Canada.

If the revenue generation at the site or the tax revenues can be increased, the requirement for general appropriations is consequently reduced. Various options for these are as follows:

a. There are different ways of restructuring the Air Transportation Tax. Removal of the ceiling on the tax would raise an estimated $50 million annually.

b. Domestic flights have traditionally been charged lower landing fees than international flights, reflecting government support for domestic transportation. Removal of the differential would raise about $460 million in the 10-year period 1985-1995, rising annually in steps from $23 million in 1985 to $60 million in 1995.

c. The uniform landing and general terminal fees set by Headquarters prevents airports from adjusting them to meet costs. This inflexible approach does not allow for the possibility of increasing revenues.

d. Airport revenues from commercial operations are also limited by the practice of limiting airport land use to aviation purposes. It can be argued that if these rules were relaxed, without in any way compromising safety and security, extra revenues could be generated. No estimate of this extra revenue is available.

e. Government policies have constrained the ability of airport management to aggressively pursue the revenue maximization goal. For example, for the 3-year period of 1982/83 to 1984/85, the fee increases which normally were 15 per cent annually, were limited to 6 per cent and 5 per cent by the administered prices program. This resulted in foregone revenues of approximately $30 million.

f. Currently, there exists only limited internal cost recovery from other governmental users of airports, such as Coast Guard and DND. If these costs were recovered, the revenue could be increased at airports by about $6-10 million annually.

From the above, it is evident that there exist several avenues for increasing airport revenues. The study team believes these should be pursued in a decentralized fashion, with local airport management deciding how to proceed.

Airport revenues are very sensitive to the traffic volume as measured by the enplaning/deplaning (E/D) passenger count. In the group of 23 airports, the E/D passengers varied from under 200,000 at Gander to over 14 million at Toronto. Only the top few airports with a large traffic volume showed any cash surplus; other airports were in a deficit situation. The Airport Revolving Fund (ARF) provided a mechanism to cross subsidize the low traffic volume airports from the revenues of the high traffic volume airports; this form of cross-subsidization is not the appropriate solution.

In the short term, some form of cross-subsidization will be necessary in the Canadian airport system but to achieve self-sufficiency through a businesslike approach to airport planning, an assured source of revenue must be made available for each airport.

Presently, a major portion (40 per cent) of total revenue at the principal airports is deemed to be derived from the allocation of the Air Transportation Tax. The continuance of this allocation, through legislation, and a payment of same to the airports, is necessary in the short term to provide the necessary revenues at the airport level.

In the longer term, however, the ability of airport management to maintain financial self-sufficiency or independence could be threatened by the lack of control over the legislation levying such tax.

We believe that there should initially be some form of explicit cross-subsidization through a weighted allocation and payment of the air tax; however, this should only be an interim measure to assist airports in achieving full financial independence.

A method of explicit cross subsidy, which this study team supports, was proposed in the Report of the Task Force on Airport Management. In their proposal, the air transportation tax would be allocated to airports by the following (per passenger) formula:

(77-78$)

$8.00 for first 200,000 E/D passengers
$1.60 for next 800,000
$ .46 beyond 1 million

According to the report, the ARF method "... does not recognize that airports function as a system nor does it recognize that smaller sites contribute to the activity at larger sites and that smaller sites have higher unit costs and fewer sources of revenues." We believe that a similar weighted allocation formula should be developed.

The goal should be full user-pay. Airports should set landing and general terminal fees (and other fees such as a "head tax") in accordance with market forces.

The present reliance on appropriations creates uncertainty in airport management and capital expenditures are made not in a timely fashion according to the real property requirement but more on the basis of availability of funds and on other government objectives. According to Transport Canada estimates, a total of $2.5 billion for the 23 principal airports is required in the next 10 years from 1985/86 to 1994/95, only part of which will be financed through airport cash surpluses.

The substantial requirement for government outlays under the present system should be met through alternative means. Locally constituted bodies to run independent airports in a commercial fashion could open the doors to other sources of funding.

The federal government has become involved in the development of a national system of airports. It has made a huge investment in these facilities and it is, therefore, logical to expect that the government will play a significant role in the protection of the integrity of the national system of airports. In addition, the federal government must retain the right to intervene where national objectives are paramount, such as war, the protection of human and language rights, and accessibility to transportation by remote communities. The study team believes it should intervene only when market forces and general economic factors do not produce the required change. The principal responsibility of the federal government should be in providing the air navigation services and for the regulation and enforcement of safety.

The study team recommends to the Task Force that the government should consider limiting its role to the following:

- provision for aviation safety and aviation security;
- responsibility for air navigation facilities and integration of services with airport development;
- facilitation of an international and interprovincial movement of goods and peoples;
- responsibility for international agreements in the area of safety, security and protection of environment and commerce; and
- responsibility and right to intervene in the operation and management of the airports where the need arises due to considerations related to national interest, such as a national emergency.

The federal role can be maintained without federal ownership or operation of airports. Moreover, there is no statutory obligation for the Minister of Transport to own or operate any airports.

During the transitional stage to local autonomy, the government would retain the responsibility for the collection of the air transportation tax and for its weighted allocation and payment to individual airports. This would assist airports by assuring a certain source of revenues as they plan and move towards full independence.

Having introduced the concept of financial independence for Canadian airports, it would be useful at this time to examine the role of the national government in other western countries. The following summary of the United States, British, German, French and Australian airport systems is taken from a DOT report, the Federal Role in Airports (May 1980):

a. In all systems examined, the central government retains responsibility for aviation safety and air navigation services.

b. The central government operates airports in very few nations.

c. There is a high degree of local involvement in most nations.

d. Central government appropriations on airports range from zero (for ground-side facilities) in the United States to cost sharing programs for local airports in Australia.

e. In all systems examined, the central government retains responsibility for the regulation of air carriers and, therefore, controls the role of the airports.

f. Most nations have airport legislation defining the role of the central government and of airport operators.

g. In most nations the major airports are financed commercially and have a commercial type management structure.

With respect to Item e., it should be noted that the trend now is towards deregulation.

The above survey underscores the fact that Canada is alone in its centralized public service approach to airport management. Moreover, our principal airports, to say nothing of our regional and local airports, are particularly dependent upon central government appropriations.

Current developments in Britain, Japan and the United States reinforce the observation that Canada is not moving in the same direction:

a. The British government has stated its intention to extend the involvement of the private sector in the management and financing of airports. The Transport Committee of the House of Commons has concluded that an increase in private sector investment would be beneficial.

b. The United States Secretary of Transportation has introduced a bill to create a regional airport authority to acquire Washington National Airport and Dulles International Airport from the federal government. This would remove the only two major commercial airports presently operated by the United States government. The commission advising the Secretary of Transportation recommended that the new authority assume any existing debt and repay the United States Treasury over a period of 30 years.

c. Airlines serving Denver have presented a plan to build the most modern airport in the United States by 1995. The airport would replace the existing airport and the total cost of some three billion dollars (including land acquisition) would be financed by the airport-authority through the bond market.

d. The new Kansai International Airport in Japan will be owned and administered by a newly formed separate entity. Two-thirds of the share capital will be provided by the national government, one-sixth by local government and one-sixth by independent private companies. It is thought that this system will enable the airport to establish links with the local community, utilize the energy of the private sector and allow an enterprise form of management.

Private sector participation in airport funding is clearly the trend outside Canada.

Financial self-sufficiency for commercial airports is a reality viz. an overwhelming majority of United States commercial airports. In Canada, the Edmonton Municipal Airport (EMA) stands out as a very clear example of a non-federal government airport which is financially self-sufficient. This airport does not receive any part of the federal Air Transportation Tax. EMA covers all operating, debt and capital costs through direct revenues at the airport. It receives no subsidies from the City of Edmonton. Instead, the airport contributes upwards of $2 million annually to the City.

Edmonton Municipal Airport revenues include a form of passenger head fee (charged to the air carriers) which is one of its major sources of revenue. Although EMA does not pay the federal government for air traffic control and other air navigation expenses associated with the airport operation, the imputed cost of these services is only a fraction of the net income of the airport. The number of staff at EMA is reported to be only one-third what it is at comparable Transport Canada airports. Edmonton Municipal

Airport is in most key areas similar to the United States airport commissions.

The success of the Edmonton form of airport management was also evident to this study team in their visit and inspection of United States airports. Local responsibility and accountability for all aspects of airport management, compliance with licensing regulations, user pay, and financial self-sufficiency were the rule.

Within the Air Administration, there have been a number of internal studies[3] by the Task Force on Airport Management on the viability of decentralizing authority and maximizing local autonomy. The Final Report by the Task Force recommended an Airport Crown Corporation concept for each of the 23 principal airports; however, the Task Force was constrained to federal ownership of airports. The recommendations of the Task Force were considered but never accepted.

We have studied the Task Force and other reports, visited airports both in the United States and Canada, and consulted officials from both the Department of Transport and the United States Federal Aviation Administration, as well as other airport specialists. We conclude that the major issue for Canadian airports is centralized control over airport management versus local autonomy. All the evidence points to the desirability and need for local autonomy.

Therefore, the study team recommends to the Task Force that the following conclusions be considered:

a. Airports should be locally owned and managed;

b. Air traffic control services should remain a federal responsibility and airports should not bear these costs;

---

3 We refer to the following three reports:

a. Task Force on Airport Management, Progress Report, July 1979.
b. The Airport Authority Concept, Task Force on Airport Management, January 1980.
c. The Financial Proposals of the Task Force on Airport Management, August 1980.

c. Federal controls on airport licensing, safety and security should continue;

d. All airport revenues should eventually be under the control of the airport operator and they should not be dependent on the federal Air Transportation Tax. In the short-term, the federal goverment should ensure, through legislation, a weighted allocation and payment of the Air Transportation Tax (as noted earlier in this report;

e. The airport operator should have the freedom to raise revenues through various mechanisms such as passenger head fees;

f. The airport should be financially self-sufficient for operating expenses, for debt servicing and for capital projects;

g. The airport operator should be free to raise capital from the public, lending institutions, etc.; and

h. The airport operator should be able to enter into agreements with the air carriers, as is the case in the United States, to secure loans or bonds;

It all comes down to recognizing that airports are an integral part of the local or regional financial, commercial and social infrastructure. If they are to be truly successful they must be responsive to local conditions and opportunities and not constrained by a central government. Local management should determine how revenues are to be secured and what costs are incurred.

What will the federal government get out of local airport autonomy? Besides the increased cost-efficiency and revenue generation at the airport level, the government will be able to avoid the potential liability for continuing airport cash shortfalls. Annual savings in excess of $50 million (without taking into account interest savings on future indebtedness) are possible. In addition, it may be possible for the federal government to realize a return on its sunk costs for some airports through the terms and conditions relating to the transfers of ownership.

The options described below would represent a very significant change in the federal government's role in airports. Implementation of the change would likely require extensive involvement by every major interest group at each airport e.g. all levels of government, airline industry, users, unions, etc. There are multiple courses of action which may be taken to achieve the objective. It is imperative that the process not be deflected by transitional or intermediate steps.

OPTIONS

The study team recommends to the Task Force that the federal government consider:

- adopting an airport policy which in both form and substance requires local ownership and operation of commercial airports. If such an approach were adopted, the transfer of ownership or custody and the management of all federally owned airports to a designated local entity would be made on the condition that each airport be required to become financially self-sufficient for all costs, capital expenditures, financing, and debt service;

- where financial self-sufficiency is not immediately attainable by any particular airport, steps should be considered by the federal government to provide the minimum financial assistance required for the airport to attain selfsufficiency in the shortest possible time; and

- airports which cannot be expected to reach financial self-sufficiency within a reasonable time should be re-examined. If there are compelling reasons to keep any of these airports operating, the costs should be recognized as a social subsidy. All others should be promptly closed or divested.

APPENDIX A

SELF-SUPPORTING AIRPORTS FINANCIAL SUMMARY ($ Millions)

Airports by Region	Estimated Replacement Value	Operating Expenses	Revenues	84/85 Real Property Capital Expend.
Charlottetown	47.5	4.4	1.0	4.5
Fredericton	34.9	4.4	1.4	.6
Gander	204.4	12.5	2.4	3.3
Halifax	121.7	14.1	12.3	3.0
Moncton	83.9	6.7	1.7	.4
Saint John	39.2	4.9	1.4	3.4
St. John's	92.4	8.5	3.9	3.5
Sydney	51.9	4.4	1.3	.3
Atlantic	675.9	59.9	25.3	19.0
Dorval	409.0	37.8	51.4	20.3
Mirabel	459.0	36.3	23.0	1.3
Quebec	55.4	9.5	4.8	1.4
Quebec	923.4	83.6	79.2	23.0
London	61.3	5.6	1.8	1.9
Ottawa	209.4	17.0	16.6	18.9
Toronto	684.2	66.1	131.8	9.7
Windsor	45.2	3.9	1.9	2.7
Ontario	1,000.0	92.6	152,1	33.2
Regina	55.9	7.3	4.5	15.6
Saskatoon	89.0	6.9	4.5	.9
Thunder Bay	35.8	5.9	3.0	5.0
Winnipeg	290.5	19.2	19.1	5.7
Central	471.2	39.3	31.1	27.2
Calgary	333.8	26.7	40.4	3.4
Edmonton	189.5	17.0	21.1	2.5
Western	523.3	43,7	61.5	5.9
Vancouver	476.3	29.5	61.8	5,0
Victoria	67.3	6.3	4.3	2.0
Pacific	543.6	35.8	66.1	7.0
TOTAL	4,136.8	354.8	415.4	115.4

Note

1. The O&M expenditures include:

   Direct O&M ($191.5)
   Air traffic control charges ($84.6)
   Management and specialized support services ($54.3)
   Grants in Lieu of Taxes ($23.4)
   Interest ($0.9)

   but exclude depreciation ($62.8).

For FY 84/85, an additional appropriation of $121.7 million was made to cover Special Recovery Capital Projects Program and other capital expenditures. This was comprised of $26.7 million SCRPP funding plus $95 million to cover the possible shortfall beyond the $80 million statutory drawing authority (noted earlier in this report).

APPENDIX B

SELF-SUPPORTING AIRPORTS PROFIT-LOSS STATEMENT ($ Millions)

Airports by Region	Revenues	Direct O&M Grants in Lieu of Taxes	Net before Other Items
Charlottetown	1.0	2.1	(1.0)
Fredericton	1.4	2.0	(0.6)
Gander	2.4	7.9	(5.6)
Halifax	12.3	8.3	4.1
Moncton	1.7	3.1	(1.5)
Saint John	1.4	2.4	(0.9)
St. John's	3.9	4.7	(0.8)
Sydney	1.3	2.2	(0.9)
Dorval	51.4	25.1	26.3
Mirabel	23.0	26.1	(3.1)
Quebec	4.8	4.2	0.6
London	1.8	2.3	(0.5)
Ottawa	16.6	9.4	7.2
Toronto	131.8	44.8	87.1
Windsor	1.9	2.1	(0.2)
Regina	4.5	3.6	0.9
Saskatoon	4.5	3.1	1.5
Thunder Bay	3.0	2.4	0.7
Winnipeg	19.1	10.9	8.2
Calgary	40.4	16.9	23.5
Edmonton	21.1	10.6	10.5
Vancouver	61.8	17.7	44.1
Victoria	4.3	3.1	1.3

Net before interest and other items			200.5
Other items:			
management overhead	54.3		
terminal control	84.6		
interest	0.9		
		(139.9)	
Net before depreciation		60.6	
Depreciation		(62.8)	
Net operating profit (loss)		(2.2)	

FINANCIALLY DEPENDENT AIRPORTS

Transport Canada

OBJECTIVE

To develop and operate a network of regional and local airports that enables all areas of Canada to have reasonable access to air transportation.

To recover costs from airport users to the extent feasible.

RESULTS/BENEFICIARIES

One hundred and thirty-one regional and local airports are owned and/or operated by Transport Canada. These airports handle 7 per cent of the passenger traffic in Canada.

Over 150 airports are owned and operated by other jurisdictions which receive subsidies from Transport Canada.

The major clients/users are the domestic air carriers as well as the general aviation community. The major beneficiaries are the local communities which use the airports.

AUTHORITY

BNA Act
National Transportation Act
Aeronautics Act

These define the specific responsibility of the federal government as follows:

a. provision for aviation safety;
b. provision of air navigation services and for the integration of air navigation facilities and services with airport development;
c. facilitation of the inter-provincial movement of people and goods.

There is no statutory obligation on the Minister to own or operate airports. However, the Aeronautics Act gives the Minister the authority to construct and maintain all government aerodromes and air stations, if he so chooses.

AGREEMENTS

Nouveau-Québec Agreement
Labrador Coast Airstrips Construction Program Agreement
Agreement Between N.W.T., Yukon, DIAND, Environment, and Transport.

RESOURCES (millions of current dollars)

	84/85
Operating Expenses	$134
Capital Expenditures	
- real property	$113
- equipment (est.)	$ 26
Grants and Contributions	$ 47
Revenue (incl. air tax)	$ 97
Person-Years	
- at airports	913
- headquarters (total airports)	1226

REAL PROPERTY ASSETS

Estimated Real Property Replacement Value: $3.4 billion.

Inventory	No.	Area (000s) sq.m.
Air Terminal Buildings/Shelters	80	55
Runways	155	11,825
Taxiways	237	2,099
Aprons	115	3,999

Note - The inventory is incomplete, and includes information for only 87 airports.

PROGRAM DESCRIPTION

Transport Canada owns and is responsible for the operation of 131 regional and local airports, including the national airports located at Yellowknife and Whitehorse.

Financial assistance is provided to regional and local airports operated by other parties.

Transport Canada's Management Services Unit provides for the regional and NHQ person-year resources in support of the total airports activity, including self-supporting airports.

The following table summarizes the financial situation of the 131 Financially Dependent Airports (FDA) owned by Transport Canada, as of FY84/85:

($Millions)

Region	**Estimated Replacement Value**	**O&M**	**Revenues**	**FY 84/85 Real Property Capital Expend.**	**FY 85/88 Real Property Capital Expend.**
Atlantic	$ 707.0	$12.3	$ 7.4	$ 7.8	$ 30.8
Quebec	791.7	12.2	5.6	22.9	57.6
Ontario	282.1	5.4	5.1	37.1	42.2
Central	436.8	12.4	2.6	6.7	61.9
Western	714.3	16.0	7.1	26.3	92.1
Pacific	514.1	10.6	7.2	12.4	28.1
TOTALS	$3,445.9	$69.0	$35.1	$113.2	$282.7

The annual costs of operating the FDAs are about twice the revenues generated on-site (including allocation of the Air Transportation Tax).

The resources expended in the departmental operation of the 131 FDAs as well as the regional and headquarters management for the total airports activity were as follows:

Region	FDA PY	FDA On-Site O&M ($Millions)	All Airports Headquarters PY	All Airports Headquarters O&M ($Millions)
Atlantic	207	$12.3	138	$ 9.4
Quebec	169	12.2	143	7.2
Ontario	81	5.4	127	5.9
Central	41	12.4	131	7.4
Western	219	16.0	160	6.8
Pacific	196	10.6	131	7.2
NCR (NHQ)			396	20.7
TOTALS	913	$69.0	1,226	$64.6
Recovery		$35.1		$49.6
Net Cost		$34.0		$15.1

The Financially Dependent Airports planning element is credited with the following revenues and recoveries (FY 84/85):

a. Revenues from the airports operated by the department, totalling $35.1 million (including $13.2 million allocated from the Air Transportation Tax).

b. The portion of the Air Transportation Tax corresponding to airports not owned or operated by the department, totalling $12.0 million.

c. A recovery from the Airports Revolving Fund to pay for the management services provided by the FDA planning element to the Self-Supporting Airports, totalling $49.6 million; this is applied against the $64.6 million total cost of management services.

d. A recovery of $0.5 million from the Environmental Services Program for weather services.

These totalled $97.2 million for the entire planning element.

A comparison between the Self-Supporting Airports and the Financially Dependent Airports owned by Transport Canada may be instructive:

	23 Self-Supporting Airports	131 Financially Dependent Airports
Percentage of total traffic	86%	7%
On-site PY Resources	2,535	913
Direct O&M Expend.	$191M	$69M
Revenues	$415M	$35M
FY84/85 Real Property Capital Expend.	$115M	$113M
FY 85/88 Real Property Capital Expend.	$384M	$283M
Estimated Replacement Value	$4.1b	$3.4b

Notes

a. Revenues include implicit allocation of the Air Transportation Tax.

b. Direct O&M excludes air traffic control charges, management overhead, depreciation, grants in lieu of taxes or interest normally included as expenses in the Airports Revolving Fund.

Thus the 23 Self-Supporting Airports had 12 times the passenger traffic and revenue of the 131 FDAs owned by Transport Canada. On the other hand, the direct operating expenditures were only three-fold, and the capital investment is only one-third higher, in terms of both estimated replacement value and planned capital expenditures.

The planning element Financially Dependent Airports also provides grants and contributions to support airports which are operated through other jurisdictions. The number of airports thus supported are as follows:

a. fourteen airports under the Nouveau-Québec Agreement (27 September 1983);

b. fourteen airports under the Labrador Coast Airstrips Construction Program Agreement (12 July 1982);

c. forty-nine airports in the NWT and Yukon under the Arctic Airports Agreement (25 October 1978);

d. thirty-eight airports in the south, covered under the 1972 Financial Assistance Policy;

e. for FY84/85:

   1. fifty-five under the Financial Assistance Program for Local/Local Commercial Airports, Transport Canada,

   2. twenty under the Special Employment Initiatives Program, CEIC (1984/85),

   3. seven under the Laprade Envelope, EMR (1984/85),

   4. eight under the Special Recovery Program, MSERD (1984/85),

   5. Ste-Anne-des-Monts, Quebec under ARFA/MFRA, Transport (1984/85), and

   6. Fogo Island, Nfld, Newfoundland Transport Envelope, Transport Canada (1984/85).

The Northern Quebec/Nouveau Québec Airports Development program is a joint federal/provincial program to develop airports in the James Bay and Northern Quebec area. Infrastructure at three Cree and 11 Inuit communities will be covered. The infrastructure at the Cree communities will be totally funded and owned by Transport Canada but operated by the Cree. The province will own and operate the facilities at the Inuit communities. The Inuit group are funded on a 60/40 (federal-provincial) cost-sharing basis.

Under the Labrador Coast Airstrips Construction Program Agreement, the federal government will contribute 100 per cent of the actual direct construction costs of aviation facilities in nine Labrador coast communities. Airstrips already constructed or under construction in five other communities are also included for upgrading purposes. Eleven of the 14 will be operated by Labrador and the remainder by Transport Canada.

The Memorandum of Understanding between the Northwest Territories, Yukon, Department of Indian and Northern Affairs, Department of the Environment, and the Department of Transport stipulates that:

a. DOT provide and fund air transportation facilities and equipment, fund the maintenance and operation of airports, and fund training programs.

b. DIAND fund the provision of the joint community airport maintenance equipment, etc.

Basically, the northern airports would be operated by NWT and Yukon, but funded by DOT.

The Financial Assistance Policy for the 38 southern local airports provides financial assistance equal to 100 per cent of approved capital expenditures as well as 100 per cent of operating deficits up to a level approved by DOT in accordance with certain criteria.

The Local/Local Commercial Financial Assistance Program provides funds in accordance with Ministerial direction, for planning of airport capital improvement projects at local or local commercial airports not owned by the federal government.

The following table outlines the grants and contributions for FY84/85:

Operating Contributions	**($Millions)**
Local-Northern	$ 4.8
Local-Southern	4.4
Regional	7.2
	$16.4
Capital Contributions*	
Labrador and Nfld Local	$13.7
Northern Quebec Local	3.6
Regional Airports	0.2
Other Local Airports	13.4
	$31.0

*Includes allocations of $5.6 million for the Special Recovery Capital Projects Program expenditures.

OBSERVATIONS

The federal government's involvement in airports started in 1927 when it built two civil airports at St. Hubert and Rimouski, Quebec. During the 1930s depression, the federal government constructed 50 airports as unemployment relief projects. At the start of World War II, nearly all airports, regardless of ownership, were mobilized by the federal government and large sums of monies were spent on enlargement and modifications. At the end of the war, a number of municipalities declined to take their airports back, leaving the operating and financial responsibilities with the federal government.

Into the 1960s, the federal policy was to encourage municipal airport operation. However, the choice before the communities was to operate the airports directly with subsidies, or to have then run federally at substantial gain to the communities. The results were inevitable.

In summary, the federal role has been one of ever increasing operational, regulatory and financial involvement. Ownership, operation, regulation and subsidization covers virtually all licensed airports.

This program assessment covers 131 regional and local airports owned and/or operated by the federal government. These airports cover 7 per cent of the passenger traffic in Canada. Also included in this review are over 150 airports owned and operated by other jurisdictions which receive subsidies from the federal government.

Currently the 131 airports are managed as a centralized public service operation. This form of management does not recognize that airports are an integral part of local or regional financial and social infrastructure. If they are to be truly successful they must be responsive to local conditions and opportunities. We believe that all airports should be locally managed and where feasible, locally owned or under local authority with each airport entity required to be financially self-supporting.

For the airports operated by the federal government, the shortfall between revenues and on-site O&M was $34 million for the fiscal year 84/85. Real property capital expenditures were $113 million for FY 84/85 and is estimated to average $95 million for each of the following three fiscal years. Over the 4-year period, the federal government will need to appropriate over half a billion dollars for these airports. This does not include $100 million for other capital requirements (such as equipment).

Grants and contributions to support airports which are operated through other jurisdictions amounted to about $47 million in FY 84/85. Only about half of this amount is required to subsidize isolated communities.

Several features of the current management structure makes it very difficult to reduce costs. These are discussed below:

a. Since airports are administered centrally, there are higher over-head costs due to duplication of work. The removal of the airport operation from the federal system would eliminate the need for excessive checks and balances which are prevalent in the federal bureaucracy.

b. Central planning for airports provides a more uniform level of service, irrespective of the operating costs and the ability of airports to afford it. We must recognize local conditions as a factor in determining the level of service.

c. The existence of national labour agreements creates rigidities in pay and work practices which limit the individual airports' opportunities to effectively manage and control their costs. Again, the need to recognize local conditions.

d. Airports are dynamic enterprises and should be in a position to take timely action to meet their individual opportunities and problems. The public service environment and government organizational and administrative structure do not accommodate this need. Local management enthusiasm is denied and buried under the federal bureaucracy.

So long as the on-site airport management is not challenged to be self-supporting, the need for ever increasing federal funding will continue.

Under current arrangements, site revenues at virtually all airports in this planning element do not cover operating costs. The books are balanced partially by an implicit allocation of the Air Transportation Tax and the rest through appropriations. This tax is special in that the revenues are earmarked for the Air Program in the Department of Transport.

There exist several avenues for increasing airport revenues. For example:

a. If the ceiling on the tax is removed, increased revenues will result.

b. Airport revenues from commercial operations are also constrained by the practice of limiting airport land use to aviation purposes. If these rules are relaxed, without compromising the safety and security aspects, extra revenues can be generated.

c. The government's policies have constrained the ability of airport management to aggressively pursue the revenue maximization goal. So long as the local management are not challenged, they will continue their dependence on federal largesse.

d. The uniform landing and general terminal fees set by "Ottawa" prevents local airports from adjusting them to meet costs. This inflexible approach does not allow for the possibility of increasing revenues.

The above avenues should be pursued in a decentralized fashion, with each individual airport deciding how to proceed.

Currently, these airports do not receive any explicit cross-subsidy from either the Air Tax or from the revenues of the principal airports. Thus, it is not recognized that smaller airports contribute as "feeders" to the activity at larger airports; moreover, smaller airports have higher unit costs and fewer sources of revenues.

In the short-term, some form of cross-subsidization will be necessary in the Canadian airport system; but to achieve self-sufficiency through a businesslike approach to airport planning, smaller airports would need to be guaranteed explicit allocations from the proceeds of the air tax.

In the longer term, however, the ability of airport management to maintain financial self-sufficiency or independence could be threatened by the lack of control over the legislation levying such tax. This is particularly true since the tax represents a major portion (almost 40 per cent) of total revenues at the 131 local and regional airports.

The study team recommends to the Task Force that initially some form of explicit cross-subsidization through a weighted allocation and payment of the air tax should be considered by the government; however, this would be only an interim measure to assist airports in achieving full financial independence. The goal should be full user-pay. Airports should set landing, general terminal and head fees in accordance with market forces.

Airports which serve remote and isolated communities or which are low passenger volume, may not be able to reach financial self-sufficiency. If there are judged to be compelling reasons to keep these airports operating, the costs would be borne by the local/regional community or recognized as a social subsidy.

Airports are capital intensive operations which must respond to market demand for facilities. Capital expenditures over the next three years are projected at almost $400 million. Because these airports currently compete with a wide variety of other programs for federal government capital appropriations, they face a high degree of uncertainty and unnecessary delay in capital projects. Greater flexibility in tapping sources of capital (i.e. private markets) would allow the projects to be tested in the market place and substantially reduce the uncertainties and delay.

The federal government must retain the right to intervene where national objectives are paramount, such as war, the protection of human and language rights, and accessibility to transportation by remote communities. It should, however, intervene only when market forces and general economic factors do not produce the required change. The principal responsibility of the federal government should be in providing the air navigational services and for the regulation and enforcement of safety.

An examination of the approach by other western countries to local or regional control of airport operations, reveals a major degree of "decentralization". Canada is notable by the extent to which it has centralized airport ownership and operations. In general, other countries vest a high level of operating and financial autonomy in local authorities. Central government financial involvement ranges from zero to capital cost sharing programs. The management, operations and finance are largely modelled on private sector commercial principles.

Within the Air Administration, there have been a number of internal studies on the viability of decentralizing authority and maximizing local autonomy. Several of these studies have recommended the transfer of responsibility for airport management to local authorities. Examples of these studies and general conclusions are discussed below:

a. The "Transfer of Responsibility for Local and Local Commercial Airports" report dealt with 898 airports but more particularly with the 77 Southern Local and Local Commercial airports where DOT had a financial or ownership involvement. It recommended that local and local commercial airports be operated by provincial, municipal or private operators. If none of these groups were interested, the need for the site was to be re-examined.

b. The "Non Revolving Fund Airports Study" dealt with 47 airports in a non-revolving fund group where Transport Canada had a direct involvement either by ownership, operation or subsidy. It concluded that the federal government was over-extended in its involvement in regional airports.

   It recommended the transfer of the 47 airports to other owners/operators, typically the Provinces and Municipalities.

c. The Federal Role in Airports study concluded that four forms of involvement were not essential to the achievement of federal responsibilities:

   1. airport ownership;
   2. airport operation;
   3. involvement in the decision-making process at the airport level; and
   4. training of airport personnel.

Financial self-sufficiency for commercial airports is a reality, viz. an overwhelming majority of United States commercial airports. In Canada, the Edmonton Municipal Airport (EMA) stands out as a very clear example of a non-federal government airport which is financially self-sufficient. This airport does not receive any part of the federal Air Transportation Tax. EMA covers all operating, debt, and capital costs through direct revenues at the airport. It receives no subsidies from the City of Edmonton. Instead, the airport contributes upwards of $2 million annually to the City.

Edmonton Municipal Airport revenues include a form of passenger head fee which is one of its major sources of revenue. Although EMA does not pay the federal government for air traffic control and other air navigation expenses associated with the airport operation, the imputed cost of these services is only a fraction of the net income of the airport. The number of airport staff is much lower than at comparable Transport Canada airports. Edmonton Municipal Airport is in most key areas similar to the United States airport authorities.

The success of the Edmonton form of airport management was also evident to this study team in their visit and inspection of United States airports. Local responsibility and accountability for all aspects of airport management, compliance with licensing regulations, user pay, and financial self-sufficiency were the rule.

We have studied several internal government reports, visited airports both in the United States and Canada, and consulted officials from both the Department of Transport and the United States Federal Aviation Administration, as well as other airport specialists. We conclude that the major issue for Canadian airports is centralized control over airport management versus local autonomy. All the evidence points to the desirability and need for local autonomy.

Therefore the study team recommends to the Task Force that the following conclusions be considered:

a. Airports should be locally owned and managed;

b. Air traffic control should remain a federal responsibility and airports should not bear these costs;

c. Federal controls on airport licensing, safety and security should continue;

d. All airport revenues should eventually be under the control of the airport operator and they should not be dependent on the federal Air Transportation Tax. In the short-term, the federal government should ensure, through legislation, a weighted allocation and payment of the Air Transportation Tax;

e. The airport operator should have the freedom to raise revenues through various mechanisms such as passenger fees;

f. The airport should be financially self-sufficient for operating expenses, for debt servicing and for capital projects;

g. The airport operator should be free to raise capital from the public, lending institutions, etc.; and

h. The airport operator should be able to enter into agreements with the air carriers, as is the case in the United States, to secure loans or bonds;

It all comes down to recognizing that airports are an integral part of the local or regional financial, commercial and social infrastructure. If they are to be truly successful they must be responsive to local conditions and opportunities and not constrained by a central government. Local management should determine the levels of service, how revenues are to be secured and what costs are incurred.

How will the federal government benefit from local airport autonomy? Besides the increased cost-efficiency and revenue generation at the airport level, the government will be able to avoid the liability for continuing airport cash shortfalls. Annual savings in excess of $100 million are possible (without taking into account interest savings on future indebtedness).

The options described below would represent a very significant change in the federal government's role in airports. Implementation of the change would likely require extensive involvement by major interest groups at each airport, e.g. all levels of government, airline industry, users, unions, etc. There are multiple courses of action which may be taken to achieve the objective. It is imperative that the process not be deflected by transitional or intermediate steps.

OPTIONS

The study team recommends to the Task Force that, in the case of airports owned or operated by Transport Canada, the federal government consider a fundamental change in airport policy from ownership and centralized public service operation to non-federal ownership and non-federal operation.

For airports not owned or operated by Transport Canada; it should be recognized that a number of airports will be required to support otherwise isolated communities. These should be clearly identified and funded separately as a social subsidy. Otherwise, grants and contributions should be phased out.

For airports owned or operated by Transport Canada, it is recommended to the Task Force that the government consider transferring ownership or custody and management of all federally owned airports to a designated local entity on the condition that the airport is required to become financially self-sufficient for all costs, capital expenditures, financing and debt service.

Where financial self-sufficiency is not immediately attainable by any particular airport, steps should be considered for the federal government to provide the minimum financial assistance required for the airport to attain self-sufficiency in the shortest possible time.

Airports which cannot be expected to reach financial self-sufficiency within a reasonable time should be re-examined. If there are compelling reasons to keep any of these airports operating, the costs should be borne by the local/regional community or recognized as a social subsidy. All others should be promptly closed or divested.

AIR NAVIGATIONAL SERVICES

Transport Canada

OBJECTIVE

To provide for "adequate safety of aircraft... throughout Canada, by effective development, operation and maintenance of ...air navigation components".

RESULTS/BENEFICIARIES

Aviation Industry (Domestic, International, Military)
Air Travellers

AUTHORITY

BNA Act
National Transportation Act
Aeronautics Act

RESOURCES (millions of current dollars)

	84/85
Capital	$8.2

REAL PROPERTY ASSETS

	No.	
Area Control Centres	7)	Estimated Replacement
Terminal Control Units	9)	Values Included with
Airport Control Towers	61)	Relevant Airports
Flight Service Stations	114)	
Surveillance (Radar) Sites	22)	
Navigational Aid Sites	923)	No Replacement
Communications System Sites	339)	Values Estimated
Field Maintenance Units	28)	

PROGRAM DESCRIPTION

Within the Air Navigational Services (ANS) Activity, these are three planning elements:

a. Air Traffic Services
b. Technical Services
c. Aviation Services

Only the first two planning elements above have real property components:

a. Air Traffic Services operates the following facilities in the indicated regions:

FACILITY	ATL	QUE	ONT	CTRL	WEST	PFC	HQ	TOTAL
Area Control Ctrs	2	1	1	1	1	1		7
Terminal/Enroute Control Units	1	1	2	4	1	-		9
Airport Control Towers	9	9	13	7	11	12		61
Flight Service Stations	16	18	13	21	29	17		114
General Office Space	1	1	1	1	1	1	1	7
TOTAL	29	30	30	34	43	31	1	98

b. Technical Services maintains equipment at the following locations:

	ATL	QUE	ONT	CTRL	WEST	PFC	HQ	TOTAL
Surveillance (Radar) Sites	4	3	6	4	2	3	0	22
Navigation Aid Sites	116	202	127	163	189	126	0	923
Communication System Sites	36	64	50	55	61	73	0	339
Field Maintenance/ Office	4	4	4	7	5	4	0	28
TOTAL	160	273	187	229	257	206	0	1312

Each region is managed by a Regional Administrator with line authority from the Air Administrator over the ANS planning elements in his region. At headquarters, the Assistant Administrator, Air Navigation, reports to the Air Administrator and exercises line authority over the Headquarters Directors of Air Traffic Services, Facility Engineering and Systems Development, Air Navigation System Requirements, etc. Each headquarters Director exercises functional control over his regional counterpart.

OBSERVATIONS

Air Navigational Services has only a minor involvement in real property:

a. For capital projects with real property aspects, the activity appropriates the funding except where the facility is an integral part of an air terminal building and the funding for the real property facility would come out of the Airports Activity.

b. The Airports Activity is responsible for the design, construction and maintenance of all building infrastructure required to support ANS equipment or personnel, whether these are on or off airports.

c. Where the sites are off airports, site acquisition by purchase, lease or other arrangement is performed by the Airports Activity. This is currently a very small activity, given the absence of expansion in the number of sites.

For FY 84/85, the Total Estimated Cost of all approved capital projects was $1.1 billion, of which $1.0 billion will be spent on restoration due to physical or functional obsolescence and the remainder for capacity expansion. Of the $1.1 billion, approximately $92 million ($59M - SSA, $34M - Other Airports) represents the value of the real property portion.

The Technical Services planning element (1,945 PYs) mandate is to develop, implement and maintain the physical plant (including surveillance, communication, navigation and telecommunications systems) component of the ANS activity.

It also provides services to others for the design, implementation and continuing maintenance of designated Airport and Canadian Coast Guard electronic systems. Selected services are also provided to DND, Environment, other federal departments, domestic airlines, provincial, territorial and municipal authorities.

The ANS Activity receives the following revenues and recoveries:

Revenue	**($ millions) FY 84/85**	
Air Transportation Tax	30.3	
Rentals and Concessions	0.5	
Other revenue	15.9	
		46.7
Recoveries		
Air traffic control charge	84.6	
Coast Guard helicopters and telecommunication services	0.9	
Environmental Services (weather)	1.3	
		86.8

a. The activity receives 14.4 per cent of the Air Transportation Tax to cover enroute navigational services.

b. Other revenues come from international flights on North Atlantic and polar air routes and from non-air traffic telecommunication services.

c. The air traffic control charge represents the recovery from the Airports Revolving Fund for services in the vicinity of the 23 self-supporting airports.

OPTIONS

Design, construction and maintenance of all real property for Air Navigational Services is performed by the airports activity, whether these are on or off the airports.

SECTION 12 - OTHER TRANSPORTATION PROGRAMS

MOTOR VEHICLE TEST CENTRE

Transport Canada

OBJECTIVES

To contribute to the reduction in deaths, injuries and property damage through improved safety of motor vehicles.

To contribute to a reduction in health impairment caused by exhaust emission levels.

To contribute to energy conservation by reducing the average fuel consumption of new motor vehicles.

RESULTS/BENEFICIARIES

The motor vehicle industry is under scrutiny, with the general public being the ultimate beneficiary.

AUTHORITY

Motor Vehicle Safety Act
Motor Vehicle Tire Safety Act

RESOURCES (millions of current dollars)

	84/85
Operating Expenses	$2.9
Capital	0
Revenues	$0.2
Person Years	29

REAL PROPERTY ASSETS

Land - 546 hectares
Estimated Replacement Value of Test Centre - $41 million.

PROGRAM DESCRIPTION

The Motor Vehicle Test Centre at Blainville, Québec was opened in May 1979 to provide test facilities for the Road Safety and Motor Vehicle Regulation Group. Real property facilities include tracks, administration and specialized buildings, and specialized areas for testing purposes.

Of the 29 PYs (mostly engineers and technicians) operating the test centre, two are allocated to the real property management and administration function. The on-site maintenance is contracted out through Public Works Canada. In the pre-approval planning stages, there are capital expenditures forecasted for the next three fiscal years of $4 million, of which $3.8 million represents the real property component to be handled through Public Works Canada.

The major activities undertaken at the Test Centre include the testing of vehicles, components, emission levels, and fuel economy.

As scheduling permits, facilities are made available for use by outside clients, e.g. universities, provincial governments, motor vehicle industry. Fees are charged to recover the incremental costs. The current fee schedule was established under Order in Council P.C. 1981-237.

OBSERVATIONS

A July 1979 Evaluation of the Motor Vehicle Test Centre examined the project management aspects, including the original justification, project construction and planning for its use. It found that although the original concept was very modest, it grew very quickly before an engineering estimate was finalized. Subsequently, changes due to operational requirements and inflationary increases due to delays in the approval process escalated the costs even more. However, the evaluation report recommended that the Test Centre operate as planned, subject to various constraints.

Transport Canada constructed the Test Centre because there was no equivalent facility of this nature available in Canada where motor vehicle safety compliance testing could be conducted. There was insufficient demand by either government or industry to enable the private sector to establish such facilities on a commercial basis in Canada. The establishment of the Test Centre has encouraged both research and development testing on the part of Canadian industry but to date the level of activity is still insufficient for the Test Centre to operate as a commercial venture (client fees average $150-250,000 annually). Fees are maintained at a level that will encourage the use of the facilities to stimulate motor vehicle R&D in Canada, and yet not provide unfair competition for any commercial establishments that provide testing services.

The external demand for use of the Test Centre is not all that active. It could double in absolute terms if more PY resources could be freed to service the demand. Presently, it is estimated that about two PYs in total are devoted to the external testing requirements. Departmental priorities would suffer if the external use of the Test Centre were to be expanded under the present person-year allocation.

As a physical plant, the Test Centre could be used more extensively. Certainly, the program could perform more testing if more PY resources were approved. However, there is the possibility of generating additional revenues through higher usage by clients with their own staff.

From the real property point of view, there are some options to the status quo:

a. Closing the Test Centre would force the department to go back to the United States to contract with test facilities there. Given the sunk cost of the facilities, there would be no significant savings.

b. Selling the Test Centre to private interests, given the department would be the main user, would mean that the government would end up paying the return on the capital investment. Furthermore, any future testing requiring specialized equipment might require guarantees of minimum usage, sufficient to recover full costs.

c. Setting up a Joint Venture, whereby private interests would market the excess testing capacity to a wide range of potential clients, hire staff to assist with testing programs and share profits with the government. It is not known what the potential would be for such an enterprise; however, the Test Centre does already allow private firms to use their own testing staff at the facility and has contracted out the operation of some of the facilities.

OPTIONS

The study team recommends to the Task Force that the government should explore more aggressively opportunities for better usage of facilities under full cost-recovery schemes.

TRANSPORTATION TRAINING FACILITIES

Transport Canada

OBJECTIVE

To deliver technical and non-technical training programs which are national in scope.

RESULTS/BENEFICIARIES

Training for air traffic controllers, marine traffic regulators, electronic technicians, flight service specialists, transportation managers, coast guard officer cadets, etc.

AUTHORITY

Financial Administration Act, Section 7.

RESOURCES (millions of current dollars)

Canadian Coast Guard College	**84/85**
Operating Expenses	$1.4
Capital	$5.9
Revenue	$0.1
Person Years	3

Transport Canada Training Institute	**84/85**
Operating Expenses	$5.4
Capital	0
Revenue	$2.6
Person Years	23

REAL PROPERTY ASSETS

	Coast Guard College	Transport Training Inst.
Replacement Value (Estimated)	$32 million	$67 million

PROGRAM DESCRIPTION

Training is provided at Sydney, N.S.-Canadian Coast Guard College (CCGC), and Cornwall, Ont.-Transport Canada Training Institute (TCTI).

CCGC is planning $20 million in capital expenditures over the next three fiscal years, mostly in real property. TCTI plans $11 million in capital expenditures over the same period, but nothing in real property.

TCTI provides technical training for air traffic controllers, marine traffic regulators, electronic technicians, and flight service specialists, as well as tranportation management training. These total some 100,000 student-days a year.

CCGC prepares officer cadets as navigating or engineering officers in the Canadian Coast Guard. The cadets follow a 3-year course, with a 300-member student body of whom 61 are expected to graduate in the summer of 1985.

TCTI serves as a conference/seminar centre both for government and non-government agencies. This amounts to about 15,000 residential days per year.

OBSERVATIONS

The TCTI charges $20 per student day for all government departments, $32 for non-government clients, and $35 for foreign nationals. These fees cover only direct costs such as food, maid, security and switchboard services. For foreign nationals, there is an additional charge of $110 per day for facility use.

The CCGC charges foreign nationals $20 per day for room and board, and $80 for training facilities. Proposals to increase these to $35 and $125, respectively, are being discussed. This would be full cost recovery for operations.

According to departmental briefing notes, the cost at TCTI per student day varies from $50 for conferences to $240 for technical training (for an average of $160), if all O&M expenses, including TCTI teaching staff, were to be recovered. The corresponding cost varies from $85 to $325 (for an average of $225) if the costs of capital investment also had to be recovered.

Since the status quo is to charge only for the direct costs related to room and board, the options are:

a. To move towards full cost-recovery by recovering all TCTI O&M expenses, but not the costs of capital investment. Such charges would be well below market rates and should not diminish the cost-efficiency of TCTI operations (1984 occupancy rate exceeded recommended 85 per cent level).

b. To move to full cost-recovery by recovering all costs, including capital. Such charges would be comparable to market rates and might decrease the demand for TCTI facilities.

It should be noted, however, that since non-government clients represent 1-2 per cent of TCTI student-days, the additional revenues would not be significant.

For comparison, Public Works Canada charges $55-$70 per day for its facilities at Heron Rd and in Arnprior; these are based on full operating costs (not including costs of capital).

OPTIONS

The study team recommends to the Task Force that the government consider instituting charges for foreign nationals based on full recovery for all operating costs at the Canadian Coast Guard College. The government should also consider instituting charges (for all users) based on full recovery for all operating costs at the Transport Canada Training Centre.

SECTION 13 - NATIONAL DEFENCE SERVICES PROGRAMS

INTRODUCTION

DND has a comparatively well-managed and effective but cumbersome real property function. Improvements and considerable cost avoidance could be achieved by:

- rationalization of DND's infrastructure;
- increased contracting out of civilian design, and operation and maintenance activities, accompanied by a phased reduction of civilian employees, taking attrition into account;
- simplification of and improvements to internal DND real property management processes; and
- increased use of PWC by DND for in-house design and realty services.

BACKGROUND

In the period from 1939 to the mid 1960s, DND acquired and became the custodian of the largest and most diverse inventory of real property in the Government of Canada. Although there was some modest reduction in the early 1970s DND's inventory remains the largest today.

Changing military requirements have created a situation where much of this infrastructure has become redundant. Nevertheless DND continues to operate and maintain it, partly out of its own volition, but primarily in response to government direction, to avoid the possible socio-economic disruption that could be caused by infrastructure rationalization.

The Defence Services Program in total is funded on a formula basis intended to allow DND to focus its resources on Canada's military priorities. However, as far as its management of real property is concerned, the focus on and adjustment to military priorities has not been fully achieved.

The results of this situation are that DND has too much infrastructure and this oversupply is causing wasteful expenditure and manpower utilization.

Given the Defence Services Program funding formula, costs avoided or savings made through the rationalization of real property management in DND could assist the funding of military priorities, thereby minimizing possible increases in the overall cost of the Defence Services Program.

OBSERVATIONS

The provision and management of real property in DND is based on the concept that the Department must establish and maintain an environment which promotes the military way of life and military esprit de corps. The application of the concept to the real property function provides the Department's rationale for both the scale, range, diversity and cost of its inventory and its mode of real property management.

DND is the custodian of the largest inventory in the Government of Canada in terms of building area (with almost 10.7 million square metres of space) with the largest number of buildings (more than 36,000 of which more than 24,000 are married quarters). It is the third largest landholder in the government, with more than two million hectares.

DND's funding formula is based on Canada's commitments to NATO of 3 per cent per annum real growth in defence spending, an agreed total program resource level (dollars and military and civilian person-years) and a capital allocation of approximately 27 per cent of the total program level. Within this formula the Department retains the flexibility to adjust resource allocations so as to maximize effort on primary military requirements, although it cannot shift resources between capital and operational votes without Treasury Board approval, nor switch civilian to military person-years.

To ensure that as far as possible available resources go first to military priorities, DND employs an elaborate and extensive needs definition, planning and approval process, a central feature of which is a rigorous prioritization exercise. Pressures exist within the Department to allocate resources towards the equipping and operation of the Forces and to minimize expenditures on real property except where they are judged to be critical to military effort.

DND is permitted to employ civilians in a support role to military functions. The theory is that this arrangement allows the military personnel to be concentrated primarily on military duties. A large number (10,070 or 28 per cent) of DND's 36,000 civilian employees work in the real property function chiefly under the supervision of military personnel in Operation/Maintenance functions. The total number of military personnel involved in real property (construction engineering) activity is 2,280 or 2.7 per cent of the Forces.

In dollar terms the proportion of real property workload done in-house by the 12,350 military and civilian personnel is as follows:

- design 25 -30 per cent
- construction 10 per cent
- operation and maintenance 70 per cent

Grants-in-lieu of taxes on DND properties are paid on DND's behalf by PWC from the PWC program and are not charged back to DND. PWC provides 263,000 square metres of office and storage space for DND in the National Capital Region including NDHQ, and smaller amounts of office space in other centres across the country. PWC also provides DND with some of its recruiting centres. PWC generally acts as DND's agent for leased office and recruiting centre space. PWC acts as the government's agent for disposal of surplus DND properties.

Recent audits and evaluations, most notably those of the 1982 Barton Report on Defence Procurement and the Auditor General in his 1983-84 report have commented favourably on DND's real property acquisition and management generally. The Auditor General (AG) also made a number of observations.

DND has moved to eliminate the problems identified by the AG which are in its power to resolve. However, at this stage it is still wrestling uncomfortably with the most difficult and intractable policy issue: how to identify separately and show clearly the total costs of meeting strictly military real property requirements versus the heavy additional costs of meeting government's broader socio-economic considerations through defence infrastructure.

If military requirements were the only criterion, DND internal documents indicate that the number of bases in Canada could be reduced by at least seven from the 33 which currently exist, and the number of stations could also be reduced substantially.

In the final analysis, prolonging indefinitely the life of defence installations with no essential military function is not the way to encourage the social and economic evolution of host communities; the costs to all outweigh the benefits.

A systematic medium and long term infrastructure rationalization plan is needed. Such a plan should include provision for cooperative planning with provinces and local communities for the socio-economic adjustments which would have to made. It should also include provision for rationalization of utilities and municipal services which DND currently provides for itself.

In addition to socio-economic considerations, the military philosophy that lies behind DND's approach to real property management also tends to foster a situation in which DND has more property than it really needs and expends more manpower on real property development, operation and maintenance than is necessary.

The basic notions that form this philosophy are that only the military knows and can decide what the military needs. The military must be self-dependent and self-sustaining, ready in peace-time to mobilize instantly for war conditions.

These arguments are used for example to justify the retension by DND of redundant infrastructure to meet mobilization contingencies. They are also used to support DND's claim that its civilian in-house architectural and engineering activity is militarily essential.

However, an alternative approach to accommodation for mobilization which would entail a combination of prefabricated building, canvas and designated civilian buildings would appear to offer a much more cost effective yet practical solution than maintaining redundant facilities. No in-house design work would be necessary under this alternative approach.

Similarly it should be noted that although DND argues that an in-house civilian architectural and engineering division is needed for buildings of primary military function, most of the in-house designs on which this unit actually works are for buildings that have no special military purpose, such as officers' quarters etc., while construction projects to support new equipment purchases, such as the ship repair unit in Base Halifax and the hangars for the F18 fighter plane have been contracted out for design by consultants.

Equally important in understanding DND's real property function is recognition of DND's determination to "stay out of trouble politically". To do this, DND has developed an elaborate "fail-safe" property management process, which is designed to ensure full compliance with government and departmental administrative policy.

The process is particularly heavy and lengthy at the front end (the construction project justification and development phases). It could be simplified and shortened without serious risk, and with immediate benefits in terms of speedier project implementation, an enhanced relationship with the private sector, and reduced overhead.

Given that 70 per cent of the operation and maintenance is done in-house by 10,000 civilian employees, and that much of this is simply routine maintenance, there is considerable scope for contracting out this work to the private sector. The target should be the elimination of all DND civilian in-house operation and maintenance except that which can be justified for military operations. The reduction of civilian employees should be phased and should take attrition into account.

Increased effectiveness, significant cost avoidance and a substantial freeing up of resources for redeployment in support of military priorities could be achieved through phased application of the four themes identified in this overview; infrastructure rationalization; increased contracting out; process simplification; and increased use of PWC by DND for in-house design and realty services.

DEFENCE SERVICES PROGRAM
(REAL PROPERTY MANAGEMENT AND ORGANIZATION)

INTRODUCTION

The aim of this background report is to outline briefly the nature of the Defence Services Program and to describe and comment generally on the provision, management and organization of real property and related professional and technical services in DND. A series of accompanying reports describe various aspects of DND's real property provisions and management in greater detail, viz:

Defence Services Program (Infrastructure)

Defence Services Program (Quartering)

Defence Services Program (Design and Construction)

Defence Services Program (Works)

Defence Services (Properties and Utilities)

National Defence Headquarters

There is also a related report on the Crown Corporation Defence Construction Canada (1951) Ltd.

OBJECTIVE

The objective of the Defence Services Program is to ensure the security of Canada and contribute to the maintenance of world peace.

The program has a number of sub-objectives. Those which affect the provision and management of real property are:

- to provide effective control, management and administration of all activities of the Department and the Canadian Armed Forces;

- to provide the resources necessary to ensure adquate supply and technical support of the Department and the Armed Forces, and

- to provide for all levels of training of the Canadian Armed Forces.

Implicit in these statements is the following sub-objective:

- to provide defence infrastructure appropriate to the size, structure and roles of the Canadian Forces.

RESULTS/BENEFICIARIES

National Defence Headquarters, Commands, Bases and Stations, and Personnel Support Infrastructure appropriate for the Canadian Forces.

Professional and technical real property services associated with the life-cycle management of 33 bases and 24 stations of the Canadian Forces in Canada and abroad.

The preparation in peacetime of Forces personnel trained to operate in the fields of combat engineering and construction engineering during wartime.

The direct beneficiaries of these results are the 82,000 military and 36,000 civilian personnel of the Candian Forces and their families and the 21,000 members of the primary reserve. Indirect beneficiaries in peacetime are the communities and regions within which Canadian Forces are located, the Canadian people, and Canada's allies. Beneficiaries in wartime are the Canadian people and Canada's allies.

AUTHORITY

National Defence Act.

RESOURCES

	84/85	**85/86**
Capital	$150	$161 million
Operating	520	526 million
Revenues	83	84 million

Person-Years	
military construction engineering	2,280
civilian construction engineering CFT	9,070
civilian construction engineering term	1,000
military combat engineering	1,060
Non-Public Fund	$25 million
Defence Construction Canada (1951) Ltd.	
Operating	$14.6 million
Person-Years	260-340

PROGRAM DESCRIPTION

The Defence Services Program brings together in a single program all the activities and resources which enable the Department of National Defence and the Canadian Forces to carry out their roles.

Military Philosophy

DND's basic philosophy and concept is to establish and maintain an environment which promotes the military way of life i.e. which:

- maintains Canadian sovereignty and security;
- facilitates peacetime preparation for wartime readiness and response;
- provides for life-time military careers;
- fosters military esprit de corps; and
- supports as necessary the social needs of the military and their dependents.

The application of this concept has led to the emergence and development of the military almost as a closed and separate society within the greater Canadian society with a discipline and mores that differ to a certain extent from those found in the Canadian society generally.

Real Property Management

The provision and management of real property in DND is based on this concept. The application of the concept to the real property function provides the Department's rationale for both the scale, range, diversity and cost of its inventory and its mode of real property management.

DND is the custodian of the largest inventory in the Government of Canada in terms of building area (with almost 10.7 million square metres of space) with the largest number of buildings (more than 36,000 of which more than 24,000 are married quarters). It is the third largest landholder in the government, with more than two million hectares.

The DND real property inventory is probably the most diverse and is amongst the most complex in government. With 33 bases and 24 stations (which includes firing ranges, messes, colleges, schools, hospitals, water, hydro and sewage plants, etc.) DND acts as a community administrator as well as a provider and manager of real property supporting the wartime and peacetime activities of its 82,000 military, 36,000 civilian staff and 21,000 reservists.

Real Property Management Issues

DND has succeeded in acquiring almost total management control over its real property, because it has convinced central agencies and successive administrations with various arguments. According to DND, real property is an essential and integral component of defence, therefore of the Defence Services Program. Program needs (which are exceedingly broad because the program is broad) drive the real property function.

DND states that the military must be able to practice construction engineering (i.e. perform professional and technical real property activities) and receive professional, technical and supervisory construction engineering training in peacetime, in order to be ready to convert instantly to war conditions. A further argument is that the total real property function must be and must remain in (or associated with) DND because it is essential for those providing the service to understand and be able to comply with the military's requirements.

A consequence of DND's success in gaining management control over its real property has been the almost total internalization of the challenge function within the Department, and the withering of the challenge function outside the Department in the central agencies. Central agency analysts have scant knowledge of DND's real property function and are unable to provide a meaningful critique.

The military therefore is able to define and supply its own real property needs to its own standards and within its own cost criteria.

In justifying its own real property standards, scales and cost criteria to itself, DND frequently falls back on a vague concept, known as the "minimum military requirement (MMR)". What the minimum military requirement is, no one knows: it has not been defined. It is DND's equivalent to similarly vague philosophical concepts to be found in other federal departments who refer to "federal image" or "federal presence" or "broader government objectives" to justify projects which they wish to put in place.

Real property infrastructure and related professional and technical services are needed to support the "Force Posture": this is the term used in DND to describe the size, structure, composition and geographical distribution of the Canadian Forces. Changing strategic and technological conditions have outdated the existing Force Posture which was last approved in 1975. Changes in military requirements may have made some of DND's real property redundant.

A further consideration which strongly influences the amount and use of real property in DND is that military criteria (efficient and effective service to support program objectives) are not the only criteria the government employs. Socio-economic criteria (regional development, job creation, etc.) are applied heavily to DND's program, with the consequence that the Department has been expected by government to continue to sustain Bases and Stations for which it no longer has a military requirement.

Program Resource Allocations

DND's funding formula is based on Canada's commitments to NATO of 3 per cent per annum real growth in defence spending, an agreed total program resource level (dollars, and military and civilian PYs) and a capital allocation of approximately 27 per cent of the total program level. Within this formula the Department retains the flexibility to adjust resource allocations so as to maximize effort on primary military requirements, although it cannot shift resources between capital and operational votes without Treasury Board approval, or switch civilian to military PY's.

To ensure that as far as possible available resources go first to military priorities, DND employs an elaborate and extensive needs definition, planning and approval process, a central feature of which is a rigorous priorization exercise. Pressures exist within the Department to allocate resources towards the equipping and operation of the Forces and to minimize expenditures on real property except where they are judged to be critical to military effort.

Military - Civilian Interface

DND is permitted to employ civilians in a support role to military functions (as well as to support the Deputy Minister's role of policy advice and financial and personnel administration). The theory is that this arrangement allows the military personnel to be concentrated primarily on military duties. A large number (10,000 or 28 per cent) of DND's 36,000 civilian employees work in the real property function chiefly under the supervision of military personnel. The total number of military personnel involved in real property (construction engineering) activity is 2,280 or 2.7 per cent of the Forces.

In dollar terms, the proportion of real property workload done in-house by the 13,350 military and civilian personnel is as follows:

- design 25 - 30 per cent
- construction 10 per cent
- operation and maintenance 70 per cent.

Although DND's inventory is not growing appreciably, DND retains the authority and the capability to acquire land and property on its own account. DND also leases married and single quarters (and occasionally other facilities) directly. The Department negotiates utility and local service agreements directly with municipalities as necessary.

DND handles contracts under $30,000 in value through DSS. Contracts over $30,000 are handled on DND's behalf by the Crown corporation, Defence Construction Canada (1951) Ltd. DCC obtains consultant, construction and maintenance contracts for DND (approximately 1300 contracts annually) and employs 260 to 340 staff, according to workload volume. (See the program review on DCC for further details.)

DND-PWC Interaction

Grants-in-lieu of taxes on DND properties are paid by PWC on DND's behalf from the PWC program and are not charged back to DND. PWC provides 263,000 square metres of office and storage space for DND in the National Capital including NDHQ, and smaller amounts of office space in other centres across the country. PWC generally acts as DND's agent for leased office and recruiting centre space. PWC acts as the government's agent for disposal of surplus DND properties.

Delegated Authority

Based on its managerial credibility, DND has obtained the most extensive delegation of spending authority which Treasury Board has assigned. This authority has been sub-delegated within the Department and the Forces for construction and maintenance projects as follows:

- Treasury Board (over $10 million);
- Minister of National Defence ($1 to $10 million);
- ADM (Mat) and/or CCP (up to $1 million);
- Command Commanders and/or CCE's (up to $400,000);
- Base Commanders and BCEO's (up to $100,000).

Financial Considerations

The DND real property budget consists of approximately $160 million in capital funds and $520 million in operating and maintenance funds. The regular $150 million capital program is largely a replacement program. However, in addition to this program, capital funds for real property construction projects required to support major new equipment (e.g. fighters, frigates) are included in the budgets for those projects; ranging from $10 - 25 million annually.

There is also a Non-Public Fund financed by the military personnel themselves, through which a further $25 million is expended annually on certain elements of the social infrastructure required for military personnel and their dependents (e.g. CANEX's and recreational facilities for DND families).

DND obtains some offsetting capital contributions from NATO for capital projects which serve NATO forces generally (e.g. the new Ship Repair Unit in Halifax). Rent is charged for Housing provided by DND to its personnel which is paid into the Consolidated Revenue Fund. Other offsetting revenue (approximately $1.5 million) comes from the sale of DND infrastructure services (water, sewage, hydro) to small municipalities surrounding certain bases. In turn, DND pays a small amount of capital and operating contributions to municipalities which provide social and recreational facilities used by DND families (approximately $1.5 million).

ORGANIZATIONAL STRUCTURE FOR CONSTRUCTION ENGINEERING

The Defence Services Program brings together in a single program all the activities and resources which enable the Department of National Defence and the Canadian Forces to carry out their roles. The diagrams in the attached Annex A describe the program and organizational structure of DND.

Materiel Support is an activity of the Defence Services Program under the authority of the ADM Materiel (ADM Mat). He reports to the Deputy Minister (DM) and the Chief of the Defence Staff (CDS). The DM is the senior civilian advisor to the Minister, responsible (a) for ensuring that all policy direction emanating from the government is reflected in the administration of the Department and in military plans and operations, and (b) for financial and personnel administration. The CDS is the senior military adviser to the Minister responsible for the effective conduct of military operations and the state of readiness of the Canadian Forces.

In DND the acquisition, operation, maintenance and disposal of real property is a centrally managed functional component of the Materiel Support activity at Headquarters (NDHQ). The responsible official reporting through both the civilian and the military lines of authority, is the Chief of Construction and Properties (CCP).

CCP is responsible for advising the CDS, through ADM (Mat), with regard to Construction Engineering (CE) services for the Canadian Forces, and for taking appropriate action on behalf of the CDS in regard to CE activities, i.e. the military aspects of the real property function.

CCP is responsible to ADM (Mat) for:

- formulating plans and programs for design and construction of new buildings and facilities;
- operation, maintenance and evaluation of existing accommodation, fixed facilities, and utilities;
- provision of fire prevention and protection services;
- implementation of approved programs;
- management of real property and utility services;
- formulating related policies, procedures and directives; and
- providing the necessary control and guidance for policy application.

CCP is responsible for providing functional advice to the ADM Personnel (ADM Per), in support of the ADM (Per)'s responsiblity for training (including training and educational facilities) and for provision of social support infrastructure, including messing, married and singles quarters, medical dental and other facilities on or related to Canadian bases and stations. ADM (Per) is also functionally responsible through Command and Base Administration Officers for civilian cleaning staff.

The CCP's Military Engineering Branch in NDHQ is divided into four divisions, as follows:

- Director General Quartering (DGQ);
- Director General Construction (DGC);
- Director General Works (DGW); and
- Director General Properties and Utilities (DGPU).

CCP and his Directors General have functional relationships with Commanders in the field, and provide functional guidance to the Command Construction Engineers (CCE). CCE organization consists of the following primary functions:

- Engineering (Civil, Architectural, Mechanical, Electrical, Draughting);
- Quartering (Base Development, Program Planning, Administration and Financial Control, Property Management); and
- Works (Base Maintenance, Contract Administration, Fire and Crash Protection).

These functions are further divided into sub-functions to suit individual command requirements. CCE's are responsible to their commanders for monitoring and advising on the operation and maintenance of accommodation, fixed facilities and utility plants; engineering design and preparation of plans and specification in support of base projects; coordination of CE budgets and programs; monitoring base CE administrative procedures; real property management within the region of CHQ; and fire protection services.

The CCE's have a functional relationship to the Base Construction Engineer Officers (BCEO's) at the bases within their commands. The role of BCEO's is to control the activities of construction and maintenance of works and buildings, operation of utility plants and systems, provision of fire protection services and real property management.

Field Engineering Operations

At the present time the Canadian Military Engineers have five field units - four Combat Engineer Regiments (CER) operating in direct support of Mobile Command (Army) field formations and the brigade in Germany and 1 Construction Engineering unit which is capable of undertaking design and construction world-wide under all conditions.

Under the normative planning process two additional units will be formed - an airfield damage repair (ADR) unit and a task force engineer support regiment - and 1CEU will be expanded from a design/site supervision type of operation to a unit with a full field construction capability.

The CER's, the ADR and the task force engineer regiment are the staff responsibility of the Director General Military Engineering Operations (DGMEO) and 1CEU is an NDHQ unit under the Director General Works.

Although the primary function of the CER's is the close support of Army combat units, which includes the traditional tasks of demolition, mine warfare, equipment bridging and water supply, they are also charged with the construction and repair of roads, bridges, airfields, port facilities, bases and storage facilities in the forward area under war-time conditons.

An important aspect of the training of these units is therefore the need to gain practical engineering and construction experience. At the present time they are given only limited opportunities to undertake construction projects for various reasons - the most significant of which, aside from field commanders' reluctance to lose their engineer support for extended periods, is resistance from the civil sector to DND undertaking jobs with soldiers which can be done by private contractors and labourers.

Although good training projects may be offered from time to time by municipalities or other organizations, - the City of Whitehorse recently requested assistance in the construction of a 170 foot suspension bridge - DND has had to turn them down for this reason.

On the other hand 1CEU, and the other two field units when formed, are primarily slanted toward construction projects in support of military operations. In this context, 1CEU is the design authority for the North Warning System Short Range Radar Stations (NWS/SRR) and will build the prototype and three operational SRR's between 1986 and 1992.

Personnel in these units remain current through these projects and by rotational postings within the Construction Engineering organziations at NDHQ, Command Headquarters, Bases and Stations.

The CE function at these various levels is therefore essential to the maintenance of a trained cadre of construction personnel for field units and as a basis for war-time mobilization.

ANNEX A

DEFENCE SERVICES PROGRAM ORGANIZATION

Figure 1. Activity Structure

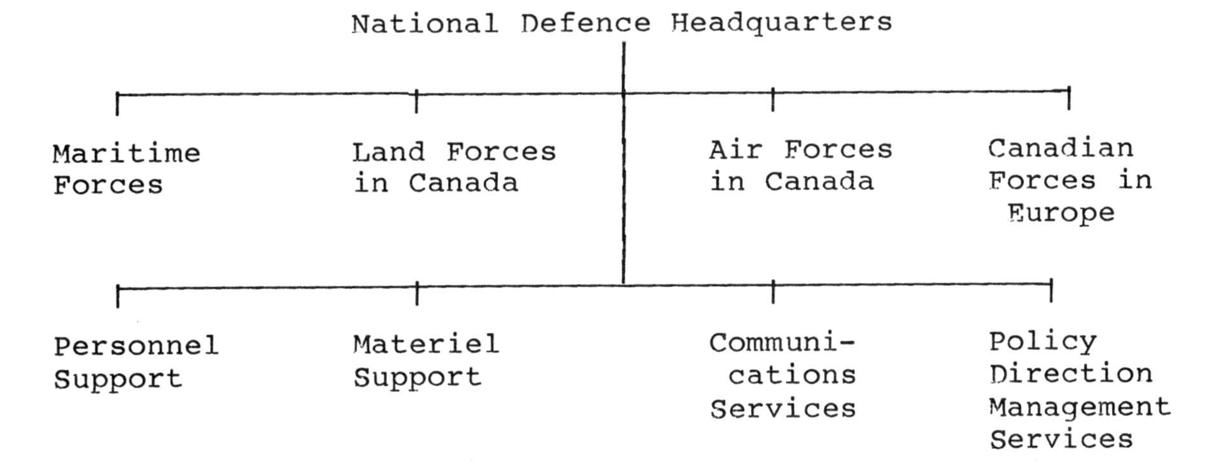

Figure 2. Organization of National Defence Headquarters (NDHQ)

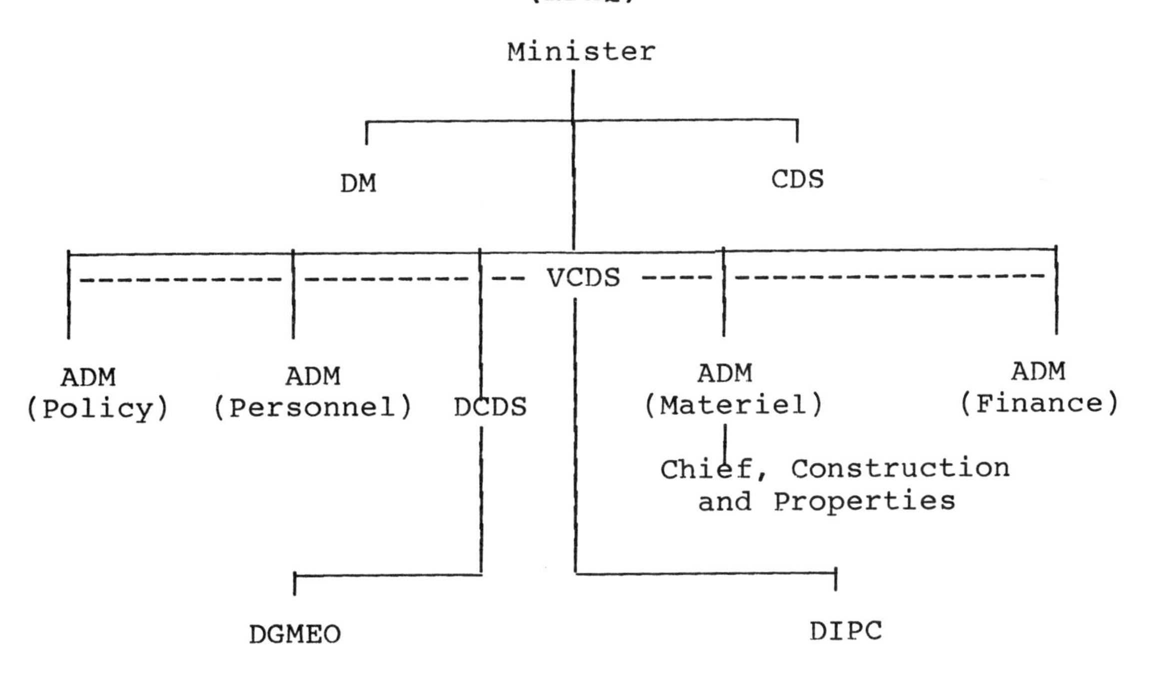

DEFENCE SERVICES PROGRAM ORGANIZATION

Figure 3. Construction Engineering Branch (NDHQ)

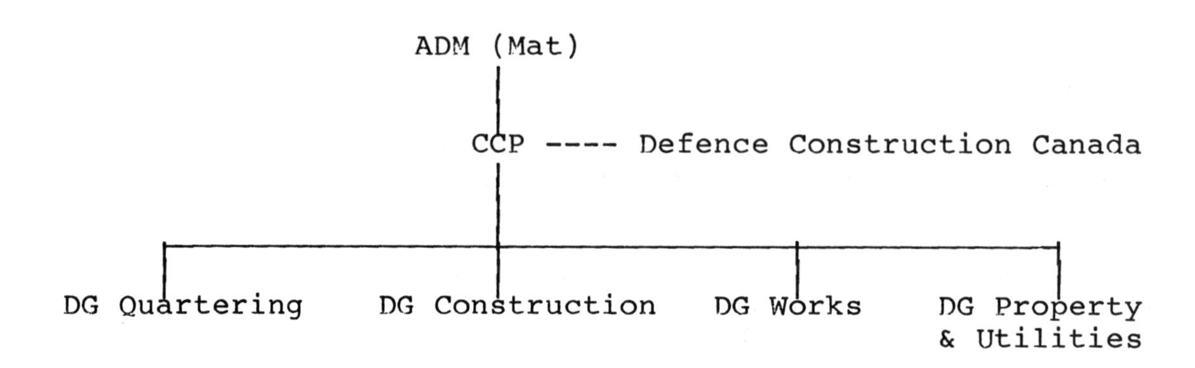

Figure 4. Construction Engineering Functional Relationships

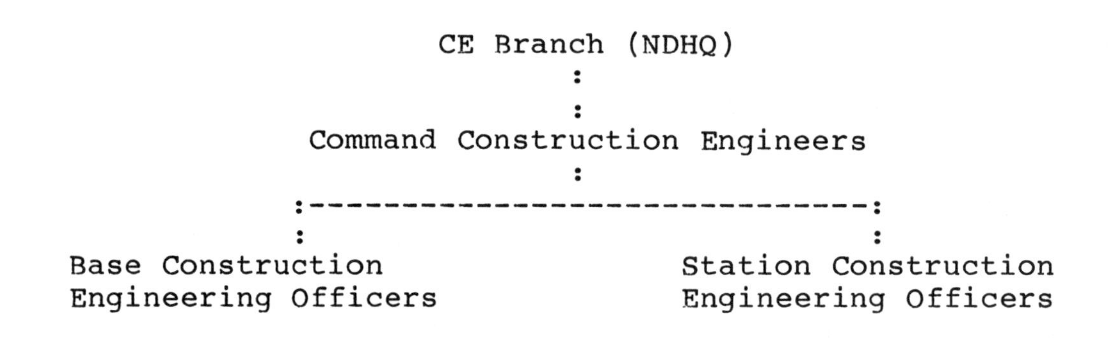

Note - The acronyms used in these diagrams are explained in the paragraphs following Organizational Structure for Construction Engineering.

DEFENCE SERVICES PROGRAM (INFRASTRUCTURE)

OBJECTIVE

To provide defence infrastructure appropriate to the size, structure and roles of the Canadian Forces.

RESULTS/BENEFICIARIES

National Defence Headquarters, Commands, Bases and Stations, and Personnel Support Infrastructure appropriate for the Canadian Forces.

The direct beneficiaries are the 82,000 military and 36,000 civilian personnel of the Canadian Forces and their families; and the 21,000 reserves. Indirect beneficiaries in peacetime are the communities and regions within which Canadian Forces facilities are located, the Canadian people, and Canada's allies. Beneficiaries in wartime are the Canadian people and Canada's allies.

AUTHORITY

National Defence Act.

RESOURCES

	84/85	85/86
Capital	$150	$161 million
Operating Expenditures	$520	$526 million
Revenues	$ 83	$ 84 million
Person-Years	12,500	12,500

REAL PROPERTY ASSETS

Land	2 million hectares
Number of Buildings	36,000 (including 24,000 married quarters)
Area of Buildings	10.7 million square metres

PROGRAM DESCRIPTION

This report describes components of the Defence Services Program that are concerned with managing the overall DND inventory of real property infrastructure.

The report will focus on:

a. the nature of the infrastructure;
b. the strategic management of the infrastructure;and
c. the provision of personnel support infrastructure, particularly housing.

Infrastructure

DND's infrastructure constitutes the largest inventory of real property in the Government of Canada in terms of building area (with almost 10.7 million square metres of space) with the largest number of buildings (more than 36,000 of which more than 24,000 are married quarters). It is the third largest landholder in government with more than 2 million hectares. (Annex A attached provides a description of DND Bases and Stations in Canada.)

The DND real property inventory is probably the most diverse and is among the most complex in government. With 33 bases (including one in Lahr, Germany) and 24 stations, DND acts as a community administrator as well as a provider and manager of real property supporting the wartime and peacetime activities of the Canadian Forces.

In terms of its size, distribution and disposition, the infrastructure inventory has been quite dynamic as it has been adjusted over time to meet the changing roles and requirements of the Canadian Forces. There have been three periods of substantial growth: 1939-45, 1950-55 and 1955-60; and a period of some reduction; 1970-75. (Annex B attached provides a list of closures over the past 15 years.) Based on the remaining life expectancy of the existing buildings in the inventory, DND reports 15 per cent will have to be replaced within the next 10 years, and a further 25 per cent in the following 20 years.

Since 1976, the total size of the inventory has remained fairly stable; only two installations (Renous and Churchill) have been closed, and no new installations have been added, although new facilities have continued to be acquired, and old facilities replaced, modernized or renovated.

DND has recognized that the gradual reconfiguration of infrastructure has not kept pace with the decrease in size of the Canadian Forces which occurred within the last 15 years (from 120,000 down to the current 82,000) nor with changing operational requirements.

Strategic Management of Infrastructure

The Director Infrastructure Planning and Coordination (DIPC) at NDHQ reporting to the Vice Chief of the Defence Staff (VCDS) is responsible for guiding the strategic management of the infrastructure. The DIPC develops long-range policy directives and guidelines for the department; coordinates infrastructure activities; provides guidelines from the military perspective for the development of base development plans, and monitors their implementation; plans joint use and occupancy of Canadian forces installations by civil authorities and foreign military powers; and provides advice to other staff agencies on base planning matters.

DIPC consults with all levels of staff within NDHQ, and the field, other government departments and national and foreign military agencies on matters related to DND infrastructure. The directives and guidelines which he prepares for VCDS' signature (e.g. for Base Development Plans) provide a framework for the activities of the CE Branch and CE units in the field.

Personnel Support Infrastructure and Utilities

Two other aspects of DND's infrastructure are the personnel support or social facilities provided to meet the social needs of DND personnel and their families and the provision of utility services for military installations.

Personnel support and social facilities are seen by DND to be necessary to support the military way of life, particularly at remote or isolated installations, and to foster military esprit de corps generally. DND's self-provision of utilities was orginally necessary to support isolated installations where such services were not available from surrounding communities, and is also necessary in some instances to meet emergency requirements.

The locations of many of DND's installations were determined before or during the Second World War and during the 1950s, prior to or in the early phases of the great wave of urbanization which occurred in Canada in the 30 or so years from 1945 to the 1970s. Consequently, many Commands, Bases and Stations that were orginally remote or separate from urban communities and services are now physically linked to or surrounded by urban development. Many of the services which DND once needed to provide for its personnel can now be supplied either by local governments (municipal or provincial) or by the private sector.

In some instances, the location and growth of defence installations in unsettled areas stimulated the development of communities around them. Today, most of these communities remain dependent upon DND for their continued existence.

The traditional military ethos of self-dependence and a certain separation from larger society combined with the need to keep troops occupied has contributed both to the proliferation of personnel support services in the Forces, and to the evolution of the whole elaborate structure of real property management, operation and maintenance in DND.

Nevertheless, DND has attempted to adjust philosophically and conceptually to its changing relationship with the larger Canadian society and with host communities, and to rationalize the management and disposition of its personnel support, social and utilities infrastructure in keeping with this evolving relationship. It has, for example, classified its installations into three categories, (urban, semi-urban, and isolated: see Annex D attached) in order to establish the kinds and levels of service which it will continue to provide for itself as opposed to those which it will now expect to obtain from the surrounding community. It has entered into agreements with municipalities both to obtain and provide services.

The personnel support facilities required to meet the needs of DND personnal and their families are provided in two ways. Facilities which are defined as being directly related to the work of the Forces, or to maintaining the health education and fitness of the Forces are provided through the Defence Services Program. A range of other facilities which are essentially social or commercial in character are financed by military personnel, through the Non-Public Fund.

Facilities which fall into the first category, (Defence Services Program funded) include colleges, schools, medical and dental facilities and hospitals, messes, primary physical education facilities and housing (married quarters and singles quarters).

The Non-Public Fund

Facilities which fall into the second category, (Non-Public funded) include municipal type recreation facilities, cultural, hobby and social recreation facilities, specialty interest recreational facilities (equivalent to private clubs) and CANEX retail outlets. CANEX retail outlets include exchanges, groceterias, service stations, concessions (banks, credit unions, barbershops, etc) and cafeterias, snack bars and lunch rooms. All these kinds of facilities are funded in whole or in part by the military personnel themselves through fees, dues, leases and purchases.

There are arrangements in place for joint use and joint funding of facilities between the Defence Services Program and the Non-Public Fund where considered appropriate.

For example, DND is responsible for provision of messes at public expense. Any additions, changes or renovations in excess of approved scales are made at the expense of the NPF fund. All facilities which are NPF funded are maintained by or through DND Construction Engineering staff, with NPF's share of the costs prorated to the fund. (See Annex E for details.) Grants in lieu of taxes are paid by DND on NPF facilities.

The provision of facilities, the degree of maintenance support, and the provision of utilities and basic services is dependent on the group into which the facilities fall and the category (urban, semi-urban or isolated) of the base.

DND Housing

At the present time the most difficult and visible problem related to the personnel support infrastructure is the management of DND housing. As long as it provides housing the department must face constant adjustment to changes in demographics, social patterns, Force requirements, housing standards, community environments and market conditions. With over 24,000 PMQs (permanent married quarters) owned and rented, and over 22,000 single quarters (SQ), and faced with some 16,000 - 20,000 personnel transfers annually, the logistics of utilizing and operating this housing are difficult, as exemplified in the annual vacancy rate of approximately 10 per cent for PMQs and close to 20 per cent for SQs.

The difficulties are compounded by the fact that from the point of view of equity, DND must also take into account the impact of housing market conditions and costs on personnel stationed at or transferred to or from those (urban) bases where housing is not provided, and personnel are expected to find their own.

Recognizing the problems, DND recently convened a Task Force to review the PMQ situation and to recommend revisions to PMQ management. CMHC has been providing support for the Task Force. The team has been quantifying PMQ requirements based on the following criteria: (a) military personnel needs; (b) Base category; (c) market availability; and (d) military operational requirements. The team will also evaluate a 10 per cent sample of the stock, and assess the direct and indirect costs of operating and maintaining the housing inventory.

In the meantime three trial projects in Ottawa, Cold Lake and Val Cartier will lead to an assessment of alternate management methods, including the concept of a self supporting housing fund.

The preliminary findings of the Task Force are that DND requires almost all the PMQs it now has, that there are surpluses and shortages of units at various installations across the country, and that DND's worst problems are in and between the urban centres, where wide fluctuations of housing availability and costs have occurred.

The Task Force plans to submit its proposals to DND Executives in June/July, and to obtain a decision on the future management of PMQ by September 1985.

Responsibility for the overall management of Personnel Support Infrastructure and the Non Public Fund is with the ADM Personnel (ADM Per). The Non Public Fund is controlled by a Board of Directors, including CDS, VCDS, ADM (Per), ADM (Fin), and the Commanders of the major Commands.

The Chief of Construction and Properties and the Construction Engineering Branch in NDHQ provide functional support to ADM (Per), and CE units at Commands and Bases carry out operation and maintenance of the Personnel Support facilities.

OBSERVATIONS

DND has too much infrastructure, and this oversupply is causing wasteful expenditure and manpower utilization.

The oversupply is the result of a number of causes, including:

- changing military requirements;
- powerful local socio-economic pressures, which hitherto have led government to direct that installations which DND wishes to close should remain in operation;
- slow adjustment by DND to changing urban/community conditions; and
- lack of a powerful challenge function outside DND in central agencies.

The unit charged with the strategic planning of the infrastructure (DIPC) is distracted from this major responsibility because it is required to handle "fire-fighting" situations: e.g. the proposed Chatham Base closure.

The Defence Services Program is subsidizing the Non-Public Fund.

In the view of the study team, management of DND housing needs overhaul. A more flexible, economic and efficient form of housing support for military personnel should be found. Options which should be considered include increased contracting out (including increased leasing), or the establishment of a separate housing corporation, or the transfer of housing to Provincial Housing Corporations. Surplus housing should be transferred to Provincial Housing Corporations, or leased, or sold.

DND should assess its utilities and municipal-type services, vis-à-vis services available in surrounding municipalities and develop a 3-year Rationalization Plan.

OPTIONS

The study team recommends to the Task Force that the government should consider asking DND to develop medium (1 to 5 years) and long range (5 to 10 years) infrastructure rationalization proposals. The rationalization plan should include provision for cooperative planning with provinces and local communities for the socio-economic adjustments which would have to be made.

DND should adopt a revised form of housing management, which should be incorporated in any overall reform of federal housing which may be recommended and approved as a result of the Housing Task Force study team.

DND should develop and implement a 3-year Utilities and Municipal-type Service Rationalization Plan.

ANNEX A

MAJOR INFRASTRUCTURE DISTRIBUTION

Province	Base	Station	Detachment/ Installation
British Columbia	Chilliwack Comox Equimalt	Aldergroves Baldy Hughes Holberg Kamloops Masset	Chilcotin Nanaimo Nanoose Rocky Point Vernon
Alberta	Calgary Cold Lake Edmonton Penhold Suffield	Beaverlodge Wainwright	Primrose Range Jimmy Srange Sarcee
Saskatchewan	Moose Jaw	Alsask Dana Yorkton	Dundurn Baurdick Primrose Range
Manitoba	Portage Shilo Winnipeg	Beausejour Fin Flon Gypsumville	St Charles
Ontario	Borden Kingston London North Bay Ottawa Petawawa Toronto Trenton	Carp Falconbridge Lietrim Lowther Sioux Lookout	Connaught Ipperwash Meaford Merrick
Quebec	Bagotville Montreal St Jean Valcartier	Chibougamau Lac St Denis Moisie Mont Apica Senneterre	Nicolet Farnham
New Brunswick	Chatham Gagetown Moncton		St Margarets Mill Hill Tracadie

Province	Base	Station	Detachment/ Installation
Nova Scotia	Cornwallis Greenwood Halifax Shearwater	Barrington Mill Cove Newport Corner Shelburne Sydney	Aldershot Bedford Debert Granville Ferry Victoria Branch
Prince Edward Island	Summerside		
Newfoundland		Gander Goose Bay St Johns	
Yukon			Komakuk Point Shingle Point Whitehorse
Northwest Territories		Inuvik Alert	Broughton Island Byron Bay Cambridge Bay Cape Dyer Cape Hooper Cape Parry Cape Young Clinton Point Dewar Lakes Gladman Point Hall Beach Jenny Lind Island Lady Franklin Longstaff Bluff Mackar Inlet Nicholson Peninsula Pelly Bay Tuktoyaktuk Yellowknife Frobisher Shepherd Bay

ANNEX B

A DECADE OF INFRASTRUCTURE REDUCTIONS

1970	Ville La Salle
1971	CFB Clinton CFB Gimli CFB Rivers Coverdale Radio Station London Supply Depot and Workshop Cobourg Supply Depot Ladner Radio Station
1972	CFS Lamacaza CFAD St Therese CFS Gloucester
1973	
1974	CFS Ramore CFS Armstrong CFS Foymount Patricia Bay
1975	CFS Moosonee
1976	CFS Val D'Or
1977	
1978	CFAD Renous
1979	
1980	CFS Churchill
1981	

DEPARTMENT OF NATIONAL DEFENCE

ANNEX C

SUMMARY OF INSTALLATIONS, DEFENCE EXPENDITURES AND DIRECT EMPLOYMENT BY PROVINCE AND TERRITORY

Provinces	Bases	Stations	Cadin Pinetree Radar Sites	Other[1]	Expenditures 1981/82			Direct Employment (as of March 1982)			% of Total Pro-Vince Employment (1981)
	(Possible Reduction/Closure Bracketed)				Total ($000's)	%of Total	Per Capita	Civilian	Military	Total	(Annual Average)
Newfoundland	-	3	(2)	-	42,778	0.9)	$ 76	257	870	1,127	.6)
Prince Edward Island	1	-	-	-	47,332	1.0)	$390	275	927	1,202	2.5)
Nova Scotia	4	5	(2)	5	722,398	)21.6 15.4)	$862	6,727	12,497	19,224	)3.3 5.9)
New Brunswick	3 (1)	-	(1)*	3	199,139	4.3)	$289	1,670	4,217	5,887	2.3)
Quebec	4 (1)	5	(5)	2	726,005	15.6	$114	5,420	11,159	16,579	.65
Ontario	8 (1)	5	(3)	4	1,639,216	35.0	$192	13,684	23,896	37,580	.88
Manitoba	3 (1)	3	(2)	1	282,566	6.0)	$278	1,698	3,972	5,670	1.3)
Saskatchewan	1	3	(3)	3	83,915	1.8)	$ 88	609	1,618	2,227	0.5)
Alberta	5 (1)	2	(3)*	3	388,135	8.3)	$176	2,692	7,240	9,932	)1.0 1.0)
British Columbia	3 (2)	5	(3)	5	529,779	)27.8 11.3)	$195	4,387	8,039	12,426	1.0)
Yukon	-	-	-	2	797	-)	$ 35	0	21	21	
Northwest Territories	-	2	-	20	20,547	0.4)	$460	37	483	520	
TOTAL IN CANADA	32	33	(24)	48	4,682,607	100.0	$194	37,456	74,939	112,395	1.0

1 Refers mostly to communications centres.
* Radar sites in Chatham, N.B. and in Penhold and Cold Lake, Alberta are part of the bases for administrative and control purposes.

ANNEX D

DND BASE CLASSIFICATION

Urban Locations

Calgary
Edmonton
Esquimalt
Halifax
Kingston
London
Moncton
Montreal
North Bay
Ottawa
Royal Roads Military College
Shearwater
St.Jean
St.John's
Toronto
Winnipeg

Semi-Urban Locations

Aldergorve
Bagotville
Borden
Carp
Chilliwack
Chatham
Comox
Falconbridge
Farnham
Gagetown
Greenwood
Kamloops
Leitrim
Moose Jaw
Nanaimo
Penhold
Portage
Petawawa
Shilo
Summerside
CFS Sydney
Trenton
Valcartier
Val d'Or

Isolated Locations

Aldershot
Alert
Alsask
Argentia
Baldy Hughes
Barrington
Beausejour
Beaverlodge
Chibougamau
Cold Lake
Cornwallis
Dana
Debert
Dundurn
Gander
Goose Bay
Gypsumville
Holberg
Inuvik
Ipperwash
Lac St Denis
Lowther
Masset

ANNEX E

DND PUBLIC/NON-PUBLIC PARTICIPATION GUIDELINES

Cost Element	Item		Messes			Physical Education and Recreation							CANEX				
			Officers	WO's and Sgts	Junior Ranks	Military Colleges	Physical Education	Municipal Type	Social Hobby Cultural	Specialty Urban	Specialty Semi-urban	Specialty Isolated	Urban	Semi-urban	Isolated	Europe	Operational
1. Provision of Facilities	1.1	Original Capital Cost	P	P	P	P	P	S	S	N	N	N	N	N	P	N	P
	1.2	Use of Available Facilities	P	P	P	P	P	P	P	P	P	P	P	P	P	P	P
	1.3	Renovations to Scale	P	P	P	P	P	S	S	N	N	N	N	N	P	N	
	1.4	Renovations in Excess of Scale	N	N	N	N	N	N	N	N	N	N	N	N	N	N	
2. Maintenance of Facilities	2.1	Routine Maintenance	P	P	P	P	P	P	P	N	N	P	N	S	P	P	P
	2.2	Major Maintenance	P	P	P	P	P	S	S	N	N	N	N	N	P	N	P
3. Cleaning Services	3.1	Routine to Scale	P	P	P	P	P	P	N	N	N	N	N	N	N	N	P
	3.2	Required in Excess of Scale	N	N	N	N	N	N	N	N	N	N	N	N	N	N	P
4. Utilities Services	4.1	Installation	P	P	P	P	P	S	S	N	N	N	N	N	P	P	P
	4.2	Heat	P	P	P	P	P	P	P	N	S	P	N	S	P	P	P
	4.3	Electricity	P	P	P	P	P	P	P	N	S	S	N	S	P	P	P
	4.4	Water	P	P	P	P	P	P	P	N	S	P	N	S	P	P	P
	4.5	Sewage	P	P	P	P	P	P	P	N	S	P	N	S	P	P	P
5. Base Services	5.1	Security	P	P	P	P	P	P	P	P	P	P	P	P	P	P	P
	5.2	Fire Protection	P	P	P	P	P	P		P	P	P	P	P	P	P	P
	5.3	Routine Snow Removal	P	P	P	P	P	P	P	P	P	P	P	P	P	P	P
	5.4	Snow Removal Outdoor Rinks	-	-	-	P	P	P	-	-	-	-	-	-	-	-	-
	5.5	Garbage Removal	P	P	P	P	P	P	P	P	P	P	P	P	P	P	P

CODE: N NON PUBLIC; P PUBLIC; S 50/50 PLIT

DEFENCE SERVICES PROGRAM (QUARTERING)

OBJECTIVE

The objective and role of the Construction Engineering Branch under the Chief Construction and Properties (CCP) is to provide construction engineering support to the Canadian Forces and Forces of other countries carrying out construction in Canada; conduct and coordinate the implementation of approved construction programs; and to provide functional direction on construction engineering (CE) matters.

The objective and role of the Quartering Division under the Director General Quartering (DGQ) as part of the CE Branch is to define departmental requirements for accommodation and fixed facilities; manage Construction and Properties budgets and programs; formulate policies for program and project control; manage the CE financial and term labour resources; and evaluate accommodation facilities.

RESULTS/BENEFICIARIES

Approved programs, plans and budgets to meet military construction engineering requirements and delivery of approved construction projects on time and within budget.

The beneficiaries are the Canadian Forces and Department of National Defence.

AUTHORITY

National Defence Act.

RESOURCES (DGQ only)

		85/86
Operating		$1.9 million
Person-Years:	Military	18
	Civilian	26

PROGRAM DESCRIPTION

This review describes and analyzes one component of Construction Engineering in DND, the Quartering function.

Construction Engineering is the term used in DND for real property provision and management. Quartering is essentially the real property planning and control function.

A companion report (Defence Services Program: Real Property Management and Organization) describes how the Construction Engineering Branch (CEB) fits into the structure and organization of NDHQ, and the functional relationship between CEB and the Command Construction Engineers at the five Command Headquarters across Canada and in Europe.

The Director General Quartering and his Division, reporting to the Chief Construction and Properties (Head of the CE Branch), are responsible for:

- Accommodation planning and studies;
- Accommodation scales and standards;
- Base Development Plans;
- Construction and real property requirements definition;
- Project definition;
- Preparation of Project approval documents;
- Project management;
- Departmental construction and maintenance programs (3 year programs: MYOPs, etc.);
- Construction engineering (budget and project) financial control; and
- Special CE programs in support of government initiatives.

Construction Engineering Capital and Operations Funding Formulae

The DND real property inventory is not growing, except for new facilities to support "equipment projects" (i.e. new fighters, new frigates, etc.). Capital construction levels are therefore based on the plant replacement value (PRV) except for "equipment projects" which are funded within the new equipment budgets.

However, in the past 10 years, DND has not been able to provide funding commensurate with the Construction

Engineering Branch's desired norm of 2 per cent of PRV. Capital funding levels currently stand at about 1.2 per cent of PRV. The acceptability of this funding formula for DND management purposes has not been tested to the knowledge of the study team, and it is therefore not possible to state whether the shortfall is significant or not.

The same is true for operation and maintenance funding levels, where again the desired level of 1.8 per cent of PRV has not been achieved, and levels are hovering around 1.4 per cent.

The above situation has placed pressure on DND to ensure that its Construction Engineering funds are expended as optimally as possible on the area of greatest need. Consequently, the department has developed an elaborate construction planning and priorization process in order to achieve this goal. Many standards for various types of facilities are in place to support this process. The process places strong emphasis on needs definition and requirements definition.

The notable features of the management process are:

- the lengthy, elaborate, multi-layered project identification, challenge and approval process;
- the risk-free, fail safe approach to acquisition, design and construction;
- the application of a lengthy (50-year) fully costed life-cycle project development, operation and maintenance concept;
- in the implementation phase, a strong emphasis on project control (time, quality, quantity and cost) which entails an extensive monitoring and inspection process of work done on contract, by either DND or DCC personnel or both.

Requirements Definition

Effective and efficient provision of real property services depends upon clients having the clearest possible concept of their requirements. In DND, the military are the clients and their definition of real property requirements is dependent upon having a clearly articulated and government approved force structure in place which meets Canada's defence and foreign policy.

The basis for the present force structure was defined in 1975 and is now considered by the Department to be somewhat outdated. This makes it difficult to relate capability levels to the achievement of roles and objectives. Furthermore, when the model was designed several important factors, including infrastructure, operations and maintenance were not adequately defined.

Base Development Plans

The department has determined that 40 Base Development Plans (BDP) should be prepared. Each BDP is initiated by the provision of guidelines reflecting the military requirement which are prepared by the Director of Infrastructure Planning and Control (DIPC) and approved by the Vice Chief of the Defence Staff (VCDS). Planning factors taken into consideration include the role, missions and tasks of the Base, and the units, elements and personnel establishment to be accommodated, the physical planning, functional analysis and economic factors.

The Auditor General (AG) was critical of BDPs in his 1983/84 report, saying that the cost of contributions to wider social, economic and environmental objectives is usually not addressed (although DND guidelines call for "regional socio-economic factors" to be taken into account). The AG also commented that BDPs do not address the efficient use of the real property involved, in terms of the economic value of the land for alternative uses.

To date, 10 BDPs have been approved, four are expected to be completed during FY 1985/86, another 10 in 1986/87, with the balance (16) in future years. The total number contemplated (40) includes Bases which the department knows will continue to have an important role in the revised force structure as well as some for which there may no longer be a military requirement.

Most BDPs prepared to date have involved the appointment of planning and engineering consultants who work on a multi-disciplinary team basis under the guidance of a DND Project Manager provided by DGQ with input from a Base Liaison Officer. The consultant contract costs for preparing these plans is in the $1 to $2 million range (i.e. equivalent to the cost of a medium-sized municipality's development plan).

Plans usually do not specify detailed architectural, structural or servicing designs, but indicate the mass, volume and siting of proposed structures, gross floor areas, assumed unit costs and the general quality of construction anticipated. Plans designate the use or re-use of land and buildings, and indicate the volume, location, cost and phasing of development, including supporting major services in water, sewer, energy and transport.

Within the parameters of BDPs, Bases develop individual project proposals which are put forward in major program submissions to Commands for roll-up in Command Major Program submissions, for review by the Construction Priority Screening Committee (CPSC) at NDHQ. The CPSC establishes an annual construction priority list for approval by the Program Control Board (PCB), a senior executive committee in DND. From this approved priority list DGQ establishes the 3-year Major Construction Program for approval by PCB.

Project Management

The Construction Engineering Branch has developed a 3-stage Construction Engineering Project Management System (CPMS) which is essentially a process for the development, approval, design, construction and commissioning of capital projects within the approved major construction program.

Project Management and financial control throughout all stages rests with DGQ. DGQ provides a Project Manager (equivalent to a Development Manager in the private sector) who remains in charge of the project throughout its complete development phase.

An individual Project Manager may have six or seven or more projects in various stages of development under his control at any one point in time. He oversees the projects through a matrix team organization. The team will consist of representatives from the user and NDHQ sponsor as well as from the CE organization, and other functions as necessary.

Team leadership changes from one stage to the next as follows:

Stage 1	Project Definition Stage: Team Captain from DGQ.
Stage 2	Project Design Stage: Team Captain from DGC. Consultant contract administration by DCC.
Stage 3	Project Construction Stage: Team Captain from DGQ. Construction contract administration and on-site supervision by DCC.

Once DGQ has secured project approval he passes responsibility over to the Construction Division for Design either in-house or by consultant. The completed design is then transmitted to DCC for contracting. DCC supervises the construction and administers the contract. The completed structure is handed back from DCC to DGQ for commissioning, and after certification, DGQ passes responsibility to the Command (or Base) for operation and maintenance of the facility.

In addition to his planning, project management and project financial control responsibilities, DGQ is also responsible for setting accommodation scales and standards and for evaluations.

DGQ's division has an establishment of 44 PYs and is organized in two directorates. The Director of Construction Engineering Requirements (DCER) is responsible for ensuring that the user/sponsor have defined the project requirement satisfactorily and in accordance with scales and standards, and also for project management and Base Development planning. He has a staff of approximately 26 PYs, most of them military and mostly professionals. The Director of Construction Engineering Control secures project approvals and maintains funding control and acts as liaison with NATO and NATO funded CE projects. He has 18 PYs.

OBSERVATIONS

In his 1983/84 Comprehensive Audit, the Auditor General concluded that capital construction is managed satisfactorily in DND. He found that DND generally complies with applicable legislation, Treasury Board requirements and departmental policies respecting management of capital construction projects, but suggested that economic analysis of projects and post-completion reviews should be improved. DGQ has moved to improve post-completion reviews and strengthen feedback. He has also increased the involvement of Operations and Maintenance functional advisers (from DGW) during the development phases of capital projects.

DND's Management Audit (e.g. in the Petawawa supply facility audit) has criticized the uneven quality of project management, commenting that program managers' approach to their tasks varies from strongly proactive and management/control oriented, to passive and reactive. It should be noted that the experience and qualifications that project managers bring to their assignments vary. Some project managers are career-oriented construction engineering specialists; others are rotating through and will move on to other areas of the Forces. Again, DGQ is acting to alleviate these deficiencies through the publication of a Project Management Manual, planned for 1986.

DND's Management Audit has also commented that the general approach to the capital program is focused too much on the justification and implementation of individual projects and lacks a comprehensive assessment of the costs and benefits to be achieved by the proposed or approved program versus other alternatives. The difficulties of articulating a comprehensive construction engineering strategy in the absence of an approved Force Posture and approved long range Infrastructure Plan have been discussed in the accompanying Program Review on the Defence Services Program (Infrastructure).

In this respect it is worth noting that the Construction Program occasionally contains sizable capital projects on Bases that may be redundant from the military perspective (e.g. an $8 million project for a combined mess for Summerside, slated for design in 1985/86).

A contributing factor to the lack of a comprehensive program overview may be the split of responsibilities between DGQ, DGC and DGPU. DGC and DGPU both have responsibilities which logically should be integrally linked with DGQ's program and planning responsibilities, namely, the estimates function of DGC and the maintenance of the inventory database by DGPU.

OPTIONS

The study team recommends to the Task Force that the government consider strengthening the effective program and project management and control function which DGQ performs for construction engineering in DND by DGQ taking over the preplanning and estimates function of DGC and responsibility for maintenance of the inventory database from DGPU, these being functions logically related to DGQ's planning and control role.

DEFENCE SERVICES PROGRAM (DESIGN AND CONSTRUCTION)

OBJECTIVE

The objective and role of the Construction Engineering Branch under the Chief Construction and Properties (CCP) is to provide construction engineering support to the Canadian Forces and Forces of other countries carrying out construction in Canada; conduct and coordinate the implementation of approved construction programs; and to provide functional direction on construction engineering (CE) matters.

The objective and role of the Construction Division under the Director General Construction (DGC) within the CE Branch is to develop plans, policies, and standards for engineering and architectural design activities in support of the construction and maintenance of accommodation and facilities in the department, and for the execution of designs for NDHQ controlled projects.

RESULTS/BENEFICIARIES

Architectural and Engineering Designs for Construction Engineering projects: Estimates; A&E Policies for Design Activities: Advice.

The beneficiaries are the military and DND generally, and specifically Defence Construction (1951) Ltd., the Construction Engineering Branch in NDHQ and CE units at Commands and Bases.

AUTHORITY

National Defence Act.

RESOURCES (DGC only)

	85/86
Operating Expenses	$5 million
Person-Years (civilian)	109

PROGRAM DESCRIPTION

This review describes and analyses one component of Construction Engineering in and for DND, the design and construction function.

Construction Engineering is the term used in DND for real property provision and management. The design and construction aspects of real property provision and management are performed in or for DND as described below.

Design

Architectural and engineering design is carried out at several levels of the organization depending on the size, complexity and security considerations of the projects. The design of large, complex and/or sensitive projects is controlled at NDHQ (generally projects over $1 million). Design authority for projects between $400,000 and $1 million is delegated to Commands and design authority for projects below $400,000 to Bases.

Judgement is exercised on whether project designs should be done by in-house professional and technical resources or contracted out in whole or part to design consultants in the private sector. The criteria for doing the work in-house include (a) complexity/security; (b) in-house workload and technical capabilities; (c) operational urgency; (d) approval stage of project; and (e) need for in-house resources to maintain awareness of the state-of-the-art. All design work and estimates required for the preplanning stage are done in-house. Approximately 70 per cent of the total value of projects is normally contracted out.

Almost invariably, before moving to the construction phase, DND satisfies itself in exhaustive detail that the full design meets its requirements: i.e. design is taken to the full working drawing stage. Projects generally are treated as individual design challenges. Although the department has many accommodation standards and scales, it has few standard designs.

The department rarely applies the design/build or performance specification methods to facility acquisition. Design/build or performance specification methods are those in which the client provides a statement of his need and/or a specification of the performance characteristics which he desires for the facility, then leaves the design and construction responsibilities substantially or entirely to the contractor. These methods reduce the level of internal checking and inspection to a minimum and place accountability and liability clearly with the contractor to supply a finished product which meets the specified standards and scale.

Design Organization: NDHQ

The unit responsible for design is the Construction Division under the DG Construction (DGC) in the Construction Engineering Branch at NDHQ. (Although called the Construction Division, it is not involved in construction nor in project management.) The division of 109 PYs at NDHQ (including 20 architects, 30 engineers, and technicians, draftsmen and support personnel) is staffed entirely by civilian employees of DND.

DGC performs his responsibilities through a mix of in-house design and contracting out. He decides (in consultation with CCP, DGQ and others) which projects shall be done in-house and which by contracting out. Consultants contracts are obtained and administered for him by the Crown Corporation DCC after ministerial approval of consultant selection. The short list for selection is drawn up with his advice. Contracted design for NDHQ controlled projects is done under the supervision or inspection of his division.

In Stage 1 of the CE Project Management System (CPMS), i.e. the project definition stage, DGC is responsible for pre-planning of all construction projects as input to the design brief and approved statement of requirement which are the responsibilities of DGQ.

Once a project is approved, it moves into Stage 2 of the CPMS, the project design phase. DGC provides a team leader (or Design Manager) who manages the production of the design under the project manager provided by DGQ. At the end of Stage 2, the completed design enters Stage 3, the construction phase. It is passed from DGC to the Crown Corporation DCC to be contracted out for construction. DGC still maintains the team captaincy of the project team during this phase though responsibility has now passed the Crown Corporation.

The DGC's division is organized in three directorates: (a) Architecture; (b) Engineering; and (c) Construction Materials. Between 20 and 25 designs are done in-house annually. The organization spends approximately 50-55 per cent of its working level time on projects (which includes 5 per cent on pre-planning). It prepares 600-650 cost estimates a year, of which approximately 90 per cent are for pre-planning. Another 5 per cent of its working level time is spent on liaison with DCC and site visits, and 5 per cent is devoted to providing advice to Commands and Bases. Five per cent of its time is spent on construction materials testing and certification. (The balance of time goes on training, management and administration, sickness, vacation, etc.)

Construction

Almost all new construction (90 per cent plus) and most reconstruction is contracted out to the private sector. The contract process is handled for DND by the Crown Corporation Defence Construction Canada (1951) Ltd. DND does little of its own construction. For military training purposes, however, a small number of small construction projects are built by the Combat Engineering Units, usually at a rate of only one a year.

Although DND arranges to have a separate agency (DCC) manage its construction contracts, DND monitors contract progress as it deems necessary, either by CE field units or NDHQ or both.

Design and Construction Organization: Field

In the field, design authority for projects under $1 million is delegated to Command Headquarters. Engineers who are responsible for preparing engineering studies, design, cost estimates, plans, drawings and specifications for command construction projects, and monitoring major design and construction contracts in conjunction with DCC Branch Managers. Again, DCC is responsible for the actual award and administration of design and construction contracts.

OBSERVATIONS

With respect to the design and construction aspects of DND's Construction Engineering function, a number of comments are worth noting.

Within DND, civilian employees perform many of the tasks related to design and construction activity. They understand the forces' requirements but they are not inherently military themselves.

DND splits off much of the actual design and virtually all construction to the private sector.

The private sector consultants and contractors who work for DND are professionals who seek to understand and are capable of satisfying the needs, not only of DND, but of all their clients, including other federal departments and agencies.

Scrutiny of the DND construction program list shows that while there is a small number of projects which perhaps could be said to have a special, technically complex military aspect, the majority of projects have no particular uniqueness (i.e. hospitals, gymnasia, married quarters, food services buildings, maintenance facilities, supply buildings, etc.)

Construction contractors working on security projects must be bonded and must have security clearance. The same principles could be extended more fully, perhaps completely across the DND design activity without serious risk.

Under the conditions noted above, the study team is of the opinion that there is scope to privatize design activities further.

Even where there are projects which have a special military character, the essential task is for the users/sponsors to be able to articulate their statements of requirement precisely. Professional designers in the private sector can and have worked to these specifications.

With further contracting out DND would still be able to maintain control through its CE Project Management System, and specifically through (a) a clear statement of approved requirement, (b) good project management, and (c) inspection and certification of completed projects.

OPTIONS

Tasks of DGC which are essential to sound requirements definition are preplanning and related estimating. The study team recommends to the Task Force that the government consider retaining these in DND and transferring them to DGQ.

DGC's design management activities are either duplicative of work being done by the private sector consultants and contractors, or would not be necessary if greater accountability were to be placed on the private sector with less double-checking by the government. DGC's design management activity should be phased out. If needed, DGQ can contract design management services through DCC.

DGC's remaining in-house design activity should be transferred to the common Architectural and Engineering service in PWC.

DND should adopt greater use of design/build or general performances specifications. This approach would simplify and speed up the design process in DND and DCC and would take advantage of the private sector's ability to respond to a knowledgable client.

DEFENCE CONSTRUCTION CANADA

OBJECTIVE

To contract for major military construction and maintenance projects and professional services required by the Department of National Defence.

RESULTS/BENEFICIARIES

Works and buildings at DND Bases and Stations. Professional Services through Architectural and Consulting Engineering Firms.

The beneficiary is the Department of National Defence.

RESOURCES	**84/85**
Operating	$14.6 million
Person-Years	260-340

PROGRAM DESCRIPTION

Defence Construction (1951) Limited is a Crown corporation named in Schedule C of the Financial Administration Act. With the exception of the qualifying shares of its six (unpaid) Directors, the Company's shares are held by the Minister of National Defence in trust for her Majesty. The Company reports directly to the Minister.

The Company's chief responsibilities are to obtain and manage contracts in the design and construction field above $30,000 in value on behalf of DND. It is responsible for three categories of contract:

- Architectural and Engineering (A&E) design consultants;
- Hard Construction (new); and
- Maintenance (including re-construction).

During 1984/85, the Company awarded 1,276 contracts having a total value of $240 million. The number and value of contracts by category, and the estimated expenditures were:

	Number of Contracts	Value $ millions	Expenditures $ millions
A&E Consultants	423	11	8
New Construction	295	142	97
Maintenance	558	87	95
TOTAL	1,276	240	200

Approximately 50 per cent of the contracts handled by DCC are small: under $100,000 in value. The number of large contracts ($1 million plus) normally ranges from about 15 to 20 annually.

Program delivery is organized through the Head Office with 61 PYs located in Ottawa, and five regional offices located in Halifax, Montreal, Toronto, Winnipeg and Victoria with 212 PYs. There is also a European office of 13 PYs in Lahr, Federal Republic of Germany. The composition of DCC's staff as of Feb 1985 was:

Professional	66
Administrative	11
Technical	140
Support	69
TOTAL	286

A&E Consultant Contracts

As the custodian, project sponsor and design authority, DND is responsible for providing Defence Construction Canada (DCC) with plans, designs and specifications for its construction contract requirements.

Internally, DND decides whether a project should be designed in-house, or should be contracted out to design consultants. If it is to be contracted out, DND requests DCC to draw up contracts with the approved consultants. DCC then administers the contracts, but technical direction and supervision of the design is carried out in DND, by Construction Engineering Branch in NDHQ or Construction Engineering Officers at Commands and Bases.

The authority levels for consultant selection are:

DCC: up to $25,000
Minister: up to $100,000
Treasury Board: over $100,000

The proposal call route is followed for projects over $100,000 in value.

Above $25,000, consultants are selected by the Minister based on lists of names submitted to him by DCC in consultation with DND. The process of consultant selection can be lengthy and time consuming.

The Manager of Consultant Contracts in the Head Office is responsible to the President for arranging the terms of contracts for consulting services.

Hard Construction Contracts

Following design approval, DND requests DCC to tender for the hard construction contracts. Although it is not bound to do so and in contrast to other Crown corporations, DCC follows Government Contracting Regulations. Calls are national in scope, and, to date, have always been opened in Ottawa at DCC Head Office.

DCC obtains the contracts but Treasury Board or DND approves them. The authority levels for construction contract approval are:

Treasury Board	$10 million plus
Minister	up to $10 million
NDHQ	up to $1 million
DND Commands	up to $400,000
DND Bases	up to $100,000

The Engineering Division in DCCHQ is responsible for the administration of both construction and repair and maintenance contracts. This involves the calling and review of tenders, recommendations to award, the award and issuance of contracts and the inspection of work, including certification for payment. Before going to tender, DCC checks designs to assure itself that they are biddable and buildable.

DCC Regional Managers are responsible for the actual supervision and control of work at the various sites in each region. Site Representatives (equivalent to Project Managers in the private sector) are responsible for the day-to-day inspection of the work and the on-site administration of the contracts. Site Representatives are named at every Base where DND has an active construction program. At Bases with very large programs (e.g. CF Base Halifax at the present time) there could be four or five Site Representatives on the job.

Maintenance

The process and the authorities for maintenance contracts are very similar to those followed for new construction. In the maintenance category DCC and DND also have an arrangement for a fast-tracking or short tender call (STC), mainly for single trade jobs up to $50,000, with negotiation up to $100,000. In these cases contract supervision is provided by DND.

DCC - DND Relationship

The relationship between DCC and its client, DND is governed by a Memorandum of Understanding (MOU) first signed in June 1965, and last revised in July 1981. The MOU specifies:

a. that the Construction Engineering (CE) organization of the Canadian Forces will be fully responsible for all design. Design standards are developed by National Defence HQ CE staff in cooperation with DCC;

b. that where the scope or the intent of the work is not clear CE (with the assistance of DCC) will ensure that clarifying action is taken;

c. that DCC is fully responsible for the administration of all contracts placed by DCC on behalf of DND. Standards for supervision and inspection of these contracts are developed jointly by DCC and CE;

d. that the technical staffs of both organizations will be utilized in such a manner that the best capabilities of both organizations are brought to bear on each project. This arrangement essentially provides for interchange of services rather than staff although the latter has been and will continue to be done where advantageous to both agencies; and

e. that in every case, it is CE's responsibility to ensure that completed projects meet the needs of users, while DCC's responsibility is to ensure that contractors meet the requirements of the contracts.

Both DND and DCC express satisfaction with the current organizational form of DCC and the present arrangements between the two organizations. They stress four principles that they feel are important in understanding DCC's role and capability, and in comprehending its relationship with DND. These are:

Specialization. DCC is essentially a contracting agent running a competitive tendering process and (in private sector terminology) a project manager, providing contract supervision and quality assurance.

Dedication. Since it has only one client, DCC is able to concentrate on knowing and understanding that client, and on meeting its needs and priorities.

Separation. The separation of DCC as an organization superficially independent of DND provides both a measure of protection for the department from political pressures related to contracting and an effective intermediary between the military and the consulting and construction contracting industry.

Flexibility. Both DCC and DND feel that as a Crown corporation, DCC has greater flexibility than a government department would have to respond to its client, and to adjust its workforce (by project and/or skill) in accordance with the geographical distribution, volume and nature of the workload.

DCC and DND have developed a contracting process over which they are able to maintain a full measure of control and through which risk has been almost totally eliminated. It appears, however, to be expensive. DCC costs alone for hard construction contract supervision are approximately 7 per cent.

It is not possible to quantify the full cost of project design and construction supervision in DND, given the complexity of DND's project approval and implementation process, the nature of the project team matrix and the absence of comprehensive cost data.

However, from the limited data that is available it is clear that combined DND/DCC costs (as a percentage of the hard construction costs) for projects designed by consultants are at least 8-10 per cent, and for projects designed in-house are at least 13-16 per cent, depending on the size and complexity of the project. A developer in the private sector would expect to pay no more than 6 to 10 per cent for the same services (i.e. design, supervision and project management).

Although superficially separate from and independent of DND, DCC is in fact closely linked to the department. It reports to the same Minister. The Board of Directors are predominantly either military or civilian members of the department (2 ADMS and 2 Generals) and DCC is funded through the Department.

Review of DCC's workforce versus its workload confirms that DCC does adjust its staff size to the volume of business. DCC employs a "core" staff of approximately 260 to 290, which in recent years has risen as high as 310 to 340 during the peak construction period (April 15 - November 15), a fluctuation of 20 to 30 per cent or so. This variation in staffing levels compares with a variation of approximately $7 million to $17 million in the monthly value of work performed.

The fluctuation in staffing levels is not markedly different from the hiring practices of regular federal departments with contracting responsibilities, for example PWC and Parks Canada. DCC's major advantage is its ability to deploy and redeploy, hire and fire considerably faster than regular departments bound by PSC regulations.

It should be noted that many members of the DCC "core staff" have been with the Corporation for many years. Since they are dedicated to work only on DND contracts and since the majority of contracts are relatively small the question arises as to whether the more qualified and experienced employees are not sometimes under-employed.

It should also be noted that for projects under $30,000 DND does not use DCC, but uses DSS to contract. DSS simply prepares and obtains the contract but does no inspection or administration. These tasks are carried out by DND staff.

In recognition of the fact that the design, contract, project management, construction commissioning, operation and maintenance of built works is best performed as a continuum, especially on major projects, other federal departments have developed an integrated management process with a single management authority to reflect this. Private industry too has moved in the same direction with the development of integrated architectural/engineering/ construction companies or consortia.

The split of responsibilities between DND and DCC potentially breaks the continuum at two, possibly three key points: (a) at the point where design moves to construction (b) at the point where the completed project is commissioned and possibly (c) lack of feedback during construction to correct design flaws. DCC and DND go to considerable effort to coordinate their activities closely in order to eliminate any gaps in the continuum.

One way to improve the organizational response to the design/construction continuum would be to transfer the Construction Directorate (under DGC) from DND to DCC, thus bringing the design, contract tendering and contract supervision (project management) into one organization.

A second way would be to bring DCC closer to DND, but still respecting the principles of separation and flexibility described previously. This could be done by changing the classification of DCC (now Schedule C, a commercial type of Crown corporation) to Schedule B (a departmental corporation).

However, the study team is not convinced that DCC should continue indefinitely as a contracting and project management agency with only a single client. Ultimately the most economical approach is to merge DCC with the common Design and Construction organization within PWC.

At the present time PWC has sufficient management challenge on its hands dealing with the other changes it is facing. Therefore, the study team proposes, as an interim step towards the ultimate solution, that DCC be converted from a Schedule C to a Schedule B Corporation, and that it report to the Minister of Public Works.

OPTIONS

In line with the thrust of the recommendation to create a single strong consultant and construction agency in government, closely integrated with the design function, the study team recommends to the Task Force that the government consider converting DCC from a Schedule C to a Schedule B Crown Corporation, and transferring it from the Minister of National Defence to the Minister of Public Works as the Minister responsible for the design and construction process in government.

DEFENCE SERVICES PROGRAM (WORKS)

OBJECTIVE

To operate, maintain, and protect from fire, all real property in the custody of the Department of National Defence.

RESULTS/BENEFICIARIES

Real property operated, maintained and protected from fire to the standards of the Department of National Defence.

The beneficiaries are the 82,000 military and 36,000 civilian employees of DND and their families and 21,000 reservists.

AUTHORITY

National Defence Act.

RESOURCES

	84/85	85/86
Operating	$520 million	$526 million
Revenues	$ 83 million	$ 84 million
PY - military	2,280	2,280
- civilian CFT	9,070	9,070
- term	1,000	1,000
- total	12,350	12,350

PROGRAM DESCRIPTION

This report describes the real property operation and maintenance (O&M), and fire protection functions in DND.

The report covers property management and maintenance and fire services to both publicly funded and non-publicly funded facilities (i.e. in addition to funding and maintaining property provided through the Defence Services Program DND maintains and provides services to property owned by military personnel for their own social and commercial needs, and recovers some but not all of the costs from the Non-Public Fund (NPF). The NPF is owned and operated by the military personnel themselves).

Operation, maintenance and protection of real property is managed and carried out at the Command, Base and Station level under policies, procedures and standards established at NDHQ. A works O&M planning and scheduling system is in place. A computerized management information system (CEMIS) now provides information on the status and costs of projects by general categories of works. The system is being developed to provide improved management data by individual facilities which will start to become available in 2 or 3 years time.

There is no formal Base Maintenance Plan similar to a Base Development plan, but Bases and Commands work on a 3-year maintenance program. The 3-year program uses the Base Development Plan as a reference. The program is not formalized by NDHQ. Each Base submits a 3-year maintenance plan annually which is revised and approved by their respective Command. Any maintenance projects over $400,000 requiring NDHQ financial approval are submitted on an individual basis.

The works activity is managed through a mixture of 2,280 military and 10,070 civilian CFT and term personnel. Military personnel generally control the planning, budgeting, scheduling and supervision functions. Civilian personnel generally perform the bulk of the routine maintenance. The actual mix of military and civilian personnel varies from Base to Base, depending on military tradition (the navy traditionally used civilians, whereas the air force and army use military personnel more extensively) as well as Base or Station military function and category (urban/isolated).

About 30 per cent of the O&M work is contracted out, either through DCC (maintenance design and construction projects) or DSS (property management and maintenance services, often on a standing offer basis). The proportion of in-house to contracted out work varies from Base to Base, depending on the factors identified above and on the kinds of equipment assigned to Bases (e.g. availability of heavy equipment).

Firefighting, fire inspection and crash-rescue are carried out by military firefighters supplemented by civilian firefighters. Military firefighters are concentrated on facilities deemed to be of greatest military importance (e.g. all air-field firefighting services are manned 100 per cent by military personnel).

In-house, a wide-range of maintenance engineering studies and some design and construction are undertaken by the mobile Construction Engineering Unit (I CEU) stationed at Winnipeg, Manitoba. These tasks are performed on all bases and serve the dual purpose of military training and real property management.

The functional unit in NDHQ which is responsible for establishing technical policies, procedures and standards (including fire prevention, firefighting, crash rescue, O&M performance measurement, management information, and environmental protection is the Works Division under the Director General Works (DGW) in the Construction Engineering Branch.

DGW has 74 PYs organized in four Directorates: (a) Base Maintenance; (b) Canadian Forces Fire Marshall; (c) Construction Engineering Management Policy; and (d) Conservation and Environment. DGW also is responsible for the management and control of 1 CEU in Winnipeg and its 61 PYs. The Works Division is responsible for monitoring operation and maintenance costs and compliance with departmental policies and procedures by individual Base. To assist in the performance of this latter task DGW normally conducts O&M evaluations of one Command or Base each year.

The Department of National Defence bases its building maintenance budget on a formula, 1.8 per cent of the replacement value of its buildings. However, actual budgets in recent years have been funded at a lower level, approximately 1.4 per cent. The effects of this on the maintenance condition of the inventory, if any, are not known, although DND officials have stated that conditions tend to vary somewhat from base to base and according to the function of facilities.

DND design and construction is based on a 50-year life cycle concept, that is, the department is attempting to include in its project analysis the full costs of designing and building structures of sufficient quality and durability to last 50 years, including all the costs for operation, maintenance and cyclical repair.

Additionally, the department is taking steps to include the Works Division (or its field equivalents) in the requirements and design phases of all construction projects in order that O&M considerations can be taken into full account. This has not always been the case previously.

This approach enables the department to consider possible trade-offs between higher quality design and construction and hence higher development costs on the one hand and lower O&M costs and a higher level of operational effectiveness on the other.

Although the DGW is functionally responsible for O&M, one notable exception to this arrangement is the division of responsiblities for cleaning. DGW is functionally responsible for all contract cleaning, ($8 million per annum) but in-house cleaning is assigned to the ADM Personnel or is under the operational control of the Admin Officer at the Base. ADM Personnel has functional responsibility for 2,600 CFT civilian cleaning staff at an estimated salary cost of $48 million. These staff members are included in the resources profile with this assessment.

As noted in a previous paragraph, the bulk of maintenance is done by civilians. The civilian work force is hired through Canada Manpower Centres. DND tries to ensure that so far as possible civilian employees have provincial trade certification before they are hired. The civilian work force is aging and will reach a significant retirement peak in the next 2 or 3 years.

DND does not put the same effort into career planning and training for its civilian employees as it does for its military personnel. The Auditor General commented that the size and composition of the civilian establishment generally is not determined in the light of current or future military requirements. However, in the CE field long-serving civilian employees do provide continuity to offset the effect of military rotations.

In the last year for which the data is available (1983/84) DND utilization of CE civilian PYs fell 312 PY below authorization (6470 established on an authorized base of 6782). Base/Station Management and Production Overhead costs, excluding NDHQ and Command overhead, represented 19 per cent of actual expenditures including salaries.

OBSERVATIONS

On the available evidence it appears that DND's operational management of the O&M function is sound, and that the current state and general condition of the DND inventory is fair to good, with some variation Base-to-Base. There is, however, a lack of cost and performance data by individual building or facility, which makes it impossible to draw conclusions about DND's overall management or to draw comparisions between DND and industry standards. DND is moving to improve its construction engineering management information system (CEMIS) but it will be several years before the required data base will be in place.

DND has never met its own maintenance funding formula. Nor has there has been any empirical testing of the DND maintenance funding formula in comparison to actual levels, and it is therefore not possible to conclude if the maintenance activity is appropriately resourced. Although there is currently little evidence that the condition of the inventory is deteriorating, there is some jeopardy that deterioration could happen in future years if there is in fact underfunding in this area.

Normally the operation and maintenance of the inventory does not receive the same level of corporate scrutiny and attention at NDHQ as the capital side of the construction engineering activity. Rather it appears that central control is tightened (or loosened) somewhat arbitrarily to correct problem areas, for example, to adjust incidences of possible over maintenance, or to repair deficiences.

DND currently does not appear to manage its civilian CE workforce as effectively as its military personnel, nor to determine its civilian resource requirements in relation to the operational requirements of the military. The department says that these considerations are being taken into account in the Normative Planning process and that it will relate the peace and war structures into a more detailed definition for civilians as a result of the process.

OPTIONS

The study team recommends to the Task Force that the government consider directing DND to increase the amount of O&M contracted out to the private sector; a target should be the elimination of all DND civilian in-house maintenance, except that which can be justified for military operational requirements. The achievement of such a target could be phased and should take attrition into account.

DND should assess to what degree full rationalization of fire and other municipal type property services between Bases/Stations and surrounding or adjacent municipalities could be achieved; then develop and implement a 3-year phased plan of rationalization.

The validity of the maintenance funding formula, and the possible future implications of the current funding level should be assessed.

Construction Engineering Branch in NDHQ should continue its efforts to complete as soon as possible the further development of CEMIS, and to establish a database by individual building and structure.

ANNEX A

DND DEFENCE SERVICES PROGRAM

Real Property Operation and Maintenance (83/84)

BASE/STATION LEVEL PERSONNEL STATISTICS

Category	Military		Civilian		Total	
	Auth	Actual	Auth	Actual	Auth	Actual
Establishment						
Tech & Admin	799	787	1288	1185	2087	1972
Operations	266	255	1392	1336	1658	1591
Firefighters	574	610	690	686	1264	1296
Tradesmen	408	429	3412	3263	3820	3692
Cleaners				2600		2600
Subtotal	2047	2081	6782	9070	8829	11351
Term				1068		1068
TOTAL		2081		10138		12419

Definitions: Category of Personnel

a. **Tech and Admin. Support** - Tech and Admin. Support personnel refers to civilian and military personnel working in the Engineering Services, Requirements, Administration and Utilities offices in support of CE activities.

b. **Operators** - The operators category usually refers to those persons directly involved in the daily operations of water, sewage treatment, power and heating plants.

c. **Firefighters** - This category strictly applies to persons hired and employed as firefighters.

d. **Trademen** - The tradesmen category usually refers to those persons employed in the several trades shops found in CE Base Section, such as the carpenter shop, the plumber shop, etc. These personnel support the daily routine maintenance of the Base and are also employed on Base funded projects.

e. **Cleaners** - CFT civilian employees under the management of Base Admin. Officers, reporting functionally to ADM Personnel.

Term Employees

a. These civilian employees are appointed for a specified period. Hiring is arranged locally through the Civilian Personnel Officer.

b. Term personnel may be employed by CE under the following conditions:

1. to implement approved CE projects for which work by contract is not considered practicable, provided that the term element has been included in the project cost estimate;

2. to prepare designs, estimates, drawings, specifications or bills of material which are in direct support of CE projects;

3. for activities where the use of term personnel is specifically authorized by higher authority; and

4. to augment established staffs of certain seasonal activities or periods of abnormal workload.

DEFENCE SERVICES PROGRAM (PROPERTIES AND UTILITIES)

OBJECTIVE

To provide real estate service in support of the management of DND's real property infrastructure.

RESULTS/BENEFICIARIES

Property acquisitions, property and facility records, property disposals, utilities agreements with municipalities and other sources.

The beneficiaries of these results are the 82,000 military and 36,000 civilian personnel of the Canadian Forces and their families.

AUTHORITY

National Defence Act.

RESOURCES (DGPU only)

		85/86
Operating		$1.3 million
Person-Years	civilian	29
	military	3

PROGRAM DESCRIPTION

The activities described in this report are real estate service activities carried out at NDHQ and in the field in support of real property management.

Although DND's real property inventory is relatively stable, there is a sporadic need to acquire new property (by purchase or lease), and a need to dispose of surplus property.

The locations of many of DND's installations were determined before or during the Second World War and during the 1950s. Installations that were originally remote or separate from urban communities and services are now physically linked to or surrounded by urban development. DND is moving to transfer to municipalities utility services which it once needed to provide for itself.

Functional responsibility for these real estate services rests with the Properties and Utilities Division in the Construction Engineering Branch at NDHQ. The Director General Properties and Utilities is responsible for:

- ensuring the maintenance of a property registry and inventory database for all DND owned or occupied real property;
- buying or leasing properties required for DND owned or occupied real property;
- managing all utilities and municipal service agreements over $25,000 in value; and
- administering the military airfield zoning program (basically a sporadic activity).

A task associated with DGPU's inventory database responsibilities is to manage the annual estimation of the present replacement value (PRV) of the total inventory. This estimation is done by CE units in the field on an individual facility basis, then rolled up by Station, Base and Command to produce a national figure, which is issued for resource allocation purposes. Property acquisition tends to be an unpredictable and sporadic activity. Currently, for example, the DGPU is spending 50 per cent of his time on three active property dossiers; Calgary, Downsview and Cold Lake.

In addition to negotiating land and property purchases DGPU arranges leases for housing, and on occasion has obtained leases normally negotiated by PWC when PWC has not been able to act in a timely fashion.

With respect to utilities agreements with municipalities the DND thrust is to transfer responsibilities to municipalities when and where possible. Currently the DGPU is negotiating with Calgary, London, Edmonton and five other municipalities with a view to handing over all municipal type infrastructure to them.

The DGPU has a staff of 32 PYs in NDHQ, almost all civilians. His organization is divided into three Directorates: (a) Properties; (b) Property Records and Legal Services; and (c) Utilities and Municipal Services.

Operational control and administration of these activities at the Command and Base level rests with Command Construction Engineer Officers and Base Construction Engineering Officers. They are assisted in the execution of these duties by Regional and Base Property Officers.

OBSERVATIONS

Property acquisition and leasing is a service which has no particular military character, and which could be transfered to the common service realty agency, Public Works Canada.

The remaining functions of DGPU (inventory maintenance, and administration of utility and municipal service agreements) could be transfered to DGQ and DGW respectively.

OPTIONS

As an activity with no particular military character, duplicating a service provided by the common service agency PWC, DGPU's real property acquisition function should be transferred to PWC. Therefore, the study team recommends to the Task Force that the government consider instructing DND to use PWC as its agent for property acquisition.

As activities integral to the program planning and management function of DGQ, the responsibility for maintenance of the inventory database and management of utilities and municipal agreements could also be transferred from DGPU to DGQ.

DND should be directed to develop and implement a plan to speed up and complete the transfer of utilities and municipal services to local governments and their agencies.

NATIONAL DEFENCE HEADQUARTERS

OBJECTIVE

A National Defence Headquarters (NDHQ) which meets the operational requirements of DND and is consistent with the accommodation strategy of the government for the National Capital Region (NCR).

RESULTS/BENEFICIARIES

The direct beneficiary would be the Department of National Defence. Indirectly the Government of Canada would also benefit from the provision of an appropriate NDHQ because of the NCR accommodation inventory rationalization that could occur.

AUTHORITY

Public Works Act. National Defence Act.

RESOURCES

Present NDHQ accommodation (263,000 square metres of space) is provided for DND by PWC under the PWC Accommodation Program, at a gross "shadow" rent of $43 million in 1985/86.

PROGRAM DESCRIPTION

Currently DND has space in all or portions of 32 buildings dispersed across the NCR, of which space in 21 buildings is leased from the private sector and space in 11 buildings is Crown-owned (exclusive of Canadian Forces Base Ottawa which is owned by DND).

From the 1940s through the 1960s, National Defence Headquarters was partly housed in A, B and C buildings on Cartier Square with the remainder scattered throughout the Ottawa area. This unsatisfactory arrangement and the poor standard of office space led the department and the government to plan in 1967 for a consolidated facility at LeBreton Flats. But in 1969 the department was advised that instead DND would occupy the smaller building at 101 Colonel By Drive, then under construction for Transport Canada. The new building was occupied in 1973 but accommodated less than half the NDHQ staff. The remainder were dispersed in some 25 other sites in Ottawa and Rockcliffe.

The 1970 government decision to decentralize to Hull created a surplus of office space in downtown Ottawa by 1978. DND was approached and agreed to fill some of the space by relocating most of the Rockcliffe elements, providing that DND was allowed to consolidate in two or three major buildings including the Centennial Towers. Consolidation did not occur. Instead, DND was dispersed into various buildings in the core area. By 1982, with the move about half completed, DND was told to stop; there was no more rental space left as the situation had changed completely, downtown rents had increased dramatically, (by over 200 per cent in some instances) and there was a shortage of suitable office space.

At this point in 1982, the President of the Treasury Board suggested to the Minister that, because of the high costs of rentals in the Ottawa-Hull area, DND should consider relocation to a permanent new purpose-built headquarters complex outside the core area. The Minister agreed and a Task Force was established in DND to consider various options including locations such as Rockcliffe, Uplands or elsewhere on the outskirts.

The present highly dispersed accommodation for NDHQ is operationally inefficient, inhibits secure communications links and the comprehensive use of information systems, and leaves NDHQ vulnerable to the threat of terrorism. It is therefore appropriate for DND to have its Task Force prepare options for a consolidated complex.

However, the issue goes well beyond DND and affects both Treasury Board, as the government's general manager, and Public Works Canada as the current supplier of both office and non-office accommodation in the National Capital Region. Yet DND is not consulting either of these organizations at this stage.

The provision of a consolidated new NDHQ outside the Ottawa-Hull downtown core is seen by both PWC and the study team as one of the keys, perhaps the key to the rationalization of the government's office inventory in the NCR.

Relocating DND out of leased space in the centre would support the thrust to increase Crown ownership in the National Capital, and would provide the government with the flexibility to retain, replace or terminate expiring leases as appropriate. It would also provide the opportunity for other major government departments to be consolidated; for example Transport Canada could be relocated from the leased space in Place de Ville to 101 Colonel By.

Preliminary analysis of the proposed future complex indicates that there would be long term accommodation savings and cost avoidance in comparision to the present situation.

The funding source for the new NDHQ would have to be assessed. Currently PWC is the funding source for all accommodation in the NCR both office and non-office. The study team is recommending that the capital funds for single or special purpose (non-office) projects be transferred from PWC to the sponsoring department, with the capital for general purpose office projects remaining in PWC.

Since a new NDHQ would be essentially an office complex a case could be made for funding to come through PWC, especially given the strength of the real property inventory rationalization aspects of the issue. If, however, NDHQ were deemed to be a non-office project then DND would have to justify and obtain funding directly from Treasury Board. In any event, the source of funding should not be an issue which blocks this project.

The study team supports the investigation into the development of a new NDHQ consolidated complex, built on a phased basis, within the NCR but outside the downtown cores of Ottawa-Hull.

OPTIONS

The study team recommends to the Task Force on Program Review that the government consider broadening the DND Task Force for a new NDHQ to include representatives of Treasury Board Secretariat and PWC; DND and PWC should submit to Cabinet within 1 year the options for the development of a new NDHQ within the NCR but outside the downtown cores of Ottawa-Hull.

DND should justify the long-term NDHQ requirements to Treasury Board for a phased development. PWC should be responsible for the design and construction contracting aspects of the project with DND providing the Project Manager.

PWC should plan the rationalization of the NCR real property inventory around the phased development of the new NDHQ.

SECTION 14 - EXTERNAL AFFAIRS

REAL PROPERTY ABROAD

External Affairs Canada

OBJECTIVE

To effectively and efficiently provide accommodation abroad.

RESULTS/BENEFICIARIES

The Department of External Affairs has custody of and operates official residences, chanceries (offices) and staff quarters for 119 posts in 90 countries. The direct beneficiaries of this program are our representatives abroad. The indirect beneficiaries are any Canadians living or travelling abroad.

AUTHORITY

There is no authority provided in the External Affairs Act for the control, management and administration of real property.

RESOURCES (thousands of current dollars)

	84/85	85/86
Operating Expenditures	$15,800	$16,500
Capital Expenditures	$47,700	$43,400
Revenue	$10,200	$11,000
Person-Years	309	311

REAL PROPERTY ASSETS

Number of Buildings	646
Estimated Replacement Value	$800 million

PROGRAM DESCRIPTION

The Bureau of Physical Resources was established in 1975 in the Department of External Affairs (DEA) to satisfy the property requirements of the department in its operations abroad and to respond to the need to achieve long term rent savings through ownership of a significant proportion of offices and accommodation.

The bureau performs the following functions: management of the inventory of real property resources, property acquisition, property valuation, property administration and development, architecture, engineering, construction and property disposal.

The following table shows the property managed.

Description	Crown Owned	Crown Leased	Privately Leased	Total
Official Residence	75	45	1	121
Chancery	40	120	0	160
Staff Quarters	439	1,287	326	2,052
Others	80	117	0	197
Land Vacant	12	4	0	16
TOTAL	646	1,573	327	2,546

The Director General, Bureau of Physical Resources, who reports to the Assistant Deputy Minister of Administration is authorized to use 309 person-years. There are 273 person-years involved in real property management with the remaining 36 being involved in material procurement and transportation. Of the 273 real property person years, 102 are at headquarters; five in the Director General's office, 22 in the Policy and Advisory Directorate, and 75 in the Property and Advisory Directorate of which eight are architects, four are engineers, 18 are property acquisition specialists, and eight are interior designers.

There are 171 person-years abroad providing technical support. Tradesmen are locally engaged. At larger posts, such as London, New Delhi and Washington, maintenance activities are the responsibility of a Post Management Officer who may be on a secondment from the Department of National Defence. Other specialists from Environment

Canada, Public Works and National Defence are also called upon when required on a secondment basis.

OBSERVATIONS

Although External Affairs has been purchasing and managing real property abroad for a number of years, the External Affairs Act does not provide authority to the Secretary of State for External Affairs to have custody of any property. In the absence of specific legislative authority, the custody of federal property is to rest with the Minister of Public Works.

Since 1975 approximately $75 million has been spent acquiring crown owned property. Over the same period of time rental expenditures have been reduced by approximately $30 million. Crown ownership has produced more secure facilities which better reflect the Canadian presence.

The Long Range Capital Plan of DEA promotes the objective of obtaining ownership of all chanceries (offices) and official residences and owning 70 per cent of the staff quarters. This appears to be a high ratio as Canada's diplomatic status may change in some countries. Given the high rotation of staff abroad, staff quarters specifically purchased for large families are not always suitable for single persons, and vice versa.

The responsibility and accountability for real property management is divided between the Director General Physical Resources Bureau and the Heads of Posts who operate the embassies and consulates abroad. The bureau serves a challenge function, to the accommodation demands and controls exercised by senior staff abroad. The challenge function of the bureau is further augmented by the Treasury Board.

The bureau has established official residence standards which were approved by Treasury Board 3 years ago. There are three categories of official residences based on the need to entertain and the significance of the host country: Category A is approximately 7,000 square feet in size, Category B is 6,000 square feet; and Category C is 5,000 square feet. Although there are no cost standards relating to fit up, the bureau has interior designers at headquarters, who in conjunction with the Head of Post determine the full furnishing. The cost for fully furnishing a Category A Official Residence including renovations ranges between $150-200 thousand.

The Head of Post, although responsible for maintaining official residences, is restricted from altering representational areas without headquarters approvals. Every 10 years each residence is reviewed by an interior designer from headquarters and a major refurbishment is undertaken, at an average cost of $40 thousand per residence.

The office space and residence standards are based on personnel policies which provide that staff should have accommodations and standards of living comparable to those enjoyed in Ottawa. The department is in the process of developing office space standards comparable to those used by the federal government in Canada. Current office accommodation and in many cases private accommodation exceeds the levels of comfort currently enjoyed by the public service in Canada.

External Affairs spends about $33 million annually to lease staff quarters and it recovers approximately $11 million. Staff are charged rent not on the basis of what they occupy or what the accommodation costs, but rather based on a shelter cost formula prepared by Canada Mortgage and Housing Corporation. Based on the Ottawa-Hull market, CMHC determines an accommodation cost based on family configuration and family income bracket. Rents abroad range from $200 a month to slightly over $1,000 a month.

The real property management function within the Department of External Affairs is not a subject with high priority among departmental senior management. Generally, the level of job classification within DEA for real property management appears to be below that available in other departments. For example, DEA administrative officers are assigned as project managers to multi-million dollar construction projects as compared to the assignment of architects and engineers by other departments. This results in much greater reliance on the private sector, with much less double checking by DEA. Almost 99 per cent of the planning and design is contracted out to the private sector.

External Affairs has lost a number of opportunities to achieve savings abroad due to a limited delegation of financial, leasing and acquisition authority. By the time approvals were obtained from Ottawa, especially from central agencies, the favourable property deals were no longer available.

OPTIONS

The study team recommends to the Task Force that the government consider amending the External Affairs Act to include authority for the Minister to have the custody, control and management of real property abroad.

External Affairs should take greater advantage of the professional expertise available in the Department of Public Works to ensure that sufficient expertise is brought to bear on real property management matters.

The government should review existing accommodation cost recovery policies related to staff quarters abroad in order to increase revenues from the rentals of staff quarters.

The government should review the level of preferred crown-ownership of offices, official residences and staff quarters abroad, their quantity and quality in the long-range capital plan of External Affairs with a view towards increased economy.

SECTION 15 - ENVIRONMENT PROGRAMS

INTRODUCTION

It is well known that Parks Canada, by far the largest of Environment Canada's three property holders, operates the National and Historic Parks. It is less well known that nearly 60 per cent of the estimated replacement value of Parks Canada's non-land real property assets lies in their 2,500 miles of major roads and highways and their nine canals or that these items consumed 41 per cent of the 1984-85 Parks' capital projects budget. Clearly this large, expensive transportation infrastructure seriously distorts both the Parks Canada budget and mandate, as does the fact that Parks Canada serves as the municipal administration in the towns of Banff and Jasper. We believe that the Parks Canada program should be simplified and significant savings realized through:

- the transfer of responsibility for through-park highways and roads and historic canals and waterways to the provinces; and
- the transfer of townsite management responsibility in Banff and Jasper to the Province of Alberta.

BACKGROUND

Environment Canada is the federal government's largest custodian of raw land - some 12.8 million hectares - and is the eighth largest building occupant with approximately 635,000 square metres of floor area in 5,334 buildings. The majority of these assets are held by Parks Canada with 12.77 million hectares of land and 523,000 square metres of space in 4,817 buildings located in its 31 National Parks and 69 Historic Parks and Major Sites.

These considerable assets are not centrally managed on a departmental basis. The Directorate of Facilities Management for Environment Canada Headquarters is responsible for ensuring that real property and infrastructure required to support the department (except for Parks Canada) is provided as and where required. This directorate performs the basic functions of accommodation management and allocation; identification of real estate and infrastructure requirements and project development. It has no in-house engineering and architectural design capability and contracts for these services, all construction and all real estate services through PWC.

By contrast, Parks Canada is fully capable of performing all aspects of the real property function. Its Realty Services Branch provides full realty services in support of the parks function but relies on PWC and/or the Department of Justice, as appropriate, for other realty services in support of the common administrative function or where required by legislation. Its Engineering and Architecture Branch is responsible for all design and engineering support to Parks Canada programs. At the present time, 31 per cent of this work is done through PWC and 28 per cent by private sector consultants. All construction, maintenance and consultant contracts are let by Parks Canada Contracts Services Branch staff at regional headquarters.

The National Battlefields Commission, a Schedule B Crown Corporation, responsible to the Minister of the Environment, operates and maintains the 95.1 hectare National Battlefields Park (Plains of Abraham) at Québec City. The Commission controls nine buildings with a total floor area of 1,599 square metres.

OBSERVATIONS

Review of the past several years' expenditures suggests that Parks Canada has emphasized acquisition and development of new parks at the expense of the maintenance and recapitalization of existing assets. The recapitalization back-log is now estimated by Parks Canada staff to be in the order of $320 million. There are also indications that the initial and long-term costs of some parks are excessive and that they could have been considerably lower had the park agreement with the ceding province or territory not included such non-park items as highways, golf courses, gondolas, etc. This type of tourist development item should be developed and maintained outside the park by the province, territory or private enterprise. In spite of these problems, once a park has been established, the formal development planning process used by Parks Canada appears to be a most effective one with full functional review and senior management involvement throughout.

The Parks Canada philosophy that all park and park-related activities not central to the conservation -

preservation - display mandate should be privatized is worthy of full support. The study team is of the view that privatization of existing in-park services should be accelerated where possible and Parks Canada development of such services should be severely restricted in wilderness parks.

The 2,500 kilometres of highways and roads, the majority of which pass through, and in some cases between parks, represent a large percentage of Parks Canada's infrastructure and consume a disproportionate share of the capital budget. Analysis of the 1984-85 estimates for the National Parks program indicates that highway and road-related capital projects represent:

- 47.5 per cent ($20.4 million) of the 1984-85 major capital projects budget; and,
- 52.5 per cent ($148.5 million) of the total estimated completion value of all of the capital projects listed.

The canals, which were transferred to Historic Parks and Sites Branch from Transport Canada when they effectively ceased to be essential to trade within Canada, impose a similar distortion on the parks budget. The study team recommends to the Task Force that the government consider transferring both through-park highways and roads, and the canals to provincial jurisdiction.

Leasehold properties in the National Parks, particularly in the Mountain Parks, have been a source of controversy for years. Rents on Banff and Jasper properties are to be adjusted again in 1990. We strongly support the Parks Canada staff recommendation that a review committee, chaired by a private sector real estate expert with representation from Parks Canada, Treasury Board, Justice and the residents, be formed to recommend a fair mode of rent setting. The establishment of rents should be based on sound business principles.

The federal government has inadvertently become involved in municipal adminstration of the Banff and Jasper townsites. This is an expensive and inappropriate role for the federal government and the government should consider taking steps to transfer responsibility for townsite administration from Parks Canada to the Province of Alberta.

Residents of Banff and Jasper receive municipal services that are heavily subsidized by Parks Canada. In1983-84, the residents paid only 21.1 per cent of the cost of providing these services compared to the Alberta formula where 46 per cent of the cost of municipal services is borne by the rate-payers. Pending the transfer of townsite administration to the province, Parks Canada plans to move in steps toward the full Alberta formula should be supported.

Although there may have been good cause for the establishment of the National Battlefields Commission in 1908 to acquire, restore and operate the historic battlefields at Québec City, there appears to be no good reason for its continuance. The use of 47 person-years to operate a relatively small park in the centre of an urban area is excessive. The study team recommends to the Task Force that government consideration be given to transferring the functions to the Historic Parks and Sites Branch and contracting out the majority of the operating and maintenance activities.

There is no apparent reason for real property management to be exercised by two agencies within Environment Canada. It is considered that the Facilities Management Directorate should be absorbed by the Parks Canada Realty Services and Engineering and Architecture Branches which would then provide real property management services to the whole department.

Significant savings and considerable cost avoidance are attainable in the Environment Canada real property management function through:

- the transfer of the total responsibility for the construction, operation and maintenance of through-park highways, roads and historic canals and waterways to the provinces;
- the transfer of townsite management responsibility in Banff and Jasper to the Province of Alberta;
- pending transfer of townsite management responsibility to the province, charges for municipal services in Banff and Jasper should be increased in steps until they reach the Alberta formula of 46 per cent of costs;
- increased and accelerated privatization of visitor services in the National and Historic Parks;

- the establishment of an appropriate mechanism for setting acceptable, equitable rents for leasehold properties within park boundaries;
- the abolition of the National Battlefields Commission and the transfer of its responsibilities to the Historic Parks and Sites Branch; and
- the centralization of the real property management function in the department.

The major savings cannot however be made by the department itself. These will require Federal-Provincial negotiation which should begin as soon as possible.

PARKS CANADA

Environment Canada

OBJECTIVE

The objective of Parks Canada is to acquire and develop representative areas of the country for use by the public but consistent with the preservation of such areas in their natural state; and, to preserve, restore, and operate sites and structures of importance to Canadian history - including canals. The real property function in Parks Canada operates in support of this objective.

RESULTS/BENEFICIARIES

Parks Canada owns and operates 31 National Parks, 69 Historic Parks and Major Sites and has placed in excess of 1000 plaques commemorating persons, places and events significant to Canadian history. The beneficiaries of these activities are the communities in which they are located and the millions of Canadian and foreign tourists who visit them annually.

AUTHORITY

Historic Sites and Monuments Act, R.S.C. 1970, c.H-6.
National Parks Act, R.S.C. 1970, c.N-13.

RESOURCES (thousands of current dollars)

	84/85	**85/86**
Operating Expenses	56,387	55,174
Revenue	7,854	8,200
Capital	70,633	60,049
Person-Years	1,672	1,598

REAL PROPERTY ASSETS

Land - 12.77 million hectares
Building - 4817
Gross Floor Area - 472,796 square metres owned of which 16,396 square metres are operated and maintained by lessees or concessionaires
- 49,625 square metres of office accommodation provided by PWC

PROGRAM DESCRIPTION

According to 1982-83 figures compiled by Parks Canada, their non-land assets, which had an estimated replacement value of $3.6 billion, can be broken down as follows:

- roads (including some 2,500 km of major highways which represent the bulk of the value) - 37.7 per cent;
- marine works (primarily canals) - 21.9 per cent;
- historic sites - 17.0 per cent
- grounds - 6.6 per cent;
- buildings - 6.3 per cent;
- utilities - 5.0 per cent;
- bridges - 3.6 per cent.

Real property management in Parks Canada is exercised through the Director General Program Management who reports to the Assistant Deputy Minister Parks. The two branches of the Program Management Directorate principally concerned with real property management are the Engineering and Architecture Branch and the Realty Services Branch. These two branches are supported by the Contract Services Branch and receive guidance and direction from Program Planning and Analysis Branch.

Engineering and Architecture Branch. The branch is structured with 65 PYs at national headquarters; a total of 200 PYs in the five regional headquarters (Calgary, Winnipeg, Cornwall, Québec City, and Halifax); and approximately 1,300 general works PYs distributed among the 100 parks and major sites. These latter person-years are involved primarily in operations and maintenance and small, local construction projects. Headquarters Engineering and

Architecture (E & A) Branch performs the following functions:

- functional direction and audit of regional E&A staffs who are responsible to their Regional Director;
- provision of departmentally unique engineering and architectural expertise to regions particularly in relation to canals and restoration work;
- provision of drawing support and restoration design to PWC for their heritage structures (i.e. East Block restoration) as a free service;
- project management including "front-end" input to the project/ program planning process; and
- E&A staff development.

At the present time the E&A work is divided as follows:

- HQ staff - 7 per cent
- Regional staff - 34 per cent
- PWC (almost entirely highway work plus some dredging and shore protection but basically no "in-park" work) - 31 per cent
- Consultants - 28 per cent (for the most part engaged by regions).

With a major recapitalization program facing the department it is the intent to have the regions move toward a 20 per cent/80 per cent in-house/ consultant design ratio. This will ensure staff have sufficient work to maintain professional expertise while devoting the bulk of their resources to project management. All construction, maintenance and consultant contracts are let by the Contract Services Branch personnel at Regional Headquarters.

Realty Services Branch. As is the case with E&A Branch, Realty Services Branch operates as a headquarters staff agency with functional but not line control over professional staff in the regions. The branch has been assigned 47 PYs - 18 in headquarters and 29 in the regional headquarters. The bulk of the latter are located in Ontario and Western Regions - 11 and 14 respectively - where the vast majority of the lease-hold properties problems occur. The role of the branch is to administer and advise on Parks

Canada's interests in land. Principal branch responsibilities include:

- development and review of policies, guidelines and related procedures for the realty function and review of departmental plans for compliance;
- research titles to establish ownership of lands including Dominion, Ordnance and Admiralty Lands;
- maintenance of real property records and provision of data to the Central Real Property Inventory;
- negotiation for, review, make recommendations on and document the alienation, acquisition and disposal of land (although the branch acquires almost all of its own property, disposals are usually arranged through PWC);
- arranging for appraisals, legal surveys and appointment of agents (through PWC and the Department of Justice);
- determination of the return (rentals, rates, fees) to the Crown pursuant to realty agreements and administration and enforcement of those agreements; and
- co-ordination of the proclamation of all new National Parks and the legal establishment of National Historic Parks.

In essence, the branch provides full realty services in support of the parks function. Other realty services in support of the common administrative function are provided by PWC and/or the Department of Justice, as appropriate.

OBSERVATIONS

Review of the last several years' expenditures suggest that Parks Canada's Cabinet-approved mandate to expand the park system from 31 to 50 parks has led to heavy emphasis on acquisition and development at the expense of maintenance and recapitalization of existing assets. Funding reductions in late 1984 forced a reassessment of this approach and it now appears that, for the time being at least, acquisition and new development will cease or be dramatically reduced in scope and greater attention will be paid to the recapitalization backlog. This backlog is estimated by Parks Canada staff to be in the order of $320 million.

Although the decision-making process underlying the determination of which land forms in what part of Canada should be preserved, protected and developed is beyond the scope of this study team's terms of reference it is central to the real property management issue. There are indications that the initial and long-term costs of some parks are excessive and that they could have been considerably lower had the park agreement with the ceding province or territory not included such non-park items as highways, golf courses, gondolas, etc. It is considered that this type of tourist development item, inserted at the insistence of the ceding province should be developed and maintained by the province in question or by private enterprise outside the park rather than at the expense of Parks Canada. This issue will be referred to the study team examining Environment Canada programs. (The Gros Morne Park is an example of the problem).

Once a park has been acquired, the formalized development planning process, which contains the following components, appears to be a most effective one:

a. **Park Purpose Statements.** This is the lead document and defines whether a park is to be a largely undeveloped wilderness park on the one hand or a visitor-oriented park on the other or somewhere in between. In all cases, development planning is guided by this key document.

b. **Park Development Plans.** These are based on the Park Purpose Statements and on any agreements reached with the Province or Territory ceding land for a park, and cover a 15-year period. Projects planned for the first 5 years are costed to a Class "D" (rough order of magnitude) estimate level which is updated annually. Plans are formally reviewed by senior management every 5 years.

Individual major capital or recapitalization projects must be included in the development plans and move from the provisional statement of requirement stage through to final approval with full senior management involvement throughout by means of functional review and sign-off at each stage. Project priority setting is carried out by regional headquarters in the first instance as work is funded through the regional budgets. The ADM Parks and his Chief of Operations establish funding priorities among the regions. As is the case for development planning, the approval and priority setting function appears to be sound with appropriate senior management involvement throughout.

Privatization. The Parks Canada philosophy is that all park and park-related activities not central to the conservation- preservation-display mandate should be privatized. Under this philosophy emphasis is placed on:

a. private development of visitor services outside the parks except where park size or isolation forces their provision within the park boundries. In this latter case, these services should be privately developed under lease or concession agreements;

b. the privatization of existing park visitor/ tourist services constructed in the past by Parks Canada or required under the park agreement with the province or territory. At the present time Parks Canada operates golf courses in only three parks-Funday, Cape Breton Highlands, and Terra Nova-and will continue to do so only until such time as they become financially viable at which point their operation will be tendered to private concessionnaires; and

c. the examination of the privatization of camp grounds. Guidelines are currently being developed and it is anticipated that the first camp ground operations will be tendered to private enterprise in fiscal year 1986/87.

In remote areas where few visitors use a park and/or there is a relatively short season which render such activities unprofitable, Parks Canada operates the minimum, essential visitor services. Similarly, park operation and maintenance activities are carried out by contract where possible as are all construction and recapitalization projects.

Highways. As indicated above, Parks Canada is responsible for the operation, maintenance and recapitalization of some 2,500 kilometres of highways - including the Trans-Canada highway (TCH) through Banff. These highways which pass through, and in some cases, between parks represent a large percentage of Parks Canada's infrastructure valuation and consume a great deal of the budget. This in spite of the fact that prior to April 1, 1985 PWC at its cost:

a. funded, designed, and contracted the construction of the TCH twinning project in Banff; and

b. designed and provided contract administration for all park highway and road recapitalization projects and all bridge projects, the capital costs of which were borne by Parks Canada.

With the exception of the TCH twinning project which remains a PWC project, all of these services will be charged to Parks Canada on a cost recovery basis by PWC from April 1, 1985 onwards.

Analysis of the 1984-85 Estimates for the National Parks program indicates that highway and road-related capital projects represent:

a. 47.5 per cent ($20.4 million) of the 1984-85 major capital projects budget; and

b. 52.2 per cent ($148.5 million) of the total estimated completed value of the projects listed.

This vast expenditure on what is essentially a non-park activity should be excised from the Parks Canada budget as it seriously distorts the cost of operating the park system.

Canals. The approach taken with bridges over historic canals provides an example of how long-term, continuing costs can be reduced or eliminated. As the successor to the agency that built the canals, Parks Canada is responsible in perpetuity for the maintenance and operation of crossing places at points where the canals cut existing roads and railways. However, where these swing or lift bridges cease to meet the carrying capacity required by the appropriate road or highway authority, Parks Canada is usually prepared to contribute to the upgrading project - usually a new high level bridge-on the basis of the replacement cost of the old bridge. In exchange for this one-time contribution the highway authority assumes full responsibility for the new bridge in perpetuity. It has been suggested that a Parks Canada contribution of $1.0 million toward a $3.0 million bridge could eliminate a perpetual $50K annual direct operating and maintenance responsibility. The replaced bridge is normally demolished unless it is of particular historic or architectural interest. This is an intriguing approach which could possibly have other applications in Parks Canada programs. However savings of this nature point out the failure of government departments to appreciate that an outlay of $1.0 million will cost approximately 12 per cent ($120,000 per year) or more in interest costs.

Banff and Jasper Townsites. Two principal issues surround the Parks Canada operation of the townsites - leasehold rents and municipal services charges. Although quite separate these two issues are usually interwoven by local residents and their political representatives.

The leasehold issue has been controversial since 1887. As the National Parks Act prohibits the sale of land in a National Park all private holdings are in the form of land leases; most of which have a 42 year term. The basic outline of the situation is as follows:

a. a 1972 Supreme Court test proved that the leases cannot be unilaterally changed;
b. under most leases the rents can be adjusted by an amount approved by the Minister every 10 years;
c. residents with a "need to reside" in the parks as defined in the Act are charged $250 per year;
d. commercial leases are based on 6 per cent of the fee simple value of the land or a percentage of the business's gross sales;
e. cottage leases are based on 4 per cent of the fee simple value of the land per annum;
f. a few leases still have a review process only every 42 years and a few every 21 years. These will all be resolved in the 1990s;
g. Treasury Board believes that the rentals are far too low although they are considerably higher than they were in 1980 and the Federal Court has ruled favourably on all challenges to the levels to date;
h. various attempts have been made over the years to rationalize the situation including, in the early 1970s, the introduction of a bill to establish a Canada-National Parks Leaseholds Corporation. The bill was allowed to die on the order paper after second reading.

Parks Canada staff have recommended that the Minister of the Environment establish a review committee of interested parties headed by a private sector real estate expert with representation from Justice, Treasury Board, Parks and the lessees to recommend a mode of rent setting that is fair, equitable and acceptable to the Government of Canada. This committee would establish the format for the 1990 rent adjustment which, under the National Parks Lease and Licence of Occupation Regulations, can be made by the Minister. This would appear to be a sound approach to resolving this most difficult problem area. At the present time the leases produce $3.7 million revenue per year.

The issue of charges for municipal services is equally difficult as for years residents of Banff and Jasper have received municipal services heavily subsidized by the Canadian taxpayer. The present situation is that Parks Canada charge for the provision of water, sewer, garbage collection and fire services and has the authority to charge for streetworks. Charges were unchanged between 1968 and 1980 and fell well behind costs as a consequence. Recent attempts to achieve reasonable levels were constrained by the 6 and 5 program of the previous government. The 1983/84 expenditure/revenue situation is:

	Total expenditure	**Revenue**	**% Recovery**
Water Supply/Fire Protection	$855,900	$226,000	26.4
Sewerage	279,300	130,000	46.5
Garbage	649,100	193,000	29.7
Streets	804,000		
TOTAL	2,588,300	549,000	21.2%

Clearly this situation can not be permitted to continue. Parks Canada staff have proposed to the Minister that charges be based on the equivalent Alberta funding formula where 46 per cent of the cost of municipal services is recovered from municipal rates. They propose to increase recovery by 35 per cent in 1985/86 and to introduce streetworks as part of a review of charges for 1 April 1986. This approach is fully supported provided the move to full (46 per cent) recovery is not permitted to lag.

While all of the above activity is admirable and should have been undertaken some time ago it still does not answer the question as to whether or not Parks Canada should be in the business of townsite management. It has been estimated that Parks Canada could save at least 75 person-years, $4.5 million in operating and maintenance costs and $3.5 million in average capital investment costs per year at a cost of the loss of $1.1 million in revenues through the transfer of townsite administration to another authority. With this kind of saving to be made divesture should be a high priority item.

The nature of the National and Historic Parks system is such that a dedicated Parks Canada real property management staff is essential. The number of personnel engaged in the function could be reduced if some or all of the following alternatives were adopted:

a. **Privatization of Services.** The present policy of privatizing or contracting out all visitor services should be vigorously pursued and extended. The privatization of camp grounds should be accelerated as it offers early savings in both person-years and operating and maintenance costs. Service development in remote, wilderness parks where Parks Canada now runs minimum essential services should be severely restricted.

b. **Highways and Roads.** Through-park highways and roads, while not an integral part of the Parks Canada function or mandate, represent a disproportionate percentage of the Parks Canada assets value and expenses. These highways and roads, which would except for the existence of the park be owned, operated, and maintained by the provinces, should be excised from the Parks and transferred to the provinces leaving Parks Canada with responsibility only for those roads which directly support the parks program. Such a transfer would have to form part of some broader Federal-Provincial fiscal review as there is no incentive for the provinces to absorb costs now borne by federal departments or agencies. Should such transfers not prove to be feasible, full responsibility for funding, design, construction, operation and maintenance of highways and roads should be transferred to the appropriate department (Transport Canada) with PWC providing design and construction services. (See Section 8 - PWC - Highway Systems).

c. **Canals.** The canals were transferred to Historic Parks and Sites Branch from Transport Canada when they effectively ceased to be essential for the movement of goods within Canada. Consideration should be given to transferring the canals to the provinces. As is the case for highways, there is no incentive to the provinces in accepting the costs for a major tourist attraction they currently get for free hence any transfer would have to be part of a broader funding review.

d. **Park Leases.** The Parks Canada approach to a lease review committee should be followed to ensure the 1990 rentals are established at appropriate levels. Consideration should be given to re-examining earlier proposals for the Canada-National Parks Leaseholds Corporation as the establishment of a Crown Corporation in this area would tend to put the whole matter in a more business-like frame work freed to a large extent from political interference.

e. **Townsite Management.** Clearly Parks Canada should not be in the town management business and the following alternatives should be pursued:

   1. the rate charged for full municipal services must be brought into line with that charged in other Alberta communities; and

   2. discussions should be opened with Alberta with a view of transferring administrative responsibility to the province. This transfer would result in the saving of at least 75 person-years and $6.9 million per year. The eventual result of such a transfer - the towns would initially most probably be designated as Improvement Districts under the Alberta Municipal Act - could be the evolution of municipal self-government.

f. **Acquisitions.** The acquisitive nature of Parks Canada's mandate must be reviewed against their ability to properly maintain the real property assets now held and the realistic examination of how many parks Canada needs and can afford.

OPTIONS

The study team recommends to the Task Force that the government should consider:

- instructing Parks Canada to acquire no more parks until completion of a policy review which should include a realistic examination of how many parks Canada needs and can afford to maintain;

- accelerating the program to privatize campgrounds as it offers early savings in both person-years and operation and maintenance costs. Services provided in remote wilderness parks should be severely restricted;

- adopting the Parks Canada staff proposal on lease review to ensure that fair, equitable, acceptable rents are established for the 1990 review with a minimum of political interference;

- aligning the rate charged for full municipal services to townsites with that charged in other Alberta communities. Given that the rate will increase by 35 per cent in 1985/86, full Alberta rates should be charged in fiscal year 1987/88;

- negotiating with the provinces to transfer full responsibility for through-Park highways and roads, and historic canals to their jurisdiction. A reasonable target date for a transfer would be April 1, 1990; and

- opening discussions with Alberta with a view to transferring the administrative responsibility for the Banff and Jasper townsites to provincial administration. Transfer should be effected no later than April 1, 1990.

ENVIRONMENTAL SERVICES

Environment Canada

OBJECTIVE

To ensure that the real property and infrastructure required to support the department (except for Parks Canada) is provided as and where required.

RESULTS/BENEFICIARIES

The Atmospheric Environment and Environment Conservation Services of Environment Canada control, and operate various facilities across Canada in support of their programs. The principal beneficiaries of the real property function in support of these activities are the various Environment Canada field agencies and their clients.

AUTHORITY

Department of the Environment Act - R.S. c. 14 (2nd Supp.), ss. 2-7, 30, Sch 1.

RESOURCES (thousands of current dollars)

	84/85	85/86
Operating Expenses	6,795	7,351
Capital	10,868	14,802
Person-Years	44.16	41.78

REAL PROPERTY ASSETS

Land - 1271.34 hectares
Buildings - 517
Gross Floor Area - 112,343 square metres (two buildings - the National Hydrology Research Centre in Saskatoon and the National Water Resources Institute in Burlington - constitute 51.25 per cent of the total floor area. The majority of the remaining 515 builings, which are spread

across Canada, are water gauging stations, automatic lighthouse stations and other small buildings.

PROGRAM DESCRIPTION

The real property function for Environment Canada, (except for Parks Canada) is centralized in the Headquarters Facilities Management Directorate in Ottawa. This directorate is responsible for:

a. the preparation and maintenance of departmental property records;
b. arranging for all real estate transactions through Public Works Canada;
c. real property and accommodation requirements definition;
d. preparation of projects for screening and priority setting by senior management for entry into the 5-year program and the subsequent preparation of the appropriate Treasury Board submissions;
e. vetting plans and specifications produced by Public Works and Transport Canada prior to tender to ensure that they meet stated requirements; and
f. monitoring projects under construction to ensure that the product meets user requirements.

The directorate has no in-house capability to carry out engineering or architectural design. All construction projects are designed to Environment Canada requirements and implemented by PWC although Transport Canada has been engaged on occasions where their northern expertise was required.

To perform this function the directorate has a staff of 15 of whom four, other than the Director, are engineers employed in the engineering and construction section. The remainder of the staff is employed in accommodation management, allocation and real estate functions.

At field level, with the exception of the Atmospheric Environment Service which has three engineers to oversee projects in its regions, the property management staff are in effect the custodial and plant operating personnel for the main functional buildings. All other work is contracted out. The capital expenditure increase in 1985-86 is due to the increased cash flow on the National Hydrology Research Centre project and various other projects shown in the 1985-86 Estimates.

OBSERVATIONS

Review of the real property management program in Environment Canada outside of the Parks Canada program indicates that the function is being performed in an efficient, effective, professional manner. The staff level is consistent with the requirement for the department to maintain a capacity to define and plan its requirements and to maintain program or project control.

It is considered that an alternative to the status quo would be to merge the components of the Facilities Management Directorate with the Engineering and Architecture and Realty Services Branches of Parks Canada. Such a merger could provide some personnel savings in headquarters staff and at the same time provide one central focal point for all real property management in Environment Canada. The merged agencies should remain under ADM Parks who has the greater real property holdings.

Building management and operating staffs for the National Hydrology Research Centre and the National Water Resources Institute at Burlington - 15 person-years - could be transferred to PWC however, no advantage would be gained as there are no savings to be made by such a transfer. Eleven of the person-years involved are in the HP group and are required for plant operation in the NWRI.

OPTIONS

The study team recommends to the Task Force that the government consider undertaking further investigation to determine the personnel savings attainable through the absorption of the Facilities Management Directorate functions by the Engineering and Architecture and Realty Services Branches of Parks Canada.

NATIONAL BATTLEFIELDS COMMISSION

Environment Canada

OBJECTIVE

To acquire, restore and maintain the historic battlefields at Québec to form a National Battlefields Park.

RESULTS/BENEFICIARIES

The creation of a suitable historic park to commemorate the national battlefields at Québec.

The principal beneficiaries of the program are tourists visiting the park and the local residents who use the park as if it were a municipal park. Although the physical layout of the park precludes the conventional counting of visitors, it has been estimated that it is visited by approximately one million persons annually. Québec City benefits directly through the presence of a park in an area which has a shortage of public leisure areas and through an annual grant-in-lieu of taxes of one million dollars in 1984/85.

AUTHORITY

National Battlefields at Québec Act SC 1908, c. 57-58. Included in Schedule B by SC 1983-84, c.31 and assigned to the Minister of the Environment by P.C. 1979-1618, 5-6-79.

RESOURCES **(thousands of current dollars)**

	84/85	85/86
Operating Expenses	2,800	2,824
Capital	66	63
Person-Years	47	47

REAL PROPERTY ASSETS

Land - 95.1 hectares
Buildings - nine (one administrative, eight operational)
Building Floor Area - 1,599 square metres.

PROGRAM DESCRIPTION

The commission is a Crown Corporation within the meaning and purpose of the Financial Administration Act. It is responsible for the preservation, management and operation of the National Battlefields Park at Québec; is funded through the annual appropriations of the Department of the Environment; and, is responsible to Parliament through the Minister of that Department. The act provides for the appointment of nine Commissioners - seven by the Governor-in-Council and one each by the Government of Ontario and Québec. The Chairman is appointed by the Governor-in-Council which also appoints the Secretary. All of the commission's real property assets are in Québec City.

The program is delivered by 47 person-years (PY) all of which are located in Québec City. The majority of the work involved in operating and maintaining the park is done by commission staff. Heavy work, such as road repair and snow removal, is contracted out through Supply and Services Canada. The cost of the program, exclusive of the grant-in-lieu of taxes to the city is $1,866,000 in 1984/85.

The employment of the 47 PY is:

a. Administration - 11
b. Property management/grounds upkeep - 36.

OBSERVATIONS

The following assessment is based on conversations with Treasury Board and Parks Canada staffs and a confirmatory telephone conversation with a member of the commission staff. It is generally agreed that the commission fulfills its mandate in a most pleasing, efficient manner that effectively portrays the history it was meant to protect.

There is no apparent reason why in 1985 the National Battlefields at Québec should be administered differently than other equally important national historic parks and sites in other parts of Canada. Transfer of responsibility for this park to the Historic Parks and Sites Branch of Parks Canada would as a minimum achieve a saving of some of the direct administrative costs arising from the commission operating as a separate entity.

Review of the estimates suggests that a disproportionate amount of work is done by Commission staff rather than by contract. It is suggested that application of the Parks Canada policy of contracting out operations and maintenance activities to the greatest extent possible could reduce costs by at least 20 per cent and person-years by a minimum of 60 per cent.

There are two possible alternatives to the status quo; both requiring legislative action:

a. transfer the park to Parks Canada Historic Parks and Sites Branch; or
b. transfer it to Québec City with a grant and a requirement to preserve the site as a historic monument in perpetuity.

Transfer to the city's administration, while recognizing the fact that the park effectively serves the city as a city park with historic overtones, is not a practical proposition as the city would lose the grant-in-lieu of taxes brought in by the park and incur direct costs in its maintenance as the replacement grant would, or should, only cover the historic aspects of the park. It has furthermore been suggested that it would be totally inappropriate to transfer responsibility for a national historic site of such importance to a junior level of government.

On the other hand, transfer of full responsibility to Parks Canada would remove an administrative anachronism and offer the possibility of some small but significant financial and personnel savings.

OPTIONS

The study team recommends to the Task Force that the government consider abolishing the National Battlefields Commission and transferring its property and functions to Parks Canada and their operations and maintenance practices regarding contracting out be applied to management of the property.

SECTION 16 - SOLICITOR GENERAL

LAW ENFORCEMENT PROGRAM

Royal Canadian Mounted Police

OBJECTIVE

The program objective of the Royal Canadian Mounted Police (RCMP) is to enforce laws, prevent crime and maintain peace, order and security.

Real property is managed in support of this program objective by the Property Management Branch in Headquarters, which is part of the Services and Supply Directorate, under a Deputy Commissioner Administration.

The objectives of the Property Management Branch are:

a. To identify and acquire annually capital construction funds to provide for a construction program to meet the operational needs of the force.
b. To identify and direct the implementation of leasing projects for new or additional accommodation when capital construction is not considered practicable, to meet the operational needs of the force.
c. To update standards of accommodation and property management policy to ensure Divisions are provided with adequate parameters within which they can carry out repair, construction and other accommodation projects commensurate with their delegated authority.
d. To provide a monitoring and audit capability which will ensure maximum benefit is derived from the annual capital contruction budget.

RESULTS/BENEFICIARIES

Divisional and sub-divisional headquarters, laboratories, detachments, residences, and other buildings.

The beneficiaries are the 21,400 members and civilian employees of the RCMP.

AUTHORITY

Solicitor General Act: Royal Canadian Mounted Police Act.

RESOURCES (in millions of dollars)

	84/85	85/86
Capital	35	35
Operating Expenditures	42	50
Revenues	30	32
Person-Years	211	211

PROGRAM DESCRIPTION

Real property in the RCMP is centrally managed by the Property Management Branch, Services and Supply Directorate in Headquarters, in support of the four activities of the Law Enforcement Program:

a. enforcement of federal statutes and executive orders;
b. police services under contract;
c. Canadian police services (including forensic laboratories and the Canadian Police College); and
d. Administration.

The RCMP is the holder of the 10th largest crown property inventory (by building area) and the 5th largest space inventory in the federal government with 505,000 square metres of crown-owned and 98,000 square metres of leased space. Its accommodation profile by building is as follows:

Type	RCMP Owned	PWC Owned	Commercial Lease	Mun. Owned	Other	Total
Division HQs	12	2	1		1	16
Sub/Div. HQs	22	6	11			39
Detachments	428	16	165	87	7	703
Separate Residences*	511	244	28		1	784
Other Buildings**	821	62	198	16	69	1,166
BUILDING TOTALS	1,794	330	403	103	78	2,708
SITES	966	2	257		97	1,322

* Includes pool houses.
** Includes warehouses, labs, garages, storage sheds, radio shelters, single quarters, satellite detachments.

	RCMP Owned	PWC Owned	Leased
No. of attached married quarters -	201	1	85
No. of pool houses -		244	22

Total no. of married quarters = 784 + 201 + 1 + 85 = 1,701

The Force is the custodian and operates and maintains the majority of the space it occupies outside the National Capital Region. PWC provides most of its accommodation in the Capital Region, including the RCMP Headquarters. In a few other areas RCMP premises are provided by PWC in general purpose office buildings. Some 87 RCMP detachment facilities are owned by municipalities to whom the Force provides police service.

The policy of the Force is to occupy Crown-owned accommodation. The special features required by the RCMP such as radio rooms, shielded communication space, cells, security considerations and 24-hour operations make leasing an unattractive proposition for the private sector and lead to unacceptable lease terms and conditions being demanded.

The Force has its own capital funding, (currently at $35 million) and under its long term capital plan is moving gradually to achieve the Crown ownership policy.

The Property Management Branch has the mandate to plan, develop, implement and administer the accommodation policies and program of the Force. The Branch has 31 person-years and also has a functional relationship with the 83 staff in the Division Property Management Sections in the field. Commanding officers of the Divisions have full operational control over and accountability for all resources allocated to them, including real property.

Accommodation planning begins with the identification of needs within the 16 Divisions by Division Property Management Section personnel. Needs are priorized within each Division and submitted to headquarters. Priorities are established nationally by a Headquarters Construction Planning and Priorities Committee (CPPC). Their recommendations are submitted annually to the Senior Executive Committee (comprised of the Commissioner and Assistant Commissioners) for approval.

The RCMP uses PWC as its land acquisition, design and construction, leasing and property disposal agency. The Force and PWC have collaborated to develop land standards, standard building designs and space standards. The Force has a comprehensive set of technical standards to meet its security and operational requirements and keeps its own inventory information.

The RCMP employs a variety of methods for the operation and maintenance of its real property. The majority of the work is contracted out through DSS, using service agreements or standing offer agreements. The RCMP also use PWC in some instances. There are eight PWC/RCMP Management Agreements for RCMP complexes in existence. Preventive maintenance is contracted out through PWC as are tenant services. PWC also does some preventive maintenance in-house for the Force in remote areas. The RCMP itself has a limited in-house O&M capability of 102 people principally related to the Canadian Police College in Ottawa (17 PYs) and the Training Depot in Regina (58 PYs). The Force has been reducing these numbers gradually as staff reach retirement age and converting to contracting out.

OBSERVATIONS

The RCMP has a well managed, well organized, effective and economic real property function.

Both Treasury Board and Auditor General staff testified to this. A Treasury Board Program Analyst commented further that the relationship between the RCMP and Public Works is a model. The RCMP stated that it is generally well satisfied with Public Works as a responsive professional agent and PWC commented that the RCMP is an excellent client. This review concurs with these judgements.

The Commissioner of the RCMP commented that property management in the Force had improved substantially over the past 10 to 15 years from a low point where poor accommodation had been affecting Force morale and there had been severe criticism by the Auditor General.

The essential features of the RCMP/PWC relationship are as follows:

Knowledgeable Client. The RCMP has a good accommodation planning and management process. The Force knows what it needs, when, where, why and how much. It knows the costs. Its priorities are clear.

Professional Expertise Rests with Service Agency. The RCMP's accommodation management organization is lean, is based on modest classification levels (CR-3 to AS-4) but is efficient and effective. The Force has no A&E professional capability and makes no effort to second guess the professional and technical advice and judgement of the service agency, PWC. The RCMP has assigned 19 person-years to PWC which are used for dedicated and responsive service to the Force with respect to design and construction. This arrangement also enables PWC to provide the functional management to support these resources as necessary.

Client Controls own O&M. Control over its own O&M has removed from the RCMP/PWC relationship many of the minor irritants that commonly affect landlord/tenant, or property service agent/client relations. The RCMP claims that often it can operate its facilities better and cheaper than PWC. A limited 1981 comparative study by the Force of RCMP properties handled by PWC under the Management Agreements versus properties managed by the Force tended to confirm the RCMP viewpoint.

Nevertheless, the RCMP does not hold rigidly to this as a firm policy position. It is willing to consider changing arrangements where PWC can demonstrate that it can perform services more cost-effectively than the force. At the present time, PWC is developing a proposal to carry out cyclical/preventive maintenance and repair on RCMP properties in the north as part of a proposal to perform these services for a number of federal departments with northern property.

Although the RCMP has contracted out almost all its O&M (an estimated 90 per cent) in compliance with its perception of government policy, the Force's property managers hold that in-house janitorial services are often more cost-effective than contracted services, and are better suited to their 24-hour operations.

The RCMP net property costs could be reduced by recovering the full capital and O&M costs of accommodaton provided in support of police service to provinces and municipalities, or by requiring other levels of government to accommodate the Force fully at their expense when police service is provided to them. The change would have to be phased in with the renegotiation of policing agreements towards the end of the 1980s.

There are two other real propety issues related to the RCMP:

a. the issue of an extension to the RCMP HQ in Ottawa to permit consolidation of its management/ administration and a new Services Building; and

b. the issue of housing management.

RCMP HQ and Services Buildings

Under the existing system PWC is expected to fund these proposed RCMP projects as part of PWC's overall responsibility for accommodation in the National Capital. The RCMP recognizes that these projects do not have high priority in the PWC program at the present time in comparison to projects for certain other departments, even though the design for the Services Building exists. While the Commissioner stated that he understood and accepted the rationale for the centralization of National Capital accommodation capital responsibilities, other members expressed the view that if PWC's capital vote were split among client departments and agencies, the RCMP would be in a position to seek Treasury Board approval for these projects as best suits its own timeframes and needs.

Housing Management

The RCMP provides housing for members of the Force in areas where there is no housing market, or in isolated places where the Force has to locate. Within the RCMP real property inventory, 201 detachment buildings include residences; 284 separate residences are also provided. In addition, in the north, the RCMP has 244 separate residences assigned to it by the pool housing Manager, PWC.

While the RCMP feels that it has good control over that portion of its housing which it owns or leases for itself (and confirms that because it can plan and carry out staff rotation precisely, it has a very low vacancy rate), it is less comfortable with PWC's management of pool housing, at least in the PWC Western Region, where delays in meeting schedules occur principally because other federal users cannot plan as precisely as the RCMP and tend to overstate requirements.

In 1983, a Treasury Board Task Force on Federal Housing for Public Servants recommended that where residential markets exist or have the potential to exist, the government should reduce its pool housing levels in order to stimulate market development. Yellowknife and Whitehorse would be the two localities with the best, though still fragile, potential for market development. The RCMP has two separate residences, 59 pool and 14 single quarters in Yellowknife and six separate residences, 73 pool and four single quarters in Whitehorse.

The issues of RCMP and pool housing should be assessed by the Study Team on Housing.

OPTIONS

The study team recommends to the Task Force that the RCMP should continue to be the custodian for its own accommodation, and to be responsible for its own operation and maintenance. PWC should continue to provide the design and construction service required by the RCMP. The Force and PWC should continue to keep open the possibility that wherever PWC can prove and deliver cost-effective operation and maintenance service, additional management agreements should be negotiated.

TECHNICAL SERVICES (REAL PROPERTY)

Correctional Services Canada

OBJECTIVE

The objective of the Correctional Services Program is to administer sentences imposed by the courts and to prepare offenders for their return to the community as useful citizens.

Within this overall program objective the real property objective of the Technical Services Division is to design, construct and maintain buildings and facilities according to the needs and priorities of the service.

RESULTS/BENEFICIARIES

Sixty-one institutions (including 19 Community Correctional Centres), 122 facilities and 61 parole offices and related professional and technical services.

The direct beneficiaries are the 12,000 inmates and 7,000 parolees and the 11,100 staff of Correctional Services Canada. Indirect beneficiaries are Canadian communities and the Canadian people generally.

AUTHORITY

The Penitentiary Act. The Parole Act.

RESOURCES ($ million)

	84/85	85/86
Annual Operating Expenses	49	54
Capital Expenditures	144	173
Person-Years - (CSC staff)	679	700
CSC dedicated PY in PWC	90	90

NOTE - In addition, approximately 1,000 inmates work on property operation and maintenance.

REAL PROPERTY ASSETS/SERVICE

Land - 7,726 hectares
Area of Buildings - 797,000 gross square metres
Number of Buildings - 1,608

PROGRAM DESCRIPTION

Framework

The legislative and constitutional framework which governs the operation and administration of The Correctional Service of Canada (CSC) is set out by the Constitution Act 1867, the Criminal Code of Canada, the Penitentiary Act and Regulations, the Parole Act and various international agreements. CSC adheres to the United Nations Standard Minimum Rules for Treatment of Prisoners, the International Covenant on Civil and Political Rights and the American Commission on Accreditation.

The Correctional Service of Canada is part of the criminal justice system. This system's operation depends upon its closely inter-related components, which include the body of criminal laws, law enforcement agencies, the judiciary and correctional services. Jurisdiction over these components is shared and divided among all levels of government. At the federal level, the Correctional Service is a part of the Ministry of the Solicitor General.

CSC has limited control of its input, as the service's clients are the product of the criminal justice system. Likewise, the output is governed in large part by legislation.

Under the provision of the Criminal Code of Canada, persons sentenced to 2 years or more are imprisoned in a federal penitentiary. Anyone sentenced to less than 2 years is imprisoned in a provincial reformatory or jail. The only exceptions occur when a province and the federal government contract to exchange offenders for specific purposes, e.g. to move an offender closer to home near the end of his/her sentence, or to provide a higher level of security for a provincial inmate. As well, CSC is responsible for the supervision of federal and provincial inmates released under legislative authority and for the supervision of federal inmates released under mandatory supervision.

Departmental Mission

The mission of CSC is to contribute to the protection of society by exercising effective and humane control of offenders while helping them become law-abiding citizens. In order to meet the custodial and social-oriented implications of this overall mission, the service is required to maintain equilibrium between two potentially conflicting "driving forces", while ensuring that the related activities are carried out as effectively and efficiently as possible. The two "driving forces" are the humane control of inmates and the earliest reintegration of offenders as useful and law-abiding members of Canadian society.

Economic and Social Climate

In terms of its ability to continue to deliver quality correctional services, CSC faces important challenges in the 1980s. Increasing numbers of federal inmates and the greater fear of crime and its consequences are expected to result in public demands for more traditional correctional services. At the same time, overall economic conditions and greater restraint on public spending will make it increasingly difficult for CSC to expand traditional correctional services at the same rate experienced in the past. In addition, the focus on openness and accountability in government will require policy adjustments in correctional practices and conditional release as the full impact of access and freedom of information initiatives and the entrenchment of civil rights are felt. As well, CSC will have to respond to pressures for new services and policies to deal with special offender groups.

CSC also feels that in the 1980s it must continue to be sensitive to provincial concerns and jurisdiction and must respond to a need for greater and more direct involvement of the community at all levels.

The two driving forces of CSC's mission (humane treatment and social reintegration), the present and future economic and social climate, the legacy of buildings from the past, and the reaction of CSC management to all of these issues, are the influences that affect real property management in CSC.

CSC Accommodation Planning and Investment

In order to respond in a timely way to the pressures it perceives CSC has spent considerable effort in the past few years to improve its real property planning and management.

CSC has adopted a 10-year National Accommodation Plan based on projected population demands and inmate profiles, and taking into account the effects of cascading inmates from higher to lower-security levels. As projected populations and inmate profiles are re-evaluated and adjusted annually, the details of the accommodation plan are modified accordingly.

Just as in the 1960s there was a sudden and unexpected increase in the number of committments (which peaked with equal suddenness in 1964 leaving surplus capacity) so there has been an unforeseen growth in the inmate population in the 1980s leading to overcrowding and then to double bunking. By October 1984, 962 inmates were double-bunked and temporary facilities were in place.

In the early 1980s inmate trend analysis indicated that the original (1981) long range plan, essentially a replacement program, would have resulted in a short-fall of over 4,000 cells by 1992/93. Consequently, a National Headquarters Accommodation Planning committee was established in 1983 to develop, review and assess alternatives for meeting expansion needs.

The current plan emphasizes provision of new accommodation and the elimination of overcrowding by 1986. There has been a substantial upward revision of the CSC construction capital reference level from the $60 to $70 million per annum to the $150 - 200 million range for the duration of the plan.

Additionally, the pressures on accommodation at both the federal and provincial levels, led to the two levels of government to negotiate a number of agreements to house each others' inmates where the proper authority lacked the appropriate institutional accommodation.

Inmate Classification

For a variety of reasons (control, discipline, punishment, reward, rehabilitation), CSC has adopted a seven element security classification of inmates (Classes S1 to S7). On entering the penitentiary system all inmates are classified in accordance with the length of their sentence, their record and psychological profile, and the type of crime for which they were sentenced.

The system of penitentiaries (i.e. the accommodation) is organized to reflect the security inmate classification, and to cluster or segregate as appropriate the different security groups. The security classes are grouped into three general types of institution: minimum security (S1 and S2), medium security (S3,S4 and S5) and maximum security (S6 and S7). CSC's preference is to keep these three types of institution physically separate, although there are situations where two different types of institution are physically separate but adjacent and can share services.

Cascading

Inmate treatment, (i.e. "effective and humane control") operates on what CSC calls the cascading down principle: i.e. as inmates demonstrate good or reformed behaviour they are moved from the more harshly disciplined higher security environments to more liberally organized lower security institutions. Conversely, bad behaviour leads to opposite moves.

Transfer

The physical separation of facilities, which was described above, and the cascading down principle, leads to inmates being transferred not just from one part of a penitentiary to another, but from one institution to another, frequently in another region, and sometimes at the opposite end of the country. Some 14,400 such transfers occurred in 1983-84 for an inmate population of 11,000.

In spite of CSC's best efforts to project the size of inmate classes accurately, using very sophisticated computer modelling and statistical analysis techniques, their predictions have been inaccurate on a national scale and worse on a regional basis. Consequently, CSC finds itself in a situation where it has the wrong types of institutions, and the wrong numbers of cells, in the wrong part of the country, for the actual inmate population with which it has to deal.

Treatment

The second thrust of CSC's mission, ("the earliest re-integration of offenders as useful and law-abiding members of Canadian Society") also has strong implications for the CSC accommodation program. Under the Parole Act, inmates become eligible for parole after a certain portion of their sentence has been served and depending on their behaviour. The decision to grant parole does not rest with the CSC but with the Parole Board, an independent body. CSC's ability to predict when inmates are due to be released is reduced by the vagaries of the parole process. Again, while CSC attempts to project parole patterns, with fair accuracy on a national scale, at regional, provincial and local levels the unpredictability is greater, exacerbating accommodation problems for wardens and technical support staff.

The effort to rehabilitate inmates has led to the introduction of a wide number of economic (e.g. manufacturing, farming, realty management, etc) educational, social and recreational programs. These programs have placed substantial accommodation requirements on the CSC administration, to the point that in new penitentiaries more than 50 per cent of the built space is allocated to administrative and program functions.

Socio-Economic Considerations and Community Reaction to New Penitentiaries

Whilst a number of penitentiaries are old (some predate Confederation) the expansion of the inmate population over the last 30 years has led to the establishment of several new institutions. There are plans for still more new ones.

Government socio-economic considerations and vociferous community reaction to proposed new institutions (pro and con) have been the primary determinants of location, rather than the needs of inmates to remain close to their family and social support, or the needs of CSC to be close to the (urban) social and economic infrastructure on which the penitentiaries depend. Consequently, CSC has had to make provision for in-house services and facilities which could otherwise be obtained from surrounding communities, and has had to wait years for decisions on new institutions.

Accommodation Management

CSC accommodation is a centrally planned and managed sub-function of the Technical Services Branch in CSC Headquarters, under a Director, Accommodation Requirements and Construction (DARC) reporting to the Director General, Technical Services. DARC has 25 person-years involved in capital program planning and management, four in inventory tabulation, and six in looking after operations and maintenance plans, programs and standards.

At the regional level, the five regions have a total of eight architect/engineers between them. There are also 16 regional staff handling O&M programming. At the local level there are 672 CSC employees operating and maintaining the facilities. Approximately 1,000 inmates work on property operation and maintenance, under the supervision either of CSC staff or PWC staff or both.

CSC - PWC Interface

The CSC-PWC relationship is similar to that between the RCMP and PWC, except that at the present time it does not work quite so smoothly for a number of reasons:

a. lack of control at the administrative level over capital project decisions;
b. uncertainties and changes in project direction within CSC;
c. variances in approach in both CSC and PWC at the regional level; and
d. a cumbersome, and in some cases heavy-handed response by PWC to CSC requirements, leading to delays in meeting serious CSC deadlines, and causing CSC operational difficulties.

Both parties agree however that their relationship has improved substantially over the past 5 years, and the parties are cooperating to produce further improvement.

CSC performs the following responsibilities:

a. long and short range planning;
b. requirements definition, approval and priorization; and

c. operation and maintenance; either in-house, or through PWC or service contracts with DSS.

PWC is the design and construction contract agent for CSC and acquires the land and leases that are necessary for the department. CSC has assigned 90 person-years to PWC for dedicated delivery principally of the design and construction program.

OBSERVATIONS

In spite of substantial improvement at the administrative and operational management level in the face of severe constraints, CSC still cannot be said to be managing its property in a cost effective manner relative to its program. This is not the fault of the property managers (who have one of the most difficult real property assignments in the Government of Canada) so much as the responsibility of departmental management and a consequence of government decisions.

The department has placed enormous emphasis on its capital program, particularly on new acquisitions as relates to many of its operational problems such as over-crowding, double-bunking, and assignment of inmates to inappropriate institutions because of space problems.

In capital planning there is too much emphasis on national data; adjustments are needed to take regional sensitivities and variances into account.

Alternative measures, which potentially could alleviate the pressure to build, include an increased emphasis on the establishment of more extensive Federal-Provincial Agreements to accommodate inmates, share facilities or develop joint institutions (e.g. in Newfoundland, where neither level of government is able to justify the economics of an institution solely for its purposes). For minimum security institutions CSC should be prepared to examine seriously the option of acquiring and converting other surplus social infrastructive such as schools or community colleges as an alternative to new construction.

There is much less emphasis on operation and management, and a lack of data in this area, although new property management information systems are being developed. An obvious obstacle to improved effectiveness in operation and maintenance is the productivity of inmates, which is variable. Also CSC must continue to operate many uneconomic institutions.

Organizationally, property administration is overly centralized, with too many layers involved before decisions on day-to-day operational matters can be taken. Wardens should have full operational control over their institutions.

If the correctional system is viewed as a whole, then non-real-property solutions to some of CSC's problems should be considered as alternatives to more capital construction. This is particularly true given that the present rise in criminal activity may be peaking again. This important issue should be assessed by the Task Force Study Team on Justice.

OPTIONS

The study team recommends to the Task Force that CSC and PWC should continue to collaborate on improvements to their relationship. CSC should seek PWC assistance in sharpening its operation and maintenance management. PWC should be prepared to standardize its operational response and to adapt to the special environmental considerations in penitentiaries, including recognition of the value of making the fullest possible use of inmate labour.

SECTION 17 - INDIAN AFFAIRS AND NORTHERN DEVELOPMENT

TECHNICAL SERVICES

Indian and Northern Affairs

OBJECTIVE

The Technical Services Program provides policy direction and professional advisory services in contract administration and the planning, design, procurement and maintenance of real property and other capital assets.

The objectives associated with programs for capital expenditures on Indian lands (housing, schools, and community infrastructure) as well as on Territorial lands (northern roads) will be examined by other teams of the Task Force.

RESULTS/BENEFICIARIES

The Department of Indian and Northern Affairs undertakes architectural and engineering services to construct schools, roads, houses, airstrips, sewer and water systems for Indian and Inuit communities.

AUTHORITY

Department of Indian and Northern Development Act, 1970; Yukon Act, Northwest Territories Act, Territorial Lands Act, Land Titles Act, Public Lands Grants Act, Canada Land Surveys Act.

RESOURCES (thousands of current dollars)

Real Property Related		84/85	85/86
Operating Expenditures	- Indian Affairs	$85,000	$85,000
Capital Expenditures	- Indian Affairs	$265,000	$305,000
	- Northern Affairs	$ 28,000	$ 21,000
Person-Years		401	401

REAL PROPERTY ASSETS

Building Space - 1,487,000 square metres
Total number of buildings - 6,580
Estimated Value of Assets - $3.7 billion

PROGRAM DESCRIPTION

The Department of Indian and Northern Affairs (DINA) has a number of organizational units which are involved in real property management:

- the Northern Land Use Planning Directorate develops policies and programs that determine the department's land use planning process in the Yukon and Northwest Territories;
- the Northern Resources and Economic Planning Directorate plans and controls northern road development and infrastructure development;
- Indian Reserves and Trusts Directorate maintains an Indian Lands Registry;
- the Indian Housing and Bands Support Directorate plans and controls capital for Band housing, schools, infrastructure, and other facilities;
- the Capital Management Directorate provides a framework for capital management and the management of related operations; and
- the Technical Services Directorate which provides Architectural and Engineering Services in support of the above programs.

The Native Affairs Study Team is reviewing the expenditure programs of the Department of Indian Affairs and commenting on the real property implications related to those programs (housing, schools, infrastructure, etc.). This review will focus on the professional and technical services which support the program management.

The architectural and engineering services are delivered through headquarters (Director of Technical Services) and through the regions (Directors or Regional Managers of Architectural and Engineering Services).

The Technical Services Unit and the related regional units are responsible for the annual implementation of approximately 4,000 individual projects through contributions, contracts and other agencies (Public Works Canada). The projects represent an annual expenditure in excess of $300 million. Approximately 90 per cent of the projects are less than $250 thousand in size.

The direct beneficiaries of the architectural and engineering service are the managers of the Indian Affairs Program and the Northern Development Program who utilize these professional and technical services. The indirect beneficiaries are the clients of the programs (Indians and Residents of the Territories).

There are 401 person-years dedicated to providing services at three operating levels: Headquarters, 10 regional units and 45 district or service centres. While headquarters provides mainly policy advice and develops standards for areas such as professional services, municipal services, technical services, technological development, building and transportation services, and technical data and training coordination, both headquarters and the regions employ professional specialists in the following areas: architecture, mechanical, electrical, water and roads engineering, drafting and surveying, project management, construction management, fire inspection, and technical and administration support (project recording, document management, etc.). Headquarters provides a central pool of expertise which is dispatched to specific districts on an as required basis.

The following information, based on 1982-83 data, provides an order of magnitude overview of the utilization of architectural and engineering person-years in the department:

Type of Activity	Professional	Technical & Support	Total
Corporate Activity	37	50	87
Design & Construction	67	86	153
Technical Operations & Maintenance	50	86	136
Research and Development	1	1	2
Special Projects & Programs	4	5	9
TOTAL	159	228	387

The Technical Services Unit, in headquarters, presently utilizes 93 person-years and is responsible for functional direction and advisory services concerned with the implementation of DINA's architectural, engineering and construction, property development, property appraisal, property administration and property management requirement. In addition, it has responsibility to transfer technological information to Indian Bands, oversee fire protection and prevention on Indian reserves, and contract administration in the department. The unit also provides direct technical support and project management services in the implementation of the Northern Roads Program.

The regional offices, utilizing 308 person-years, implement DINA's capital construction program consisting of approximately $300 million capital for the construction of houses, schools, community centres, sewers, water systems, etc. on Indian lands, and $27 million for the construction of Northern Roads in the Yukon and the North West Territories.

In addition, approximately $77 million is spent annually to maintain the estimated $2.4 billion worth of capital assets on Indian reserves, the responsibility of which has been assigned to the Minister of Indian and Northern Affairs. The estimated replacement value of the Northern Affairs inventory is $1.3 billion. The cost of maintaining these assets are borne by the Territorial Government and are included in the federal transfer payments to the Territorial Governments.

A major portion of the capital and maintenance funds of DINA are spent by Indian Bands and Territorial Governments under contribution arrangements. DINA staff, indealing with Indian Bands when implementing projects, are caught between the government's requirements for cost control and accountability on the one hand, and Band requirements for control of their affairs on the other. DINA is increasing the ratio of capital contribution to Bands versus in-house capital construction. For example, 65 per cent of the total $200 million capital expenditures of 1982-83 were made via contributions to Bands; 2 years later in 1984-85 the ratio had increased to 80 per cent.

DINA enters into General Service Agreements with the Territorial Governments to establish jurisdication, responsiblity and reporting requirements regarding northern roads. It has established a Memorandum of Understanding with Public Works Canada for all design and construction work contracted to the latter department for capital project delivery.

OBSERVATIONS

As the notion of native self-government gains momentum, more and more of the Indian Affairs funding related to real property projects is being transferred from the capital budget to the contribution budget. Based on criteria which take into account a Band Council's readiness to assume construction responsibilities, each project is evaluated as to whether it can be done by a Band under a contribution agreement or by in-house DINA staff. When differences occur between the Band and DINA staff over Band readiness, the Minister resolves the dispute. The responsibility and resources for project management are being transferred to Indian Bands and Tribal Councils. Reality, however, dictates that DINA has to implement an extensive monitoring and training process for every project to ensure under the Financial Administration Act that funds are indeed spent for what they are intended and that some level of prudence and probity are observed. Contribution agreements may, over time, have a significant impact on DINA's architectural and engineering role. As Band Councils become more sophisticated, DINA's role will evolve into one of arms-length contribution management. Over time, the resource requirements for these architechtural and engineering services should be substantially reduced.

As more responsiblities are transferred to the Territorial Governments, the funding for maintenance of northern roads and for new construction will also be transferred to the Territorial Governments. Already, a workload associated with ensuring that Bands are able to deliver the projects.

Although the Bands appoint a Band Project Manager, the department also appoints a project manager, known as a "Project Officer", to oversee the Band work, and to rescue projects which run into difficulties. Resources are also devoted to training Bands how to maintain facilities once they are constructed. DINA does not, at this time, have a policy identifying an appropriate service level or the resource level required to train the Indian Bands. It does however, have a master plan identifying the type of training required in the technical and contract area for Indian Bands to effectively assume full responsibility.

There appears to be a split responsiblity between Indian Bands and the regional DINA staff over on-going operations and maintenance. Some Bands do not have the expertise or resources to maintain facilities (i.e. arenas) which have been constructed. As a result, DINA staff fill the void and undertake emergency repairs to prevent deterioration. Indians have come to expect that these types of services should continue to be provided. Although the philosophy of DINA is that DINA manages the program and the Bands are to manage and operate the assets, there is no framework in the department to determine the level of support services to be provided to the Indian Bands to bring them to the point that they are able to assume full responsibility. As long as DINA retains accountability for public funds (for example, to replace structures allowed to prematurely deteriorate), an in-house role will be required within DINA.

At headquarters and at regions, difficulties arise between DINA staff over the differentiation between capital program management (the responsibility of DINA program managers) and project management (the responsiblity of DINA technical services). For example, the answer to the question: "to what extent should the manager of the educational program be involved in the design, construction and daily operations of a school versus the overall management of the program?" has not been satisfactorily resolved within DINA. The "service" role of the architectural and engineering (technical) services group is not well understood in the department by program managers. As a result, there is some confusion and overlap of responsibility in the management of physical assets.

DINA does not do in-house design or construction contract administration for its own construction projects with a value over $500K. These are contracted out to Public Works. PWC undertakes approximately $30 million of project delivery for DINA. For projects of less than $500K value, the department contracts out approximately 75 per cent of project design. A Memorandum of Understanding outlining respective areas of services and responsiblity exists between PWC and DINA and permits a good working relationship between the two groups.

DINA does not do in-house design or construction contract administration for its own construction projects with a value over $500K. These are contracted out to Public Works. PWC undertakes approximately $30 million of project delivery for DINA. For projects of less than $500K value, the department contracts out approximately 75 per cent of project design. A Memorandum of Understanding outlining respective areas of services and responsiblity exists between PWC and DINA and permits a good working relationship between the two groups.

DINA does not have a reliable management reporting system that systematically collects and reports capital project information (physical and financial) to properly manage capital programs and projects. Although a Project Accounting System was put in place in 1982, the system is perceived as being so complex and the information it contains so suspect, that it has been almost universally rejected by the managers it was intended to serve. Improvements are being undertaken and will result in a substantially improved system later this fiscal year.

In summary, more and more in-house responsibility for capital construction and maintenance is being transferred to Indian Bands and Territorial Governments, but not the accountability. Very little hands-on design and construction is performed by Indian and Northern Affairs staff, and almost no hands-on maintenance. Design and construction is normally under contract to Indian Bands and the Department of Public Works, while maintenance is generally done by the Bands. The main emphasis of the over 400 employees (of which 30 per cent is professional) is in project management, technology transfer to Bands and providing professional advice and services to support DINA program managers. The relationship between the Bands and DINA concerning real property management and accountability requires further improvement and clarification especially concerning DINA's future direction.

OPTIONS

The study team recommends to the Task Force that the government consider:

- developing a plan to transfer knowledge of operational maintenance within the next 3 years to

Indian Bands to reduce their dependence upon departmental staff;

- developing improved funding arrangements which reduce DINA accountability for project delivery and increase the responsibility and capability of the Indian Bands and Tribal Councils. DINA should cease in-house project delivery and increase contributions;

- phasing out in-house capital construction of northern road projects and transferring responsiblity to the Territorial governments by making transfer payments; and

- decreasing DINA's in-house architectural and engineering capabilities to the level of a knowledgeable client based on broader initiatives of consolidating Architectural and Engineering Services across government. The professional and technical expertise within DINA should be transferred to Public Works and DINA should contract future requirements for these services from PWC.

SECTION 18 - HEALTH AND WELFARE

MEDICAL SERVICES BRANCH

Health and Welfare Canada

OBJECTIVE

To protect and enhance the health of those Canadians whose care, by legislation or custom, is the responsibility of the Department of National Health and Welfare. The Property Planning and Management Section operates in direct support of the branch objective.

RESULTS/BENEFICIARIES

The Medical Services Branch owns and operates:

a. eight hospitals;
b. six cottage hospitals;
c. twelve clinics;
d. ninety-six nursing stations;
e. one hundred and twenty-seven health centres;
f. one hundred and ninety-seven health stations;
g. sixty three health offices; and
h. some 200 staff accommodation buildings in support of the objectives of the program.

The principal beneficiaries of the program are Canada's Registered Indians and Inuit peoples and the non-native residents of the Yukon and Northwest Territories. Other program clients include federal public servants, civil aviation personnel, immigrants and temporary residents, and international travellers.

AUTHORITY

The mandate of the Medical Services Branch (MSB) derives from Section 91 of the Constitution Acts, 1867 and 1981. Sub-section 24 relates to the provision of Indian Health Services. Program authority for the provision of health services to Indian communities has been a matter of policy since 1945. A Privy Council decision in 1954 authorizes the provision of health services to the Yukon and Northwest Territories.

RESOURCES **(thousands of current dollars)**

	83/84	84/85
Operating Expenses	$ 2,875	$ 3,807
Capital	23,975	34,327
Grants and Contribution	6,638	9,539
Person-Years	97	97

REAL PROPERTY ASSETS

Land - 170.32 hectares
Buildings - 508
Gross Floor Area - 176,028 square metres in MSB custody
- 1,164.6 square metres directly leased (residential)
- 71,224.9 square metres PWC managed office space

PROGRAM DESCRIPTION

In the acquisition of land or office accommodation and in capital construction projects over $200,000, Public Works acts as the sole agent for the branch. The branch is authorized under the Financial Administration Act to tender and act as its own agent for projects under $200,000. Other construction projects funded through capital contribution arrangements with Indian Bands are implemented by the Bands themselves generally with no involvement by Public Works at any stage of the planning or construction. Space in these projects is leased back to the branch through Public Works. Increases in both capital and grants budgets reflect increased cash flow from the 62 construction projects shown in the approved Departmental Estimates.

The program delivery organization, which concerns itself almost entirely with accommodation requirements identification, accommodation allocation, project staffing and approvals, and on-going operations and maintenance of existing facilities, is structured as follows:

a. National Headquarters - eight personnel concerned with requirements, accommodation planning and allocation, property records, maintenance plannning;

b. Regional, zone and hospital staff totalling 89 personnel who are almost entirely concerned with the identification, resolution, and supervision of operations and maintenance activities. Forty-seven of these people are maintenance supervisors, tradesmen, and heating plant operators on hospital establishments.

The Medical Services Branch has no professional Architectural and Engineering staff. It relies totally on Public Works for this service. Public Works also arranges joint contracts for maintenance of facilities in the North where more than one government agency operates in a community.

OBSERVATIONS

The Medical Services Branch has a well-defined capital program policy, based on Treasury Board and branch-approved scales of accommodation, to ensure that health care programs are supported by those facilities necessary to maintain health care delivery and management services. The management system culminates in a user-dominated Capital Program Review Committee which:

a. reviews and recommends the capital plan portion of the MYOP to senior management;

b. reviews the long term capital plan framework annually;

c. identifies requirements for adjustments of new policies and procedures for the effective, efficient management of the capital program policy;

d. reviews major capital projects requiring Treasury Board approval; and

e. establishes methods and procedures for monitoring capital projects.

This system appears to be effective in ensuring the timely delivery of real property assets to meet program requirements and ensures that senior management actively participates in the capital development process.

The branch does however have problems in its facilities maintenance program in that it has not, until relatively recently, considered the development of a program of preventive maintenance. In all regions, except Ontario where a preventive maintenance (PM) program was established in conjunction with Public Works, maintenance is basically conducted on a failure repair basis.

The branch sees a requirement to establish a full PM system, based on a complete inventory of facilities and their condition, which does not exist at present, in all regions. While it would prefer that this program be established and operated by Public Works that agency has, other than in Ontario, declined due to lack of person-years (PY). Money is not a problem as the branch provides that resource but is unable to afford to transfer its program PYs for the purpose. To resolve this problem, the Medical Services Branch is seeking funding to contract private industry to establish and operate a full PM system for all its facilities across the country. This initiative is considered to be worthy of support as it offers the prospect of long-term maintenance savings and reduced capital outlays.

OPTIONS

The study team recommends to the Task Force that there would not appear to be any reasonable alternatives to the status quo. Real property management is effectively contracted out through Public Works and departmental staff are involved solely in program support activities.

HEALTH PROTECTION BRANCH

Health and Welfare Canada

OBJECTIVE

To ensure that appropriate accommodation is provided for the branch's laboratory functions.

RESULTS/BENEFICIARIES

The Health Protection Branch (HPB) owns and operates regional laboratories in Vancouver, Winnipeg, Scarborough and Longueil and has one regional laboratory in a portion of a converted Public Works building in Halifax. Seven additional laboratories are located in single purpose buildings owned by Public Works in the National Capital Region. The HPB is constructing replacement facilities in Burnaby (Vancouver) and Winnipeg and is planning a replacement facility in Halifax.

AUTHORITY

The HPB has no specific authority to acquire real property assets. Special purpose facilities outside the National Capital Region are funded by HPB and constructed by Public Works while special purpose buildings within the National Capital Region are funded, constructed and fully maintained by Public Works as landlord for HPB.

RESOURCES (thousands of current dollars)

	84/85	85/86
Operating Expenses	$1,060	$1,988
Capital	2,260	22,800
Person-Years	.75	8

REAL PROPERTY ASSETS

Land - 7.48 hectares.
Buildings - 4 (including the two under construction).
Gross Floor Area - 25,485 square metres, in HPB custody.
- 54,919 square metres in PWC custody,the vast majority of which is in the NCR.

PROGRAM DESCRIPTION

The HPB holdings do not warrant a formal real property management organization. Major capital projects are under the direction of the Director, Bureau of Administration. Routine property management, including operation and maintenance functions, is administered by the Regional Directors. The amount of time, and the number of person years (PY), expended on this activity will increase temporarily during the design and construction of the new laboratories. All design, construction, and maintenance functions are performed by contract through PWC.

The project delivery process is as follows:

a. HPB writes the special project brief for Public Works (PWC) and seeks Treasury Board approval to hire consultants;

b. site selection and participation in the consultants' brief review and milestone establishment are joint HPB/PWC activities;

c. HPB approves preliminary design and participates in design reviews with PWC;

d. HPB receives Treasury Board approval to construct;

e. PWC lets tenders, awards contracts and supervises construction; and

f. on project completion HPB and Medical Services Branch conduct extensive tests of air handling systems and if all is well accept the facility.

OBSERVATIONS

The program, which under normal circumstances, uses existing staff of the HPB Bureau of Administration and Regional Directors, appears to be effectively run and ensures that the best interests of HPB are protected. Given that there is no full-time staff involvement in the property management function it is difficult to see how it could be conducted at less cost. Cost increases in 1985-86 reflect the start of major cash flow on the new laboratory construction projects.

OPTIONS

The study team recommends to the Task Force that the government consider developing legislation to provide the Health Protection Branch with the legal authority to hold real property assets in their own right.

SECTION 19 - NATIONAL MUSEUMS

NATIONAL MUSEUMS OF CANADA

Department of Communications

OBJECTIVE

The objective of the National Museums of Canada is to demonstrate the products of nature and the works of man, with special but not exclusive reference to Canada, so as to promote interest therein throughout Canada and to disseminate this knowledge. The Architectural Services Directorate of the Corporate Services Division functions in direct support of this objective.

RESULTS/BENEFICIARIES

The National Museums of Canada, a Schedule B Crown Corporation reporting to the Minister of Communications, has four operating divisions.

a. the National Gallery;

b. the National Museum of Natural Science;

c. the National Museum of Man which includes the War Museum; and

d. the National Museum of Science and Technology which includes the Aviation and Space Museum.

All of these museums' display buildings are located in the National Capital Region where two new museums buildings - for the Gallery and the Museum of Man - are being constructed by the Canada Museums Construction Corporation. On completion of these projects and the renovation of some of the display building space vacated by these collections, Museums Canada's ability to display its collection will have more than doubled.

AUTHORITY

The National Museums of Canada operate under the authority of the National Museums Act: 1967-68, c.21, s.l.

The corporation has no authority to own real property in its own right.

RESOURCES (thousands of current dollars)

	83/84	84/85
Operating Expenses	$1,059	$1,094
Capital	1,946	1,115
Person-Years	19	26

PROGRAM DESCRIPTION

Museums Canada does not manage real property in the true sense as it owns neither land nor buildings in its own right. The corporation is a tenant of Public Works Canada which provides full operations and maintenance services. The Architectural Services portion of the Corporate Services program planning element is essentially involved in the identification, rationalization, and statement of Museums Canada accommodation requirements for satisfaction by Public Works or the Canada Museums Construction Corporation in either new or renovated existing buildings; and, in long-range development planning. The corporation currently occupies all or part of 39 buildings in the National Capital Region. Seven buildings are used for public display of the collections, parts of three are used for office accommodation, and 29 serve as storage, workshop, research or conservation facilities alone or in combination in support of the museums. The public display buildings are:

a. The Victoria Memorial Museum, at Elgin and Argyle Streets, which houses the National Museum of Man and the National Museum of Natural Science;

b. The Canadian War Museum on Sussex Drive;

c. The Lorne Building, on Elgin at Albert, which houses the National Gallery;

d. The National Museum of Science and Technology on St. Laurent Boulevard; and

e. The Aviation Museum which occupies three hangars at Rockcliffe.

On completion of the two new museum buildings 16 occupancies will be vacated - 11 by the Museum of Man and five by the Gallery - and five more will be vacated when the Victoria Memorial Museum is renovated for the Natural Science collection after departure of the Museum of Man. When the Museums Canada long-range plan has been implemented there will be six public display buildings or locations and four office and/or conservation laboratory sites.

Museums Canada accommodation is provided by PWC and CMCC to meet requirements defined by the user divisions through the Architectural Services Directorate. This directorate was authorized 19.5 PY in 1984/85 of which five were term positions (expiring in 1988) provided to assist in the coordination of the review of the detailed designs and working drawings for the new National Gallery and the National Museum of Man from a requirements and operational point of view and to define projects related to the occupancy of these buildings and the new Aviation and Space Museum being designed and built by PWC. Considerable effort is being expended, with the assistance of specialist consultants where necessary, in planning the renovation of existing space which will come available on completion of the new buildings.

The permanent staff working under the director includes:

a. Chief, Accommodation Management and a staff of six responsible for accommodation planning, allocation, coordination, signage, parking and telecommunications;

b. Chief, Project Coordination who is an architect charged with professional project coordination, briefing of consultants, and design review;

c. A two-person graphic arts section; and

d. A four-person office management section.

OBSERVATIONS

Review of Museums Canada long-range planning documents and various detailed project briefs clearly indicates that the Architectural Services Directorate is performing its tasks in an efficient, effective, professional manner. The directorate provides an essential bridge between the exhibit designers and the builders which would be difficult to achieve by other means.

The frequent use of consultants to augment in-house professional staff indicates a clear desire to keep staff levels to the minimum necessary to provide knowledgeable professional support to the various museums projects on a day-to-day basis.

Given the highly specialized electrical, mechanical, and lighting systems required to preserve, protect and display museum pieces it is considered that there is no practical alternative to the maintenance of a small in-house professional staff to develop detailed statements of accommodation requirement and to ensure that museum requirements are met. This is particularly necessary in an environment where both Public Works and Treasury Board standards are geared to relatively standard office buildings rather than highly specialized museum structures and where, at the operational level, Public Works staff have demonstrated a lack of training and appreciation of the nature of the museums operation in terms of the need for fast response to systems maintenance problems.

It is considered that significant savings could be made by both Museums Canada (security, administrative staffs) and PWC (building maintenance staff, cleaning contracts, etc.) through consolidation of Museum support operations in fewer, single purpose buildings. Maintenance of the current sprawl is clearly most inefficient. The Museums Canada development plan which clearly recognizes this problem and proposes a clear solution should be brought forward.

OPTIONS

There is no reasonable alternative to the status quo. It is considered essential that Museums Canada retain a capability to define and plan their accommodation and maintain project and/or program control.

NATIONAL MUSEUMS OF CANADA (NMC-1)

Real Property Management Resource Summary: Program Name and Code Number

Program Resources: ($)	83/84	84/85	85/86	86/87	87/88
Total Operating Expenditures	553,083	1,058,819	1,093,785	950,602	994,807
Revenue	-	-	-	-	-
Salaries and Wages	425,072	660,819	892,684	755,348	755,348
O&M	119,010	398,000	201,101	195,254	239,459
Grants and Contributions	9,001	-	-	-	-
Capital	800,507	1,945,600	1,114,568	1,105,608	1,302,938
Person-Years	11	19	26	22	22

Regional Distribution:

84/85	NRC	Atlantic	Quebec	Ontario	West	Other
Total Gross Expenditures	3,004,419					
Revenue	-					
Salaries and Wages	660,819					
O&M	398,000					
Grants and Contributions	-					
Person-Years	19					
Capital	1,945,600					

CANADA MUSEUMS CONSTRUCTION CORPORATION

Department of Communications

OBJECTIVE

The construction, in the National Capital Region, of buildings for the National Gallery of Canada and the National Museum of Man including the acquisition, control, administration, and disposal of the lands required for the construction.

AUTHORITY

CMCC was established as a Schedule C Crown corporation by Order-in-Council P.C. 1982-1838 on June 17, 1982. The corporation reports through a board of directors, composed of the Chairman of the Corporation, the Chief Executive Officer of the National Museums of Canada, the Chairman of the National Capital Commission, and the Deputy Ministers of the Departments of Public Works and Communications, to the Minister of Communications. The Directors of The National Gallery and the National Museum of Man act as advisors to the Board.

RESOURCES (thousands of current dollars)

	84/85	85/86
Operating Expenses	$ 2,346	$ 2,605
Capital	$ 39,654	$ 87,395
Person-Years	37	40

PROGRAM DESCRIPTION

The CMCC is constructing a building of some 39,000 net square metres for the Museum of Man in Hull and one of 32,500 for the National Gallery in Ottawa on National Capital Commission property. The approved budget for the two buildings is $191.45 million, exclusive of commissioning and fit-up costs which will be borne by Museums Canada.

The CMCC with its 37 person-years is the delivery organization. Its sole purpose is the design and construction of the two museum buildings. The staff are involved in the normal project management functions of design checks and approvals, site control, cost control, financial management and, as is the case with a project of such visibility, public relations and public information programs. Design proper is contracted to two architectural firms - one for each building. CMCC does all of its own contracting and contract administration.

OBSERVATIONS

Measured against its mandate "to construct, in the National Capital Region buildings for the National Gallery of Canada and the National Museum of Man" within an established funding level the CMCC must be deemed a failure. It is considered however that, in terms of its project management activities related to the two construction sites, CMCC is performing effectively and that staff numbers are generally appropriate to the size and complexity of the projects. A chronology which is essential background to this general observation is attached at Annex A.

The present situation is that finished buildings ready for fit-up as conceived in the approved designs can only be achieved through the expenditure of from $36.0 to $54.0 million beyond budget. The study team advances the following observations:

a. CMCC was established outside the normal system of checks and balances.

b. There was no apparent attempt to determine the total project cost - construction plus occupancy. The budget only covered the construction phase of the program.

c. In spite of the fact that the projects are presently known to be between $36.0 and $54.0 million over budget - assuming they are completed in accordance with approved designs - at the time of writing of this assessment, no action has been taken to approve the over-run and/or effect a change in management to curtail and control any further over-runs.

d. Operating outside the system of checks and balances, CMCC management should have advised Cabinet in October 1983 that the projects could not be completed within budget and that the $5.0 million estimated over-run could be expected to rise as full design was completed and the high risk "fast-track" construction process began.

e. When further funds were not forthcoming, CMCC should have developed options in 1983 and recommended those portions of the project which could be scaled down to meet budget.

In assessing CMCC as a model for the delivery of large, prestigious construction projects it can only be concluded that the public interest is better served when project control is exercised within the framework of Departmental and Treasury Board review. In this specific case there is no reason to believe that completion dates could not have been met through the Major Crown Project procedure with "fast-track" construction procedures inplemented by Public Works. It is likely that work would not have proceeded or the design would have been changed to fit the budget under this controlled approach providing the Senior Review Board was properly established.

It is considered that, at this stage of the project, a change of approach from Crown Corporation to a normal Major Crown Project control system would carry cost and time penalties in the order of $8 to $10 million. Changes could be made in senior management; however, any change in the individual project management staff would have serious consequences arising from a break in continuity. Furthermore, accountability would be confused for the remainder of the projects by shifting organizations in mid-stream.

The practical alternatives open to the government are:

a. provide sufficient funds to complete the project as approved and closely control the expenditure of the additional funds provided; or

b. complete the buildings to the extent possible within the present budget - or the present budget increased by some amount. Acceptance of this alternative assumes acceptance of partially completed buildings for an indefinite period and higher eventual completion costs.

Under either alternative, it is considered essential that a Chief Executive Officer with senior construction executive experience be appointed and given operational authority to ensure the successful completion of what is, at this stage, nothing more than a large construction project. However, one member of the senior management team might continue to be an acknowledged expert from the artistic/museums community to retain the projects' credibility with that community. This could become particularly important should it be deemed appropriate to seek public subscriptions to complete the projects as designed.

OPTIONS

The study team recommends to the Task Force that the government consider retaining the Canada Museum Construction Corporation, and appointing a Chief Executive Officer with senior construction executive experience and full operating authority. Co-incident with this appointment, a formal decision should be made on the level of funding to be provided and the degree of completion which is acceptable.

Sufficient funds should be provided to complete these projects as approved and the expenditure of these funds should be closely controlled.

ANNEX A

CANADA MUSEUMS CONSTRUCTION CORPORATION

SEQUENCE OF EVENTS

September 1981 - The decision was taken by the government to construct new buildings for the National Gallery and the Museum of Man. The funds allocated to the project - from the Government Operations reserve envelope - totalled $185.0 million over fiscal years 1982-83 to 1986-87. The budget was increased to $191.45 million in November 1983 to account for cost increases due to changes in cash flow projections ($1.6 million) and the provision of additional parking at the Gallery ($4.85 million). The $186.6 million allocated for the buildings was apparently based on a late 1970s estimate by the National Museums of Canada. This estimate was not site-specific, covered only the construction costs, and can be considered to have been no more than a Class D (rough order of magnitude) figure.

June 21, 1982 - CMCC was established, which placed it outside the normal approval system. The Board of CMCC decided that funds available for construction would be divided evenly between the two projects and the government concurred.

Eventually, the building budget for each museum was established at $80.0 million with the remainder allocated as follows:

a. Fees $14.8 million;
b. Operating costs for CMCC $11.8 million; and
c. Gallery parking $4.85 million.

May, 1983 - Government approved the design for the Gallery with the clear understanding that the projected cost of this building was $4.0 million under the base budget of $80 million.

October, 1983 - Government approved the long-term building and funding schedules for both projects. CMCC advised the government that the two projects were already - at only the preliminary design stage - a total of $5.0 million over their base budgets. Approval was based upon CMCC obtaining the additional $5.0 million from private donations.

December, 1983 - Gallery construction started.

February, 1984 - Museum of Man construction started.

May 25, 1984 - Government formally recognized that the buildings could not be completed as conceived within budget (potential over-runs in the order of $24.0 million were being reported) and authorized CMCC to make a public appeal for funds to "improve the quality of the two Museums" to quote from the auditor's notes to the 1983-84 CMCC Annual Report. CMCC has done some preliminary work on fund raising but such activities were curtailed on change of government. It also appears that there is uniform provincial opposition to federal fund raising for these projects.

December, 1984 - At the request of the Deputy Minister of Communications and the Secretary of the Treasury Board, the Department of Communications convened a Task Force to determine the additional funding required for the construction and occupancy of the new facilities for the Gallery and Museum of Man and for the occupancy of the new National Aviation Museum. In relation to the CMCC projects, the Task Force stated in its report dated February 19, 1985 that:

a. The potential construction over-run is:

   1. Gallery - $21,388,003 (26.7 per cent)
   2. Museum of Man - $14,679,252 (18.4 per cent)
   3. Total - $36,067,255 (22.54 per cent)

b. Occupancy Costs - furnishings, moving, exhibition development, etc., costs - for both projects amount to $55,505,000. These costs, which fall outside the CMCC mandate, were not considered in the decision to construct the new buildings.

c. In comparison with their present operating costs the Gallery and Museum will experience cost increases of $1,771,000 and $4,595,000 per annum respectively in the new buildings.

March, 1985 - During interviews with the Study Team, CMCC suggested that $54.0 million rather than the Task Force recognized $36.0 million was needed to properly complete both buildings as designed. Provision of this amount would re-establish realistic contingency allowances for both projects - contingency on the Museum of Man project is currently $660,000. If properly controlled all of the additional $18.0 million would probably not be committed or spent.

Percentage completion (construction only) as of April 1, 1985:

a. Gallery - 25.1 per cent (40.9 per cent contracted); and
b. Museum of Man - 10.8 per cent (25.8 per cent contracted).

SECTION 20 - OTHER PROGRAMS

SCIENTIFIC AND INDUSTRIAL RESEARCH

National Research Council

OBJECTIVE

To provide the facilities to support research in natural sciences and engineering, to build and maintain national competence and to disseminate the acquired knowledge to national and international organizations and individuals.

RESULTS/BENEFICIARIES

The results of this program are:

- maintenance of an appropriate milieu in Canada for the search for new scientific and technical knowledge; and
- maintenance of the capability to respond rapidly and effectively to forthcoming needs for expertise and in-depth scientific, technical and engineering analysis of specific problems as they are identified.

Principal beneficiaries of the program are as follows:

- Canadian Industry, R&D;
- Federal departments and agencies;
- Other Canadian governments, organizations and individuals engaged in the generation and use of scientific and technical knowledge;
- Canadian Universities; and
- International governments and organizations usually in joint or reciprocal arrangements which generally benefit Canada.

AUTHORITY

National Research Council Act

RESOURCES (thousands of current dollars)

	84/85	85/86
Operating Expenses	$38,000	$38,000
Capital	$62,000	$20,000
Revenue	$ 2,000	$ 2,000
Person-Years	260	260

REAL PROPERTY ASSETS

The current real property inventory consists of approximately 280 building and structures having an estimated replacement value of approximately $400 to $450 million, and land adjacent to the buildings and structures.

PROGRAM DESCRIPTION

The real property administered by National Research Council (NRC) consists of Office Buildings; Research Institutes; Laboratories; "National Facilities" (wind tunnels, engine test sites, observatories, a fire research station, an ocean field test site, a helicopter icing facility, a low temperature test facility); "Special Purpose Buildings" (compressors, chillers, pumps, fuel storage and blending); engineering and maintenance shops; and transmitter and receiver sites for space and earth physics.

Facilities are located at 68 different locations as follows:

a. British Columbia 5 locations
b. Prairies 23 locations
c. Ontario 19 locations
d. Quebec 10 locations
e. Maritimes and Newfoundland 11 locations

Associated with NRC facilities (particularly the observatories) are large holdings of land (e.g. 135 acres in Algonquin Park, 3,700 acres at Penticton, B.C., 176 acres at Victoria/Squamish, B.C.).

In Boucherville, the NRC has obtained a "first refusal option" on some 35 acres of adjacent industrial land for a prospective use to attract industry to co-locate with the Industrial Materials Research Institute.

The NRC also participates in the Canada-France-Hawaii Telescope Corporation (CFHT) in Hawaii, and the Tri-University Meson Facility (TRIUMF) at UBC. Funds are provided under separate contribution agreements in each case. The real property assets are owned by other entities and property operations and capital costs are not part of NRC contributions.

Annex A provides a more detailed description of the "National Facilities" managed by NRC and of the two facilities (Canada-France-Hawaii Telescope and Tri-University Meson Facility) to which NRC provides contributions.

Acquisition and management of facilities is organized on a national basis. All facilities operations are the responsibility of one of the NRC Vice-Presidents in Ottawa and are managed on-site by some 45 building managers and staff.

A national Plant Engineering Division, based in Ottawa (213 person-years) provides functional engineering, technical, and operating support directly to the respective Vice-President and through him to the managers at facilities. There is no regional organization.

The majority of Design and Construction services (architectural, engineering, etc.) are contracted out (80 per cent) with the remainder handled by Public Works (14 per cent) and by in-house staff (6 per cent). In-house expertise is used for pre-feasibility and feasibility studies, definition of requirements and project management and control. Detailed approval and management procedures were not examined.

In the National Capital Region, most operations and maintenance functions are contracted out directly to the private sector; the National Capital Commission provides landscaping, snow clearing and grounds maintenance; and Public Works provides garbage collection. In-house staff provide operating personnel and supervisory/ contract administration personnel.

Outside the National Capital Region, most operations and maintenance is contracted out or provided by Public Works, under the control of the on-site building managers.

Federal government departments are charged only "incremental costs" for use of NRC facilities. With regard to other external users, there is no NRC wide policy as to cost recovery. Apparently, agreements are on an individual case by case basis, and rental of property is governed generally by Treasury Board Administrative Policy Guidelines. (In general, property per se is not "let out"; rather, turn-key services including facilities are provided under various cost formulae to R&D clients). The current National Research Council Act allows only direct costs (excluding overhead, capital costs, etc.) to be charged to non-federal government users.

It is difficult in the case of the "National Facilities" (Annex A) to separate the use of real property from the use of all research operations by external users. However, only a small portion of total costs (O&M, capital, financing) is being recovered. The "National Facilities" having an estimated replacement value in excess of $200 million, are used extensively by or an behalf of external users. For example, wind tunnels had an estimated external user utilization of 85 per cent in FY 82/83, and for the same period: airborne facilities (77 per cent), engine test facilities and low temperature test facilities (90 per cent). Astrophysical facilities (observatories) ranged from 25 to 85 per cent external use during this period. Revenues credited to "National Facilities" (reported as rental income by NRC) were only $2 million (10 per cent of total O&M for National Facilities). External users include other federal departments, other governments, industry and several Crown Corporations (e.g. De Havilland).

In response to the discontinuation of certain research programs, the NRC has identified several surplus properties and has initiated their transfer to the Public Works surplus properties inventory.

OBSERVATIONS

With the exception of some office and administrative accommodation, the majority of facilities are designed and built for specific purposes or constitute a unique if changing facility to meet evolving scientific research needs. Given the ongoing scientific technical and engineering research programs now mandated as a federal government responsibility, the current infrastructure does not appear surplus to need. Surplus properties have been identified as specific program initiatives have been discontinued. Further reduction of the infrastructure could be undertaken only in response to discontinuation or transfer to other organizations of research programs and activities.

Notwithstanding the above general comments, specific properties have potential for alternative use or reduced federal administration and control:

- Sussex Drive Laboratories, Ottawa (a Public Works building) - if a new facility which combined the Astro-Physics, Chemistry and Biological research operations were provided in the NCR, the land and buildings could probably be converted to higher value use, with a net cost benefit. Net savings cannot be calculated without detailed study; and

- Shared and/or external ownership of certain properties (e.g. Institute for Manufacturing Technology, Winnipeg, Institute of Optics, Québec City) are now being explored by the NRC. Capital and operating savings cannot be estimated precisely at this time.

Divestiture of those "National Facilities" extensively used by external users in the private sector and/or other levels of government is theoretically possible. To do so, however, would remove from national control unique institutions and would necessitate an examination of the program mandate. Moreover, allocation of access to research facilities so divested could become subject to narrow/short term criteria (e.g. a particular company or regional interests) perhaps not in the national interest.

A detailed management review has not been undertaken. However, neither this review nor previous experience with NRC capital and operating management of real property assets indicate that internal resources are inefficiently deployed especially in view of the number and geographic dispersion of facilities. Both design and construction and O&M services are already extensively contracted out either directly or through Public Works.

Two areas merit examination with respect to cost-recovery:

- Vacant lands surrounding certain facilities are required to control safety, security and/or the

- experimental environment (buffer zones for noise, air pollution, electromagnetic interference). It is possible that these operational requirements could be met while increasing certain "higher value" public/private use of the land on a leased basis. A case by case analysis is required to determine compatable uses and revenue potential of this land; and

- External use of "National Facilities" is now subject to cost recovery. Costs recovered are for services and facilities related to the experiments/tests undertaken, cover only a small proportion of operating costs, and do not cover capital costs. This policy cannot be assessed independently of the program mandate; nor can action be taken without the amendment of the National Research Council Act. However, the NRC has estimated that increased revenues of some $5-$10 million could be generated if they were permitted to develop and charge a realistic "market-based" fee to users.

An alternative to increased charging, to be pursued on a facility by facility basis, would involve the joint ownership and control of facilities by the NRC with those external users who derive benefit from ongoing research activities. The Canada-France-Hawaii Telescope (CFHT) and Tri-University Meson Facility lend themselves as models wherein costs are shared in proportion to use by the beneficiaries and the knowledge base is shared by all participants. Precise benefits cannot be estimated without detailed study and negotiation with potential participants (universities, industry, provincial governments, foreign governments). However, if all facilities now used by external users were subject to such joint funding, annual savings to the NRC operating budget would be about the same amount ($5 to $10 million) represented by increasing charges as set out in the previous option.

Clearly a combination of the two options is also possible: shared ownership in some cases; NRC ownership and increased charges in other cases.

Implications of the above options include:

- resistance by industry, provincial and university beneficaries now accustomed to status quo;

- relationship with the international scientific community which provides for reciprocal knowledge transfer and use of other countries' facilities by Canadian scientists on a more "informal" reciprocal basis; and

- a general examination as to the appropriate Federal role in scientific research including direct (i.e. NRC) and indirect (i.e. tax expenditure) funding policies.

OPTIONS

The study team recommends to the Task Force that the government consider providing legislative authority for the NRC to charge user fees compatible with the full costs and levels of service provided.

The NRC should actively pursue joint funding and ownership of facilities with other levels of government, universities, industry, and foreign governments.

The NRC should charge user fees compatible with the full costs of the services provided.

ANNEX A

NATIONAL RESEARCH COUNCIL - "NATIONAL FACILITIES"

(Source: National Research Council, 1984-85 Estimates, Part III - Expenditure Plan)

NATIONAL FACILITIES

Engineering Facilities. NRC operates a number of major national engineering facilities to support engineering R&D in selected areas of national need and priority. A brief description of the major facilities follows:

Wind Tunnels. The National Aeronautical Establishment (NAE) operates and maintains a number of wind tunnels as national facilities for use by industry and government. The three principal tunnels are a 2m by 3m low-speed wind tunnel, which began operations in the early 1940s; a 1.5m by 1.5m trisonic blowdown tunnel, which was commissioned in 1962; and a 9m by 9m low-speed tunnel, which was commissioned in 1970. Major industrial users of these facilities are the aircraft manufacturing companies but there is increasing demand from other users for wind engineering studies on buildings and bridges, for developing urban core wind profiles, for measuring the wind drag of surface vehicles such as trucks and cars, and for other applications.

Airborne Facilities. The National Aeronautical Establishment operates and maintains test facilities mounted in specially configured aircraft, for use, primarily by Canadian aircraft manufacturers and government departments, in simulating the performance of new aircraft design features; in investigating hazardous aircraft operating conditions or failure occurrences; in conducting detailed studies of turbulence and other atmospheric conditions; in testing navigation systems; and in testing other flight-related conditions, systems, and equipment. The facilities include a flight mechanics airborne simulator, two atmospheric studies aircraft, and a remote sensing and navigation systems aircraft.

Railway Test Facilities. The Division of Mechanical Engineering operates and maintains national test facilities for use in rail-related research by railway operators, car and locomotive builders, railway users, and government regulators on problems related to lubrication, car dynamics, structures, and other specialized subjects. This research is aimed at improving the performance of locomotives, rolling stock and related equipment; and reducing wear, damage to cargo, and the incidence of train derailments. The facilities currently include a curved track simulator, a vibration test facility, a vehicle squeeze frame, and an impact test ramp. A wheel, brake, and bearing test rig is under development to permit the study of fatigue and failure of these components under controlled conditions.

Marine Testing Facilities. NRC provides national facilities in marine hydrodynamics for use by Canadian researchers in fields such as marine propulsion, manoeuvring, seakeeping, hydrodynamics, ocean environment, and Arctic modelling techniques. The main facilities currently operating in Ottawa are a towing tank, a manoeuvring basin, and a cavitation tunnel, with associated computer-based equipment for data gathering and analysis.

The growing offshore activity on Canada's east coast and Arctic regions has expanded the requirement for facilities and related expertise in all aspects of naval architecture and marine engineering, expecially as applied to northern and ice-covered waters. As a result the Arctic Vessel and Marine Research Institute is being established in St. John's, Newfoundland, and is expected to be fully operational by 1985-86. The Ottawa-base capabilities will be transferred to the new Institute, which will provide Canadian industry, governments, and universities with facilities and technical support needed for the design, development, and construction of vessels and fixed structures tests on all types of vessels and on fixed structures operating on or below ice-covered waters. The main facilities will be an ice towing tank, an open water towing tank, a computer-controlled model-making facility, and associated data gathering systems, design offices, and machine shops.

Gas Dynamics Test Facilities. The Gas Dynamics Test Facilities of the Division of Mechanical Engineering are centred around a very large air compressor and exhauster plant that generates the high volume air and gas flows needed in gas dynamics testing and research. This research focuses on the dynamics of very high temperature gases flowing developing and testing gas turbine engines and aeronautical, marine, and railway equipment and power plants. The testing facilities include combustion facilities, a propulsion tunnel, and an altitude test chamber.

Hydraulics Facilities. The national facilities maintained and operated by the Hydraulics Laboratory of the Division of Mechanical Engineering include the Deep Water Wave Basin and the Coastal Wave Flume.

The Deep Water Wave Basin provides for scale model testing of ocean engineering structures intended for use in deep water. The associated wave machines generate long and crested waves that simulate the wind and wave environments necessary for the accurate performance appraisal of off-shore oil drilling rigs, production platforms, etc.

The Coastal Wave Flume is provided for the simulation of coastal or shallow water conditions. The major problem areas are shoreline erosion and sedimentation as well as the effect of waves and currents on coastal structures such as breakwaters and other harbour facilities.

Engine Test Facilities. The Division of Mechanical Engineering operates and maintains facilities consisting of a calibrated gas turbine test cell, and engine icing test cell, and an anechoic test cell for use by Canadian industry and governments in monitoring and improving the performance of gas turbine aircraft engines. The testing capabilities include the measuring of such factors as thrust and fuel consumption, the effect on in-flight performance of passing through icing clouds, and the operating noise levels of these engines. Testing at the facilities is a means of accurately simulating flight conditions, and is among the Transport Canada Flight Certification procedures for aircraft engines.

Low Temperature Test Facilities. The Division of Mechanical Engineering operates and maintains national facilities for conducting tests on various types of machinery, primarily transportation equipment, under controlled low-temperature conditions. The facilities are used by Canadian aircraft and vehicle manufacturers, railways, and government departments and agencies. One of the three facilities is a climatic engineering test facility, a large chamber built to accommodate locomotives, railway and subway coaches, off-road vehicles, and building modules and other large structures. It can provide temperatures as low as -43°C, winds over 60 km/hr, snowfall up to 3 cm/hr, and freezing rain conditions. A second facility is the helicopter icing facility, a spray rig used to test the effectiveness of de-icing systems on full size helicopters that are flown under the continuous spray. The third facility, an icing tunnel, is used by Canadian industry and governments to test aircraft components and other equipment under low temperature conditions.

Fire Research Field Station. The Division of Building Research operates and maintains a facility located at Carleton Place, Ontario for use by government departments, regulatory agencies, and Canadian building and furniture supply manufacturers. It permits full-scale studies of the generation of spread of fire and smoke, both from room-to-room and floor-to-floor in houses, mobile homes, and high-rise buildings, and allows testing the effectiveness of fire retardant materials and extinguishing systems. The facility consists of a large hangar-like structure, 30m by 60m by 12m high; a 10-storey high-rise structure; and associated data gathering and workshop support service areas.

SCIENTIFIC FACILITIES - MANAGED BY NRC

Facilities for Space Science. To support the space science research activities of Canadian universities, industry, and government agencies in a national program, NRC provides the rocket launching facility at Churchill, Manitoba, the balloon launch facility at Gimli, Manitoba, and protable launchers at various sites including the Arctic. (These facilites have recently been declared surplus).

The Canada Centre for Space Science (CSSS) contracts with Canadian industry for design and fabrication of research payloads, and provides Canadian-manufactured rockets and high-altitude balloons to carry these payloads. The launch range and facilities are operated by Canadian industry under contract to NRC. Services include launching and tracking the vehicles and receiving, recording, and transforming the experimental data.

CCSS also coordinates and plans space science activities at the national and international level, including the provision of scientific instrumentation and systems for flights on NASA's Space Shuttle and on satellites launched by other countries.

Astrophysical Facilities. The Herzberg Institute of Astrophysics (HIA) operates and maintains the Dominion Astrophysical Observatory (DAO) in Victoria, B.C., the Dominion Radio Astrophysical Observatory (DRAO) in Algonquin Park, Ontario.

The DAO facility is an optical observatory that provides three telescopes for use by Canadian scientists (including HIA staff) in astronomical research. The detection and data processing systems include spectrographs, computers, and measuring engines. The facility is also used for processing data obtained at the Canada-France-Hawaii Telescope. DAO is a world centre of excellence in the design of large telescopes and the polishing of large mirrors. Work done at the observatory includes research into supernovas, interstellar matter, stellar atmospheres, and black holes. The DRAO facility provids two radiotelescopes for detecting and analyzing radio waves from space. Work at the observatory includes studies of the distribution and velocity of gases in order to determine the structure and evolution of objects such as galaxies and supernova remnants. The DRAO facility is the major Canadian radio observatory. It possesses the largest fully steerable parabolic reflector in North America. Work at this observatory includes research into the distribution and formation of molecules in space, and studies of quasars and distant galaxies.

Other Scientific Facilities. Other national scientific facilities include a Positive Ion Accelerator and an Electron Linear Accelerator at the Division of Physics in Ottawa, for studies on radiation effects in matter and nuclear physics. These accelerators are used for research in radiation dosimetry, for example as applied to cancer treatment in hospitals, and for studies into the physical properties of matter. The Division of Physics also operates and maintains an acoustics facility used for research into sound reproduction and human hearing. Among the more applied uses of this facility are the testing and calibration of high-fidelity loudspeakers by Canadian industry.

Scientific Facilities - Managed Externally. There are two relatively large national scientific facilities which receive funding from the federal government through NRC: The Canada-France-Hawaii Telescope (CFHT); and the Tri-University Meson Facility (TRIUMF).

Canada-France-Hawaii Telescope. The CFH telescope is jointly sponsored by the National Research Council of Canada, le Centre national de la recherche scientifique of France, and the University of Hawaii. To carry out the construction of the telescope and its subsequent operation, the three founding members entered into a tripartite agreement and formed a non-profit Corporation incorporated in the State of Hawaii. According to the terms of the agreement, construction costs of the telescope were equally shared by Canada and France, with the University of Hawaii contributing local facilities and services. Observation time on the completed telescope is shared by the partners in the proportions of 44, 44, and 12 per cent respectively. Payment of the NRC share of operating costs is in the form of a contribution to the Canada-France-Hawaii Telescope Corporation.

Tri-University Meson Facility. TRIUMF is a world class centre for research in intermediate energy physics and related disciplines. It is located on the campus of the University of British Columbia, Vancouver, and operated as a joint venture by the University of British Columbia, Simon Fraser University, the University of Victoria and the University of Alberta. The central feature is a uniquely designed sector-focused cyclotron that accelerates negative hydrogen ions to an energy of up to 500 MeV in a continuous mode. The unique design permits the extraction of proton beam through as many as six separate ports for experiments with protons, mesons and neutrons in a highly diversified program of basic and applied research.

The land, buildings and some administrative services have been provided by the universities; the accelerator, beam lines, experimental equipment and operations have been funded by the federal government. AECB was the responsible federal agency from the founding of TRIUMF in 1968 until March, 1976. NRC assumed responsibility at that time. Funds for operating, maintaining, and developing the facility are provided by NRC by means of an annual contribution. The research program is funded largely by granting agencies such as NSERC and to a lesser extent by NRC and external supporters of the applied program such as AECL, the B.C. Cancer Foundation, and NOVATRACK Inc.

AGRICULTURAL PROPERTIES

Department of Agriculture

OBJECTIVE

Scientific Research and Development - to maintain and improve the productivity of the agri-food sector through development and transfer of new knowledge and technology.

Inspection and Regulation - to ensure inputs such as feed, seed, fertilizer and pesticides necessary for agricultural and forestry production are of a dependable quality and are safe.

Regional Development - to facilitate the development of the agri-food sector in each region so that the sector can make its maximum long-term real contribution to the national economy.

Prairie Farm Rehabilitation Agency (PFRA) - to institute and undertake soil and water conservation programs and projects that will enable the preservation, management and use of the basic resource to support economic stability and growth.

Forestry Research and Technical Services - to enhance the forest resource base through discovery, development, demonstration, implementation and transfer of innovations, to solve problems and increase the efficiency and effectiveness of forest management.

RESULTS/BENEFICIARIES

Assistance to the food, agricultural and forestry sectors of the economy.

Client groups: producers; processors, distributors, wholesalers and retailers; and consumers.

AUTHORITY

Department of Agriculture Act
Prairie Farm Rehabilitation Act
Forestry Development and Research Act

RESOURCES (millions of current dollars)

	84/85	85/86
Operating Expenses (estimated)	$20	$ 20
Capital Expenditures	$97	$123
Revenue	$ 8	$ 10
Person-Years (estimated)	357	357

REAL PROPERTY ASSETS

Estimated Replacement Value: $2-3 Billion

	Dept.custody	Public Works	Leased
Land	540,000 hectares	500 hectares	434,000 hectares
Buildings	2,886	193	

In addition, the National Capital Commission has custody of 1,200 hectares of land.

PROGRAM DESCRIPTION

The Facilities Planning Section is the department's Real Property manager, comprising 29 person-years. This group is responsible for the following services:

a. Programming and Project Control for capital construction, maintenance and energy conservation, accommodation and real property management;

b. Project Management for the construction and maintenance of new and existing departmental facilities;

c. Accommodation Planning and Management, including the development and implementation of a National Accommodation Strategy comprising a $2 million Tenant Services program, Property Services and acquisition and servicing of Special Purpose facilities;

d. Development of a Major Maintenance Program; and

e. Processing of transactions for leases, lettings, disposals, easements, etc. and development of Management Information Systems for Fixed Assets.

There are about 10 engineers and one architect, plus seven associated technical staff among the 29 person-years (PY).

There are a number of planning elements which use real property assets under departmental custody to achieve their objectives. These are as follows:

a. Scientific Research and Development
b. Inspection and Regulation
c. Regional Development
d. Prairie Farm Rehabilitation (PFRA)
e. Forestry Research and Technical Services

Scientific Research and Development has 58 research facilities across the country with an estimated replacement value of $1.8 billion. Of these, 43 are major facilities and there are 15 sub-stations. Out of a total 3,594 PYs in the planning element, an estimated 179 PYs are employed in the O&M support of its real property.

During 1983/84, Research and Development produced results from long-term wheat rotations, new varieties of cereal, forage and field crops as well as horticultural varieties, and achieved significant progress in putting more efficient soil survey techniques into field operations.

Inspection and Regulation runs one plant quarantine station and 20 animal inspection stations, with an estimated replacement value of $750,000. Out of 4,198 PYs in the planning element, an estimated 26 are employed in the O&M support of its real property. In addition, the department leases six facilities at an annual cost of $10,000.

The facilities are used for animal and plant disease control and eradication.

Regional Development runs three swine test stations with an estimated replacement value of $3 million. There are 618 PYs in the planning element, but none are devoted to the real property under custody.

PFRA owns or has custody of 99 properties and leases 46 others at an annual cost of $3,000 (most of the non-owned property belongs to the provinces). The estimated replacement value is $219 million.

Of the 99 properties, 89 are dedicated to community pastures (total of about 920,000 hectares, of which almost half are leased from the provinces). These pastures are largely marginal and sub-marginal land which were taken out of cultivation for purposes of soil conservation. The land under PFRA custody reverts to the the provinces in the event of a change in use or transfer of title.

Real property maintenance involves only an estimated 22 of the 881 PYs in the PFRA.

PFRA generates real property revenues from pasture and grazing fees, and proceeds from sales of bulls. These totalled about $8 million for FY 84/85 and the fees cover the incremental costs of operating the community pastures for grazing purposes.

Forestry Research and Technical Services runs five major forest research centres, a forest pest management institute and the National Forestry Institute in Petawawa, with an estimated replacement value of $108 million. Out of 1,141 PYs in this planning element, an estimated 71 are in support of the real property operations and maintenance.

Forestry research is concentrated on cost effective protection and silvicultural methods such as biological pest control, tree genetics and micropropagation to improve forest growth and yields, and forest ecosystem research.

The total value of real property projects currently approved and in some stage of implementation is $280 million. Of this, professional services such as design, engineering and construction management amount to $32.6 million (12 per cent). Of these professional services, 85 per cent are contracted out, 13 per cent are provided by Public Works, and 2 per cent in-house. Construction activity is 100 per cent contracted out.

The Department's Capital Strategy calls for a total expenditure of a quarter billion dollars on real property facilities over 4 years (FY 85-89).

Within the National Capital Region, Public Works has custody of the Central Experimental Farm lands (457 hectares), but the National Capital Commission has custody of the greenbelt farms in Nepean (1,200 hectares). Public Works has custody of all the buildings occupied by Agriculture in the NCR.

OBSERVATIONS

The Department of Agriculture is a major player in the real property game, with custody of 540,000 hectares of land and 434,000 hectares of leased land, and an estimated 1.2 million square metres of space in accommodation and specialized facilities, including over 350,000 square metres provided by Public Works. The total estimated replacement value is $2-3 billion.

In the view of the study team the department is undermanaging its real property facilities. The Facilities Planning Section does not have reliable information on the number of buildings or locations under its custody. It has only outdated information on the PY resources required to support the property management and maintenance function and practically no information on the O&M costs of supporting its real property facilities, either individually or collectively.

There is no department-wide coordination of maintenance activities despite the often expressed opinions that funds and person years are inadequate to perform proper maintenance. There is a continuing resource trade-off between program support (e.g. maintenance) and program delivery.

This is particularly true at the experimental farms in the NCR, where Public Works is hard-pressed to properly maintain its buildings. There are an estimated 68 PYs dedicated to direct operating and maintenance activities, of which 38 are provided on location by Public Works and 30 by Agriculture. The maintenance problem has evolved over a long period of time, without a well defined set of interdepartmental operational roles and responsibilities.

However, the department has recognized these problems and has retained consultants to provide assistance as follows:

a. to develop a comprehensive National Accommodation Strategy Plan for both office and special purpose space whether owned by Agriculture or provided by Public Works;

b. to determine the requirements for an automated Departmental Facilities Inventory Management Information System;

c. to determine the feasibility of implementing a Major Maintenance Program. A Phase I study has already been completed which identifies the problems; and

d. to update the existing inventory of property and buildings.

The department has not addressed the question of alternative land use, particularly for its experimental farms.

There is no reason why PFRA community pastures could not be operated by provinces and/or local community associations, provided that the soil conservation role is assured. It is certainly within provincial jurisdication to do so.

OPTIONS

The study team recommends to the Task Force that the government consider instructing the department:

- to move more quickly to strengthen its property management function. Besides developing better strategies, information systems and maintenance programs, the Facilities Planning Section should have a better qualitative understanding of their properties and facilities, possibly through case studies; and

- to address the question of alternative land use and challenge the program need for all its real property. Where necessary, the full costs and benefits of relocating and/or consolidation should be considered.

The Department of Agriculture should be given the custody and funding to manage its special purpose facilities in the NCR.

The Agriculture Study Team has put forth the option that the Minister should enter into negotiations with provinces and/or local community associations to divest the government of community pastures, while safeguarding the land use for pasture. The study team supports this option.

COMMUNICATIONS RESEARCH PROPERTIES

Department of Communications

OBJECTIVES

Research - to advance Canada's research and development in the areas of telecommunications, space and information science and technologies.

Radio Spectrum Management - to manage the utilization and development of the radio frequency spectrum in Canada and to protect Canada's rights regarding use of the spectrum through international agreements and regulations.

Technology Applications and Industry Support - to foster the application of advanced information and communications technologies and to support the growth and development of industries that create, manufacture and employ those technologies.

RESULTS/BENEFICIARIES

Assistance to the communications industry.
Site Services for the Defence Research Establishment, Ottawa

AUTHORITY

Radio Act

RESOURCES (millions of current dollars)

	84/85
Operating Expenses	$5.1
Capital	$1.3
Revenue	$2.1
Person-Years	64

REAL PROPERTY ASSETS

Estimated Replacement Value: $80 million
Land: 582 hectares (Shirley's Bay)
20 hectares (Clyde Avenue)
Buildings: 76, including 67 at Shirley's Bay

PROGRAM DESCRIPTION

The Research Activity has the use of:

a. The Communications Research Centre (CRC) at Shirley's Bay, Ontario, which supports departmental R&D.

b. The Canadian Work Place Automation Research Centre at Laval, which will provide the research environment for the development of office automation applications.

The Radio Spectrum Management Activity administers a district office in Langley, B.C. and monitoring stations at St. Remis and St. Lambert (PQ), Thunder Bay and Acton (Ontario), and Fort Smith (NWT) and Churchill (Manitoba). It also has a laboratory on Clyde Avenue in Ottawa.

The Technology Applications and Industry Support Activity has the David Florida Laboratory at Shirley's Bay.

The Departmental Administration Activity manages the facilities at Shirley's Bay and Clyde Avenue. The total PY resources for FY 84/85 to manage and maintain these facilities were 61 PYs, of which seven were on-site and one was off-site management and administration, while 53 were in support of operational and technical functions (40), the heating plant (10) and capital works (3). There are 67 buildings and 582 hectares at Shirley's Bay. Annual real property capital expenditures were about $1.2 million in the 4-year period FY 81-85 and are projected at $2.8 million for each of the next three fiscal years.

The Research Centre at Laval will become operational in FY 85/86. The other regional facilities are managed by the Radio Spectrum Management personnel. Total PY resources for FY 84/85 were 3 PYs for on-site administration.

OBSERVATIONS

The land at CRC is required to provide the isolation from noise and other electronic interference, although about 40 hectares of the High Frequency testing range is being examined for impacts of releasing it as surplus. The Communications Laboratory at Clyde Avenue provides the facility for the testing and type approval of communications products. An electromagnetic interference study is currently underway to assess the technical feasibility of relocating to Shirley's Bay. There is the potential for releasing about 20 hectares of land at Clyde Avenue.

Currently the department contracts out about 40 per cent of the real property O&M requirements. Cyclical maintenance is contracted out, but preventive maintenance and urgent repairs are done in-house. Design and construction management is contracted out for projects over $200,000. Minor D&C and project related designs utilize in-house resources because of the requirements to have frequent contact with the research manager, the unique nature of the D&C, security and tight deadlines.

The Communications Research Centre at Shirley's Bay provides site services for the Defence Research Establishment, Ottawa. The recovery for incremental O&M costs ($1.35 million in FY 84/85) is approximately one-third of the annual O&M cost of operating the CRC, based appropriately on the DND share of the total floor space. When DOC was established in 1969, these facilities were transferred from the Defence Research Telecommunications Establishment. All renovations or extensions to DND facilities are funded by DND and managed by DOC.

The David Florida Laboratory collects fees for the testing of aerospace products. Spar Aerospace is the major private user of these facilities and fees are sometimes waived as an industrial incentive. In FY 84/85, the fee revenue was estimated at $800,000.

The cost of operating the Clyde Avenue facility and monitoring stations were included in the new fee structure for radio licenses.

The only alternative to the status quo is to charge more for the use of the David Florida Laboratory. However, these fees have been waived in the past for Spar Aerospace, and significant increases may run counter to government support for Spar. The Business Services study team observed that such assistance should be specifically recorded in order that the apparently unsatisfactory financial results of the facility are not attributed to management performance and that government assistance be reflected accurately. We support this finding from a real property perspective.

OPTIONS

The study team recommends to the Task Force that the government should consider instructing the department to proceed without delay to reach a decision on evaluation of surplus land at Shirley's Bay and Clyde Avenue. They should then take prompt and appropriate action based on the conclusions of the evaluations.

MINERAL AND EARTH SCIENCES PROGRAM

Energy, Mines and Resources

OBJECTIVE

To maximize the contribution of the minerals and metals sector to the Canadian economy.

RESULTS/BENEFICIARIES

Scientific knowledge and data, applied research, development and transfer of technology, surveys and maps in the earth and mineral related sciences, with emphasis on the mineral and energy resources of the Canadian landmass and offshore.

Industry, scientific organizations, public

AUTHORITY

Department of Energy, Mines and Resources Act
Resources and Technical Surveys Act

RESOURCES (millions of current dollars)

	84/85
Operating Expenses(estimated)	$1.5
Capital expenditures	$5.1
Person-Years	
- on-site	9
- headquarters	27

REAL PROPERTY ASSETS

The estimated replacement value is $23 million for the following facilities under Departmental custody:

Research Labs	4
Receiving Station	1
Seismic/geomagnetic stations	21
Base/Storage camps	2

In addition, there are 32 special purpose, research facilities in the NCR under Public Works custody.

PROGRAM DESCRIPTION

The Mineral and Earth Sciences Program (MESP) has a number of planning elements with real property custody:

a. the Canada Centre for Mineral and Energy Technology (CANMET), which carries out basic and applied research, development, demonstration and transfer of new technology to industry;

b. the Canada Centre for Remote Sensing (CCRS), which carries out research in the remote sensing of natural resources and the environment;

c. the Geological Survey of Canada (GSC), which carries out surveys, R&D, and information dissemination related to mineral and energy resources;

d. the Earth Physics Branch, which operates seismological, geomagnetic and geodynamic observatories, and is responsible for national gravity, geothermal and geomagnetic surveys;

e. the Polar Continental Shelf (PCS) project, which conducts scientific studies in the Arctic and assists other groups carrying out similar work;

f. the Surveying and Mapping Branch, which is responsible for the provision of geodetic, topographic and geographic information on the Canadian landmass.

The facilities under the custody of those planning elements are as follows:

a. CANMET research laboratories
   Elliot Lake, Ontario
   Calgary, Alberta

b. CCRS satellite receiving station
   Prince Albert, Saskatchewan

c. GSC Institute of Sedimentary and Petroleum Geology
Calgary, Alberta

d. Earth Physics Branch
18 seismic stations
3 geomagnetic and geodynamic stations

e. PCS base/storage camps
Resolute Bay, Northwest Territories
Tuktoyaktuk, Northwest Territories

f. Surveying and Mapping
Sherbrooke Institute of Cartography, Québec
(under construction)

The on-site property administration, operational and technical resources requires at most 9 PYs of MESP, with an estimated $1.5 million in real property operating expenses. Ninety-five per cent of operations and maintenance is contracted out, through Public Works.

There are currently four real property capital projects worth a total of $45.7 million, all contracted out through Public Works, with $5.6 million (12 per cent) for contracted design, engineering and construction management services. The major project is the Sherbrooke Institute of Cartography.

The Property Planning and Management (PP&M) Division of the Finance and Administrative Sector is a property service oriented organization, which, among other things, liaises with Public Works on property matters. There are three operating sections, plus the divisional administration (4 PYs):

a. Planning and Policy (6 PYs)

b. Project Management (7 PYs)

c. Property Services (10 PYs)

All the professional staff are in the administrative category although there happen to be four architects and four architectural technologists/technicians in the facilities management and planning functions.

The Planning and Policy section secures approvals and funding for the real property needs of the department.

The Project Management section is responsible for consulting with the user groups to develop the requirements, working with Public Works to establish realistic time schedules within cost constraints and monitoring the project on behalf of the user.

The Property Services section is responsible for the continued monitoring and maintenance of the department's facilities and provides tenant services for accommodation under the custody of Public Works.

OBSERVATIONS

The department utilizes contracted-out services to the greatest extent possible, normally through Public Works, both for design and engineering and construction management as well as operational and maintenance services.

About 75 per cent (by floor space) of EMR's research facilities are located in the NCR in space largely constructed before 1940 and provided by Public Works. In recent years the Department's thrust has shifted from basic research to more complex processes involving for example, new methods of extracting fossil fuels. This has rendered the present facilities outdated. As well, updated building codes and regulations and the use of hi-tech equipment has contributed to a number of maintenance problems.

EMR has encountered considerable difficulties in upgrading and maintaining the facilities to the higher standards required for its current work. Because Public Works as the "landlord" has a limited amount of financial and personnel resources to look after all the facilities under its custody, the need to upgrade EMR special purpose buildings competes for priority with all general purpose office accommodation facilities and other special purpose facilities.

Treasury Board has now approved a project whereby EMR, with support from Public Works, will review its research facilities with the aim of bringing them to an acceptable level and to maintain that level in subsequent years. This will require a considerable investment since the properties have been allowed to badly deteriorate. A comprehensive long range upgrading, replacement and maintenance schedule, with funding requirements, is expected in late FY 85/86.

This should allow the PP&M Division to plan properly and not just to react to emergencies, as has been the case.

Some of the properties in question are located on what has become high value land. Since there is little reason for these facilities to be centrally located, one option to renovation would be to relocate in a lower cost locale. The existing properties could then be declared surplus.

OPTIONS

The study team recommends to the Task Force that the government consider giving Energy, Mines and Resources the custody and funding to manage its special purpose facilities in the NCR.

The proposed review of these research facilities should also examine alternative uses of the land where some of the more obsolete facilities are situated. There is the possibility that the present high value Ottawa properties could be sold off to fund the cost of new facilities in a lower cost locale.

CUSTOMS AND EXCISE

OBJECTIVE

The Customs and Excise Program Objective is "to ensure that all duties, taxes and other relevant charges are assessed, collected, and, where appropriate, refunded; to control, for the protection of Canadian industry and society the movement of people, goods and conveyances entering or leaving Canada as required to achieve compliance with legislation; to protect Canadian industry from real or potential injury caused by the actual or contemplated importation of dumped or subsidized goods as well as by other forms of unfair foreign competition".

RESULTS/BENEFICIARIES

Canadian travellers, international travellers to Canada, importers and exporters.

AUTHORITY

The Minister of National Revenue has no authority to own or administer federal real property. By existing legislation and under s.6 of the proposed new Customs Act, the Minister has authority to designate property (both public and private) to serve Customs purposes.

RESOURCES

	84/85	85/86
Capital / Operating	$2.4M	$2.4M
Person-Years	27	27

REAL PROPERTIES ASSETS

Land - 104 hectares
Number of buildings - 90
Area of Buildings - 9,000 m2

PROGRAM DESCRIPTION

Customs and Excise (C&E) runs a very small program (capital and O&M) of approximately $2.4 million per annum through which they own, operate and maintain 90 small (1-2 persons) ports of entry. These facilities are situated in isolated locations. C&E asks PWC to undertake the capital repairs for these facilities.

C&E obtains the rest of its accommodation from several other federal landlords; PWC, Canada Post Corporation (CPC), Transport Canada (Air), Ports Canada and 11 international bridge authorities (all in Ontario).

PWC provides the capital and builds (to C&E priorities), renovates and maintains 44 border crossings across Canada on C&E's behalf. Other federal departments which have a functional requirement to co-locate with C&E are frequently accommodated in these facilities: e.g. Agriculture, Health and Welfare and Immigration. PWC also provides general purpose office accommodation and related facilities for C&E's Regional administration, and customs and excise functions. These properties (a total of 207,000 m^2 of space) are operated and maintained by PWC.

In addition, PWC acts as an agent between C&E and Canada Post Corporation, C&E's second largest landlord providing 35,000 square metres of space. C&E has a functional requirement to co-locate with CPC at designated locations across the country in order to maintain customs and excise control over mail. In other instances, C&E occupies space in CPC properties not for any functional relationship between the two, but because of the past grouping of federal departments in Government of Canada buildings now owned by CPC.

C&E also has a functional requirement to occupy space in airports administered by MOT(Air), in ports administered by Canada Ports (combined total 24,000 square metres) and in property owned by 11 international (US-Canadian) Bridge authorities (9,000 square metres).

To define, plan and control C&E's property requirements, the department has established a small real property management function of 16 PYs led by a Chief in the Administration Directorate of the Corporate Management

Branch controlled by an as Assistant Deputy Minister. There are also 11 property management officers in the field.

Property requirements are formulated in the field and rolled up into a national program at Headquarters through the MYOP process.

OBSERVATIONS

No external audits or evaluations of C&E's property function have been carried out in recent years. However, a C&E internal audit performed in 1981 drew attention to a confusion in roles between the Administration and Operating Branches, a lack of overall requirements planning and accommodation standards, and insufficient management supervision over the maintenance and inspection of C&E owned facilities.

Although a number of management improvements have been introduced, Treasury Board staff observed to the study team that there is still at the present time a lack of standards and there is no long term capital plan. C&E have been asked and have agreed to remedy these deficiencies.

C&E has indicated, for example, that it is working with PWC to develop standard designs for C&E facilities, is developing a property inventory, and is attempting to achieve space savings through space optimization projects (principally in the National Capital Region where C&E is accommodated in eight buildings).

C&E is also exploring with PWC and US authorities the feasibility of developing joint facilities with US Customs in certain areas. This is a sensitive issue since it involves questions of national sovereignty and different approaches to law and order. A pilot facility may be built.

C&E states that its relationship with PWC is satisfactory. The relationship with MOT is also reasonable. C&E has no difficulty in obtaining the space it requires in new or expanded airports; however, there is crowding in some existing airports where traffic volumes and customs workload have increased and space is a constraint.

C&E indicates that generally, the relationship with CPC is reasonable. However, C&E is apprehensive about sub-standard space in some older CPC buildings, which CPC (because of constraints) at present has no plans to renovate. C&E has experienced staff unrest in these facilities, and is concerned that there may be walk-outs.

A similar kind of situation exists in the old property owned by bridge authorities. Employees' standards have changed with respect to the facilities they expect (e.g. lunch rooms, washrooms, etc.) but these amenities have not been provided by the property owners. C&E has been examining ways and means to remedy these problems (and has asked for PWC assistance); however, in the case of the bridge authorities, there does not appear to be a single easy answer, as each authority is different; some are Canadian, some US-owned, some joint, and some are privately owned, although all were established by Order-in-Council under the Bridges Act.

If Airports and Ports are devolved to local governments it is likely that they would wish to charge C&E rent for the space it occupies in their facilities. In that event, C&E should be allocated the funds for the rents. C&E may wish to retain PWC as its agent for negotiating leases on its behalf with the local Airport and Port Authorities.

OPTIONS

The existing C&E program is minor and should remain with C&E. The existing relationship with PWC should continue. C&E will continue to be at the whim of CPC.

FISHERIES MANAGEMENT AND OCEAN SCIENCE

Department of Fisheries and Oceans

OBJECTIVE

To provide facilities in support of programs whose objectives are to undertake, promote and co-ordinate policies and programs: for the conservation and management of the aquatic renewable resources of Canada and their habitats; for the sustained economic utilization of these resources, taking into account the dependence of Canadian Communities on them; and for the conduct of surveys and research in support of Canada's economic and scientific interests in the oceans, including the safe use of Canada's navigable waters and environmentally acceptable utilization of other marine resources.

RESULTS/BENEFICIARIES

The result of the program are specialized facilities which house and/or enable:

- the development of research results and data pertaining to the maintenance and improvement of fish stocks;
- development and assistance programs to enhance fish harvesting and processing;
- the delivery of marketing and quality improvement programs;
- the delivery of fish inspection programs;
- the publication of hydrographic charts and other publications; and
- the development and dissemination of marine science information, advice, data, and technology.

Principal Beneficiaries include:

- Canadian fishermen, processors, fishing communities and consumers;
- Canadian ocean industries, shipping interests, energy and other transportation industries;
- Native groups, and environmental interests;
- International organizations, (e.g. FAO), aid programs, international consumers of Canadian fish products, distant fishing nations;

- The national and international scientific community; and
- Other federal departments (e.g. DND, DOT, EMR, DOE), and provincial governments.

AUTHORITY

The main legislative base of the department is the Government Organization Act (1979) and the schedule of statutes attached thereto, including the Fisheries Act, the Fisheries Development Act, the Fish Inspection Act, the Fishing and Recreational Harbours Act, the Coastal Fisheries Protection Act, the Fisheries and Oceans Research Advisory Council Act, the Territorial Sea and Fishing Zones Act, the Canada Shipping Act regarding charts and publications, regulations, and several international treaties and conventions. Under the Government Organization Act (1979), the duties, powers and functions of the Minister of Fisheries and Oceans include responsibilities for hydrography and marine sciences, and for the coordination of the policies and programs of the Government of Canada respecting oceans.

In addition, other multilateral/bilateral treaties and federal/provincial undertakings exist, the most important of which is the Canada/U.S. agreement - The Great Lakes Fisheries Convention.

RESOURCES (thousands of current dollars)

	84/85	85/86
Operating Expenses	$12,000	$12,000
Capital	25,000	25,000
Revenues	680	680
Person-Years	147	147

REAL PROPERTY ASSETS

The department's real property inventory reflects the highly specialized and multi-varied operational nature of the programs it delivers. Included in this inventory are laboratories, hatcheries and offices having replacement values estimated at $298.5 million, $164.7 million and

$50.7 million respectively, plus various others such as bait storage facilities, fishways, docking facilities, spawning channels, research camps, sea lamprey dams, all estimated to have a replacement value of $90.6 million.

Table 1 summarizes the distribution of property holdings by region and form of ownership/control. Holdings are highly dispersed, often in non-urban areas.

PROGRAM DESCRIPTION

Real property is delivered through 11 regional offices by Regional Directors General who report to their line ADM at Headquarters. Details of the regional structure are at Annex A. Approximately 120 person-years are employed in the regions directly in support of real property operations, on-site.

A small complement of professionals (20 person-years) is maintained in-house largely in support of highly specialized design and contruction aspects of the Salmonid Enhancement Program in British Columbia.

At Headquarters two small units, Architecture and Engineering (7 person-years) and Realty Management (4 person-years) provide policy and program direction and liaison with PWC and other agencies respecting real property transactions and issues.

Apart from front-end requirements and client project control, all design and construction work on major projects is either on direct contract with the private sector or through DPW. Minor projects engineering is done by both in-house and external resources. O & M is carried out mainly by contract using in-house resources for supervision and the operations of sensitive systems within laboratories and research institutes.

A proposal has been made by DFO to consolidate Headquarters asset management functions, including real property of this program within an assets management directorate, reporting to the Deputy Minister. This is in response to their perceived need to upgrade control and to assist senior managers in their decisions concerning assets investment and management.

DFO has a Realty Management Manual which sets out policies and authorities consistent with government policies. Management information systems to provide managers with periodic and/or ad hoc decision making and monitoring information are now in the planning stages.

There is limited scope to recover costs of realty assets which tend to be in direct support of specialised DFO programs. Where appropriate, costs are recovered on a market rental basis.

Property related information is not available and the data for this review required a specific effort to collect and the development of order-of-magnitude estimates. The department is in the process of developing an information system at this time.

OBSERVATIONS

Without examining the rationale and scope of the Fisheries and Oceans programs themselves, we cannot question the appropriateness of the real property holdings.

Real property is highly specialized and program specific for the most part. General office space administered directly by the department represents only about 10 per cent of the value of the inventory. As well, DFO provides some 75 housing units usually in remote locations to resident managers. The investment in residences is approximately $9 million or less than 2 per cent of the inventory value.

The use of in-house/PWC/private sector resources appears to be generally in balance considering the special nature of the facilities and their geographic dispersion.

OPTIONS

The study team recommends to the Task Force that the department's current proposal to upgrade assets management, control and information systems be encouraged.

TABLE 1

1984/85 DFO REAL PROPERTY RESOURCES

Region	Properties Administered by DFO					Leased Properties		PWC Properties		
	Properties No.	Approx. Replac. Value ($000)	Annual O&M incl. salaries ($000)	Revenues ($000)	Capital ($000)	Properties No.	Annual Rental ($000)	Properties No.	Annual Rental Value ($000)	PY No
Atlantic	424	278,000	5,800	110	4,400	26	22	166	5,200	58
Inland (Prairie Prov., NWT, Ont.)	34	54,000	1,500	-	270	4	16	29	1,900	13
Pacific (BC, Yukon)	230	275,000	4,500	573	20,000	43	70	117	3,600	65
Headquarters (NCR)	-	-	-	-	-	-	-	6	5,000	11
TOTAL	688	607,000	11,800	683	24,670	73	108	318	15,700	147

Capital Investment planned for the three Fiscal Years 1985/86 to 1987/88 is approximately $54 million of which $37 million is planned for the Pacific Region.

ANNEX A

DFO REGIONAL STRUCTURE

REGION	GEOGRAPHIC TERRITORY
Atlantic	
Newfoundland Region, Atlantic Fisheries Service	- covers all of eastern Newfoundland and most of Labrador
Scotia-Fundy Region, Atlantic Fisheries Service	- covers all of Nova Scotia except that portion draining into the Gulf of St. Lawrence - southwestern half of Province of New Brunswick - Province of P.E.I.
Gulf Region, Atlantic Fisheries Service	- that portion of New Brunswick, Nova Scotia and Newfoundland draining into Gulf of St. Lawrence - that portion of Labrador adjacent to Strait of Belle Isle
Quebec Region, Atlantic Fisheries Service	- Province of Quebec
Atlantic Region, Ocean Science and Surveys	- Four Atlantic provinces and eastern Arctic
Quebec Region, Ocean Science and Surveys	- Province of Quebec
Inland	
Western Region, Pacific and Freshwater Fisheries Service	- three prairies provinces (Alberta, Saskatchewan, Manitoba) and the Northwest Territories
Ontario Region, Pacific and Freshwater Fisheries Service	- Province of Ontario

REGION	GEOGRAPHIC TERRITORY
Inland (cont'd)	
Central Region, Ocean Science and Surveys	- area covering Great Lakes and Hudson - area covering Central Arctic
Pacific	
Pacific Region Ocean Science and Surveys	- area covering Pacific Coast - area covering Western Arctic
Pacific Region Pacific and Freshwater Fisheries Service	- coastal areas of British Columbia and Yukon Territory

SECTION 21 - BACKGROUND DOCUMENTS

REAL PROPERTY RESPONSIBILITIES AND EXPENDITURES

The federal government manages some 30 million square metres of building space and 21 million hectares of land. The value of federal government real property holdings has been estimated at $40 to $60 billion. The tabulation of data collected on organizations covered by the study team's review shows total resources expended during 1984-85 on real property as:

Total Operating Expenditures	$4.152 billion
Salaries and Wages	$0.967 billion
Operation and Maintenance	$2.829 billion
Grants and Contributions	$0.356 billion
Revenue	$2.302 billion
Capital	$1.801 billion
Person-Years	34,826

The year was typical except that capital expenditures were about 33 per cent above normal levels because of the SRCP program. The distribution of expenditures by region was:

- Capital Region - 19.8 per cent
- Atlantic - 14.9 per cent
- Quebec - 17.8 per cent
- Ontario - 15.7 per cent
- West and Territories - 31.8 per cent

Custodianship of Crown properties is assigned to Ministers by Acts of Parliament. The Public Works Act gives custodianship to the Minister of Public Works for all properties except those which are assigned to other Ministers by other specific acts. Other acts have given separate authorities to some 46 different departments, agencies and corporations of the federal government. Almost 20 of the separate authorities use the Department of Public Works (PWC) as their agent for general purpose office space. In addition, 90 other organizations are exclusively tenants of PWC.

The major departments with separate authorities are National Defence (bases), Environment (parks), External Affairs (overseas properties), Transport (airports and harbours), Indian Affairs and Northern Development (Indian reserves), Correctional Services (penitentiaries), RCMP (stations) and Agriculture (research facilities).

Crown corporations with separate authority can be divided into two general categories. First are those corporations which have been set up with a prime objective of managing federal property; major examples are the Canada Lands Company Ltd., the National Capital Commission (NCC) and Ports Canada. Second are corporations established to meet other purposes but which are authorized to hold, operate and maintain property in support of their operations and/or as an asset base; major examples are Canadian National and Canada Post. (The study team has included programs of the first category in the review, but has excluded programs from the second category.)

The allocation of responsibility differs between the National Capital Region and other locations in Canada. In the National Capital Region, the National Capital Commission has use control of all federal lands and custody of most federal lands. PWC has responsibility for all buildings except the airport, the military base, properties of Crown corporations and buildings on NCC lands. In the rest of Canada, PWC responsibility is generally limited to office complexes; most real property is managed by user organizations under their separate authorities although they may use PWC services in support of their responsibilities.

Appendix A contains a complete list of government organizations classified by the Schedules of the Financial Administration Act. Subsidiaries of Crown corporations and joint venture organizations are not included. The information provided on each organization's property responsibilities and holdings was obtained from the Central Real Property Inventory maintained by PWC. Information on several Crown corporations was not available because these corporations do not report their holdings to PWC.

APPENDIX A

ORGANIZATIONS WITH REAL PROPERTY PROGRAMS

Schedule A	1 DPW Provided	2 Ind. Auth.	No. Bldgs.	Bldg. Space (Sq. Metres)	Type of Facilities	Land Area (Hectares)
Agriculture		X	2,621	835,968	Research Facilities, Lands	875,269
Communications		X	71	32,033	Research Labs, Monitoring Stations	931
Consumer & Corporate Affairs	X					
Employment & Immigration	X					
Energy, Mines & Resources		X	123	25,700	Research Facilities	902
Environment		X	6,316	654,166	Parks, Historic Sites, Heritage Canals, Research Facilities, Weather Facilities	12,826,995
External Affairs		X	1,832	23,211	Overseas Residences and Chanceries	42
Finance	X					
Fisheries & Oceans		X	862	191,948	Research Facilities, Small Craft Harbours, Fishing Harbours	2,665
Indian Affairs & Northern Development		X	1,827	546,068	Indian Reserves, Northern Properties	13,404

Note 1 – Organizations listed are those which have all their requirements provided through Public Works owned or leased real property.

Note 2 – Organizations listed are those which have real property authorities separate from Public Works. In many cases, the office space requirements of these organizations, particularly in the National Capital Region, are provided by Public Works. The independent authority is reserved for special program specific real property.

N/A – Information Not Available

APPENDIX A

ORGANIZATIONS WITH REAL PROPERTY PROGRAMS

Schedule A	1 DPW Provided	2 Ind. Auth.	No. Bldgs.	Bldg. Space (Sq. Metres)	Type of Facilities	Land Area (Hectares)
Insurance	X					
Justice	X					
Labour	X					
National Defence		X	29,273	10,669,586	Military Bases and Stations	2,005,784
National Health & Welfare		X	732	174,546	Indian and Northern Medical Facilities, Research Laboratories	169
National Revenue		X	225	18,309	Customs Facilities	106
Public Works	X		4,700	7,944,203	General Accommodation, Special Purpose Buildings, Marine Facilities, Surplus Properties	4,552,753
Regional Industrial Expansion	X					
Secretary of State of Canada	X					
Solicitor General	X					
Supply & Services	X					
Transport		X	4,267	1,277,878	Airports, Harbours, Training Facilities	184,618
Veterans Affairs		X	27	5,505	Medical Facilities	42
Treasury Board	X					

ORGANIZATIONS WITH REAL PROPERTY PROGRAMS

Schedule A	1 DPW Provided	2 Ind. Auth.	No. Bldgs.	Bldg. Space (Sq. Metres)	Type of Facilities	Land Area (Hectares)
Office of the Auditor General	X					
Canada Labour Relations Board	X					
Canadian Human Rights Commission	X					
Canadian Intergovernment Conf. Sec.	X					
Canadian International Development Agency	X					
Correctional Services of Canada		X	1,608	794,100	Penitentiaries	7,726
Canadian Radio-Television Commission	X					
Canadian Sentencing Commission	X					
Canadian Transport Commission	X					
Office of the Chief Electoral Office	X					
Commission of Enquiry into Marketing Practices - Potato Industry in Eastern Canada	X					
Commission of Enquiry on Equality of Employment	X					
Commission of Enquiry on the Canadian Sealing Industry	X					
Commission on Pacific Fisheries Policy	X					

ORGANIZATIONS WITH REAL PROPERTY PROGRAMS

Schedule A	1 DPW Provided	2 Ind. Auth.	No. Bldgs.	Bldg. Space (Sq. Metres)	Type of Facilities	Land Area (Hectares)
Criminal Code Revision Commission	X					
Federal Provincial Relations Office	X					
Investment Canada	X					
Immigration Appeal Board	X					
Ministry of State for Science & Tech.	X					
National Energy Board	X					
National Farm Products Marketing Council	X					
National Film Board	X					
National Library	X					
Northern Pipeline Agency	X					
Office of the Administrator Under the Anti-Inflation Act	X					
Office of the Commissioner for Federal Judicial Affairs	X					
Office of the Commissioner of Official Languages	X					
Office of the Co-ordinator, Status of Women	X					

ORGANIZATIONS WITH REAL PROPERTY PROGRAMS

Schedule A	1 DPW Provided	2 Ind. Auth.	No. Bldgs.	Bldg. Space (Sq. Metres)	Type of Facilities	Land Area (Hectares)
Office of the Governor General's Secretary	X					
Office of the Grain Transportation Agency Administrator	X					
Office of the Information & Privacy Commissioners	X					
Petroleum Compensation Board	X					
Petroleum Monitoring Agency	X					
Privy Council Office	X					
Public Archives	X					
Public Service Commission	X					
Public Service Staff Relations Board	X					
Registry of the Federal Court of Canada	X					
Registry of the Tax Court of Canada	X					
Restrictive Trade Practices Commission	X					

APPENDIX A

ORGANIZATIONS WITH REAL PROPERTY PROGRAMS

Schedule A	1 DPW Provided	2 Ind. Auth.	No. Bldgs.	Bldg. Space (Sq. Metres)	Type of Facilities	Land Area (Hectares)
Royal Canadian Mounted Police		X	2,058	603,122	Detachments and Training	1,106
Royal Commission of Economic Union & Development Prospects for Canada	X					
Royal Commission of the "Ocean Ranger" Marine Disaster	X					
Statistics Canada	X					
Statute Revision Commission	X					
Supreme Court of Canada	X					
Tariff Board	X					
National Parole Board	X					

ORGANIZATIONS WITH REAL PROPERTY PROGRAMS

Schedule B	1 DPW Provided	2 Ind. Auth.	No. Bldgs.	Bldg. Space (Sq. Metres)	Type of Facilities	Land Area (Hectares)
Agricultural Stabilization Board	X					
Atomic Energy Control Board	X					
Canada Employment & Immigration Commission	X					
Canadian Centre for Occupational Health & Safety	X					
Crown Assets Disposal Corporation	X					
Director of Soldier Settlement	X					
Director, The Veterans' Land Act	X					
Economic Council of Canada	X					
Fisheries Prices Support Board	X					
Medical Research Council	X					
National Battlefield Commission		X	9	1,599	Plains of Abraham	95
National Museums of Canada	X					
Natural Sciences & Engineering Research Council	X					
Science Council of Canada	X					
Social Science & Humanities Research Council	X					
National Research Council of Canada		X	277	267,385	Research Laboratories, Lands	2,065

APPENDIX A

ORGANIZATIONS WITH REAL PROPERTY PROGRAMS

Schedule C (Part 1)	1 DPW Provided	2 Ind. Auth.	No. Bldgs.	Bldg. Space (Sq. Metres)	Type of Facilities	Land Area (Hectares)
Atlantic Pilotage Authority	X					
Atomic Energy of Canada Ltd.		X	448	405,088	Administrative, Manufacturing, Research	10,822
Canada Deposit Insurance Corporation	X					
Canada Lands Company Limited		X	7,690	725,109	Mirabel, Vieux Port du Montreal, Vieux Port du Quebec	29,891
Canada Mortgage & Housing Corporation		X	86	79,335	Administrative, Housing	479
Canada Post		X	3,078	2,168,457	Administrative, Stations	491
Canadian Arsenals Limited		X	130	98,750	Administrative, Manufacturing	431
Canadian Commercial Corporation	X					
Canadian Dairy Commission	X					
Canadian Livestock Feed Board	X					
Canada Harbour Place Corporation		X			No Facilities, Construction Ongoing	
Canadian National (West Indies) Steamships, Ltd.	X					

ORGANIZATIONS WITH REAL PROPERTY PROGRAMS

Schedule C (Part 1)	1 DPW Provided	2 Ind. Auth.	No. Bldgs.	Bldg. Space (Sq. Metres)	Type of Facilities	Land Area (Hectares)
Canadian Patents & Development Ltd.	X					
Canadian Saltfish Corporation	X					
Cape Breton Development Corporation		X	N/A	N/A	Administrative, Operational	N/A
Defence Construction (1951) Limited		X			No Facilities, Contracting Agent	
Export Development Corporation	X					
Farm Credit Corporation	X					
Freshwater Fish Marketing Corporation	X					
Great Lakes Pilotage Authority	X					
Harbourfront Corporation		X	N/A	N/A	Toronto Harbourfront Development Lands	N/A
Laurentian Pilotage Authority	X					
Loto Canada Inc.	X					
National Capital Commission		X	1,402	84,754	Park, Administrative, Housing, Historic Facilities, Lands	45,570
Northern Canada Power Commission		X	201	34,809	Administrative, Operational	10,745

ORGANIZATIONS WITH REAL PROPERTY PROGRAMS

Schedule C (Part 1)	1 DPW Provided	2 Ind. Auth.	No. Bldgs.	Bldg. Space (Sq. Metres)	Type of Facilities	Land Area (Hectares)
Pacific Pilotage Authority		MOT Provided				
Pêcheries Canada Inc.		F&O Provided				
Royal Canadian Mint		X	2	14,317	Administrative, Manufacturing	59
St. Anthony Fisheries Limited		F&O Provided				
The St. Lawrence Seaway Authority		X	277	55,403	Administrative, Bridges, Seaway	10,849
Societa a Responsibilita Limitata immobiliare San Sebastiano		External Affairs Provided				
Standards Council of Canada	X					
Uranium Canada Ltd.	X					
VIA Rail		X	N/A	N/A	Stations	N/A

ORGANIZATIONS WITH REAL PROPERTY PROGRAMS

Schedule C (Part II)	1 DPW Provided	2 Ind. Auth.	No. Bldgs.	Bldg. Space (Sq. Metres)	Type of Facilities	Land Area (Hectares)
Air Canada		X	N/A	N/A	Administrative, Operational	N/A
Canada Development Investment Corporation		X	N/A	N/A	Commercial Facilities	N/A
Canada Ports Corporation		X	372	1,163,192	Port Facilities and Lands	36,749
Canadian National Railway		X	N/A	N/A	Stations, Hotels, Developmen Lands, etc.	N/A
Halifax Port Corporation		X	N/A	N/A	Port Facilities and Lands	N/A
Montreal Port Corporation		X	N/A	N/A	Port Facilities and Lands	N/A
Northern Transportation Company Limited		X	2	35,207	Administrative, Operational	341
Port of Quebec Corporation		X	N/A	N/A	Port Facilities and Lands	N/A
Petro-Canada		X	N/A	N/A	Administrative, Operational	N/A
Prince Rupert Port Corporation		X	N/A	N/A	Port Facilities and Lands	N/A
Teleglobe Canada		X	23	20,668	Administrative, Operational	1,144
Vancouver Port Corporation		X	N/A	N/A	Port Facilities and Lands	N/A

APPENDIX A

ORGANIZATIONS WITH REAL PROPERTY PROGRAMS

Exempt	1 DPW Provided	2 Ind. Auth.	No. Bldgs.	Bldg. Space (Sq. Metres)	Type of Facilities	Land Area (Hectares)
Bank of Canada		X	N/A	N/A	Administrative	N/A
Canadian Broadcasting Corporation		X	485	394,615	Administrative, Operational	1,870
Canada Council	X					
Canadian Film Development Corporation		X	N/A	N/A	Administrative	N/A
Canadian Wheat Board		X	N/A	N/A	Adminstrative, Operational	N/A
International Development Research Centre	X					
National Arts Centre		X	N/A	N/A	Administrative	N/A

RECORD OF CONSULTATION

WITH OTHER GOVERNMENTS RE: ORGANIZATION AND MANAGEMENT PRACTICES

United Kingdom	- Property Services Agency
United States	- General Services Administration
British Columbia	- British Columbia Building Corporation
Ontario	- Ministry of Government Services
Quebec	- Société Immobilière du Québec
Newfoundland	- Department of Public Works and Services

WITH PRIVATE ASSOCIATIONS/FIRMS RE: GOVERNMENT INTERFACE

Association of Consulting Engineers
Canadian Construction Association
Canadian Institute of Public Real Estate Associations
Royal Architectural Institute of Canada
Murray & Murray, Griffiths & Rankin (Architects)
Neish, Owen, Rowland & Roy (Architects)
Bregman & Hamann (Architects)
Page & Steele (Architects)

WITH ORGANIZATIONS RE: TRANSPORTATION PROPERTIES

City of Edmonton Airport
Virginia Airport Authority
Minneapolis Airports Commission
Airport Operating Council International (Washington)
Federal Aviation Administration (U.S.)
Virginia Port Authority
American Association of Port Authorities